W9-CMS-269

THE AGE OF
STONEHENGE

Colin Burgess was born in London and educated at the University of Wales. In the years immediately after publishing *The Age of Stonehenge*, the author gave up digging and any serious interest in British prehistory, and turned to the archaeology of the Mediterranean, and particularly of the Sea Peoples and the Phoenicians. In the years 1986–1993 he directed a major fieldwork project in the Evora area of central Portugal, and in recent years he has been very much concerned with the archaeology of Sardinia. In the early 1990s he took early retirement, eventually moving with his wife to France. He still returns to the University of Newcastle upon Tyne for three months every winter to teach adult education students in his old department, now the Centre for Lifelong Learning. He is President of the Bronze Age Studies Group, an informal association of European friends professionally interested in later prehistory.

Also by Colin Burgess

Bronze Age Metalwork in Northern England, c. 1000–700BC
Prehistoric Man in Wales and the West (ed. with Frances Lynch)
Au Temps de Stonehenge (ed. with Ann MacSween)
Between and Beyond the Walls: Essays on the Prehistory and History of North Britain in Honour of George Jobey (ed. with Roger Mivet)

THE AGE OF STONEHENGE

Colin Burgess

CASTLE BOOKS

For Norma,
Christopher and Simon,
Who have lived with it all
for so long

This edition published in 2003 by Castle Books ®,
A division of Book Sales Inc.
114 Northfield Avenue
Edison, NJ 08837

This book is reprinted by arrangement with
Orion Publishing Group Ltd.
Orion House, 5 Upper St Martin's Lane, London WC2H 9EA

Originally published in Great Britain by
J.M. Dent in 1980
Also published by Phoenix Press in 2001
A division of The Orion Publishing Group Ltd.

A CIP catalogue record for this book is available from the
British Library

ISBN: 0-7858-1593-7

Printed in the United States of America

Contents

List of Plates

List of Line Drawings

Acknowledgments

The author and publishers would like to thank the following for their permission to reproduce photographs in this book:

P. Topping/Scottish Development Department Excavation (Plate Ia); R. Moss/Scottish Development Department Excavation (Plate Ib); Professor M. J. O'Kelly (Plate II); C. Burgess (Plate III); Dr J. Evans/Professor R. J. C. Atkinson (Plates IVa and IVb); Plate V is copyright National Museum of Antiquities of Scotland, Edinburgh; G. J. Wainwright/Department of the Environment Excavation (Plates VIa, VIb, VIc); A. L. Pacitto/Department of the Environment Excavation (Plate VII); Plates VIII and IX are Crown copyright, reproduced by permission of the Controller of Her Majesty's Stationery Office and the Royal Commission on Ancient and Historical Monuments in Wales, F. Lynch/Department of the Environment; the late J. Radley (Plate X); R. Bradley (Plate XI); J. Barber/Scottish Development Department Excavation (Plate XII); A. Fleming (Plate XIII); G. Jobey/Scottish Development Department Excavation (Plate XIV); Plate XV is copyright Airviews Ltd, Manchester Airport; Plate XVI is copyright National Museum of Ireland, Dublin; Plate XVII is copyright Ashmolean Museum, Oxford; London Museum (Plate XVIIIa); P. Baker (Plate XVIIIb); Plates XVIIIc and d, and Plate XIX appear by permission of the Trustees of the British Museum.

NOTE TO THE PHOENIX PRESS EDITION

'Change everything or change nothing' is probably the only solution when writing a short introduction to the paperback edition of a book one wrote twenty-one years ago. Of course I could change much, but it would be impossible even to list here the most important new discoveries, new sites, and new publications since 1980. Essentially, though, I think they complement rather than change or disprove what I published in 1980.

To refer just to the new literature on Stonehenge would exceed my limit, but in the Internet age, reader, there is much you can pursue yourself. I would have addressed particularly the question of absolute chronology and C14 dating, which need a less idiosyncratic treatment than I gave them in 1980. There is no space, alas, to alter the chronological framework of the book, which quickly jarred with me. I soon realised how artificial was my use of named periods, by which I attempted to emulate R.J.C. Atkinson and avoid the use of 'Three Age' terminology. Well, it is still very much with us, and so much less cumbersome than my system. So the Meldon Bridge period would become the Late Neolithic, the Mount Pleasant period the Copper Age (just about everyone else has one, and we should, too, as Christopher Hawkes urged in his 1960 *Scheme*), and Overton is first or earlier EBA (avoiding confusion with the Burgess/Needham numbered metalworking phases). Bedd Branwen must go, because its C14 dates are clearly too late for its early urns and the period it was meant to describe; the Loose Howe period would fit better for what is second or later EBA. The Knighton Heath period is the Middle Bronze Age, and the dramatic changes of the Penard period must take us into the Late Bronze Age, and not stay part of the MBA, if we are to march with the rest of Western Europe. As to the broad trends, contrary to many recent writers I cannot see much of a role for indigenous Mesolithic communities in shaping the early Neolithic of these islands, in the light of Jared Diamond's *Guns, Germs and Steel*. About Beakers I have not changed my mind: that they represent some totally extra-cultural, and immensely seductive, phenomenon; this after observing the Beaker package fitting happily into so many disparate local contexts throughout Europe. Finally, I remain convinced that there were major dislocations in later prehistory, the important ones for this work coming at the end of the Copper Age in the late Third Millennium, and in the 12th century BC, ushering in the Late Bronze Age, both of them part of much wider Old World changes that I have since written about in more detail.

The Age of Stonehenge has long been unobtainable, but the enquiries I still receive, from within Britain and from abroad, suggest the publishers may be right in thinking there is a market for a reprint. It is of course extraordinary that after twenty years I should feel it does not need a total re-write, but that is because it is traditional archaeology of the kind that has been unfashionable in our universities for the past two decades. During that time the witch doctor syndrome that passes as the New Archaeology has prevailed to a point where there are few left teaching prehistory in Britain who know anything, want to know anything, or dare to confess they know anything, about the material remains which dictionaries seem to think archaeology is all about. In the 1970s when I put the book together British archaeology desperately needed new philosophies and goals. Instead it was sucked into an American-inspired emperor's new clothes craziness (thanks for that notion, Paul Bahn) in which the proponents of the new thinking felt it necessary to cloak their ideas in an impenetrable, mind-numbing mist of jargon, newspeak, and invented and misused words, to the amazement of our European colleagues. And the establishments cheered the emperor's new wardrobe with the rest of them, filling our universities and publications with 'new' persons and 'new' ideas oblivious to an essential requirement of communication: clarity. To paraphrase someone – was it George Orwell? – there is nothing worth saying that cannot be explained in simple words. But these have become so unfashionable that good men and women have felt it necessary to keep their heads below the parapet, or in my case retire abroad to escape death by boredom. With little or no teaching role themselves, they can only grieve the fact that there will soon be very few teachers left here who know anything about the basics that must be at the heart of our business. All this comes to a head just when *Time Team* (for all that it misleads) has created such a public thirst for dirt archaeology. Pity those who set off eagerly to seek it in our universities, but instead will be told by their professors, by word and in print, that philosophy is the most important thing in archaeology, and that an understanding of the basic processes and raw materials (which some of the teachers appear to know little about) very much takes second place. This must be putting the archaeological cart before the horse. I wonder, though: have my publishers got wind of the rumoured swing of the pendulum back towards 'real archaeology' in our universities? Finally, reader, if you must read one thing which illustrates what has happened to British archaeology in the last two decades, then seek out *Landscape History*, 1997 and Frances Lynch's brilliant review of Christopher Tilley's *Phenomenology of Landscape*; and as a rare critique of the New Archaeology, Paul Courbin's *What is Archaeology?* (1988).

Colin Burgess, Centre for Lifelong Learning,
University of Newcastle upon Tyne,
and Haute-Vienne, France, March, 2001.

Chapter I

Before Stonehenge

Our understanding of Stonehenge has changed dramatically over the last two decades, in keeping with a much wider transformation in attitudes to the prehistory of the Third and Second Millennia. The old familiar concepts of migrations and invasions, of contacts with distant lands, of incessant folk movement in empty, undeveloped lands criss-crossed by traders, raiders and prospectors, have all given way to more abstract ideas, of exchange and distribution systems, constant culture contact, communities of tradition and independent development. This is not to say that adventurers and settlers never ran their boats up on to the shores of these islands, merely that we have too often taken the easy way out, and interpreted prehistory in terms familiar to the modern world. In primitive societies completely different, and to us alien, mechanisms are often at work. Thus stone axes, much like those in use when Stonehenge was built, are today spread over great distances in Australia and New Guinea, not by organized trade, which for long has been held to account for the distribution of similar axes in prehistoric Britain, but by more complex processes such as exchange at tribal frontiers, and the handing on of axes from one tribe to the next.

There is no sure way that prehistorians can prove beyond all reasonable doubt that these complicated systems operated in a given instance, but they frequently fit the evidence far better than the traditional solutions. In recent years there has been growing disillusionment with the traditional diffusionist views of prehistory, and the new attitudes are very much part and parcel of this. They are also a spin-off from the 'New Archaeology' which has exercised such a profound influence on prehistorians in the last dozen years. Nevertheless it is important that the pendulum should not swing from one extreme to the other. New concepts do not automatically negate all established ideas, and can confirm and modify as well as destroy.

These changing attitudes have also owed much to the application of scientific methods and aids to prehistoric study, and to the greatly increased resources allocated to the discipline in recent years. This has meant not only a lot more evidence from a lot more sites, but, even more important, a much more detailed and extensive examination of individual sites. Our understanding of their meaning, and thus of what happened in prehistory, has broadened accordingly.

One of the major problems in any study of prehistory is the question of terminology, because there are no proper names in prehistory, nor any dates closer than the nearest century or even millennium. The fact that an established terminology is convenient can lead to its retention long after its obsolescence has been recognized. Thus the 'Three Age' system, invaluable to those who devised it in the nineteenth century as a means of classifying museum collections, has long been recognized as obsolete. Yet it has survived as a convenient shorthand; it is neater to refer to 'Bronze Age burial traditions' than to 'burial traditions of the Third, Second and First Millennia BC'. Its continued use, however, has encouraged specialists to become excessively compartmentalized by periods, so that they are reluctant to follow their research across period boundaries even when continuity is indicated. All sorts of artificial divisions have resulted. Nevertheless, the Three Ages retained some validity; so long as the underlying technological changes appeared to accompany invasions of new peoples. First came the 'Beaker Folk', bringing knowledge of metals and turning Neolithic into Bronze Age; later came iron-using Hallstatt settlers, whose arrival separated Bronze Age from Iron Age. Such was the preoccupation with invasions and the 'Three Age' system that the full ramifications of the Beaker and Hallstatt settlements, or indeed of wider social, economic and political issues, were hardly explored.

Only in the last dozen years has disenchantment with this 'invasion hypothesis' set in. In fact the pendulum has swung to the opposite extreme, so that now scarcely any prehistoric immigrations into these islands seem acceptable. Both the Beaker and Hallstatt immigrations have been casualties, and their demise removes the principal props on which rests the entity of the Neolithic, Bronze and Iron Ages.

If these traditional agencies of change are now suspect, what can be put in their place, and how can our later prehistory be more usefully divided? This should involve changes right across the spectrum, in house types, settlement patterns, social systems, economic organization, burial/ritual customs, material equipment and so on. Changes in all these areas, especially if sudden, *could* indicate immigration, but short of a new physical type and new language, prehistoric invasions are singularly difficult to demonstrate beyond all reasonable doubt. There are, after all, well-attested invasions in history which have left scant trace in the archaeological record, whether Anglians in Northumberland or Celts in Asia Minor.

The most significant scissions in prehistory will thus be marked by disruption of the entire social fabric and the advent of new cultural traditions. On this basis very different divisions of our later prehistory can be suggested. The first began about 4000 BC with the introduction of farming, and lasted for much of the Fourth Millennium. The most notable signs of this age of the first farmers are the causwayed enclosures of southern England, the megalithic and earthen long tombs spread throughout Britain and Ireland, and simple, round-bottomed pottery. Towards the end of the Fourth Millennium striking innovations in burial and ritual monuments and material culture herald the age with which this book is concerned. The Age of Stonehenge saw a remarkable development of burial, ritual and public monuments. Above all this was the age of the round burial mound, both chambered and unchambered, forming one of the most numerous and familiar relics of our prehistoric past. These round mounds epitomize an era which saw great social, economic and spiritual changes, but with an essential continuity scarcely disturbed by the arrival of metallurgy and the Beaker tradition after 3000 BC. Its subdivisions will be considered in due course. About 1200 BC, at a time when the whole of the Old World was experiencing traumatic upheaval, and great civilizations were tottering in the east Mediterranean, far-reaching change again swept Britain and Ireland. This time the disruption was so extensive as to suggest immigrants from the Continent. The dominant monuments of this new age were its hill-forts and hill-top settlements, and it is characterized by much that was formerly regarded as 'Iron Age'. Cultural development in this age of hill-forts can be seen as a continuum in which the arrival of iron around 700 BC was no more than a technological gloss. It lasted from about 1200 BC until it was brought to an abrupt halt by the Roman Conquest.

The absolute chronology of prehistoric Britain and Ireland depends largely on radiocarbon dating up to *c.* 1500 BC, but from then on cross-dating with the literate civilizations of the Mediterranean and the Near East becomes increasingly important. Indeed it was long thought that the use of radiocarbon dating in later prehistory was not worthwhile because cross-dating would always be more accurate. A mounting flow of radiocarbon dates since the mid-1960s has shattered this myth, revealing a tangled web of misconceptions and misunderstandings, and necessitating a complete re-appraisal of later prehistory. Chronologies of key sites and artefacts were shown to be in error by up to several centuries. For example, 'Iron Age' hill-forts and pottery, the epitome of their period, were shown to have emerged before 1000 BC, half a millennium before the 'Iron Age'. Now it appears that much 'Late Neolithic' material belongs to a period when not just copper but also bronze was in regular use. This sort of re-arrangement of the raw material of prehistory has demanded sweeping changes in attitude. Time-scales have been lengthened in some cases and compressed in others, but always the results have emphasized continuity at the expense of sudden change imposed from the outside.

In recent years radiocarbon dating has been dramatically affected by tree-ring calibration. During the 1950s it was observed that C14 assays carried out on Egyptian samples were consistently younger than their known historical dates. At first there was a possibility of error either in the radiocarbon method or in the Egyptian historical dates, but subsequent programmes of C14 checks on the annual growth rings of very old trees confirmed a discrepancy between calendar years and radiocarbon years. This was caused, apparently, by past fluctuation in the atmospheric radiocarbon level. A solution to this problem appeared to lie in dendrochronology. By carrying out C14 checks on dated tree rings it should be fairly simple to build up a graph showing the divergence between tree ring dates and radiocarbon dates back through the centuries, thus providing a calibration curve for correcting C14 dates to calendar dates (assuming, as at present seems to be the case, that tree ring dates correspond with calendar dates). The discovery in 1955 of the astonishing bristle-cone pine, *Pinus longaevia*, in the White Mountains of California, a tree thousands of years older than any other species known, gave scientists an opportunity to extend their calibration curve back into prehistory. The oldest bristlecone pine so far discovered is nearly five thousand years old, and by cross-matching the rings of dead specimens with the living it has been possible to extend the curve back more than eight thousand years. Problems remain, and other radiocarbon shocks are undoubtedly to come, but for the moment calibrated dates appear to fit our conceptions of prehistory and conform reasonably well with historical dates from mediterranean and Egyptian contexts.

It is now usual to denote an uncalibrated C14 date by the convention 'bc' instead of the usual 'BC', to show that it is uncorrected and expressed in radiocarbon years. As far as later prehistory is concerned, uncalibrated C14 dates must have 100–200 years added in the first half of the First Millennium, 200–500 + years in the Second Millennium and 500–800 years in the Third Millennium if they are to approximate to calendar dates 'BC'. Thus a C14 date of 900 bc represents a true date of *c.* 1100 BC but a C14 date of 2000 bc calibrates to *c.* 2520 BC. Unfortunately the process is not entirely simple, for although calibrated C14 dates and historical dates tally very well in the Third Millennium BC, in the Second Millennium BC they do not conform at all happily, whether Egyptian or Aegean samples are used. As a temporary expedient, until this anomaly is explained, McKerrell has used the historical dates to construct an alternative historical calibration curve particularly for use in the Second Millennium. Whatever its rights and wrongs, and this solution has been bitterly criticized, it does much less violence to Second Millennium prehistory than conventional tree-ring calibration. The historical curve gives a much smaller difference between raw C14 dates and calendar dates, only some 200 years back to 1800 bc, but then the two diverge sharply, and the historical curve matches the tree-ring curve by *c.* 1950 bc. As there is comparatively little difference between tree-ring and historical calibration in the Third and First Millennia the historical curve has been used throughout for the sake of consistency. This also seems sensible when there are so many rival tree-ring calibration curves, and fundamental disagreement about their respective merits. Indeed, there are still doubts about the whole calibration issue, but until these are resolved the researcher can only make the best use of the available data.

The implications of calibrated dates are enormous. Only twenty-five years ago, Professor Piggott, without C14 dates, suggested in his standard work on *The Neolithic Cultures of the British Isles* (1954) that the Neolithic in Britain and Ireland began about 2000 BC and merged into the Bronze Age about 1500 BC. Now, after calibration, the Neolithic begins before 4000 BC, and metal appears to have been introduced by 2500 BC. The immediate effect of lengthening time scales to this extent was that evidence previously crammed into a few centuries had to be spread over much longer periods, which in itself made inevitable a lengthy re-appraisal of the material.

The radiocarbon revolution was by no means the first shock to prehistoric research in recent decades. Another much less-publicized revolution was the post-war boom in the teaching of archaeology in universities, which dramatically swelled the numbers of active researchers from the late 1950s, and resulted both in increasingly rigorous scrutiny of the available evidence and the development of new attitudes and methods. The upheaval was felt in all periods. From the point of view of the Second and First Millennia BC, metalwork studies were thought to be particularly fruitful, as they offered the best prospects for cross-dating with the historic civilizations. Perhaps the most fundamental discovery affected what for most people were most familiar relics of the 'Bronze Age', a wealth of pottery, especially food vessels and cinerary urns, and the round barrows and cairns in which they were found. Like so much in British prehistory these pots are entirely indigenous in character, do not occur on the Continent, and are not, therefore, susceptible to cross-dating. Hitherto they had been sorted typologically and spread through the whole period: food vessels followed Beakers in the 'Early Bronze Age', 'enlarged food vessels' and 'early' Collared Urns filled the 'Middle Bronze Age', and 'developed' or 'devolved' Collared Urns, Cordoned, Encrusted and Biconical Urns were 'Late Bronze Age'. By 1960 exhaustive examination of the associations of these pots, especially of the metal grave goods, had revealed that this whole sequence rested on a tissue of suppositions, circular arguments, misconceptions and doubtful associations. In fact not one of these categories of pots, and thus the burial monuments with which they were associated, could be placed in the Middle, let alone the 'Late Bronze Age'. Simultaneously the problem of the Deverel-Rimbury culture was attacked through its metal associations. This south English phenomenon, unique in British archaeology in that it is represented by both burials and settlements, had traditionally been regarded as the product of a 'Late Bronze Age' invasion from the Continent around 750 BC. By 1959 its floruit had been pushed back into the 'Middle Bronze Age', and it was being hailed as an indigenous development having little or nothing to do with invasions.

Traditional concepts in archaeology die hard. Although these were upset twenty years ago and the point has been stressed in innumerable papers ever since, it is still not uncommon to hear or see a reference to a 'Middle Bronze

Age Collared Urn', or a 'Late Bronze Age Encrusted Urn'; and any crude, bucket-shaped pot, especially if it bears fingertip impressions or a cordon, is still likely to be labelled 'Late Bronze Age', a relic of the days when all such vessels were Deverel-Rimbury, and thus 'Late Bronze Age'. But for some prehistorians these discoveries of the late 1950s and early 1960s made it clear just how precarious was the whole chronological framework of later prehistory, and in this atmosphere radiocarbon dating suddenly became an urgent necessity. In the last fifteen years it has brought many more shocks, but it has also confirmed the earlier ones. Pulling back so much material into the 'Early' and 'Middle Bronze Age' left yawning gaps in the later phases, but further radiocarbon dates brought the equally startling discovery that much supposed 'Iron Age' material, especially hill-forts and pottery, had to be pushed back to fill these voids. There are still notable blanks to be filled; radiocarbon dates have revealed the weaknesses of the older framework, but prehistorians have not yet had time to respond with appropriate excavation programmes.

There are other problems which dog the student of prehistory in Britain and Ireland. Firstly, the evidence is perversely uneven. A period with a plethora of burial and ritual sites but few settlements, such as the Second Millennium, will be followed, in the First Millennium, by an era in which settlements abound but burial and ritual sites are elusive. Seldom do both coincide. There is also great inequality in the geographical spread of the evidence. By and large there is much more material from lowland England than other regions, partly because lowland zone soils are kinder to relics of the past, and partly because of the 'southern syndrome' which has always ensured a greater expenditure of archaeological activity and resources in the south. There has been a tendency for conclusions reached essentially on the basis of southern evidence to be applied automatically and unthinkingly to the rest of these islands. This has led to some notable red herrings, for example over the introduction and significance of lead-bronze in Second and First Millennium metalworking.

The traditional picture of later prehistoric Europe is of a thinly populated, under-developed landscape with plenty of room for volatile peasant societies to roam at will. This canvas has generally been peopled with 'cultures', of variable and uncertain character, which appear and disappear, and contract and expand in rather mysterious fashion. 'Invasion' and 'migration' are the sort of terms used in discussing their appearance and disappearance. The evidence no longer supports such a simplified picture. The governing concept of this book is that by the Third Millennium Britain and Ireland (and probably much of Europe too) had already been divided fairly rigidly into territories by stratified societies, which, confined within their borders, were much more static than has usually been conceived. Only those with maritime boundaries had appreciable room for manoeuvre and direct international contact. This model is dependent on accepting a much more settled and highly developed landscape and much larger population figures than those usually entertained.

More static societies do not mean stagnant societies. It is quite clear that maritime territories maintained regular and vigorous contact with lands across the water, and would have been the first to receive exotic ideas. Those communities bordering the Channel had perhaps more in common with the groups inhabiting north-west France and the Low Countries than those in the north and west of Britain and in Ireland. This is just the picture which emerges from a reading of Caesar. The close, cousinly cross-Channel relationships that existed in his day were clearly nothing new. Comparatively little attention has been devoted to this period of prehistory in northern France, but it is clear that societies on both sides of the Channel developed along remarkably similar lines, an eloquent testimony to the incessant criss-crossing of boats which kept the two lands in constant touch with each other.

The long-distance trader has been a popular figure in prehistoric studies, but there is surprisingly little evidence for his activities in the Third and Second Millennia. In a world carved up into distinct territories new patterns of contact and distribution have to be envisaged. The sort of mechanisms that might be involved are familiar from studies of recent primitive societies, which show that ideas as well as artefacts can be spread from territory to territory over vast distances in a matter of years, passed on by contacts, both informal and formal, at tribal frontiers. An idea will be disseminated within the territory at whatever gatherings are part and parcel of the fabric of society in that territory: at fairs, markets, festivals, ceilidhs and so on. Within the territory there may be traffic in the actual artefacts representative of the idea, bartered at these gatherings, or distributed by tinkers and travelling crafts-men. The idea will thus permeate the territory, and eventually spread to neighbouring territories. Casual contact between those living along territorial borders may suffice for this, but there are good ethnographic parallels for more formal regular inter-tribal meetings, which provide further opportunities for communicating an idea. If an innovation involves artefacts the originals may vanish quickly from circulation. The further from the source the greater will be the reliance on local versions of the artefact, and the more an idea will be adapted to fit local circumstances. As soon as a concept is introduced in a territory, whether it comes from within or without, it is potentially available for transmission within the territory and to adjoining territories. The merits of each development and the circumstances of the age will govern the speed and extent of its dissemination. But this culture contact between territories must be seen as a constant process, not an intermittent one. Each territory will be in a state of 'constant culture contact' with its neighbours. The territories of Britain and Ireland can be likened to a cellular structure in which each cell (or territory) develops in sympathy with its neighbours. Thus the inhabitants of any territory will be aware of developments not only in adjoining territories but indirectly in others much further removed. An innovation in any indi-vidual cell may repercuss on adjacent cells, in which case it will ripple through the cellular structure until its force is dissipated. Those cells or territories it touches will together form a 'tradition block'. Innovations can appear at any point within the cellular structure, so while some may affect identical or similar cell clusters, others will overlap only partly or not at all. Cells, or territories, which consistently share a wide range of traditions will together form a 'community of tradition'. In many ways this will be similar to the idea of a 'culture' as conceived by Childe fifty years ago, but many notable 'cultures', such as the Beaker 'culture' have proved to be nothing of the sort, and for the same reason they cannot be classed as communities of tradition.

Such a model can be applied equally at the local, British and European level, and can be illustrated by an example central to the study of our period. The familiar categories of 'Bronze Age' pottery, Beakers, food vessels and cinerary urns, have traditionally been ascribed to separate peoples who extended in turn over the whole or parts of Britain. Just how this worked, where each group came from and what was its fate, was never made clear. Applying the 'constant culture contact' model, we can see that it is not the people within their territories who change, but their ideas, which adapt to each innovation. The various categories of pottery become representative of different burial traditions, not different peoples, each spreading from its own territorial origin. The Beaker tradition, already ancient when food vessels and cinerary urns emerged, was the first to succumb, then the food vessel tradition was squeezed into ever smaller areas, for it was in-urned cremation that proved to be the expanding force in the early Second Millennium.

Ideas of constant culture contact and communities of tradition make equal sense extended to the Continent, where the classic sequence Únětice-Tumulus-Urnfield-Hallstatt can be seen as stages in the development of a central European community of tradition. With peripheral fluctuations this encompassed the whole region from the Carpathians to eastern France, though territories at its edges were likely to be variably influenced by adjoining communities of tradition. Central Europe might seem a long way from Devizes, Doncaster or Donegal, but what happened in the region between the Rhine and the Danube very often in later prehistory repercussed on developments in Britain and Ireland. That is the nature of constant culture contact.

Prehistorians have scarcely had time to catch up with the implications of recent developments, especially wholesale radiocarbon dating, but it is possible to construct a provisional chronological scheme for later prehistory which eschews the 'Three Ages' and technological references. This distinguishes successive periods of fundamentally different character, each named after a site, which first epitomizes the essential spirit of its era, and also has a reasonably certain chronology. In the earlier periods this demands a series of radiocarbon dates, and the uncertainties of radiocarbon dating constitute one of the main problems of the scheme.

The major dividing points of later prehistory have already been alluded to.

Following the age of the first farmers, which began in the Fifth Millennium and ended in the late Fourth, came the age of Stonehenge with which this book is concerned. This commenced with the Meldon Bridge period, with radiocarbon dates of *c*. 2700/2500–2150 bc, or *c*. 3200–2750 BC in calendar years. Some old-established traditions survived, frequently in modified form, but much was new. Thus the building of long tombs and causewayed enclosures ceased and the emphasis switched to round burial mounds, such as passage graves, and new 'public' monuments, including enclosures, cursūs, henges and stone circles. It was in this period that the first phase of Stonehenge was built. There were new traditions of burial, such as cremation cemeteries, major changes in settlement and economy, and new, decorated ceramics came to the fore: Grooved wares, Peterborough styles, Carrowkeel pottery and the like. The great timber-walled enclosures of Meldon Bridge, Peebles, present all the salient features of this period, supported by a large number of C14 dates between *c*. 2700 and 2150 bc. The Mount Pleasant period which followed, from *c*. 2150 bc, was marked by the introduction of metallurgy and the Beaker tradition, but these were no more than a gloss on existing traditions which, by and large, continued from the previous period. Mount Pleasant in Dorset is typical of the great ditch and bank enclosures built in southern England at this time, possibly as territorial centres. Inhumation burial reached its apogee, at least among those who practised or qualified for formal burial, but cremation was still widespread. Before the end of this period copper had everywhere given way to bronze. A growing population and increasing pressures on the land may be indicated by spreading territorialization and land enclosure, the latter reflected in great field systems such as those at Fengate, near Peterborough.

There were fundamental changes towards 2000 BC (*c*. 1700 bc) as the Mount Pleasant period drew to a close amidst far-reaching social and spiritual upheaval. Chambered tombs throughout Britain and Ireland were blocked up, often after a thousand years or more of use, while at Stonehenge, where an ambitious modification of the site had been instituted, there was a dramatic change of plan. Work on the partially-completed double bluestone circle was suddenly abandoned and the stones removed to make way for the even more grandiose sarsen structure. Such was the atmosphere of change at the beginning of the Overton period. It is only at this point that 'Bronze Age' traditions emerged, such as the food vessels and cinerary urns which are so indicative of new sepulchral attitudes. Beakers continued, but apparently with diminished status. They were deliberately eschewed by the Bush Barrow 'Wessex Culture' chieftains, whose emergence as the new aristocracy of Wessex typifies the changing social orders of this period. Round mound burial dominated, with cist graves in northern Britain, and a more even mix of inhumation and cremation as shown at the eponymous site of West Overton G6b in Wiltshire. But cremation spread remorselessly as time went on, and the Bedd Branwen period, from about 1600 BC (*c.* 1450 bc) is marked by its total domination, as seen at the Anglesey cemetery mound. The Beaker tradition had finally petered out, food vessels survived only in their traditional areas such as East Yorkshire, and cinerary urns were much in evidence. There was little interest now in the old ritual traditions represented by henges, stone circles, stone rows and the like. Modifications begun at Stonehenge did not proceed very far. There is also evidence for abandonment of traditional lowland farmlands, and the opening up of extensive upland tracts. All this was leading up to the Knighton Heath period, beginning about 1400 BC (*c.* 1250 bc), which shows a fundamentally different character from the previous periods. The whole fabric of ostentatious burial and ritual, represented by the megalithic rings and rows, and the burial sites with their privileged dead and prestigious sepulchral vessels, all vanished. Cremation continued in flat and barrow cemeteries similar to that at Knighton Heath in Dorset, but now associated with the crude plain urns of which the southern Deverel-Rimbury vessels are the best-known representatives. These had long been both sepulchral and domestic pottery to the less privileged elements in the population. Their new prominence, coupled with the disappearance of the prestigious urn and 'Wessex Culture' burials of the previous period, suggests major social upheaval affecting the whole of Britain and Ireland. As yet few equivalents to Deverel-Rimbury ceramics and sites are known in many regions. The disappearance of the rich array of burial and ritual sites of the Bedd Branwen period means that over much of Britain and Ireland the Knighton Heath period is represented only by its metalwork. Stonehenge, like megalithic sites everywhere, lay deserted. The end of an era was approaching.

In the thirteenth and twelfth centuries BC the whole east Mediterranean region was gripped by troubles which resulted in the collapse of the great Hittite and Mycenaean-Minoan Empires and even threatened Egypt. The ripples of these disturbances spread throughout Europe, and by 1200 BC the effects were being felt in Britain. The extent of the changes which took place at this time is so striking that here if anywhere a case can be made out for immigration from the Continent. At the very least there was an intensification of cross-Channel contacts which left scarcely one aspect of Knighton Heath traditions untouched. Hill-forts began to appear on eminences from Berkshire to Yorkshire. The Age of Stonehenge had given way to the age of hill-forts.

The physical background

The earliest literary mention of Britain and Ireland, in the lost *Massiliote Periplus* of the sixth century BC, refers to the two islands as Albion and Iernē. Allowing that these are Greek version of Celtic originals, similar names were probably used by the islands' inhabitants for their homelands in the early First

Millennium and perhaps for a long time before. For Pytheas of Massilia, voyaging to the islands in 325–323 BC, they were known collectively as the Pretanic Islands, a name perhaps worth reviving in deference to modern political geography.

The Pretanic islands, in spite of their relatively small size, are extraordinarily diverse in climate, scenery, relief and soils. It is remarkable in these days of rapid transport that regional differences remain so strong. They must have been much greater in prehistoric times, when movement was restricted and the ability to adapt environments limited. It is important to know something of these regional physical characteristics in order to understand the economic and social contrasts observed in later prehistory.

The simplest physical division is the one made by Fox either side of a line running roughly diagonally from Dorset to the mouth of the Tees. To the north and west is the Highland Zone, where the rocks are hard and old, pre-Cambrian and Palaeozoic, and where much of the land is hilly and above six hundred feet. To the south and east the rocks are softer and younger, secondary and tertiary, little is above six hundred feet, much below three hundred, and the relief is generally flat or gently undulating. Taking this further we can expect the old, hard Highland Zone rocks to give thinner, poorer soils than the soft Lowland Zone rocks.

But geology is only one half of the story. The other is climate, where the dividing lines are more complex. It must be remembered at the outset that a major climatic deterioration occurred during later prehistory, from a climate appreciably better than today's, to the damp, cool conditions of modern times. Observations based on our present climate are thus directly relevant only for the last stages of prehistory, so that it is important to establish when and how this worsening of the climate occurred.

The major climatic factors are precipitation and temperature, but these determine evaporation rates, which, together with sunshine and wind, also have to be taken into account. Since our weather is essentially oceanic, and comes mainly from the west, the west is much wetter than the east, while latitude determines that the north is cooler than the south. But climate depends as much on local factors as on geographical position, with altitude, aspect and gradient particularly important. Altitude has a more dramatic effect than latitude in increasing windspeed, which governs the level of exposure and precipitation, and in decreasing the evaporation rate and temperature. A fall in temperature of about 1°F for every three hundred feet is very important when only 4°F or less separates the sea level summer temperatures of most of Britain and Ireland. With so much of the west and north above six hundred feet, the climatic advantages of the south and south-east are even further emphasized.

Regional climatic differences are much greater in spring, summer and autumn than in winter, and more important in human terms. The differences between south and north are much more obvious than between south and west. Physically and climatically the south-east is the region most like Continental Europe. Indeed the gulf between north and south is greater than that between the south of Britain and north-west France, so that crossing the line from north to south, as Jacquetta Hawkes has observed, often means more than crossing the Channel. If we compare areas at similar altitudes in the north and south the absolute differences seem slight at first: perhaps a couple of degrees in temperature. But they are differences which can be felt rather than expressed in figures; wind, sunshine and evaporation are less tangible, but make all the difference when it comes to crop ripening and human comfort. And of course over so much of the north and west altitude adds the extra dimension which amplifies the differences in human terms. The geographical position of the British Isles is such that it is a marginal region for cultivation, especially of wheat and barley, the main crops of prehistory. The critical limits for their economic growth are below thirty inches annual rainfall and the July 60°F isotherm. Only south-east England and the Midlands fall comfortably within these limits and have enough sunshine, a sufficiently high evaporation rate and level land, to make cereal cultivation an economic and safe proposition. Parts of north-east England and east Scotland are amongst the most fertile lands of Britain, and have a sufficiently low rainfall for cereal cultivation but these are marginal and the difference between success and failure narrows rapidly with altitude so that only slight annual variations in temperature and precipitation can lead to crop failure. Britain's climate is nothing if not variable, from year to year and region to region. Wettest year can follow driest year, hottest year follows coolest, there can be drought in the south and a sufficiency of water in the north (as happened in 1976) or vice versa. In addition these short term variations have to be seen against longer cyclical periods of climatic change. With much of these islands marginal for cultivation the results can be disastrous, as we know from recent history.

Thus, in modern times as in the past arable farming has been concentrated in the Lowland Zone while much of the north and west has been given over to pasture of varying qualities. The significance of this pastoral-arable dichotomy may not amount to much in our industrial society today, but in prehistoric times must have resulted in profound human differences.

The Highland Zone does have some appreciable areas of low, flat or undulating land, but, even disregarding the crucial climatic disadvantages, these lower areas are individually too small and scattered. Their soil is often too poor or difficult for them to provide a basis for agricultural wealth and thus dense population. The extensive arable tracts of the Lowland Zone, so richly endowed with the tractable soils sought by early farmers, help to explain the differences in population and wealth which have always separated the Highland and Lowland Zones. There are no population figures for prehistoric Britain, but there is some reason to believe that Domesday population levels may already have been attained during the First Millennium BC, and possibly approached more than once in earlier times. Medieval figures of two per square kilometre over much of northern England, compared with nine to eighteen over much of the south, should provide a guide to the situation in prehistory. To the physical advantages which made the Lowland Zone wealthier and more populous than the Highland Zone we can add the benefit of geographical position. The south lies closest to the Continent, and was usually the first to feel the impact of Continental developments. Conversely northern England and Scotland, in addition to their physical disadvantages are furthest from the outside world. Thus they were least affected by exotic influences, showed greater resistance to change, and usually lagged behind the south in economic terms. Western regions not only have a kinder climate than the north but are exposed to external influences transmitted via the Atlantic sea routes. Inevitably there was a reverse side to all this. The south-east being closest to the Continent was most open to raiding and immigration, whereas the north was least at risk.

Physical changes since prehistory

We have so far been concerned with the physical situation very much as it is now, and it is well known that both climate and physiography are constantly changing. There have been important physical changes since later prehistoric times, though not enough to invalidate the general physical picture discussed above. The physiographic changes are less important than the climatic differences. The basic form of Britain and Ireland was established in geological times, the Ice Ages considerably modified their relief, and post-glacial movements adjusted sea and land levels, thus altering the peripheries of the map. But Britain was finally severed from the Continent in the Mesolithic, two thousand years before the Age of Stonehenge, and post-glacial adjustments were well advanced by that time, though not over. The movements were complex, both eustatic and isostatic, their intricacies and significances even now not fully understood. A post-glacial tilting process has been claimed to take place from an east–west line extending roughly from the Humber to Anglesey. North of this line the land has been rising above the sea, leading to the phenomenon of raised beaches, and especially the 'Twenty-Five Feet' raised beach so familiar all round the shores of Scotland and Northern Ireland. South of the pivot line the effect has been entirely the opposite, with coast lines slowly submerging or at best remaining stable. This accounts for the extensive post-glacial submerged forests around the shores of southern Britain, and the drowned settlements along the eastern littoral. There are many coastal sites of our period which are now below the high water mark, for example those at Clacton, Essex, rich in Grooved ware and Beaker pottery. These adjustments went on throughout later prehistory, and are still being felt today.

Thus a prehistoric map would have had coastal margins rather different from today's. North of the pivot line inlets were bigger and the Irish Sea and North Sea marginally wider, but to the south, coastal flats would have been more extensive and the Channel rather narrower. These are important facts to bear in mind when considering movement and migration in prehistory.

Sea level movements are better documented in some areas than others. The Fens of eastern England after being subject to marine transgression in the Fourth Millennium experienced considerable regression in the Third and Second. As the fen peat dried out so it became increasingly attractive for settlement, and the intensity of activity is reflected in the vast number of finds of these two millennia. Subsequently, towards the Roman period, there was further marine incursion. A similar pattern of transgression and regression can now be traced in other areas, such as the Norfolk Broads, the Thames Estuary and the Somerset levels.

Otherwise the changes have been those which are still going on. Rivers have shifted course, and primitive prehistoric drainage patterns meant wider, shallower water courses, with more extensive marshy margins. The sea has nibbled away at the littoral, especially down the east coast; lakes have silted up, and delta formation has gone on. But it is the appearance of the countryside which has changed most dramatically, and here the hand of man has increasingly to be taken into account alongside natural factors. The school book picture of prehistoric landscapes covered by primeval forest is clearly far from the truth. In the Third Millennium the treeline may have reached its greatest elevation, up to three thousand feet, but by this time farmers had been clearing the land for two thousand years, and had made considerable inroads into the forest cover. It is quite clear that the landscape from the Third Millennium onwards was much more open than has been supposed, and by the Second Millennium farmers were already tilling some of the heavier, less favourable soils. Extensive field systems and land divisions are known to occur from the Fourth Millennium onwards, and in the Age of Stonehenge are seen all over Britain and Ireland. Careful reading of classical writers such as Caesar is worthwhile, leaving no doubt that much of the countryside was open by later prehistoric times.

Early farming communities of the Fifth and Fourth Millennia

Early farming communities were established in Britain and Ireland by the end of the Fifth Millennium BC (from *c.* 3500 bc). How many colonists came, and from where on the Continent, is not clear, although radiocarbon dates leave no doubt that by 4000 BC agriculture was well established from Cornwall to northern Scotland, and from Norfolk to Co. Sligo. The traditional picture of this era is of small farming communities scratching a precarious living in clearings in the primeval forest, then, after exhausting the soil, moving on to clear a new area and start all over again. This 'slash and burn' agriculture may well have characterized an early pioneering stage, and would explain the scatter of small-scale clearances with early radiocarbon dates known from many parts of Britain and Ireland. But rising population levels must quickly have led to ever-larger clearances and more sophisticated farming methods. Old ideas of primitive hoe agriculture in forest clearings have been jolted by the discovery of criss cross ard-marks beneath the long barrow at South Street, Wiltshire (*c.* 2810 bc). Such marks are known in many parts of Britain in the Second and First Millennia, evidence for a long tradition of cross-ploughing, perhaps already with a two-ox plough. Palynological and faunal evidence from beneath many Wessex long barrows suggests large tracts of the chalk were open by *c.* 3500 BC. The earliest of the extensive 'celtic' field systems of the region may have been laid out at this time, for in Ireland whole landscapes of this period, neatly divided into walled fields, are coming to light beneath the blanket peat. The Behy-Glenulra system in Co. Mayo, covering hundreds of acres and still running on under uncut peat is intimately connected with a court cairn (*c.* 2510 bc), and provides a remarkable example of land management before 3000 BC. Such measures were perhaps forced on farmers facing increasing pressures on resources. There is evidence from many parts of Britain and Ireland that during the Fourth Millennium more areas were reverting to scrub and forest, a sign, perhaps, of a mounting agricultural and population crisis as the carrying capacity of the land was exceeded.

The earliest farmers not surprisingly practised a mixed economy growing cereals, mainly emmer and naked barley according to soil type, and keeping cattle, sheep and/or goats, and pigs, in that order of importance. Farming patterns changed with local circumstances. Pollen and soil studies in many parts of Britain and Ireland have revealed a complex sequence of clearances and abandonments, from arable to scrub to grazing and back again. It was a pattern dictated no doubt by soil degradation, by human factors and by climatic variation. For example, at Ballynagilly in Co. Tyrone, mixed farming from *c.* 3600 bc had by *c.* 2930 bc given way to pastoralism. The Behy-Glenulra fields were also designed for stock raising. The light dry soils of the southern chalk must soon been exhausted and turned into grassland and scrub. As they were lost so ploughing for cereal cultivation switched to the lower slopes and valleys.

Settlements of this period were small, a pattern of farmsteads housing families or enlarged family groups which was to dominate in most regions for nearly three thousand years. Not many houses are known, but they are wide-scattered, and are always rectilinear and of timber, varying in shape from rectangular, as at Ballyglass, Co. Mayo, to almost square, as at Ballynagilly,

Co. Tyrone, and Fengate, Peterborough. There was considerable variation in construction. Wall slots for timbers are common, and the Ballynagilly house was plank-built, but at Mount Pleasant, Glamorgan, Carn Brea, Cornwall, and Haldon, Devon, there were rectangular stone footings. Recent large-scale excavations at sites such as Fengate and Ballynagilly have provided the opportunity to examine the surroundings of single houses, but have failed to locate evidence for more extensive settlements. The importance of rectangular buildings in this period is confirmed by the frequent discovery of rectangular mortuary structures under the southern long barrows. Some, such as the one at Nutbane, Hampshire, must have strongly resembled the houses of everyday life. This introduces one of the enduring features of later prehistory, a running together of life and death. In the Fourth Millennium we see this juxtaposition at Ballyglass, Co. Mayo, where a court cairn was built on top of a fine rectangular timber house, and it is possible that some funerary structures may have started out as domestic buildings.

Most of the known houses are in western areas, where plough damage has been relatively slight. Not surprisingly in the south and east of England they have seldom survived, and settlement traces are more likely to consist of a scatter of pits, hearths and post-holes making no coherent pattern. The site at Hurst Fen, Mildenhall, Suffolk, is typical, with pits and post-holes thickly scattered across the two hundred square metres excavated, but not one recognizable building plan. Structures have been similarly lacking on the southern causewayed enclosures. The storage pits characteristic of the Hurst Fen type 'pit and post-hole' settlements are concentrated in the same southern and eastern areas as 'Iron Age' storage pits two thousand years later, reflecting the age-old difference between arable Lowland Zone and pastoral Highland Zone. This is an over-simplified classification, however, for there have been recent discoveries of important storage pit sites in the north, at Thirlings in Northumberland; Meldon Bridge near Peebles; and in vast numbers on the Yorkshire Wolds. The earliest are of the Fourth Millennium, but most belong to the Meldon Bridge and Mount Pleasant periods. These new finds, following the quickening pace of excavation in the north, show how a gross imbalance in distribution may in part reflect a lack of fieldwork and excavation.

Among the best known monuments of the early farmers are the enigimatic causewayed enclosures of southern England. Their function is not obvious, and over the years they have been interpreted as enclosed settlements, as stock corrals, especially for autumnal round-ups and selective butchering, as ritual sites, as regional centres serving much the same function as medieval fairs, and as territorial centres. Until recent years they were mainly a feature of the southern chalk, and it was possible to envisage a common function, but aerial photography has now shown them to be widespread at least as far north as Lincolnshire. They vary so enormously, in siting, in size and form, in the number of interrupted ditches and existence of additional perimeter works, and in the results they yield to excavation, that they may have served a variety of uses. It is possible that the characteristic interrupted ditches were less important than the banks piled up from the excavated spoil. The banks seldom survive, but appear to have had far fewer gaps than the ditches, and may in at least some cases have been continuous. This removes one obvious argument against a defensive function. The siting of some sites, such as Windmill Hill, Wiltshire, does not make best use of the ground for defensive purposes. Other recently excavated examples suggest defensive intent, such as Crickley Hill in Gloucestershire, which had a continuous bank and ditch cutting off a promontory in one phase, Hambledon Hill in Dorset, which has defensive works cutting off the approaching spurs, and sites such as Orsett, Essex, where perimeters incorporate palisades, as well as banks and ditches. The absence of interior buildings and domestic structures need not preclude occupation, as most causewayed enclosures have been so eroded and ploughed as to remove all but very sizeable interior features. The wealth of refuse at many sites suggests prolonged activity. Some may well have had a resident population, augmented at times by travellers coming for ceremonies or ritual, or to participate in fairs and festivals. In such cases we may be dealing with territorial foci, but the presence of burials at other sites, both articulated and disarticulated bones, in interiors and especially in ditches, has suggested these were mortuary enclosures, where bodies were exposed. Examples include that at Offham, Sussex, which had comparatively little domestic rubbish, in contrast to sites such as Windmill Hill, and Whitehawk in Sussex, which produced both burials and evidence of intensive activity. Clearly the sepulchral aspect is worth considering in the case of sites such as Hambledon, where the ditches have produced inordinate quantities of human bones.

Not all the enclosures of this era had causewayed ditches. At Lyles Hill, Co. Antrim, and Carn Brea, Cornwall perimeter walls surround hill-top enclosures on rock which was too tough for ditch digging. Carn Brea has produced rectangular stone structures, and seems best interpreted as a walled settlement at present unique.

We must turn next to the material culture of the early farming communities. There is no definite evidence for textiles in Britain and Ireland before the Mount Pleasant period, but many other crafts and technologies continued apparently unchanged from their introduction by early farmers down to the Second Millennium. Radiocarbon dates from flint mines such as Blackpatch, Sussex (*c.* 3140 bc) and Cissbury, Sussex (*c.* 2780–2700 bc) show that flint mining was carried on from at least 4000 BC, and at centres such as Grime's Graves in Norfolk and Easton Down in Wiltshire that intensive mining was still taking place in the Mount Pleasant period. The stone-working sites of the Highland Zone had a very similar history. Some, particularly in Cornwall, seem to have been worked from the earliest farming times, and during the course of the Fourth Millennium an increasing number of sites throughout the Highland Zone were exploited (e.g. Great Langdale, West-morland, 2730 ± 135 bc). Some rock sources, such as preselite, the spotted dolerite from the Prescelly Mountains of Pembrokeshire (Group XIII), and Camptonite from Worcestershire (Group XIV), provided material both for unperforated 'Neolithic' axes and, later on, perforated implements, so were worked at least down to the Overton period. Other sources, especially Cornish rocks, have produced only imperforate implements, and may therefore have been abandoned before perforated battle-axes and axe-hammers were intro-duced in the Third Millennium. Those such as the Hyssington picrite of the Shropshire-Montgomery border, seem to have produced only perforated implements, and thus only began to be exploited from around 2000 BC. It is becoming increasingly likely that glacial erratics, often hundreds of miles from the parent rock, may often have been the source of raw material in axe manufacture. How profoundly this will affect long-held notions of stone-axe 'factories' and long distance traffic is not yet clear.

Woodworking can be expected to have benefited from the introduction of metal tools, but it was centuries before an appreciable range of metal car-penter's tools became available. Associations make it clear that the standard 'Neolithic' stone axe-head, like many other Neolithic stone implements, remained in use at least down to the Overton period. Our knowledge of the woodworking skills of the early farmers is very tenuous, because so little wood has survived. We know nothing, for example, of any skill or interest in wood carving, but bonework has survived, and this is generally of a very plain and unimaginative nature. Pottery gives the same impression: that these early farmers may have been competent craftsmen, but they had little artistic spirit.

The early farming communities put a lot of their energy into burial, ritual and ceremonial activities. These were very complex matters, often involving great feats of field engineering and implying a working knowledge of basic surveying methods. The structure of society is of course a matter for specula-tion, but it has always been regarded as egalitarian and classless, as indicated by the prevalence of collective burial and the absence of obvious signs of wealth differentials. However, it is now clear that only a favoured few could have qualified for burial in the splendid funeral monuments of the period, which suggests some degree of social stratification. Other elements were disposed of much less formally, such as those deposited in the ditches of causewayed enclosures. It would be a mistake to read too much into the apparent absence of personal wealth, for riches in peasant societies are often expressed in terms which leave little or no trace for the archaeologist: in women, cattle, salt and produce or other perishable possessions. It has been suggested that already Wessex had been carved up into separate chiefdoms, and certainly it seems inconceivable that the great monuments of that region, such as the Dorset cursus, the West Kennet chambered tomb and Silbury Hill, could be con-structed except by well-organized societies, with an individual or class at the top very much in control. Other areas have not been so exhaustively studied, but many have their architectural extravagances, like the great megalithic tombs. Faced with sites such as Brennanstown near Dublin and Tinkinswood, Glamorgan, with prodigious capstones weighing forty tons or more perched several feet in the air, who can doubt that their builders were well-organized and firmly led. A similar impression of order is given by the great field systems.

The best-known funerary monuments of the early farmers are the long tombs. Megalithic chambered long cairns of a variety of forms dot the stony lands of the west and north, while in the south and east there are the long barrows, built of earth, timber, turf and chalk. The radiocarbon chronology of the long barrows is well established, but there are far fewer dates for the megalithic tombs. Furthermore, unlike the long barrows, they had burial chambers which were accessible after their mounds were thrown up, and thus they could be and were used over very long periods. Nevertheless there is no doubt that construction of both long barrows and long chambered cairns had ceased by *c.* 2500 bc.

A complication in dating the long chambered tombs is that some at least were of multi-period construction. Only in the last fifteen years has it become clear that many of the long, imposing monuments we see today began as much more modest tombs, with simple chambers and roughly circular, 'minimal' mounds. Their incorporation into more grandiose cairns, the addition of further chambers and galleries, and enlargement and modification to their present form, may have taken place over centuries. Even after they reached their final form they continued in some sort of use, not necessarily that for which they were first designed, down to the Mount Pleasant period. The problem with radiocarbon samples from these tombs is thus to know where they belong in the sequence of development. Although the few radiocarbon dates for the construction phases of the main long tomb groups – court cairns in Ireland, Clyde-Solway tombs in Scotland and Cotswold-Severn tombs in south-west Britain – are all in the range 3300–2500 bc, much the same as the dates for the long barrows.

Small chambered tombs with simple chambers and 'minimal' cairns are common in most megalithic regions and have often been regarded as 'degenerate' and late. The fact that very similar sites underlie so many long tombs reveals the danger in this generalization. Thus the 'entrance graves' of the Scillies, Cornwall and south-east Ireland have tended to be dated very late on the basis of undoubtedly late burials which some contain. For example, cremations in the famous Scilly site of Knackyboy were accompanied by grave goods dated around 1500 BC. But it is the nature of chambered tombs that they can be used time and time again, and such burials need be only the latest in a long series. Less doubt now attends the 'portal dolmens' found on both sides of the Irish Sea. These are amongst the most impressive of chambered tombs, often with spectacular capstones, but with modest mounds where any survive. They have long been regarded as late tombs by Irish scholars, but one was incorporated into a long tomb at Dyffryn Ardudwy, Merioneth, and the finds and morphology seem more appropriate to an early than a late date.

It is now clear that chambered cairns meant much more to the community than simply places to inter the privileged dead. Though nominally 'collective tombs' they are never piled high with human remains as might be expected of mortuaries used incessantly over centuries. From northern Scotland in particular there is evidence that chambers were periodically cleared to make way for new interments. How often this happened is unknown. At some sites it has been postulated that burials were deposited on just a few occasions, perhaps only once, involving very special people on very special occasions. Access to chambers would then be maintained to meet the needs of ceremony, not to permit constant deposition of new burials. The happenings at chambered tombs were clearly as varied and complex as the tombs themselves, and they appear to have been the focus of all manner of communal rites and ceremonies. In this sense they may have been more important as territorial and community centres than tombs, fulfilling some of the purposes of the southern causewayed enclosures of Britain.

The burial rite of the chambered tombs was generally inhumation in southern Britain, and a mixture of cremation and inhumation in northern Britain and Ireland. The long barrows present a similar contrast, with inhumation predominant in the south, but more cremation in the north. For long barrows as with chambered tombs the term 'collective' burial can be misleading. Many long barrows were built over only a few bodies, some covered single crouched inhumations, such as the Heddington 3 and Barton Stacey sites in Hampshire, and some, including the recently excavated Beckhampton Road and South Street in north Wiltshire, yielded no burials at all. Although frequently described as 'unchambered', and contrasted with the megalithic tombs, long barrows appear often to have covered some sort of mortuary structure, though being of such materials as wood and turf these have left ambiguous traces. They also yielded evidence of complex pre-barrow stages, frequently involving mortuary enclosures where bodies may have been exposed or stored.

The burials from southern long barrows include both articulated inhumations and disarticulated bones. The latter are reminiscent of the groups of bones from several causewayed enclosures, and the two types of site may well have been interconnected in funerary rites which included exposure of the body. Northern long barrows are generally similar to the southern examples in form and sometimes rite, but more usually cover burnt bodies. Some seem to involve formal cremation, with cases of flue cremation and crematorium trenches, but others may be inhumations burnt in the firing of a mortuary structure.

Three aspects of burial practice which for long were thought part and parcel of Beaker traditions, now prove to have much earlier beginnings: the round barrow, crouched individual inhumation and grave goods. Round mounds, in the form of the minimal cairns covering many early chambered tombs, are perhaps as old as farming itself. Many early farming communities in northern Britain certainly favoured round barrows and cairns, and famous examples include Pitnacree, Perthshire (*c.* 2860 BC), and the Ford barrow, Northumberland, both producing the plain, round-based Grimston vessels characteristic of the north; also Copt Hill, Houghton-le-Spring, Co. Durham, where the mound covered a crematorium trench like those under the Yorkshire long barrows. Cremation was characteristic of these northern sites, but in Yorkshire round barrows are frequently associated with inhumations in a distinctive local tradition which will be considered more fully below. The significance of round mounds in the south is more ambiguous, partly because they have always been linked axiomatically to Beaker intruders. There are large numbers of round barrows scattered throughout southern England covering both single and multiple inhumations, both articulated and disarticulated. Most have no grave goods and there are practically no radiocarbon dates, which makes it difficult to dispute ascriptions to 'Beaker Folk'. A few have yielded finds potentially of Fifth-Fourth Millennium date, such as Tarrant Launceston 4, Dorset, and Blackpatch 3, Sussex, where crouched inhumations were accompanied by leaf-shaped arrowheads. But these were in use at least down to the Overton period, so hardly provide firm dating evidence. More hopeful is the Whiteleaf Barrow, Buckinghamshire, which covered a disarticulated inhumation and produced great quantities of Fourth Millennium pottery, both plain and decorated.

If the importance of round barrows in the south is uncertain at this time there can be no doubt that both individual crouched inhumation and grave goods occurred. Crouched burials have been found at several causewayed enclosures both in the ditches, as at Windmill Hill, Offham and Hambledon Hill, and in interiors, as at Abingdon. At Whitehawk, the crouched remains of a woman and child were found in a rough cist of chalk blocks in one of the ditches. Other Whitehawk inhumations were accompanied by simple grave goods. A burial from Pangbourne, Berkshire, is important because it raises the spectre of a class of unmarked graves. Here the body of an old woman was accompanied by a vast Abingdon-style bowl, an antler hoe and animal bones. A more recent unmarked burial pit at Fengate contained three disarticulated burials and one crouched, the latter with a leaf-shaped arrowhead still sticking between the eighth and ninth ribs. Such finds are an effective reminder that there was much more to burial in the Fifth and Fourth Millennia than chambered tombs and long barrows.

The material equipment of the early farmers is well-known and only the pottery deserves extra comment. Round-based, plain vessels in a variety of local styles were common everywhere. Ornamentation was generally simple, and decorated wares were less widespread. The southern Ebbsfleet pottery demands special mention because of its significance for later developments. The characteristic hollow neck, slack shoulder and ornament of short repetitive motifs, betray an ancestry in other southern decorated styles during the Fourth Millennium, and this in turn led to the multitude of 'Peterborough' styles which were to be such a feature of the Meldon Bridge and Mount Pleasant periods. Flat bases must also be mentioned. Although round-bottomed pottery seems completely dominant, flat bases are known both from the Windmill Hill causewayed enclosure and beneath the bank of the great enclosure at Avebury. Flat-based pots recovered from burial sites, such as the Dyffryn Ardudwy chambered tomb, may also date as early as this. In the subsequent Meldon Bridge period the use of flat-based pottery mushroomed, but not until the Overton period did it finally oust round-bottomed vessels.

The physical characteristics of these early farmers are familiar, for these were the gracile, dolichocephalic 'Neolithic' types who have so often been contrasted with the shorter, more robust brachycephalic 'Bronze Age' population. Three important points must be stressed before proceeding further. Firstly, the dolichocephalic individuals who have attracted so much attention are mostly from the long barrows and megalithic tombs, and we have seen that these held a small, select and not necessarily representative, segment of the population. Secondly, there was clearly much more variation in these 'dolichocephalic' types than has been admitted, with cephalic indices ranging up to mesocephaly and overlapping with the 'Bronze Age' series. Thirdly, these two series are separated by the several centuries of the Meldon Bridge period, when very little is known about the development of British and Irish physical types. But it is clear that there was ample time for the 'dolichocephaly' of the Fourth Millennium to develop naturally into the 'brachycephaly' of the later Third–Second Millennia, without recourse to 'Beaker Folk' or other invaders.

This, then, was the state of Britain and Ireland when, towards 3000 BC, there were sweeping innovations in material culture, in burial and in ritual practices, and new forms of 'public' monuments appeared coinciding with the rundown of long-established traditions. What brought these changes about is not clear, but they signal the beginning of our story. Not for the first time we are faced with the riddle of practices familiar for a thousand years petering out. Until recently invasion would have been a ready answer, but in today's climate of opinion such simplified explanations must be more rigorously scrutinized.

Chapter II

The Prehistory of the Third Millennium: the Meldon Bridge and Mount Pleasant Periods

The last causewayed enclosures, long barrows and long chambered cairns were built by 2500 bc. Their construction may simply have ceased because every group who needed these monuments now had them. A more realistic explanation is a change in spiritual fashions and, possibly, social organization, for the dates of the latest of these old-style monuments overlap with the earliest dates for new forms of enclosure and burial monuments.

The prehistory of the Third Millennium has a unitary quality in terms of social and economic systems, material culture and spirituality, but can be divided into two around 2150 bc on the basis of a major technological innovation, metallurgy, and the emergence of the mysterious Beaker tradition. In absolute terms this means a Meldon Bridge period lasting from rather before 3000 BC to *c.* 2750 BC, giving way to a Mount Pleasant period which continued to *c.* 2000 BC. The fact that so many traditions, in terms of sites and artefacts, remained unchanged through both periods makes for uncertainty in assigning individual sites or events to one or the other period. For this reason radiocarbon dates are very important in Third Millennium prehistory.

Material culture

Since so much material culture is common to both periods it is best considered first. The plain, round-bottomed bowls, so widespread among early farmers, remained in fashion throughout the Meldon Bridge and Mount Pleasant periods, but their relative importance declined. The existing simple decorated styles petered out, although some contributed to the new range of decorated wares which were characteristic of the Third Millennium. In Britain two principal new traditions emerged (Figure 2.1), Grooved wares and Peterborough wares. The latter, with thick, coarse fabrics, heavy complex rims, cavetto neck, and profuse decoration, developed out of the Ebbsfleet ware of

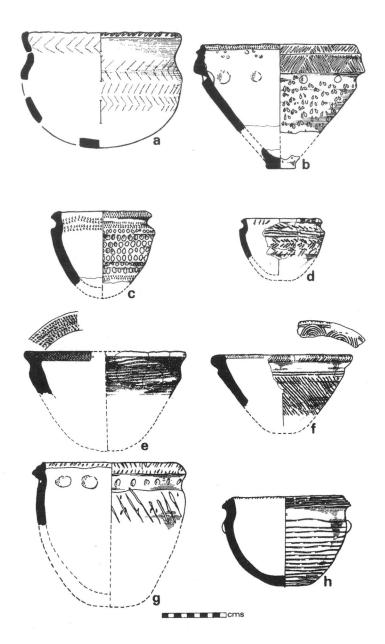

Figure 2.1 Styles of 'Peterborough' pottery: a. Ebbsfleet; b. Fengate; c–d. Mortlake; e–f. Meldon Bridge; g. Rudston; h. Dundrum. (a. Windmill Hill, Wilts., after Smith, 1965; b. and c. West Kennet, Wilts., after Piggott, 1962; d. Risby Warren, Lincs., after Riley, *PPS*, 1957; e. Meldon Bridge, Peebles, after Burgess, 1976; f. Ford, Northumberland, after Longworth, 1969; g. Rudston, Yorkshire, after Manby, 1975; h. Rath, Co. Wicklow, after Case, 1961)

the Fourth Millennium. Various Peterborough styles have been distinguished, some of them regional, but all had the traditional bowl-shaped body and round base except for the Fengate style. This had a collared rim, a trunconic body, a slight neck with circular impressions at intervals and a flat, often precariously small, base. Southern Peterborough styles, of which Mortlake ware is best known, are characterized by heavy T-, hammer-shaped and hooked rims, generally of rather rounded outline, combined with deeply cavetto necks. The rims of northern styles, namely the Rudston style of Yorkshire and the Meldon Bridge style of the Borders and eastern Scotland, can be similar, but are more often angular, expanded outwards, and have a slight chamfer on the outside and a flat top or internal bevel. This was the rim-form later to be displayed in the food-vessels of the Overton period, a point to which we shall return below. These northern styles, especially Meldon Bridge, frequently have shallow, sometimes almost imperceptible, necks and shoulders. Lines of horizontal cord are prominent in the Meldon Bridge style whereas Rudston material is characterized by incised ornament.

Too little Peterborough ware has been found in Wales and south-west Scotland to do more than record its existence, while in the Highlands and Islands completely different ceramic traditions predominated. In Ireland some Sandhills wares look very much like local versions of Peterborough pottery, especially the Dundrum style. But Ireland also had its own decorated wares, such as the thick, coarse Carrowkeel pottery, typical of passage graves (Figure 2.2), and characterized by simple, hemispherical, neck-less shapes, unexpanded rims and crude, all-over decoration; and Ballyalton bowls, often richly decorated, with a distinctive constricted mouth carinated like that of the Beacharra vessels of southern Scotland. The Scottish Highlands and Islands also have distinctive decorated traditions. The Rothesay ware of the western mainland, with decorated collared rims and plain hemispherical bodies, is found both in chambered tombs and settlements (at Rothesay *c.* 2120 bc), and resembles some Irish Sandhills ware. In the Hebrides very deep baggy vessels are found with multiple body cordons or ridges, covered with rich incised or grooved patterns.

Northern Scotland and the Northern Isles have their own wares. The stalled chamber cairns of the Fourth Millennium produce the very distinctive wall-sided Unstan bowls, but around 3000 BC Grooved wares emerged. These are found mainly in central southern England, East Anglia, Lincolnshire and east Yorkshire, and are then more thinly distributed through north-east Britain as far as the rich Orcadian finds. They are quite common in south-west Scotland, but rare or absent over the rest of western Britain. The distribution is thus very similar to that of Peterborough wares, except in the far north. Indeed, the two frequently occur at the same sites and must have been at least partly contemporary. Grooved wares have simple bucket, barrel and flower-pot shapes, with the typical grooved ornament arranged generally in geometric patterns, but

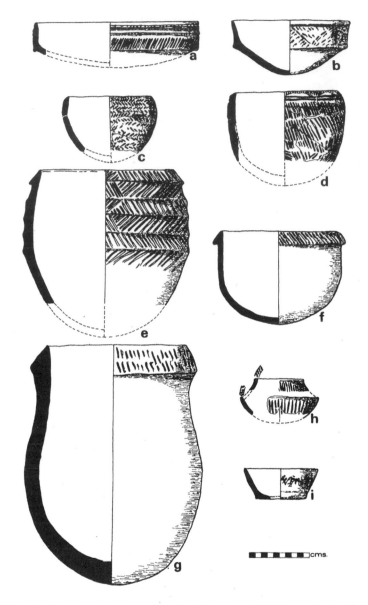

Figure 2.2 a–b. Unstan bowls; c–d. Carrowkeel bowls, e. Hebridean style, f. Rothesay style; g. Ronaldsway pot; h. Ballyalton ('Beacharra') bowl; i. Ronaldsway cup (a. Midhowe, b. Taversoe Tuack, Orkney, after Piggott, 1954; c–d. Loughcrew, Co. Meath, after Piggott, 1954; e. Eilean an Tighe, North Uist, after Lindsay Scott, 1950–1; f. Rudh an Dunain, Skye, after Piggott, 1954; g. Ballateare, i. Ronaldsway, Isle of Man, after Piggott, 1954; h. Ballyutoag, Co. Antrim, after Case, 1961)

with occasional spirals. The name does conceal abundant use of relief ornament, mainly vertical ribs, horizontal cordons and wavy lines. Impressed
ornament, including rustication is used especially to infill zones, or applied to
cordons. Completely plain vessels are also found. Various styles of Grooved
ware have been identified, but although some show regional bias none are
regionally exclusive, and it is one of the major puzzles of this pottery that
individual styles are distributed from the Orkneys to southern England. Its
origins are also shrouded in obscurity. Radiocarbon dates at present hint that
the Grooved wares of the far north are earliest, in which case an origin may be
sought in the Unstan ware of the Fourth Millennium, which frequently
employed grooved ornament. In this case Grooved ware will have developed
there early in the Meldon Bridge period. Because it is found in the south only
from the beginning of the Mount Pleasant period, and not a single piece occurs
in the intervening site of Meldon Bridge, suggests it may have had a long
gestation in the far north, spreading southwards only at the end of the Meldon
Bridge period.

The fact that Peterborough and Grooved wares overlapped from Yorkshire
southwards raises the possibility of complementary uses within the same
community. Grooved wares have practically never been found with burials and
are rare at burial sites. They come mainly from domestic sites, and from the
great southern enclosures of the Mount Pleasant period, which seem to have
included a domestic function amongst many others. Peterborough wares, on
the other hand, are frequently found at sepulchral sites, and do accompany
burials. We may therefore be dealing with a distinction between domestic and
sepulchral pottery, an idea made attractive by later developments. In the
Overton period we find just such a distinction between food vessels and
cinerary urns, lineal descendants of Peterborough wares and primarily for
burial purposes, whereas Deverel-Rimbury and similar, simple pottery,
derived from Grooved Wares, which served both domestic and sepulchral
functions, and, in some communities, may have been wholly domestic. More
practical, functional differences between Grooved and Peterborough wares are
another possibility but not yet obvious. Local chronological differences may
also be involved for the Meldon Bridge evidence shows that Peterborough
wares were in use as far north as the Borders by an early stage of the Meldon
Bridge period.

Whether Wales and Ireland had local versions of Grooved ware is not yet
clear. In both regions coarse, simple bucket and barrel shaped vessels are
well-known in the Third Millennium, for example the Lough Gur II, Kilhoyle
and Rockbarton pots of Ireland (Figure 2.3), but although these may have
been equivalent to Grooved wares, any relationship has yet to be demonstrated.

Artefacts which continued unchanged in form from the Fourth into the
Third Millennium, included the polished stone axe and a range of flint work

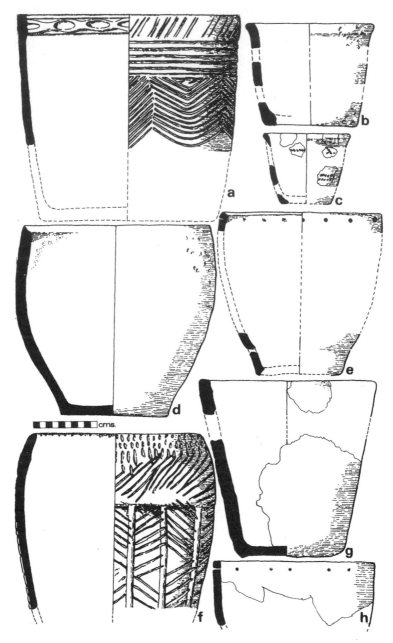

Figure 2.3 a., f. Grooved Ware; b., c. Kilhoyle pots; d, e, h. Lough Gur Class II ware; g. Bucket-shaped urn. (a. Clacton, Essex, after Piggott, 1954; b. Lyles Hill, Co. Antrim; c. Ballybriest, Co. Derry; d., h. Knockadoon, Lough Gur, Co. Limerick; e. Dyffryn Ardudwy, Merioneth; f. Durrington Walls, Wiltshire; g. Monknewtown, Co. Meath; b, c, d, h. after Case, 1961; e. after Lynch, 1969; f. after Wainwright and Longworth, 1971; g. after Sweetman, 1976)

including leaf-shaped arrowheads and scrapers. But the Meldon Bridge period is also characterized by novelties, such as lozenge, rhomboid, and transverse and hollow-based arrowheads, including lop-sided forms. Polishing was extended to a wider variety of tools including flake and discoidal knives. Edge-polished scrapers and perforated 'maceheads', both of antler and stone, also became increasingly familiar.

Settlement, farming and social organization

By the beginning of the Meldon Bridge period clearance and agricultural development had been going on for fifteen hundred years. Large parts of Britain and Ireland, especially the lighter soils on chalk and gravels, had been opened up, and clearance was biting deeply into less-favoured areas. Over the centuries since 3000 bc increasingly large tracts had been exhausted and had reverted to scrub and forest, so that a considerable agricultural crisis had developed. In all probability there were still fresh lands which could be exploited, sufficient to stave off complete disaster, but not enough to avoid a check in rising population levels and possibly even some slump. Farming patterns were changed in order to adapt to new circumstances, and the need to make the best possible use of the land compelled the enclosure of increasingly large areas in field systems. In Ireland large-scale enclosure had started even before the Meldon Bridge period to judge from the Behy-Glenulra fields, but whether any of the large British systems are as early as this has yet to be proved. By the opening of the Mount Pleasant period great areas on the river gravels of England were divided into field systems with ditch and hedge-bank margins, and land holdings were already being demarcated by pit alignments. The field system at Fengate, Peterborough, stretching over hundreds of acres, was established at this time, and even larger systems are now known stretching down the Fen Edge, sometimes, as at Billingborough Fen in Lincolnshire integrated with settlements. Aerial photography has revealed similar systems on many river gravels in the Midlands, but how many of these, or of the well-known field systems on the southern chalk, are as early as this is not clear.

Another problem of the Meldon Bridge period was increased waterlogging of low-lying areas. In the Somerset Levels new trackways had to be built in the period *c.* 2500–2200 bc, but whether this increased wetness was due to a damper climate or to drainage patterns being disturbed by interference with the natural forest cover is open to question. Certainly the scale of clearance in Ireland contributed to the significantly wetter soil conditions apparent there in the Mount Pleasant period. Blanket peat began to grow, and, in the centuries thereafter gradually cloaked, and choked, much of the landscape. As early as the Mount Pleasant period, farmers who had previously ploughed their fields found they had to dig lazybeds in the damp soil, as we see at Belderg Beg in Co. Mayo.

The pattern of settlement in the Third Millennium remained one of small, scattered farmsteads housing families or enlarged family groups. Even the largest field systems were worked from small farmsteads to judge from the discoveries at Behy-Glenulra and Fengate. But the form of houses may have changed, at least in some areas. The rectilinear timber houses of the early farmers are not so much in evidence in the Third Millennium, for round buildings became increasingly popular. The great enclosures of the Mount Pleasant period, Durrington Walls, Marden, Waulud's Bank and Mount Pleasant itself, all produced traces of round timber structures, in some cases of spectacular size. These were specialized sites, but ordinary farmsteads also had circular buildings. At least some of the ring ditches so plentiful on the gravels of English river valleys began life as settlements, and only later were converted into burial sites. Examples at Fengate, at Warren Farm, Milton Keynes, Buckinghamshire, and a triple ring ditch at Stanton Harcourt, Oxfordshire (Figure 5.1), are amongst those considered in greater detail in Chapter V. Surviving buildings within these heavily ploughed lowland sites are circular, and of a variety of structural forms.

Some Third Millennium settlements had both rectilinear and curvilinear structures, for example at Willington in Derbyshire, Hunstanton, Norfolk and Belle Tout, Sussex. These last two are among a number of enclosed settlements known from the Mount Pleasant period. Both bank and ditch and stockade perimeters are found, in some cases combined, as at Playden, Sussex. Rectangular bank and ditch enclosures have been excavated at Barford, Warwickshire, Sonning, Berkshire, and Belle Tout, while at Hunstanton a rectangular stockade without a ditch was discovered. Other palisade enclosures as far north as Bleasdale, Lancashire, and Lockerbie, Dumfriesshire, may also belong to this era.

Such settlements at present are uncommon. Too often all that survives is the 'pit and post-hole' site already familiar from earlier times, consisting of occupation areas with pits, gullies, post-holes and hearths scattered apparently at random, often rich in domestic refuse but without identifiable structures. Examples may be cited as far apart as Ballynagilly, Co. Tyrone, and Flamborough in Yorkshire. Tent-like structures are unlikely, except as temporary dwellings for seasonal activities, for the nature of society demanded more permanent buildings. These may often have been stake-built, covered with wattle and daub, and unlikely to survive except where excellent conditions occur.

Most of the settlements mentioned so far can be assigned to the Mount Pleasant period, but there is no reason to think that the settlement pattern of the Meldon Bridge period was very different. Some of the ubiquitous 'pit and post-hole' sites with Grooved and Peterborough wares must belong to this earlier part of the Third Millennium. At Meldon Bridge itself clusters of domestic pits and sporadic post-holes mostly pre-date the great timber wall and ritual features. The remnants of pottery linings in some of the pits suggest they were used for storage, but they all eventually became rubbish pits, just like the much larger storage pits of the late First Millennium.

Clues to the structure of Third Millennium society are provided by the scale of its 'public' works and the organization of the landscape. The enormity of monuments such as Silbury Hill in Wiltshire (*c.* 2725–2145 bc), the Dorset cursus, or the vast Irish passage graves such as Newgrange (*c.* 2585–2465 bc) and Knowth (*c.* 2795 bc, 2449 bc), leave no doubt that society was remarkably well organized, with powerful and capable ruling élites who could both command and carry out such undertakings. Furthermore, these demands for labour, and the way that increasingly large tracts of countryside were being enclosed, would have left less and less room for shifting populations of the sort that have traditionally peopled prehistoric Britain. As the landscape was brought under control so society, too, had to be organized. The agricultural crisis of the Fourth Millennium, leaving so many long-settled areas exhausted, may well have reduced the room for manoeuvre of small social units. The result in the Third Millennium was increasing delineation of territories, still more land allotment, and the formalizing of ruling élites. In the sense that the bounds of each territory limited the mobility of its population, society became increasingly static, and this would have been emphasized by the demands of more ordered agricultural systems and the labour requirements for the great public works. Wessex offers the best evidence for territorial division, going back to the early Fourth Millennium. It has been argued that the Wessex chalk was divided into five or six major territories of up to one thousand square kilometres. Each was marked by a cluster of tombs belonging to the leading elements in local society, and had a centre or 'capital', first causewayed enclosures, then enclosures of Durrington Walls type. These would house the paramount chief of the territory and serve as a focus for the scattered population, for the great 'public works' would demand some mechanism for bringing together the people. They would house meetings and rallies which would provide a means of communicating directly with the populace, but they would also accommodate fairs, markets, festivals and entertainments required by a scattered society.

Both forms of enclosure are sited peripherally to their barrow clusters, near the edge of the chalk, suggesting they served both chalk upland, the preserves of pastoral communities, and the lower chalk and adjoining lowlands occupied by more sedentary cultivators. Modern ethnographic parallels admit a completely different explanation of such a siting. Not all fragmented societies focus on territorial centres, and there are parts of the world where both internal and inter-tribal gatherings take place regularly at territorial boundaries. It is possible that these enclosures served just such an inter-territorial function.

In some areas, notably Yorkshire, round barrows had long been familiar, but with the decline of long barrows and long cairns there was an even greater emphasis on round mounds. The foundations were laid for the great round barrow cemeteries which became an increasingly dominant feature of the landscape. Although causewayed enclosures remained in use, new forms of enclosures were introduced belonging to the rag-bag classification termed 'henges'. These indicate changes in ethos, and perhaps in society itself. The first 'henges' lacked the standardized forms typical of later periods. Some early examples, for example at Dorchester, Oxfordshire, Barford, Warwickshire and Arminghall, Norfolk show multiple ditches, both continuous and segmented, separated and superimposed. Internal banks and external ditches were also common, occurring on a number of the more conventional, single-entrance (Class I) henges such as Llandegai A, Caernarvonshire and Stonehenge itself.

These small enclosures clearly served very different purposes from the 'causewayed camps', but the Meldon Bridge period also saw the development of new forms of large enclosures. At Meldon Bridge itself (Figure 2.4), the massive timber wall, five hundred metres long, was built only late in the period, but it closed off a gravel promontory between two valleys which had been densely occupied since the beginning of the period. Like the causewayed enclosures, and the great southern enclosures which followed in the Mount Pleasant period, the Meldon Bridge site served a variety of purposes. Its avenue entrance, standing posts and standing stones, all suggest ritual and ceremonial uses, while cremation pits are widespread in the interior. Some of the rubbish-filled storage pits belong to the enclosure phase, suggesting that some elements, whether rulers or holy men, actually lived in the site. One can speculate that Meldon Bridge dominated a large territory based on the Upper Tweed, in which case similar sites can now be expected to come to light. Indeed, a recent aerial discovery on river gravels at Forteviot, Perthshire, appears to be just such a site, with a post-pit perimeter approached by an avenue, and its interior filled with small hengi-form features. Such sites suggest that north Britain, too, was now being carved up into territories. These post-pit enclosures may have been the northern equivalent to the bank and ditch enclosures which appeared in the south at sites such as Broome Heath in Norfolk. This also lies on a river terrace, a bi-vallate earthwork along at least part of its length, its inner bank timber-reinforced at the front and crowned by a palisade. Here, as at Meldon Bridge, the defensive intent is clear. Broome Heath in its valley siting is reminiscent of two much larger C-shaped earthworks, Waulud's Bank in Bedfordshire and Marden in Wiltshire. Waulud's Bank, undated but associated with Grooved ware, has an external ditch, and could therefore have been founded in the Meldon Bridge period. Marden was one of the four new style large enclosures built in Wessex early in the Mount Pleasant period, all having the internal ditch and external bank of

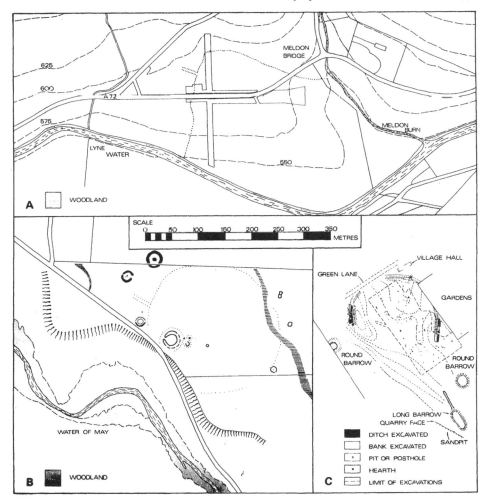

Figure 2.4 Enclosures of the Meldon Bridge period; A. Meldon Bridge, Peebles (after Burgess, 1976); B. Forteviot, Perth (after St Joseph, 1978); C. Broome Heath, Norfolk (after Wainwright, 1972)

the Class II henges which were now being built. Three of the four are adjacent to causewayed enclosures, and thus likely to have taken over their functions. The new Class II henges, with two opposed entrances, were much more standardized in form than the disparate sites which had been built hitherto.

Amongst the largest and most remarkable 'public' sites of the Third Millennium are the enigmatic cursus monuments. These linear bank and ditch sites usually extend across country for two or three kilometres, but the Dorset Cursus extends for no less than 9.6 kilometres, and emphasizes again the ability of these prehistoric societies to marshal large labour forces. Cursūs are notoriously difficult to date. The Dorchester-on-Thames example produced

Abingdon style pottery of the late Fourth Millennium, but one of the Rudstone cursūs in east Yorkshire and one near Stonehenge, were not built until the Mount Pleasant period. The development of the class as a whole may therefore have spanned the Meldon Bridge and Mount Pleasant periods.

Since large enclosures are found only in a few regions, other forms of monument must have performed their functions elsewhere. Chambered tombs were much more than mere sepulchres, and may have served as a focus for all manner of ceremonies and events vital to the life of their communities. This is indicated for example by the intense activity lately revealed around the fringes of the great passage graves of Newgrange and Knowth in Co. Meath. Most regions have notable complexes of monuments which may have served as territorial foci. Among the new 'public' monuments of the Third Millennium there were the first stone rings, and the great mound at Newgrange lies within what must be one of the earliest examples. Another at Stenness in Orkney (*c.* 2356, 2238 bc), within a Class I henge, lies amidst one of the most remarkable concentrations of monuments in these islands: the Rings of Brodgar and Bookan and the astounding Maes Howe passage grave all lie within a mile radius. There is room to mention only a few other notable complexes of the Third Millennium: the Callanish rings and stone avenues on Lewis, the Lough Gur sites in Co. Limerick, the Dorchester-on-Thames complex, and the Stanton Drew and Priddy circles in Somerset. All may have had the same relationship with their territories as Durrington Walls and the other great Wessex enclosures had with theirs.

Burial traditions

Burial, ritual, ceremony and religion were inseparable in the lives of the Third Millennium population. The regional diversity of burial customs is astonishing, and cannot be done justice in a few pages. In most areas both cremation and inhumation were practised, and this mixture persisted well into the Second Millennium, but the criteria which governed the choice of rite are seldom clear.

Round burial mounds came to dominate the Third Millennium landscape just as long mounds had dominated the Fourth. This applied to megalithic and non-megalithic areas alike. No more long chambered cairns were built after *c.* 2500 bc, which is exactly when passage graves under round mounds came into their own. Some of the largest and most complex of these appear to be the earliest, notably Newgrange (*c.* 2585, 2550, 2465 bc) and Knowth (*c.* 2795, 2449 bc). Knowth is ringed by mini-passage graves which were added during the Third Millennium, one, Site 13, having a date of *c.* 2208 bc. The construction of passage graves in Ireland appears to have gone on through the Meldon Bridge period and into the Mount Pleasant period, to judge from the dates for the Mound of the Hostages at Tara, Co. Meath (*c.* 2310–1930 bc) and Slieve Gullion, Co. Armagh (*c.* 2005 bc). This chronology can be extended to the similar Welsh passage graves. These unfortunately have no radiocarbon dates, but the Bryn Celli Ddu site on Anglesey was built on top of a henge monument, while Bryn yr Hen Bobl, a round mound chambered tomb but not strictly a passage grave, was built over a domestic site which produced Peterborough and Beaker sherds.

Most numerous of the Irish chambered tombs and decidedly odd men out are the wedge-shaped tombs concentrated in the south-west and west (Plate II). They are also the tombs about which least is known, mainly because finds have been so sparse and ambiguous. Like the entrance graves of the Scillies and south-east Ireland they have sometimes produced late material which may have clouded their overall chronology. Beaker and Kilhoyle pottery has come from several examples, and much has been made of their complementary distribution to food vessel cist burials in the Second Millennium. This would place them in the Mount Pleasant and Overton periods, possibly surviving as late as the Knighton Heath period to judge from the mould fragments found in several tombs, and the date of *c.* 1160 bc from that at Island, Co. Cork. But doubts remain about the stratigraphic position of all this late material, and its relationship to the construction and original use both of the 'wedges' and the entrance graves. Seldom are later burials so clearly secondary as in the case of the in-urned cremations dug into the entrance grave at Harristown, Co. Waterford (Figures 2.5 and 2.6).

A preponderance of cremation burial characterizes the wedge tombs in accord with the general trend in Irish chambered tombs, but their westerly orientation contrasts with the easterly attitude of all other Irish tombs. This odd orientation is paralleled in the Clava passage graves of north-east Scotland, which present similar problems of affinity and chronology. In the past the classic corbelled 'tholos' chamber of the Clava tombs has invited comparison with passage graves in Atlantic Europe, amongst which are the earliest megaliths ever built. Unfortunately excavated examples have produced practically no finds, but the suggestion of an early date is contradicted by the relationship of Clava tombs to other sites in their region. They are so closely integrated in a local ritual-ceremonial mosaic with cup-marked stones, stone circles, especially recumbent stone circles, ring cairns and other features of the late Third–Second Millennia that it seems impossible that they were of a vastly different date.

The other passage graves of Scotland, in the Hebrides, the northern mainland and the Orkneys, are more conventional, and like those in Wales and Ireland belong mainly to the Third Millennium. Construction probably lasted into the Mount Pleasant period to judge from the date for the Embo tomb in Sutherland (*c.* 1920 bc). Dates for the varied and often architecturally sophisticated passage graves of Orkney suggest a development lasting right through

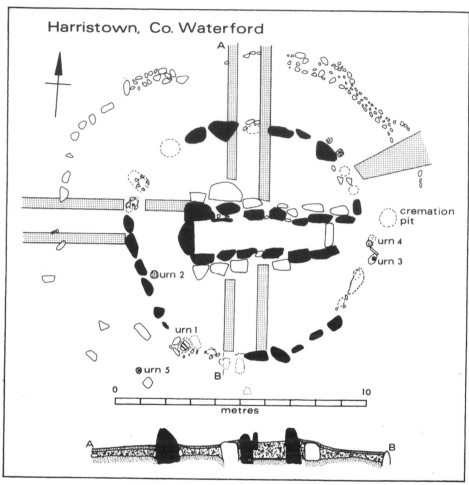

Figure 2.5 Entrance grave with secondary cremations, Harristown, Co. Waterford (after J. Hawkes, 1941)

the Meldon Bridge and into the Mount Pleasant period. For the magnificent Quanterness tomb the range is *c.* 2640–1920 bc, for the similar Quoyness *c.* 2315 and 2240 bc, while Maes Howe, greatest of all the Orkney tombs, yielded dates of *c.* 2185 and 2020 bc, from the base of its encircling ditch. Stalled cairns on the island of Rousay, and by implication those on the mainland, have given a similar range of dates from *c.* 2390–2055 bc, but they are associated with Unstan ware, and some of them are under long mounds, so their construction and early use may have preceded that of passage graves earlier in the Fourth Millennium. Stalled cairns are named from the massive upright slabs built to project from their chamber sides at intervals, dividing them into 'stalls'. In Caithness stalled chambers are incorporated into long

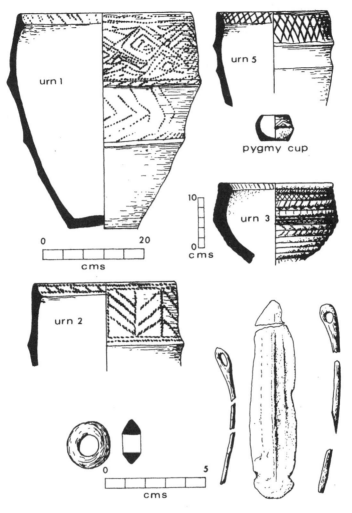

Figure 2.6 Pottery and other finds associated with cremation burials, Harristown, Co. Waterford (after J. Hawkes, 1941)

horned cairns at sites such as Yarrows and Camster Long, perhaps another indication of Fourth Millennium beginnings.

Much less is known about the scattered Hebridean tombs. Excavated examples have produced quantities of the baggy vessels, often richly decorated with incised ornament, which typified western Scotland in the late Fourth–Third Millennia.

The burial rites in these late chambered tombs varied from region to region. Cremation was overwhelmingly used in the Irish tombs, and often large numbers of individuals are represented, but inhumation was not unknown, and became more common in the Mount Pleasant period. Cremation also occurs in the Welsh tombs, but in Scotland both rites occur: cremation predominating on the mainland but inhumation in the Hebrides and Orkneys, where the recent Quanterness excavations suggest the bodies were exposed elsewhere and brought to the tomb as disarticulated bones.

In view of the scanty human remains found in many chambered tombs with long and complex histories it seems likely that they were cleaned and re-used time and time again. This applies particularly to many of the Scottish tombs, and means that excavated finds may reflect only the latest activities in a site's history.

Nevertheless it is strange that no tomb was ever filled with human remains to anything like its capacity, not even the Irish passage graves where considerable accumulations of burnt bone are common. It is likely that the burials at these sites were only part of a much wider range of ceremonial and ritual functions, and that they were certainly not intended to act as charnel houses for successive burials. For example it has been claimed that some of the Irish passage graves were closed off soon after an initial series of burials was deposited. At some of these sites, a slot, rather like a megalithic letter box, has been found above and behind the sealed entrance, too small to permit easy access. The most famous example, the Newgrange 'roof-box', has a closing block of quartz which could have been moved and replaced after a visit. It has been suggested that these slots may have been oracles, an opening through which questions could have been shouted and the muffled 'reply', the echo, bounced back. The Newgrange roof box was cunningly positioned so that fleetingly on Midwinter's day the rising sun would pierce through it and along the twenty metres length of the passage to strike an observer standing in the central chamber. Clearly these were not arrangements for simple sepulchres.

At Newgrange and equally massive Knowth, excavations have revealed the scale of the activities which went on round the main mound. Unfortunately, few other tombs have had their peripheries excavated. The hearths and buried ox carcass in the forecourt of Bryn Celli Ddu show that ritual acts took place outside the passage graves but their nature can only be guessed at. Similarly hearths, burning, deposits of animal and human bones and of artefacts in the forecourts of long tombs raise interesting questions about their later use. Radiocarbon dates and finds make it clear that although none were constructed after *c.* 2500 bc they remained centres of activity throughout the Third Millennium. There are dates for late forecourt activity at several long tombs, including Irish court cairns in Co. Armagh at Annaghmare (*c.* 2445 bc), Ballymacdermot (*c.* 1710, 1565 bc), at Ballyutoag. Co. Antrim (*c.* 2170 bc); and at the Clyde tomb of Monamore on Arran (*c.* 2240 bc).

The latest of these dates, together with the Beaker pottery associated with the blockings and sealing deposits from many sites, suggests that activity continued at chambered tombs, and they were not finally sealed off, until the end of the Mount Pleasant period.

In southern and eastern England a similar situation developed, with round barrows proliferating as long barrow construction petered out around 2500 bc. It has long been axiomatic that the round burial mound and individual crouched inhumation burial were introduced into these islands by immigrant 'Beaker Folk'. This has totally confused the early history both of this class of monument and of the burial rite. The persistence of such myths is all the more surprising in view of the contrary evidence which has been plentiful since Victorian times. Leaving aside the frequent presence of round mounds over chambered tombs, which was somehow considered not relevant to the wider problem of round mound beginnings, many nineteenth century excavations of round barrows and cairns revealed 'Neolithic' burials. In northern Britain, at sites such as the Ford barrow in Northumberland, the use of cremation could admit the possibility of a genuine 'Neolithic' aberration, but further south, where inhumation usually prevailed, the fixation with Beaker influence generally resulted in these sites being dated to a period when it could be invoked. Any round mound covering an unaccompanied inhumation was immediately dated not earlier than the Beaker period. Even where such typical 'Neolithic' grave goods as polished stone axes or leaf-shaped flint arrowheads were present, these were explained away in terms of survival.

If there were no Beaker Folk then this whole equation must be re-examined. That individual crouched inhumation, sometimes accompanied by grave goods, was a venerable insitution long before the Meldon Bridge period is made clear by the burials from causewayed enclosures and long barrows. This is southern evidence, but it is not yet so easy to establish an equally long ancestry for southern round barrows. The problem is a lack of datable artefacts and the natural reluctance to apply radiocarbon dating to unaccompanied burials. Yet in addition to the many round barrows over individual inhumations there are others which cover multiple inhumations very much in the 'Neolithic' tradition; for example three skeletons at Winterborne St. Martin 34b, five at Winterborne St. Martin 5c, and six at Winterborne Came 18b, all in Dorset. Even 'Neolithic' finds are inconclusive, for these are generally long-lived types which remained in use well into the Beaker period. Thus at Tarrant Launceston 4 in Dorset, there was a leaf-shaped arrowhead, while at Blackpatch 3 in Sussex, two crouched skeletons with leaf arrowheads, flint axes and other flint tools had a cremation scattered over them. That many of these could belong to the Meldon Bridge period, and even earlier, is made clear by those few round barrows which are indisputably pre-Beaker. A notable example is the Whiteleaf barrow in Buckinghamshire, which covered a disarticulated skeleton and much Fourth Millennium pottery. We may therefore be able to interpret literally the stratigraphic evidence from sites such as Linch Hill in Oxfordshire and Handley Down 26 in Dorset, where Beaker deposits are secondary to 'Neolithic' burials. Both of these ditched round barrows covered inhumations accompanied by 'Neolithic' jet belt sliders. At

Linch Hill a much smaller ditched barrow was subsequently constructed on one corner of the existing site. This new monument covered a similar crouched inhumation, but now accompanied by a Beaker and other typical 'Beaker' grave goods. At Handley Down the vital evidence comes from the fill of the barrow ditch, where Peterborough pottery was stratified below Beaker pottery. There is now reason to think that such jet sliders, and the burials and monuments with which they are associated, go back at least to the early part of the Meldon Bridge period. What is most urgently needed now is a systematic programme of radiocarbon dating of unaccompanied inhumations, both individual and multiple, under round mounds in southern and eastern England.

The evidence from northern England is much more positive. Characteristic of 'Bronze Age' burial traditions in the north were inhumations, single and multiple, sometimes with cremations, all placed in one or more graves, often pit-graves (Pl. IX), or on the old ground surface, under round barrows. All these permutations were introduced long before the Meldon Bridge period. For example, 'Bronze Age' barrows typically cover pit graves containing successive interments, as at Garton Slack 75 (Figure 7.1), but these are matched by pit graves with successive burials under 'Neolithic' mounds such as the giant Duggleby Howe on the Yorkshire Wolds (Figure 2.7), except that these have 'Neolithic' grave goods. In the case of Duggleby Howe we are dealing with a very early example of the rite, for one burial was accompanied by a Towthorpe bowl, a type which emerged long before the Meldon Bridge period. At Duggleby Howe, as under so many 'Bronze Age' round barrows, there were cremations as well as inhumations, here mixed together in a cemetery in the covering mound.

Undoubtedly some of the 'Neolithic' round barrows in Yorkshire were raised in Beaker times, for there are here few Beaker-accompanied burials which can be assigned to the Mount Pleasant period. But equally others, for example with Towthorpe pots at Towthorpe 18 and Aldro 94, must go back at least to the Meldon Bridge period.

Burials in stone cists, another common 'Bronze Age' tradition in Yorkshire and the Pennines as in other Highland Zone regions, may also have had much earlier beginnings, for there are numbers of cist burials with 'Neolithic' artefacts such as those at Burythorpe in Yorkshire, and Liffs Low in Derbyshire.

Further north, beyond the Tees and in Scotland, round barrows and cairns have equally early origins, although they usually covered cremations. Cremation round barrows at Pitnacree, Perthshire, and Ford, Northumberland, belong to the early Fourth Millennium on the evidence of their Grimston pottery and the former's radiocarbon date of 2860 bc ± 90. Another north-

Figure 2.7 Round barrow, Duggleby Howe, Yorkshire (after Mortimer, 1905) (various scales)

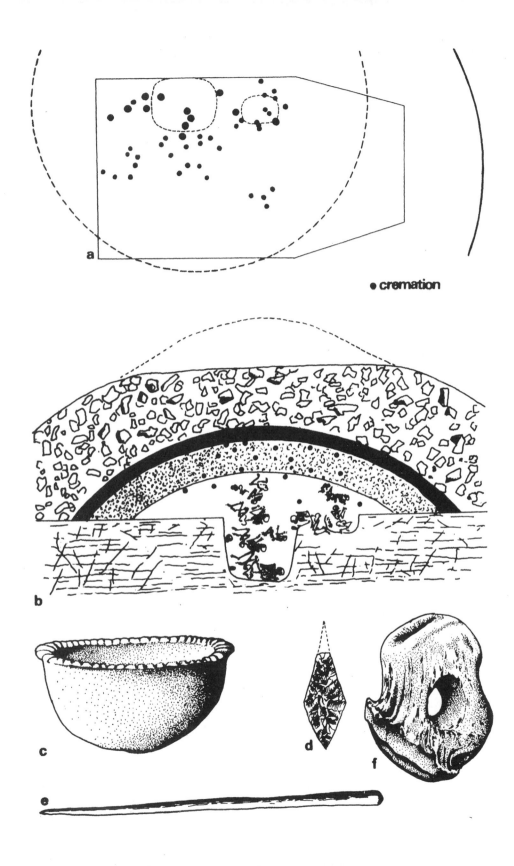

● cremation

a

b

c

d

e

f

eastern round barrow, at Copt Hill, Co. Durham, covered a cremation trench very similar to those found under some Yorkshire long barrows. Long mounds are so rare in north-east England and eastern Scotland that burial under round mounds may always have been more important here than in other parts of Britain. But the most puzzling burial tradition of these regions is the so-called flat cist grave that is such a dominant feature in the Mount Pleasant and Overton periods. The origin of these cists, which were probably covered at least by low tumps, is at present an insoluble problem. The difficulty is much the same as we face in tracing the beginnings of individual crouched inhumation under round mounds: the earliest datable grave goods are Beakers, and this has coloured the dating of the whole series. It is now tempting to speculate that the cists, like the round mounds, were introduced long before Beakers, but it is a speculation at present without any positive evidence, and one which urgently requires checking by a programme of radiocarbon dating of unaccompanied cist burials.

In Wales few burials of the early farmers other than a comparatively small number of chambered tombs have been recognized, so here too round mound burial may have started early. Wales does have some notable examples of another type of burial site belonging to the Meldon Bridge and Mount Pleasant periods; deposits in caves, fissures and rock shelters. Not surprisingly such burials are also abundant in the limestone areas of the Pennines. Close dating is difficult given the present imprecision in dating the 'Neolithic' finds from these sites. At a few, such as Dowel Cave in Derbyshire, the presence of Beaker sherds points to the Mount Pleasant period rather than the Meldon Bridge period, but at some deeply stratified burial caves, such as Elbolton in Yorkshire (Figure 7.11), the earliest interments must be appreciably earlier than Beakers. Notable cave and fissure burials include those at Gop Cave in Flintshire, and Ash Tree and Church Dale Caves in Derbyshire. Multiple inhumations were normal, often placed in stone chambers or cists built inside the cave. Articulated skeletons have been found, but the remains are frequently disarticulated and fragmentary, and it is not always possible to distinguish between formal burial, informal deposits, and the results of accidents.

Some Pennine round cairns cover cist burials recessed into rock shelves or clefts, as if in imitation of these cave burials, or preserving some memory of them. Such a site was Bee Low Cairn cist 1, Derbyshire (Figure 2.9), built into a crevice and containing multiple inhumations, all very reminiscent of the Gop Cave tradition. Yet the only accompanying artefact was an All Over Cord Beaker, providing a graphic demonstration of the way in which Beakers were adopted by local communities to fit into their sepulchral traditions.

This assimilation can also be seen in the notable Irish site of Caherguilla-more, Co. Limerick, which blends a variety of traditions, including cave burial. Here a crouched inhumation, possibly under a low mound, stood guard

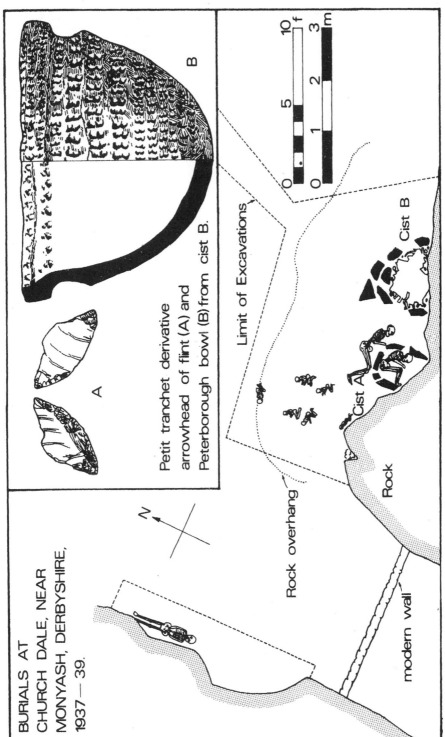

BURIALS AT
CHURCH DALE, NEAR
MONYASH, DERBYSHIRE,
1937—39.

N

A

B

Petit tranchet derivative
arrowhead of flint (A) and
Peterborough bowl (B) from cist B.

Limit of Excavations

Rock overhang

Cist A

Cist B

Rock

modern wall

0   5   10 f

0   1   2   3 m

Figure 2.8   Rock shelter cemetery, Church Dale (Calling Low Dale), Derbyshire (after Piggott, 1953) (inset scale: rim diameter of bowl 15.2 cm)

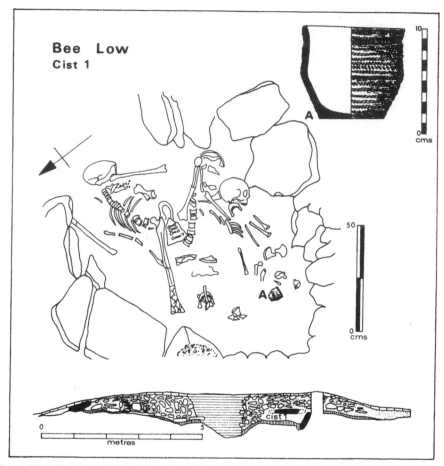

Figure 2.9 Bee Low, Derbyshire: cist with multiple inhumations and Beaker (after Marsden, 1970)

at the mouth of a chamber formed by a massive slab leaning against a cliff face. This chamber was full of jumbled bones, bone pins and decorated vessels of types familiar from passage graves. Rockbarton vessels, which are usually linked to Beakers, were also present, and fragments of a crude Beaker were found on a ledge on the cliff above the chamber. The crouched burial outside the chamber was accompanied by a decorated bowl, similar to those found with another distinctive group of Third Millennium burials. These are the tombs of Linkardstown type in eastern Ireland, large round mounds raised over chambers of megalithic proportions. These contain individual inhumations, sometimes disarticulated, as at Linkardstown and Baunogenasraid in Co. Carlow (Figure 2.10), sometimes articulated, in which case the body may be extended, as at Jerpoint West, Co. Kilkenny, or partially contracted, as at Drimnagh, Co. Dublin. One of the most notable features of all these sites is

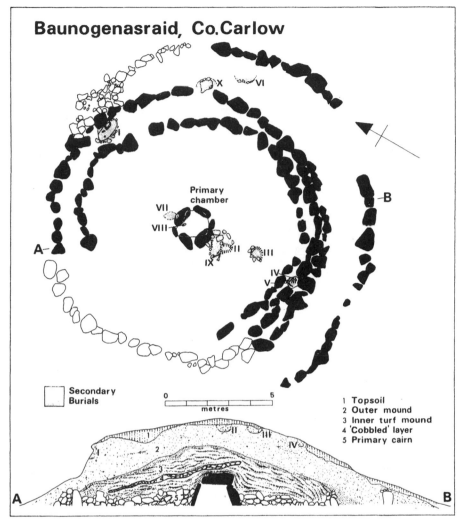

Figure 2.10 Tomb of Linkardstown type, Baunogenasraid, Co. Carlow (after B. Raftery, 1974)

the richly decorated bowl with which each is associated (Figure 2.11). Most sites had their mounds enlarged in the Overton and Bedd Branwen periods to take further burials, sometimes inhumations, sometimes cremations, some with food vessels, some in urns. In the absence of closely datable grave goods and radiocarbon dates the Linkardstown tombs suffer from the chronological uncertainties which affect so much in the Meldon Bridge and Mount Pleasant periods. They clearly represent a mixture of influences, but in the present state of knowledge it would be rash to speculate further.

As if this kaleidoscope of burial practices was not enough, there is another

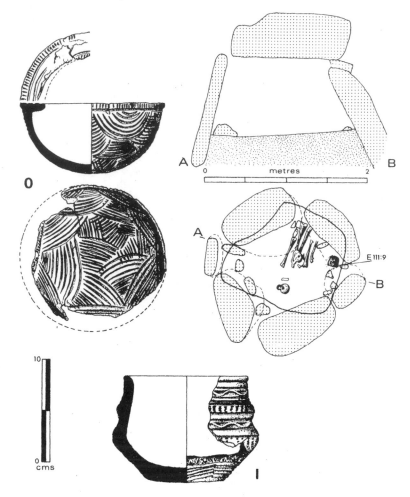

Figure 2.11 Baunogenasraid, Co. Carlow: o. decorated bowl from primary burial; plan and section of primary cist; i. food vessel from secondary burial (after B. Raftery, 1974)

important form of burial which appeared in the Meldon Bridge period and became a long-lasting tradition in Britain and Ireland. This is the flat cremation cemetery, whose existence alongside the range of more ostentatious burial sites discussed above, raises interesting social questions. The origins of this cremation rite unfortunately are no more certain. As pottery and grave goods are seldom present, radiocarbon dates are required to distinguish between cemeteries of the Meldon Bridge period and those of the Mount Pleasant period. Some may have spanned both periods.

The rise of the cremation cemetery in the Meldon Bridge period is closely linked with that of the heterogeneous group of enclosures which includes the early 'henges'. A number of these have produced cremation burials, such as

Llandegai A in Caernarvonshire and Stonehenge itself. The Stonehenge cremations appear to have been deposited over a considerable period, like those in some of the Dorchester sites and at Llandegai A. Here they came almost entirely from a segmented ring of shallow pits (*c.* 2530 bc) immediately outside the entrance of the henge (*c.* 2470 bc). At Meldon Bridge cremations were sparsely scattered over a large area, usually in pits marked by standing stones or posts. One exceptional site consisted of a cremation pit placed centrally within a ring of post-holes.

At Cairnpapple in West Lothian a cremation cemetery was established on the site before a double-entrance Class II henge was built in the Mount Pleasant period. Cremation cemeteries also occur in Irish enclosures. The great embanked site at Monknewtown in Co. Meath produced scattered cremations in pits, in cists, and, in one case, within a ring ditch. Some of these burials may have been appreciably earlier than extensive occupation deposits found associated with Beaker pottery and a pear-shaped house (*c.* 1860 bc). The Monknewtown cremations were broadly contemporary with the cremations in the great passage graves which lie a few miles to the south in the bend of the Boyne. Amongst these there are more enclosures, like Monknewtown but unexcavated. Perhaps here there is evidence for social distinction, between those buried modestly in cremation cemeteries, and those ostentatious interments in the passage graves. Again a structured society is suggested by contrasting burial customs, a recurring theme in later prehistory, and one we shall see still further exaggerated in the Second Millennium.

Cremation cemeteries also existed on the Isle of Man in the Meldon Bridge period. The Ronaldsway societies of the Third Millennium lived in farmsteads based on sunken sub-rectangular buildings, sprinkled across a no doubt well-organized landscape. The well-known Ronaldsway pottery is characterized by deep, baggy vessels with collared rims, related both to Irish Sandhills ware and west Scottish ceramics such as Rothesay ware. There were also flat-based cups, again with west Scottish parallels. Much of the material culture is found in other Irish Sea lands, including mushroom-headed bone pins and stone plaques decorated with geometric ornament. The dead were buried in small cremation cemeteries, two of which now have radiocarbon dates: at Killeaba (*c.* 2431, 2350 bc) and Ballaharra (*c.* 2283, 2275 bc).

The bewildering variety of burial customs which emerged in the Meldon Bridge period in part reflects the very complex structure of society at that time. More intelligible patterns may emerge when more radiocarbon dates are available, and deeper understanding of the material culture permits closer dating of individual sites and finds. Much of this complex mix of burial, ceremonial and ritual persisted after *c.* 2150 bc, when the Beaker tradition began to filter in from the Continent. This affected most societies only superficially, but its arrival provides a convenient point at which to divide

Third Millennium prehistory, the Meldon Bridge period from the Mount Pleasant period.

Traditionally the appearance of metallurgy and Beakers heralds the arrival of immigrants from the Continent, Beaker Folk, who were physically different from the indigenous Neolithic population, transformed existing institutions, and quickly relegated the natives to a subordinate role. Many of these long held notions are now seen to be questionable, including the supposed change in physical type. Others are illusory, like the change from wheat to barley cultivation which Beaker settlers are supposed to have instituted. It now seems that the basic structure of Irish-British societies, and the ways in which people lived and died, were only marginally affected by metal and Beakers. Copper tools and ornaments were introduced, but were not markedly superior to stone equipment, and the Beaker tradition added considerably to the store of ritual practices and material possessions. But people continued to live in the same settlements, farming as their forebears had for generations, with the same beliefs, burial customs and ritual monuments, and persisting with much of their old material culture. Only centuries later, long after Beakers and metal had become commonplace, were some of these long-established traditions disrupted, but by then the Mount Pleasant period had given way to the Overton period.

Beakers in Britain and Ireland

The classic Bell Beaker is a well-made, thin-walled, S-profiled vessel with a fine, usually reddish surface. Decoration is executed with a toothed comb, producing distinctive dentated line designs, or with all-over twisted cord lines (AOC). Two primary forms achieved an international distribution, the Maritime Beaker, with plain and comb-decorated horizontal bands of equal width, and AOC Beakers. In each region local Beaker series were soon developed, but the fineness and the tooth comb ornament persisted, and remained the hall-mark of Beakers as a whole.

Beakers were in use in Britain and Ireland for about a thousand years, from around 2750 BC (*c.* 2150 bc) until 1650 BC (*c.* 1450 bc), and their form and status naturally changed considerably in that time. They brought Britain and Ireland into an international tradition block which stretched as far east as Hungary, and from Denmark to Spain and Sicily. Beakers were the nucleus of an international artefact package that eventually comprised such familiar items as tanged copper daggers, stone 'bracers', barbed and tanged flint arrowheads, v-perforated buttons and double-pointed awls, together constituting the outward sign of a movement or idea the precise nature of which may never be revealed.

This Beaker package was everywhere blended into local contexts alongside local artefacts, and the absence of any accompanying international social or economic system, house or settlement type, ritual or burial tradition, argues powerfully against a great Beaker folk movement in the traditional sense. The Beaker tradition in fact was adapted as it was absorbed into local culture, so that in different countries it occurs in very different contexts. In Atlantic Europe, from Iberia to Ireland, it is found notably in megaliths and settlements; in Brittany seldom outside chambered tombs. By contrast, in northwest Europe, including Britain but not Ireland, it is associated above all with individual inhumation burials. Increasingly it appears that the form of a regional Beaker tradition was shaped partly by existing local traditions and partly by its form in the area from which it was received.

How the Beaker tradition spread is a matter for debate. It could have been passed on from territory to territory by normal culture contact, much in the way that the Peyote Cult spread from Mexico to Canada in the decades after 1850. The Peyote Cult incorporated a cult package of artefacts which swept along with it: rattles, a carved staff, a feather fan, a small drum and a crescentic altar of clay or earth. This provides an attractive analogy for the Beaker package. Alternatively we could be dealing with a prestige or fashion package, spread either by culture contact or by commerce, rather like the Gallo-Belgic beaker package more than two thousand years later. This contained all the utensils appropriate to Mediterranean eating and drinking habits, including another beaker, the Butt Beaker, and owed its success to the desire of barbarians from Lombardy to Lincoln to ape the manners, especially culinary, of the Roman world.

Whether Beakers represent a cult, a fashion or something quite different, they were special prestige vessels, requiring a technology and skill much higher than that used in normal potting. This does not rule out dissemination by culture contact, for the necessary expertise could have formed part of the Beaker package. But it admits alternatives, perhaps a corps of itinerant specialist potters, Beaker bearers or cult masters, who could integrate themselves in local communities and adapt their mysteries to the local milieu.

The origins of the Beaker tradition have been sought in Iberia, the most favoured source, in central Europe, in the Gulf of Lions, and in the Low Countries, and some have even hinted recently of beginnings in Britain. On the analogy of the Peyote Cult, Beakers could have spread over Europe in a few decades, much too short a time for radiocarbon dating to pinpoint their starting point. So their ultimate beginnings remain uncertain, although the generally accepted view is that the immediate source of British Beakers lay in north-west Europe, especially the Low Countries and the Rhineland. Whether the first were brought in the course of normal traffic across the narrow seas, or deliberately by Beaker Bearers, in the form of cult-masters, specialists or entrepreneurs, the evidence does not reveal. It is much more important to note the complete lack of proof for any major folk movement, and the way in which

Beakers, far from disrupting local traditions, were accommodated within them.

These initial imports were the only Continental Beakers to reach Britain in significant numbers. Local manufacture soon took over, though whether immigrant or local potters were involved is another matter. In the ensuing centuries British Beaker potters, while constantly mindful of Continental Beaker styles, nevertheless developed an insular tradition which diverged progressively from the Continental Beaker series.

The Beaker tradition began in Britain with AOC vessels, the primary areas of development being Wessex and the Upper Thames Valley, Yorkshire and eastern Scotland. There had been a long tradition of pottery decorated with horizontal corded lines in these and other parts of Britain and Ireland, stretching back through the Meldon Bridge period. Some of this material is clearly Peterborough pottery of various styles, for example at Meldon Bridge, but not all can instantly or easily be assigned to a recognizable class of pottery. The greatest puzzle of all are the sherds, apparently of AOC Beaker, in constructional levels at the Giants' Hills long barrow in Lincolnshire. Long barrow construction had ceased by the onset of the Meldon Bridge period, and even if Giants' Hills was one of the latest long barrows (*c*. 2460, 2370 bc), these sherds, if indeed AOC Beaker, would be appreciably earlier than any AOC vessels on the Continent. This problem clearly has too many ramifications to be solved here, but the simplest answer is that the Giants' Hill sherds have been incorrectly identified. Could they be related, for example, to the corded ware 'Protruding-foot' beakers, which precede AOC Beakers in the Netherlands and have radiocarbon dates around 2400–2300 bc?

Whatever the answer to these problems, AOC Beakers reached Britain by *c*. 2150 bc on the evidence of Dutch radiocarbon dates. A distinct interval elapsed before the arrival of comb-decorated examples, in the form of Maritime Beakers, dated from *c*. 2000 bc by Dutch evidence. These were found in appreciable numbers but only in Wessex and the Upper Thames Valley, and for a long time this was the only region of Britain to develop a local tradition of combed Beakers. A century or more elapsed before much interest was shown in tooth comb ornament elsewhere. Then mid-way through the Mount Pleasant period, from *c*. 1900 bc, there was an upsurge in interest in the tooth comb technique, and it spread inexorably throughout the country. Only then did distinctive regional Beaker styles begin to emerge, all sporting combed ornament.

This surprising initial lack of success of tooth-comb ornament may have been due to the fact that AOC Beakers had already achieved wide acceptance. Cord ornament was in any case a familiar insular technique, whereas tooth-comb decoration was a rather 'fiddly' novelty.

The Beaker tradition of Ireland provides a notable contrast with that of Britain. Beakers in Britain occur in a wide variety of contexts, but above all with inhumation burials, especially individual crouched inhumations in flat graves, cists and under round barrows. In Ireland, Beakers never occur with such burials, but have come mainly from settlements and, to a lesser extent, megalithic tombs. Here is cogent evidence of the way in which existing cultural traditions shaped reactions to the Beaker phenomenon. In Britain, as in north-west Europe, there was a long inhumation tradition, in Ireland there was not. The dichotomy may have been further emphasized by the two islands drawing their versions of the Beaker tradition from different sources.

Irish Beakers have usually been seen as an extension of the British series, which is undoubtedly true in part, for the later, necked forms in particular do echo British developments. But there are surprising numbers of early comb-decorated Beakers from Irish sites, such as Dalkey Island, Co. Dublin, and Lough Gur, Co. Limerick, which are very different in character from contemporary British Beakers. The only region in Britain with a strong combed tradition at this early stage was Wessex. How could the early Irish combed material be derived from Wessex when the intervening areas of western Britain have produced very few early combed vessels? Furthermore, some of the Irish vessels are not at all like the Wessex finds, but do share common features with Atlantic Beakers. This suggests a dual origin for Irish Beakers. The version of the Beaker tradition which reached Ireland initially came from as yet undefined areas of Atlantic Europe, where Beakers, as in Ireland, have been found principally in megalithic tombs and domestic sites. This Atlantic-based tradition was readily acceptable in a land which already had strong Atlantic contacts, and established the pattern which the Irish Beaker tradition was to follow. Midway through the Mount Pleasant period, comb decoration began to spread throughout Britain, resulting in new British Beaker styles which eventually spilled over into Ireland. Necked Beaker forms began to appear in Ireland, just like those in Britain, but by this time Irish Beaker styles were already settled and the Beaker inhumation burial so typical of Britain remained unknown in Ireland.

This idea of a dual origin for Irish Beakers is doubly attractive because it fits well with what is known of metallurgical developments during this period. A good case can be made out for an initial Atlantic source for Irish metallurgy which was only later, in the Mount Pleasant period, tempered by north-west European influences transmitted via Britain.

The typology of Beakers has attracted an inordinate amount of attention over the past century, and resulted in numerous classification schemes. The general trend in development, in Britain and Ireland, as in many Continental regions, was from the primary S-profiled 'bell' shape to taller shapes, both 'bell' and ovoid, then to necked shapes, with a distinct break in the outline between neck and body; and from simple to increasingly more complex and bold decoration. The simplest classification, whether labelled α, β, γ or A, B, C, distinguishes between bell (β, B), short-necked (γ, C) and long-necked (α,

A) Beakers, and has obstinate echoes in the more complex schemes of recent years. One of these, the intricate classification of D. Clarke, envisaged no less than seven separate Beaker immigrations in two main waves, producing seven Beaker groups of Continental origin, from which sprang eight regional British developments. An important contribution of this scheme was its recognition of three main insular traditions, first an 'East Anglian' group made up of biconical and ovoid vessels, then Northern and Southern traditions, to be equated roughly with short-necked and long-necked vessels, which dominated the later stages of Beaker development.

The importance of the alternative scheme of the Dutchmen Lanting and van der Waals was that for the first time Irish-British Beakers were viewed with a Continental eye. It was they who realized that the only intrusive Beakers in the British series were the original AOC and Maritime vessels, and that all others represented the developing insular tradition. They were also the first to treat British Beakers in terms of inter-related regional developments. Their scheme proposed seven developmental steps, running roughly in synchronism over the country as a whole (Figure 2.12). Steps 1 and 2 comprised the original AOC and Maritime imports and their immediate local derivatives. At step 3 there was a change to taller bell shapes, and also biconical and ovoid forms. Step 4 is the short-necked form, and step 5 is a long-necked form, with the neck everted and less than half the height of the vessel. Step 6 has taller, often cylindrical necks, at least half of the total height, while step 7 shows a fusing of body and neck into more biconical shapes. There are matching changes in decoration. The original preference for simple all-over or horizontal band ornament was retained right through to step 4, though a growing range of motifs was used. In step 5 mixtures of bands and panels or metopes of ornament became common, and in step 6 metopic ornament was totally dominant. Even this broke down in step 7, when decoration is usually arranged in a single zone covering the whole body, or two deep zones above and below the body angle.

Distinctive regional traditions emerged only with the ovoid and biconical shapes of step 3, which characterize both a south-east/East Anglian tradition and the beginnings of a northern tradition. Step 4 vessels are overwhelmingly concentrated in the north, and mostly represent the short-necked, developed stage in the northern tradition. Steps 5–7 are concentrated even more massively in the south, representing a southern tradition that eventually spread over much of Britain.

The chronology of this sequence rests shakily on a few radiocarbon dates and correlation with Continental chronologies. The main dividing point falls at *c.* 1700 bc, separating steps 1–4, earlier representatives of steps 5 and 6 and copper and early bronze metallurgy in the Mount Pleasant period, from later examples of steps 5 and 6, step 7, and more advanced bronze-working, in the Overton period. Grave associations confirm that the Beaker steps are chronologically distinct, apart, possibly, from steps 5 and 6. There are scarcely

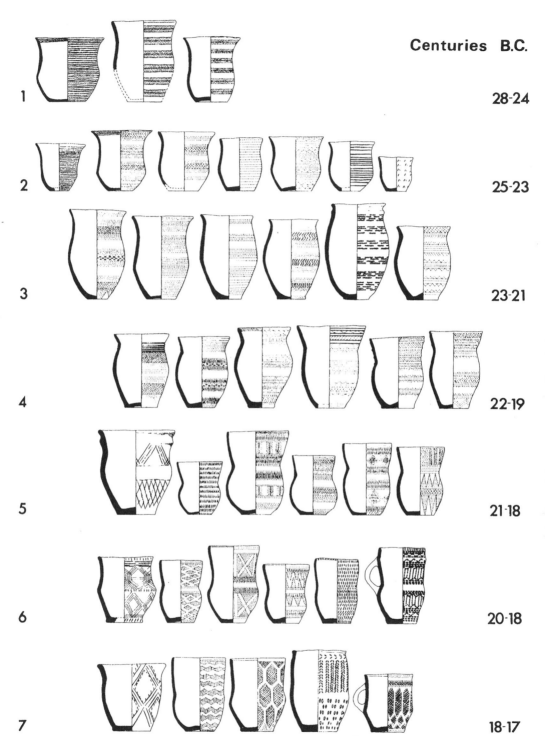

Centuries B.C.

1   28-24

2   25-23

3   23-21

4   22-19

5   21-18

6   20-18

7   18-17

Figure 2.12 British Beakers: steps in development (based on Lanting and van der Waals, 1972)

any associations for step 1, but this is hardly surprising since step 1 comprises so few vessels. Step 2, not unexpectedly, has associations with most of the elements of the international 'Beaker package', though not yet with v-perforated buttons. These appear only with step 3, and then only rarely. Step 3 shows the inevitable development of the 'package' that would have come with insularity: the 'package' artefacts still predominate, but are now joined by rivet-notched tanged knives, more trinkets, and the first belt rings. The latter, together with v-perforated buttons, became much more common in step 4, when the package still predominates, though blades now had broad riveted tangs. It is only with steps 5 and 6, in part contemporary, that the 'package' disappears, and associations take on a new look. Arrowheads are rare, wrist guards are absent and blades are of bronze and have multi-riveted heels. Only v-perforated buttons and double-pointed awls are still plentiful, the former frequently complemented by pulley rings or toggles. There are new weapons, stone battle-axes and large flint daggers and novel bronze ornaments, rings and strip armlets, but what epitomizes the transformation instituted with steps 5 and 6 is the frequent occurrence of tools, in flint, stone, bone and antler, pointing to a change in the status of Beakers and Beaker users. There are further innovations with step 7, sufficient to suggest this was genuinely later than steps 5 and 6. It is only with step 7 that daggers with thick 'plug' rivets appear, and as the associations range from the Thames valley to Scotland this was no local aberration. The other important novelty was the single-pointed awl, which subsequently was to replace the double-pointed type.

Steps 1–4 have to be spread over the centuries between *c.* 2150–1700 bc, but with so few radiocarbon dates it is very difficult to date individual steps. Steps 5–7 have to be accommodated between *c.* 1800–1450 bc, and there are more radiocarbon dates for these later vessels. For steps 5 and 6 there are dates between *c.* 1850–1473 bc from vessels found as far apart as Suffolk and the Outer Hebrides, which compare reasonably well with expected dates of *c.* 1800–1600 bc. The two step 7 dates of *c.* 1500 bc and *c.* 1330 bc compare with expected dates of *c.* 1600–1450 bc. The suggested dates for the Beaker steps in Figure 2.12 are based on both Continental and British radiocarbon dates, adapted to what is known of other aspects of the prehistory of the period.

Domestic assemblages and Beakers

Beakers were specialized prestige vessels requiring a high level of skill and expenditure of time in their manufacture. As might be expected they come mostly from burial, ritual and other sites of special significance. Equally it is not surprising, given their quality and importance that they should influence domestic pottery, though 'Beaker' sherds from domestic assemblages tend to be coarser and less finely decorated than the vessels from graves. Beaker influence is also seen in the shape of some domestic vessels, and in the use of combed decoration.

Such material can legitimately be termed 'domestic Beaker'. It occurs in varying proportions in domestic assemblages of the Mount Pleasant and Overton periods, where it often assumes undue prominence, because it is a readily recognizable element amidst the bulk of more nondescript sherds which are less easily identified. Because Beaker pottery has always been synonymous with an intrusive Beaker population, the whole of any domestic collection containing Beaker material, no matter how much or how little, is automatically labelled a 'Beaker domestic assemblage'. All its components, even the thickest, crudest, most un-Beaker-like vessels, are described as 'domestic Beaker'.

Looked at from the standpoint, not of Beaker 'folk', but of indigenous communities variably influenced by the Beaker tradition, this material takes on a completely different aspect. Instead of 'Beaker domestic assemblages' we should think of local domestic assemblages containing varying quantities of domestic Beaker. The non-Beaker elements must receive proper attention, even if they cannot be immediately categorized. The problem is less acute in the Mount Pleasant period, when the non-Beaker material usually consists of familiar categories such as Grooved and Peterborough wares, and only small quantities of Beaker. Typical are the assemblages from the many domestic pit groups around Rudston on the Yorkshire Wolds, and from occupation layers beneath round barrows as at West Overton G6b in Wiltshire, or Arreton Down on the Isle of Wight. Irish finds which belong here include the recently discovered domestic assemblages around the Newgrange and Knowth passage graves, and in the Monknewtown enclosure in Co. Meath. These all include recognizable Beaker pottery, but also less familiar wares. Some of these are thin and fine and quite likely Beaker-influenced, but others are thick and crudely decorated and of shapes which in no way resemble Beakers. It is these non-Beaker elements, in Ireland and Britain, which have to be studied and classified.

The problem is much more difficult in the Overton period, by which time familiar Peterborough and Grooved wares had disappeared. This is not to deny their strong influence on the coarse wares, as yet undistinguished, which make up much of the domestic pottery of the Overton period. Unfortunately by this time Beakers had lost something of their special status, and were figuring more prominently in domestic assemblages. Beaker shapes, fabrics and tooth-comb ornament are easily recognized, but much of this settlement pottery consists of small sherds, from vessels of uncertain shape, plain, or crudely decorated with rustication, impressed techniques or grooving, which is less easily classified. Typical is the domestic collection from the Swarkeston settlement.

Beakers and burials

The classic 'Beaker burial' is one of the most familiar concepts in prehistory: an individual crouched inhumation, accompanied by a Beaker, rarely by other grave goods, placed in a grave or cist under a small round barrow. We have seen that all the basic elements of this rite existed in many parts of Britain, as in north-west Europe, long before Beakers emerged. The novelty of the Beaker burial and what makes it so noticeable, is essentially the Beaker itself, a fine and eye-catching vessel. The idea that Beaker burial was something new is only one of the many myths surrounding interments with Beakers. Because of the nature of the Beaker tradition, Beakers appear in very different sorts of burial contexts in different parts of the country, according to local custom. Thus over much of the north and west, including Ireland, Beakers are found in chambered tombs. In many areas, especially Yorkshire and the Pennines, they frequently accompany multiple inhumations, so destroying the fallacy that Beakers are synonymous with individual burial. We should also note that Beaker burial was slow to spread in the Mount Pleasant period. Only Wessex has an appreciable number of interments with step 2 and 3 Beakers. Elsewhere there are few before step 3, and, in some regions, before step 4.

Beaker burials, whether flat graves, in cists or under small mounds, can occur singly or in cemeteries. Beakers were the preserve of a privileged élite in the population, and for every individual buried with a Beaker many more were buried without. The distinctions between those interred with Beakers and their fellow men open up a fascinating field for speculation. But the social mix was even more complex than this, for some elements in society were cremated, even when the popularity of Beaker burial was at its height in the latter part of the Mount Pleasant period. It was not always a question of inhumation and cremation in different types of burial sites, for the two frequently occur at the same site. Thus at Stockbridge Down in Hampshire, a small segmented ditched round barrow covered a large grave pit on the bottom of which reposed an inhumation with a step 4 Beaker. But higher up in the grave fill were two cremations. What relationship had these two individuals to the old woman who lay beneath them? Clearly there were complex rules which governed burial rite, and the social implications of the different styles of interment will be considered in greater detail in Chapter VII.

Flint and stonework

Much of the material culture of the Meldon Bridge period persisted after the arrival of Beakers. Flint and stone equipment, including polished axes, leaf, lozenge and transverse arrowheads, polished flint knives, plano-convex knives, and perforated mace-heads, of antler as well as stone, all remained in use, despite the impact of metal. New flint mines were opened up to obtain good quality flint, notably Grimes Graves in Norfolk (*c.* 1865–1814 bc), and many sources of stone were still being exploited in the Highland Zone, such as the preselite of Pembrokeshire.

Metalworking in the Mount Pleasant period

The bulk of the early metalwork from Britain and Ireland is made up of stray finds, lacking associations with other cultural material, so it is difficult to estimate when and how metallurgy was introduced. It was, however, well established in both islands by the time of step 2 Beakers, and if no metal artefacts have been found with step 1 Beakers, these are so few that metalworking contemporary with step 1, or even earlier, cannot be ruled out.

There are striking contrasts between the early metalwork of Britain and that of Ireland in terms of character, quantity and context, echoing the differences which separate the British and Irish Beaker traditions, and raising again the possibility of different origins. In some respects the British material is easier to deal with, because some of it comes from graves, whereas most of the Irish finds are stray or in hoards. As a result the British material can be related to the cultural sequence much more comfortably than can the Irish metalwork, which exists in something of a vacuum.

Grave goods found with step 2 Beakers show that both copper and gold were available from an early stage. The most familiar copper items belong to the international 'package', tanged daggers such as those from the Mere and Roundway burials in Wiltshire, and double pointed awls, such as that found with a Beaker burial inserted into the Thickthorn long barrow in Dorset. Goldwork found with step 2 Beakers includes basket-shaped ear-rings from Radley, Berkshire, and Kirkhaugh, Northumberland (Figure 4.9b), and gold discs, possibly button caps, as in the Mere grave. These gold ornaments were not part of the Beaker package on the Continent, although both ear-rings and discs of local forms appear widely in Europe at this time. The British basket-shaped ear-rings, made in copper as well as gold, were local versions of a tradition of more-or-less basket-shaped ear-rings which can be found in many parts of Europe during Beaker times, notably in the north-west, in Poland, in central Europe and Portugal. The general easterly distribution of the British basket ear-rings suggests that they, like the daggers and awls, were developed by an early British industry which owed much to influences coming in across the North Sea and the Channel at the same time as early Beakers. The gold discs, on the other hand, may have stemmed from Ireland, where they are much more common. Ireland is the likely source, too, for the earliest thick-butt copper flat axes (Lough Ravel type, Figure 2.13) which were reaching

British markets at about this time. Thus early British metal workshops probably developed under the influence both of central/north-west European and Irish traditions. As time went on the central European influence, received via the Low Countries, became stronger and Irish influence waned. But British workshops continued as they had started, adopting a thoroughly insular style while fully cognizant of external trends.

The beginnings of Irish metallurgy are shrouded in mystery because there are so few correlations with other cultural material. The first link comes with the hoard from Knocknague in Co. Galway, which combines Lough Ravel-type axes, and double-pointed awls with a tanged dagger of 'international' type. However, Knocknague clearly represents a mature stage of Irish copper-working. Study of the thick-butt axes suggests there are at least two more primitive typological stages, but, lacking associations, there is no means of telling how early these can be placed. The primary form is trapezoidal in shape with straight sides (Figure 2.13), rather like the trapezoidal thick-butt axes found at the start of metalworking over much of Europe and western Asia. There are plenty of possible Continental precursors early enough to have inspired pre-Beaker Irish copper-working, but there is no way of checking this possibility at present.

Whereas the earliest metalwork of Britain represents a 'light' industry, with daggers, knives, awls, trinkets and a sprinkling of flat axes, the early Irish industry concentrated very much on 'heavy' products. Firstly, great quantities of flat axes were produced, to be followed, at about the time of step 4 Beakers, by masses of halberds. The output of awls, daggers and ornaments is dwarfed by this great volume of heavy products. The contrasts with British industry are so marked that it seems scarcely credible that both could have had the same central/north-west European origins. The key to the source of early Irish metallurgy may lie with the source of Irish halberds, for central and north European halberds are too late to have influenced the Irish series. To find halberds in pre-Beaker and early Beaker times one has to turn to the Mediterranean world and especially Italy and Iberia. Atlantic Europe may also prove important, but at present little is known about the early metallurgy of that region. Iberia, however, in addition to early halberds can also provide precursors for the trapezoidal flat axes, basket ear-rings and gold discs of the early Irish industry, and also has its own branch of the international Beaker package as a source for Irish tanged daggers and double-pointed awls. Atlantic influences had permeated Ireland throughout the Meldon Bridge period, as shown by the blossoming of passage graves, and it would not be surprising to see metallurgy, and Beakers, reaching Ireland via the same Atlantic sea routes.

Flat axe typology provides the best way of following the development of early metallurgy in Britain and Ireland. We start in Stage I (Castletown Roche) with straight-sided thick-butt axes resembling the trapezoidal implements of the Continent. They are comparatively few in number, but their concentration in Munster supports the idea of Atlantic origins. One such axe occurs in the hoard from Castletown Roche, Co. Cork (Figure 2.13), which gives its name to this hypothetical primary stage of Irish metallurgy. However, Irish craftsmen rapidly developed an 'Irish' flat axe shape, shorter and broader, with curved sides, and prominent tips to the cutting edge. The second Castletown Roche axe already has slightly curved sides, and this 'Irish' shape quickly came to dominate flat axe design not only in Ireland but also in Britain.

In Stage II (Knocknague) copper axes still had broad butts, but the curved-sided 'Irish' form now predominated (Lough Ravel type). Some straight-sided implements were still produced, but now with the shorter, broader 'Irish' proportions. The Knocknague hoard, Co. Galway, shows that the first tanged daggers and double-pointed awls appeared at this stage. These occur also with step 2 Beakers in Britain, together with gold trinkets such as sun-discs and basket-shaped ear-rings. Irish axes as well as ornaments were now filtering into Britain, for there is a sparse scattering of Lough Ravel implements in many parts of the country. Irish ideas mixed with north-west European influences soon prompted the setting up of workshops in many parts of Britain, but these quickly took on distinctive local characters. In Wales and northern Britain, for example, a high proportion of flat axes had straight sides, and a butt that was thin – or pointed – in profile (Figure 2.13), instead of the Irish thick butt. Welsh products were particularly distinctive, because of their small size. Whether the thin butt was a British invention or an Irish one enthusiastically received, is not yet clear.

A Beaker grave from Dorchester near Oxford (Figure 2.13), shows that the later developments of Stage II overlapped with step 3 Beakers. A remarkable knife from this burial shows not only that rivet attachment had been introduced but also that bronze was in sporadic use, for one of its rivets is of bronze, not copper. This is confirmed by a bronze pin with a double spiral head in another step 3 Beaker grave, at Sewell, Bedfordshire. Such pins have good parallels in central Europe, no doubt indicating the source of this new metal. Despite this precocity, copper was still the metal used in the next stage of metalworking developments. Stage III (Frankford) in Ireland is characterized above all by the hoard from Frankford (Birr), Co. Offaly (Figure 2.13). This still has Lough Ravel axes, but also a new form combining the two principal insular features, the curved-sided form and the 'thin' butt (Ballybeg type). The Frankford hoard shows that halberds were now being produced in Ireland. These were large and outlandish weapons, costly in metal, that had a mixed response over much of Britain. Probably most Irish and British halberds belong to Stage III. A useful correlation with the Beaker sequence is provided by a broad-tanged knife with rivet notches in the Frankford hoard, which can be compared with the riveted, broad-tanged knives found with several step 4 Beakers (Figure 2.13).

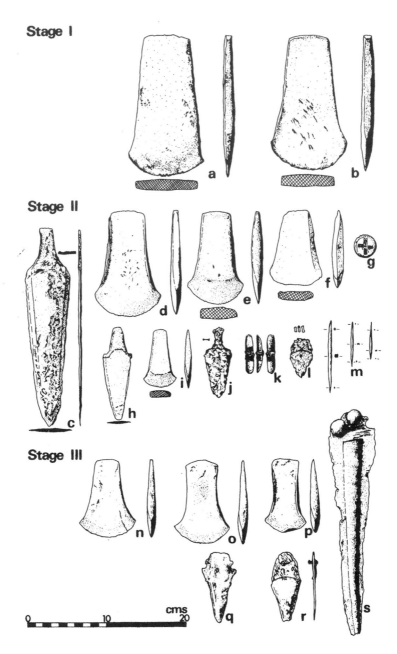

Figure 2.13 Stages in the development of copper-work: a–b. Castletown Roche hoard, Co. Cork; c. Roundway, Wilts.; d, e, h, i, m. Knocknague hoard, Co. Galway; f. Carrickshedoge ('Nash') hoard, Co. Wexford; g. Mere, Wilts. (gold); j, l. Dorchester, Oxon.; k. Radley, Berks.; n–q, s. Frankford ('Birr') hoard, Co. Offaly; r. Driffield ('Kelleythorpe'), Yorks. (all after Case, 1966, except f., after Harbison, 1968)

The independence of British workshops can be deduced as much from their halberds as their axes. Some idea of the varying popularity of this clumsy weapon can be gleaned from the numbers of finds: 10 from England, 8 from Wales, about 40 from Scotland and 175 from Ireland. The Irish figure, like all Irish bronze statistics, may have been misleadingly inflated by the amount of peat cutting, and bronze finding, that went on there in the nineteenth century, but it still shows that halberds were essentially an Irish fashion. Scotland, as so often in the centuries that followed, was much more strongly influenced by Irish practice than the rest of Britain, both in terms of numbers of halberds and the proportion of examples of Irish type. Practically all the English and Welsh halberds are of specifically non-Irish types, such as the Tonfannau type, named after two found together in Merionethshire. These have stout, straight blades, sometimes with embellished midrib, and four or five big rivets instead of the usual three. The Welsh halberds as a whole are a very individual group, just like the Welsh copper axes.

After the premature appearance of bronze at Dorchester and Sewell, a century or two elapsed before copper finally gave way to bronze. The first bronze-working, Stage IV (Migdale-Killaha), shows many signs of contact with central European metallurgy in its early Únětician, or Reinecke A1, stage, which, in radiocarbon terms, was before 1700 bc, and correlates with the latter part of the Mount Pleasant period. The main products of Migdale-Killaha metalworking were logical developments from Stage III types (Figure 2.13). Bronze flat axes, following the trend started by the Ballybeg type, had much narrower butts than copper axes, always pointed in profile (thin-butted axes). Knives and daggers had prominent arched heels, reminiscent of the broad tangs of Stage III examples, but were now bored with holes for a number of slender 'peg' rivets. Halberds of Stage III design were still circulating, for one of the Tonfannau type was deposited with a Migdale-type bronze flat axe in a grave at Sluie, Moray. However, a new type of halberd was developed by Migdale-Killaha craftsmen, the Breaghwy form, with a comparatively short, wide triangular blade and multiple slender rivets in a fairly flat heel, instead of fat 'plug' rivets in a high, rounded heel. Double-pointed awls remained in production and basket-shaped ear-rings were still worn – whether they were heirlooms or still being manufactured is not clear.

In addition to these basic items, a range of lesser products swelled the craftsman's repertoire in Britain, many of them influenced by central European fashions. The Migdale hoard itself, from Sutherland, combines the eponymous Migdale axe and a basket-shaped ear-ring with a series of ornaments based on central European types: tubular sheet beads, conical sheet bronze covers for v-perforated buttons, a strip armlet decorated with *repoussé* bosses, ribbed band armlets and a series of butt-jointed arm-rings of D-section. Both the ribbed armlets and the rings, if worn in multiples would create an effect resembling the very common spiral armlets of central Europe.

Other associations swell the range of Migdale products still further. At Mill of Laithers, Aberdeen, the butt of a Migdale axe was found with a strip armlet bearing incised decoration. Similar armlets have been found with step 5/6 Beakers, as at Knipton, Leicestershire. The type may be compared with early Únětician 'manchettes' or broad band armlets with incised ornament. There are other finds connecting Stage IV metalworking with step 5 and 6 Beakers. At West Overton G6b a step 6 Beaker was found with a double pointed awl, but now of bronze instead of copper (Figure 2.14). The hoard from Auchnacree, Angus, contained several Migdale axes and two blades, both having a prominent arched heel with multiple rivet holes for slender rivets. Knives and daggers of this form have occurred several times with step 5 and 6 Beakers, notably at East Kennet in Wiltshire and Charmy Down, Somerset. Another grave with a step 5 Beaker, at Crawfurd, Lanark, contained a bronze D-sectioned ring armlet, just like those found in the Migdale hoard but annular instead of butt jointed.

The Killaha axes of Ireland, equivalent to the British Migdale series, are markedly broader in shape. Killaha axes are rare in Britain, with only one example from Wales and perhaps three or four from Scotland, so that Irish influence must have dwindled away. Indeed, the flow of ideas was very much reversed, for it was at this time that the British Beaker tradition was exerting its greatest influence on the Irish tradition, leading to the appearance in Ireland of necked Beakers, local versions of steps 5 and 6.

The composition of some Killaha axes shows that copper was still sometimes used in Ireland, as in Britain, possibly because tin was in short supply. The Killaha hoard (Figure 2.14) combines a number of the eponymous axes with one of the new Breaghwy-type halberds and a short-tanged dagger with shoulder rivet holes and channelled blade edges. This has been wrongly compared to the later and much more sophisticated Bush Barrow daggers of England. Its true affinities lie with a similar dagger from Faversham, Kent, possibly associated with a halberd, and with another, made of copper, from Standlow in Derbyshire. This was found with a fine stone battle-axe much like those found in several graves with step 5/6 Beakers and Auchnacree-type daggers.

Before the Mount Pleasant period came to an end an even more advanced stage of bronze-working had been reached. Stage V (Ballyvalley-Aylesford) developments were mainly concerned with axes, knives and daggers. Stage V flat axes, as seen in the eponymous finds from Kent and Co. Down, instituted a new trend in flat axe development. On the practical side, shapes still approximated to those of Migdale axes, although they were sometimes subtly narrower. Much more important was the appearance of two modifications to improve hafting properties: slightly raised edges to the faces, creating in effect slight flanges, and implying the adoption of a new, bent 'knee-shaft' method of hafting; and a transverse median bevel, a rudimentary stop to cushion the

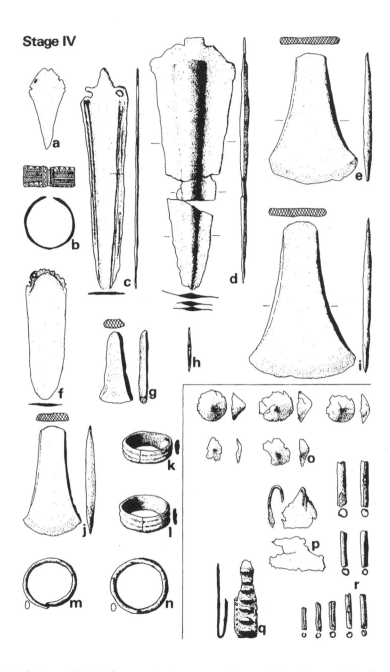

Figure 2.14 Stage IV: the first regular bronze-working: a, f. Auchnacree Hoard, Angus; b. Knipton, Leics. c, d, e, g, i. Killaha East hoard, Co. Kerry; h. Butterwick, Yorks. j–r. Migdale hoard, Sutherland. (a, f, j–r. after Coles, 1968–9; b. after Clarke, 1970; c, d, e, g, i. after Harbison, 1968) (scales : a–i, 1/5; j–n, 2/11; inset, 1/3)

impact of the axe blow. On the less utilitarian side, decoration, previously rare and rudimentary, now became commonplace, executed by hammering or punching. Evidence that such axes were in use by the end of the Mount Pleasant period comes from Mount Pleasant itself. Near the bottom of the great enclosure ditch, just above the primary silts with their Grooved ware and a radiocarbon date of *c.* 1778 bc, there was a small Stage V flat axe, still approximating to the Migdale shape, but decorated and with a transverse bevel.

One final find confirms that Stage V metalworking was making an impact by the end of the Mount Pleasant period. The Class II henge at Castell Bryn Gwyn on Anglesey was associated with pottery of the Peterborough Fengate style and a bronze awl. This was not one of the small double-pointed awls that had survived so long, but a novel type, much longer, with a round sectioned rod-like body, a single point and flattened tang. Single point awls were eventually to oust the double-pointed type in the Overton period, to which we shall turn shortly.

Chapter III

The Prehistory of the Second Millennium: the Overton, Bedd Branwen and Knighton Heath Periods

The continuity in spiritual and economic development and in settlement patterns, social systems and artefacts that lasted from the Meldon Bridge period through the Mount Pleasant period, was finally disrupted at the beginning of the Second Millennium (*c.* 1700 bc). Far-reaching social, ideological and spiritual upheavals are indicated by important changes in material culture, in burial practices, and in the fate of the great public centres of the Third Millennium. The prehistory of the Second Millennium can be divided into three main periods on the basis of changing burial customs and social patterns. The first, the Overton period (*c.* 1700–1450 bc), saw an even mixture of inhumation and cremation, but with the emphasis increasingly on the latter. The nature and status of the Beaker tradition changed, and new categories of funerary pottery – cinerary urns and food vessels – provide further evidence of changing *mores*. These circumstances created new élites, notably the Bush Barrow group of the 'Wessex Culture'. By the opening of the Bedd Branwen period (*c.* 1450–1200 bc) cremation was the dominant tradition, although pockets of inhumation survived in areas where this rite had always been most popular, such as east Yorkshire. Deep social division may be inferred from the burial record. Prestigious cinerary urns of a variety of forms probably distinguish the privileged and powerful from the poorer and less dynamic, who were buried un-urned, or in simple urns such as those of the Deverel-Rimbury group. The Knighton Heath period (*c.* 1200–1050 bc) saw a complete reversal of fortunes. The whole fabric of prestigious burial and ritual implicit in cinerary urns, grave goods and 'fancy' burial sites, vanished. The less ostentatious Deverel-Rimbury cremations continued alone, suggesting a complete social revolution. But a new agricultural crisis was threatening. Social upheaval, rising population and climatic deterioration may all have contributed, but in what proportion and in which order is not clear. Matters came to a head around 1200 BC. Throughout the east Mediterranean troubles began to build up in the thirteenth century BC. Barbarians everywhere were on the move, including the sea peoples of the Egyptian writers. Egypt herself managed to beat off their attacks, not so two other great civilizations, of the Hittites and Mycenaeans/Minoans. The ripples of these disturbances spread through Europe and eventually touched the offshore islands. The onset of the Penard period around 1200 BC ended a continuum of prehistory, stretching back two thousand years to the foundation of Stonehenge.

The Overton period: c. 2000–1650 BC (c. 1700–1450 bc)

The transition from the Mount Pleasant to the Overton period was marked by far-reaching changes, not so much in settlement and economic systems as in burial and ritual traditions, a result of social upheaval. It was only at this point, from c. 1700 bc, that there emerged those burial practices which have always been synonymous with the 'Bronze Age': cremation in a cinerary urn and inhumation or cremation accompanied by a 'food vessel'. The impetus for these developments remains a mystery. Beakers had for long been the only vessels placed with the dead, but now food vessels in a bewildering variety of forms, began to be interred in graves. Similarly cremations for over a thousand years had been placed in bags and simple holes, but now cinerary urns became commonplace.

Something of the extent of these changes can be seen at Stonehenge. At the end of the Mount Pleasant period a major remodelling of the site was begun, involving the construction of the double circle of bluestones in the centre of the old henge. But in the middle of this work there was a dramatic change of plan such as might result from a change in social and political authority. The bluestones were removed and put on one side, and work began on the even more grandiose sarsen monument, a stupendous feat requiring very capable organization and leadership.

Another sign of change around this time comes from the chambered tombs, which throughout Britain and Ireland were being sealed up after they had been centres of activity in some cases for two thousand years. Latterly Beaker pottery had been used in this context, so this sudden and dramatic change in attitude clearly had nothing to do with the Beaker tradition. Whether there was a short and sharp phase of blocking throughout the country, or whether it took time for the movement to spread is not clear. Finds and radiocarbon dates from tombs in many different parts of Britain and Ireland suggest a comparatively short episode, towards the end of the Mount Pleasant period when the Beaker tradition was already at a mature stage. At some sites, such as Beacharra in Argyll and West Kennet in Wiltshire, as if to emphasize the need to bury the past, quantities of rubbish were brought in to cover the burial deposits inside the tomb. Those responsible for the dramatic change of plan at Stonehenge, went to the Marlborough Downs, in the vicinity both of Avebury and West Kennet, for their new sarsen building material. Was the sealing up of West Kennet and the turnabout at Stonehenge due to the same upheavals? Were these events and the appearance of food vessels and cinerary urns all part of one social and spiritual revolution?

The Beaker tradition now entered its final phase, but its status had changed. In many communities Beaker-accompanied burial was still pre-eminent, and Beaker burials continued to be discriminatory and to occupy the most important position in the tomb. But in other circles Beakers were discarded in favour of the new funerary vessels. The emergence of the remarkable 'Wessex Culture' in the south speaks of new social élites, eschewing Beakers, for if 'Wessex Culture' graves included a pot then it was either a cinerary urn or one of a new tradition of accessory cups (pygmy cups). The accompaniments of late Beakers show little vestige of the international 'package' which had survived throughout the Mount Pleasant period. New associations suggest new attitudes, in particular the frequency with which late Beakers are found with tools, pointing to craftsmen, sometimes leatherworkers, sometimes metalworkers.

In the early part of the Overton period Beakers are of steps 5 and 6, sometimes provided with a handle, and with bold ornament in deep zones, or panels ('metopes'), or, alternatively, covered with simple fingernail or pinched rustication. Later on these gave way to the bipartite vessels of step 7, whose decoration departs completely from the traditional zonal styles.

Burial practices

The even mixture of inhumation and cremation of the Overton period can be seen at two Wiltshire cemetery barrows, West Overton G6b and Amesbury G71. At the former (Figure 7.6) the central grave held an inhumation with a Beaker, but a cremation was included in the upper fill. Over a few months several more inhumations and cremations were interred in pits and graves dug around the central burial, two of the burnt burials in Collared Urns. Similarly at Amesbury G71 (Figure 7.2), an existing round barrow was modified in this period (c. 1640 bc) in order to receive four inhumations and two or three cremations. One of the inhumations was accompanied by a food vessel, and one of the cremations was in a Collared Urn.

The West Overton cemetery shows how a site could be left open for some time after the initial burial, before the mound was raised. Amesbury G71 illustrates how some communities would select and modify an existing mound to house fresh burials, while others, as at West Overton G6b, would select a new site. The choice was presumably dictated by local circumstances, individual belief, but above all by social status. For most Beaker burials were still granted a new mound, and the rich burials of the Bush Barrow group of the 'Wessex Culture', also tend to occupy primary graves under new barrows. The implication is that important personages in society had a good chance of a fresh burial site, but for most of the community the determining factors were much more complex.

Many Bush Barrow burials were by inhumation, showing that this rite was still popular among the leaders of society later in the Overton period, but the fact that some were cremations shows that this rite was gaining ground even among the privileged. The rite of inhumation under a round mound was most firmly entrenched in east Yorkshire, and cinerary urn burial may have penetrated this and other eastern regions later than those southern and western areas where cremation had always been more popular. Yorkshire vase food vessels were now available as accessory vessels, but Beaker burials still occupied the prime burial positions at the bottom of pit graves (Plate IX), or within a cemetery. Thus the choice of Beaker or food vessel for the grave must have been determined by social or family status. But even in Yorkshire cremations were frequently deposited with inhumations, as at Garton Slack 75 (Figure 7.1), implying that there was yet another social factor affecting choice of rite.

The food vessel inhumation rite becomes increasingly infrequent, and cremation, both with food vessels and in urns, increasingly dominant, the further west one goes from east Yorkshire. So, in the southern Pennines, north-east England and eastern Scotland, inhumation with late Beakers, food vessels, or without pottery, was only slightly less prevalent than in Yorkshire. South of the Tees round barrows and cairns were usual. In the north-east and Scotland they were perhaps becoming more common, but 'flat' cist graves, with food vessels or late Beakers, were still characteristic of these regions. However in western Scotland, north-west England and Wales inhumations, Beakers and food vessels were dramatically fewer than in the east. The proportion of cremation and inhumation in each region depended on their relative importance in pre-Beaker times, which determined the popularity of the Beaker tradition, and then of food vessel burial. Thus inhumation was strongly entrenched in pre-Beaker Yorkshire and Beakers abound there, so the strength of food vessel inhumation is not surprising. On the other hand a long tradition of inhumation in western Scotland, seen in the chambered tombs, was tempered in the Meldon Bridge period by an increase in cremation. Beakers were accepted in the region from an early date, but were often used in chambered tomb ceremonial. With this background it is not surprising that about a third of west Scottish food vessel burials are by cremation. In contrast with north-west England and Wales, where little pre-Beaker inhumation and comparatively few Beakers, meant the few local food vessels are mostly with cremations.

Irish societies reacted idiosyncratically to developments in Britain. Cist graves were characteristic of much of Ireland in the Overton period but there are notable gaps in the distribution, in the south-west, in Clare and Sligo.

These are the areas where wedge tombs are most numerous, and the result is an interesting complementary distribution pattern. Cremation was twice as common as inhumation in the cist graves, again reflecting the pre-Beaker situation, and usually only one individual is involved. Pottery, present in about half of the sites, is usually an Irish Bowl, a local equivalent of the British food vessel.

The origins of the Irish cist grave and of Irish Bowls are shrouded in uncertainty. There are no C14 dates and few associations which relate to the problem, but Irish Bowls like British food vessels, appear to have been introduced suddenly at the beginning of the Overton period. An independent origin of Irish cists is possible in view of the rough cists at sites such as Monknewtown, but British influences were permeating Ireland in the later Mount Pleasant and early Overton periods, and if these included knowledge of the British food vessel, then logically they would also have included knowledge of the burial cist in which so many food vessels are found in western Britain.

The quantity of cinerary urn and food vessel sherds recovered from secondary contexts at the great southern enclosures of the Durrington Walls type and at the causewayed enclosures, shows that activity continued here throughout the Overton period, though altered in character. The construction of round barrows within some of these sites, as at Windmill Hill, and Marden, points to new attitudes, perhaps related to the radical change of plan at Stonehenge, and events at Mount Pleasant. Here a great palisade (Plate VIa) was drawn round the hill-top, inside the existing ditch and bank perimeter (*c.* 1687 bc), but was soon burnt down (*c.* 1695 bc). These radical developments confirm the impression that the role of the ancient enclosures and henges was irrevocably changing, although whether they still functioned as ceremonial and community centres, is not clear. But just as the construction of causewayed enclosures had ceased over a thousand years before, so henge building now stopped. No new examples can be assigned with certainty to the Overton period. Small, henge-like sites were built, as at Fargo Plantation, Wiltshire; City Farm, Hanborough, Oxfordshire; and High Knowes, Alnham, Northumberland; but these represented a new tradition of sites designed more specifically for burial purposes.

This leads on to the whole question of ring cairns and related monuments, which came increasingly to the fore as interest in the traditional henges and stone circles declined. A wide variety of ring monuments was constructed in western and northern upland areas in the Overton period. Burials, usually cremations, are frequently present, but, at least to start with, may have been subordinate to the ritual functions of the sites. Some interments, especially in-urned cremations, may have taken place centuries after a site's construction, when its original purpose had long since been forgotten or changed. In fact in the Bedd Branwen period all these ring monuments may have become mere places of burial. Thus the Brenig 44 ring cairn in Denbighshire (Pl. VIII), built in the Overton period (*c.* 1680 bc), was used down to the Bedd Branwen period (*c.* 1540, 1520, 1340 bc) for rites which involved the deposition of charcoal in pits. It became a burial site only after half a millennium, when two Collared Urn cremations were deposited (*c.* 1280 bc). This urges caution in dating those other ring sites, especially stone circles, which have yielded cinerary urn burials. For example, the Druid's Circle, Penmaenmawr, produced cremations in enlarged food vessel urns, probably of the Bedd Branwen period, but without radiocarbon dates their relationship to the original construction and use of the site remains uncertain.

Burials tend to be more sporadic in stone circles than in other ring monuments, are sometimes token deposits, and are clearly peripheral to the main function of the site. The layout and siting of some stone circles, settings and alignments suggests they continued the remarkable traditions of celestial observation which can be traced back at least to the Meldon Bridge period. They clearly took over many of the functions of henges as ceremonial and social centres. All speak eloquently of the engineering skills of these prehistoric societies, and many hint at their knowledge of field geometry and surveying.

Stones at many of these megalithic sites bear cup and ring carvings, which are also found on slabs used as walls or cap-stones in Beaker and food vessel cists. At first glance this would indicate that cup and ring art was flourishing in this period. But most of these slabs are broken from larger stones, and an opposite hypothesis is feasible, that the great cup-and-ring marked outcrops had lost their former significance, and become merely easy sources of building stone.

Sepulchral and domestic pottery

Practically every familiar type of 'Bronze Age' pottery, including the vast range of food vessel and cinerary urn forms, must now be assigned to the Overton and Bedd Branwen periods. The chronological vicissitudes of much of this material have already been outlined in Chapter I. Instead of being spread over the whole 'Bronze Age' it must all be fitted now into the few centuries between *c.* 2000–1400 BC, and is not even fully representative of that period. For such vessels come almost exclusively from burial sites, and must have been specialized funerary pottery, and perhaps the preserve of the privileged minority in society. For domestic wares, and for the sepulchral pottery of the majority, we shall have to look elsewhere.

The background of cinerary urns and food vessels in the indigenous wares of the Meldon Bridge and Mount Pleasant periods is now well established. Beaker influence has been greatly exaggerated, being confined mainly to decoration. Much more at issue is why food vessels and cinerary urns emerged at all around 1700 bc. By then Beakers had been regularly deposited with the dead for several centuries, so the new traditions, contrary to long-held notions, are unlikely to have had anything to do with Beaker ideology. They must be seen in the context of much wider upheavals, reflected in the change of direction at Stonehenge, the construction of the massive palisade at Mount Pleasant, and the blocking of chambered tombs, but this still does not answer the question, 'Why?'.

Collared Urns, the most important of the cinerary urns, were developed from collared Peterborough vessels, especially the Fengate style. The Fengate vessels most like Collared Urns occur in southern England, especially Wessex, so that the Collared Urn tradition probably originated in that area. But collared Peterborough vessels were in use throughout England and Wales, which must have greatly facilitated acceptance of the new tradition as it spread from territory to territory. It made least headway in the north-east, between the Humber and the Moray Firth, where another novel tradition was emerging, represented by food vessels. These, too, were influenced by the pre-existing Peterborough styles, in this case Meldon Bridge and Rudston, which already incorporated the essential features of food vessels: the shouldered bipartite shape, the hollow neck, and 'food vessel rim', expanded outwards, with a slight chamfer on the outer margin and a bevel on the inside.

We have seen that Peterborough and Grooved wares tended to occur in different categories of sites, the former more often in sepulchral and ritual contexts, the Grooved wares in a much wider range of domestic settings, including settlements, field systems and flint mines. This distinction was perpetuated in the ceramic novelties of the Overton period. For just as food vessels and Collared Urns were developed from Peterborough wares, so Grooved wares provided the basis for a variety of coarse bucket, barrel and bipartite vessels. The best known of these are the Deverel-Rimbury pots of Wessex and Sussex, but similar developments can now be recognized throughout Britain. Clearly Grooved and Peterborough wares did not simply vanish without trace at the end of the Mount Pleasant period, but provided the basis for new traditions of domestic and sepulchral pottery.

Deverel-Rimbury ceramics emerged at about the same time as Collared Urns and food vessels, at the beginning of the Overton period. In Wessex, as in many regions, society polarized. Food vessels and cinerary urns, as specialized funerary vessels, are representative of the whole fabric of prestigious and privileged burial in this period, whereas Deverel-Rimbury pottery and similar coarse wares epitomize the more stolid majority in the population. The former denote the more dynamic, more wealthy, more flamboyant elements in society, and in Wessex these may have been groups dependent more on pastoralism than cultivation, ranging over the chalk uplands. Later in the Overton period the most ostentatious and powerful families are those represented by the Bush Barrow graves of the 'Wessex Culture'. They did use Deverel-Rimbury wares, but only for domestic purposes, as their ancestors had used Grooved wares. They contrasted strongly with groups around the fringes of the downs, and on the lower lands off the chalk: sedentary peasant cultivators who used Deverel-Rimbury vessels in life and death. Amongst these communities those who could afford a Collared Urn were indeed notable.

A similar distinction can be seen in the southern parts of East Anglia, where Collared Urn burials dominate the chalk escarpment of Hertfordshire and Cambridgeshire, while the main Deverel-Rimbury cemeteries are found in the valleys and on the coastal lowlands. In the southern Pennines the contrast is between the limestone areas, which were the preserve of late Beaker and food vessel users, and the poorer sandstones and grits, which have yielded mainly cinerary urns. In some areas, for example south-west Scotland, the distinction between coarse vessels and specialized urns seems to be a question of social differences within the community rather than between communities.

The equivalent of Deverel-Rimbury pottery in south-west England was Trevisker ware, which exhibits a similar range of bucket and barrel shapes but is more ornate and generally finer than Deverel-Rimbury pottery. Cornish handled urns constitute the prestigious sepulchral end of the Trevisker range. In Ireland plainer, coarser versions of the sepulchral food vessels are known from settlements such as Ballynagilly, but a more significant contrast may lie with coarse bucket and barrel shaped vessels which carry on the Lough Gur II and Kilhoyle traditions. These are closely associated with wedge tombs, which, as we have seen, appear to represent different social groupings from those evidenced by cist graves and food vessels.

Whatever the precise purpose of food vessels, like Beakers they were accessory vessels, designed to accompany the dead, whether inhumed or burnt. Cinerary urns, on the other hand, were designed to contain the cremated remains of the dead, and as a result had to be larger than food vessels. Pygmy cups, miniature accessory vessels, presumably had a similar function to food vessels, but were specifically for accompanying cremations, and especially in-urned cremations. They are best considered, therefore, with cinerary urns.

Food vessels

Food vessels, usually between 10–20 centimetres in height, were essentially a feature of Highland Zone regions, and thin out markedly south of a line from the Humber to the Severn. Whereas Beakers have been thought of as drinking vessels, food vessels, with their heavy bevelled rim, are patently not cups, and traditionally have been thought to hold a more solid offering.

Food vessels are usually divided into vases and bowls, the former characteristic of Britain, the latter of Ireland, with Scotland mixing vases and bowls. The distinction is difficult in practice, for there is a broad, grey area comprising vessels which can be described either as tall bowls or squat vases. Nevertheless shape is of prime importance in classifying these vessels, so the division into vases and bowls is retained here. There are regional trends in decoration as well as in form. Just as bowls were preferred in Ireland and vases and buckets in

England, so decoration in Ireland tended to be richer and more complex than in England, frequently covering the whole exterior and often the base of the vessel. In England the decoration is not only simpler but also often restricted to the upper part of the pot. The typical decorative techniques of Ireland were false relief and tooth-comb, whereas in England cord-ornament (various twists), grooving and impressed motifs tend to predominate. Scottish and Welsh vessels, as befits their geographically intermediate position, incorporate influences from both England and Ireland. But while the Welsh series retains a strongly local character, western Scotland has produced bowls and vases so like Irish vessels that some sort of direct contact, if not transportation of actual vessels, is indicated.

Using both form and decoration a number of food vessel styles can be isolated, some with a regional significance. Vases can be divided into a bipartite group, a ridged group (especially tripartite forms) and buckets, which have a simple, open shape. Bowls can be divided into British and Irish forms. Bipartite vases are the most widespread food vessel shape. Basic Bipartite Vases (Figure 3.1), are ubiquitous, and have ridged-neck and grooved-shoulder variants. Diagnostic of the most famous regional form, the Yorkshire Vase has a shoulder groove with stops, either perforated or imperforate. The decoration is twisted or whipped cord, arranged frequently in herringbone designs, with horizontal lines and triangles also common. Either the whole pot or merely the upper part may be decorated. The Southern Bipartite Vase has a more angular outline with sparser decoration (Figure 3.1), usually confined to simple impressions on the neck and shoulder ridges. Irish Vases have a much more exaggerated neck and, often, an outwards-angled rim, and their ornate decoration is characteristically Irish. There is a short-necked variant of the Irish vase with the distinctive rim treatment and a slight internal undercutting of the flat top. The Irish Rounded Vase is the most common Irish vase form, with shoulder and body slackened to a point where the bipartite profile can be lost. As with the Irish Vase, incised and scored decorations are preferred.

Ridged bucket-shaped vases may be distinguished from ridge-neck Bipartite Vases by the position of the lowest ridge, which should be at, or below, half the height of the pot, and by the spacing of the ridges so as to separate concave zones of roughly equal width. The most coherent regional version is the Northern Tripartite Vase (Figure 3.1), with two body ridges, often decorated with crude herringbone in short lengths of whipped cord. Multiple-ridged vases are also common all over the north. The dividing line between Irish examples and ridged variants of Irish Bowls is often blurred. Simple bucket shapes (Figure 3.2) are not common but are widely scattered.

Bowls can be divided immediately into the simple, rather globular British Bowl, and the generally wider, more ornate bowls of Ireland and Scotland. Irish Bowls (Figure 3.2) are richly decorated all over, including, frequently,

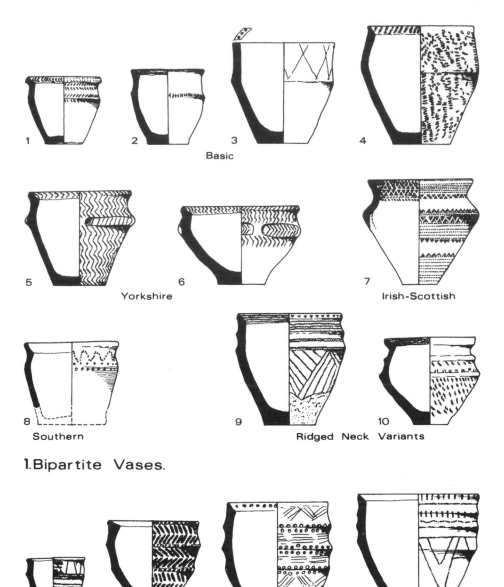

Basic

Yorkshire   Irish-Scottish

Southern   Ridged Neck Variants

1. Bipartite Vases.

Northern Tripartite

Southern   Irish-Scottish

2. Ridged, Bucket-Shaped Vases.

the base. False relief and tooth-comb are very common, but impressed motifs and grooving also appear. There are four basic versions, simple bowls, with an uninterrupted rounded profile, waisted or constricted bowls, with convex body zones, and, sometimes, lugs or stops, tripartite bowls, with two ridges dividing the body of the pot into concave zones, and ridged bowls, with a concave upper body zone, and multiple ridges encircling the body below. While all these bowl forms occur in Scotland, especially in the west, tripartite bowls are the most numerous. Some of the Scottish finds are so like the Irish material as to suggest actual pots, as well as ideas, were carried across the Irish Sea. Sheer weight of numbers suggests this traffic went from west to east, but the main flow of sepulchral ideas seems to have been in the opposite direction, taking cinerary urn burial, the basic food vessel concept, and perhaps cists, to Ireland.

Cinerary urns

Regional differences in cinerary urns tend to be a question of decoration and nuances of shape rather than distinctive local forms. Cinerary urns, having to accommodate a burnt body, are much larger than food vessels, varying between 20–50 centimetres in height, against the 10–20 centimetres of food vessels.

Collared Urns (Figure 3.3) now include all those vessels previously grouped under the defunct term 'overhanging rim urn'. Collared urns are by far the most numerous and widespread cinerary urn form, the only one found throughout Britain and Ireland. The collar, varying greatly in width and angle, is usually bevelled internally, or descends on the inside to an 'internal moulding' at about the level of the collar base. Tripartite Collared Urns are more common than bipartite examples. Decoration is usually confined to the collar and internal bevel; occurs less often on the neck, and is rare on the body. Regional variations in shape and decoration exist, but have not been published in detail. A 'north-western style', concentrated in areas from the Peak to the Scottish border, is characterized by linear incised decoration, lozenge or lattice patterns on the neck, and a row of jabs on the shoulder. Formal traits include deep, vertical necks, and cordoned or stepped shoulders. The 'south-eastern style', predominant in lowland England, but common throughout eastern

---

Figure 3.1 Vase food vessels: 1. Galley Low, and 2. Stanton Park, Derbyshire; 3. Mt. Vernon, Lanark; 4. Longridge Towers, Northumberland; 5. Goodmanham CXV, and 6. Garton Slack C62, Yorks.; 7. Greenhills, Co. Dublin; 8. Southbourne, Hants.; 9. Craignish, Argyll; 10. Ashford, 11. Monyash Moor, and 12. Lean Low, Derbyshire; 13. Stevenston, Ayr; 14. Mt. Vernon, Lanark; 15. Manorbier, Pembs.; 16. Rathbarron, Co. Sligo; 17. Dalton, Lanark; 18. Stevenston, Ayr. (1, 2, 10, 11, 12 after Manby, 1957; 3. 14, 17, 18 after Simpson, 1965; 4 after Jobey, 1968; 5, 6, 9, 16 after Simpson, 1968; 7 after ApSimon, 1958; 8 after Calkin, 1962; 13 after Morrison, 1971; 15 after Savory, 1957) (various scales)

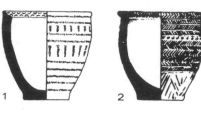

Irish-Scottish Rounded Vases   **Bucket-Shaped**

Globular Bowls

3.Rounded Vases, Bowls and Buckets.

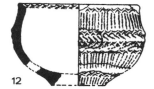

Simple   **Waisted**   **Tripartite**

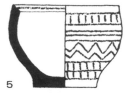

Ridged Variants

4.Irish-Scottish Bowls.

Figure 3.2 Food vessels: rounded vases, bucket-shaped and bowls. 1. Doune, Perth; 2. Mt. Stewart, Co. Down; 3. Skeldon, Ayr; 4. Cross Low, Derbyshire; 5. Hamilton, Lanark; 6. Arbor Low, Derbyshire; 7. Mt. Vernon, Lanark; 8. Omagh, Co. Tyrone; 9. Newry, Co. Down; 10. Corky, Co. Antrim; 11. Mt. Stewart, Co. Down; 12–13. Corrower, Co. Mayo. (1, 8, 10 after Simpson, 1968; 2, 9, 11 after Waddell, 1976; 3, 5, 7 after Simpson, 1965; 4, 6 after Manby, 1957; 12–13 after Raftery, 1960) (various scales)

counties as far as the Scottish border, is typified by cord ornament, use of a point-tooth comb, plain necks, and a row of corded loops or horse-shoes on the shoulder.

Collared Urns were much more important in England and Wales than in Scotland and Ireland, where their numbers were more evenly balanced by other forms of cinerary urn. The Scottish series, concentrated in south-western and central districts, presents such a mixture of 'south-eastern' and 'north-western' traits as to cast doubt on the relevance of this simple two-fold division for Scotland. The Collared Urns of Ireland have a striking easterly, and especially north-easterly, distribution, as befits a tradition drawn from Britain. Ornament is rich, in keeping with Irish traditions, but there is at the same time a relatively high incidence both of completely plain examples and of vessels with body decoration – usually scored lattice.

'Enlarged food vessels' or 'food vessel urns' (Figure 3.3), are familiar but dangerous terms, since they have a built-in assumption that is now seen to be misleading. They describe a varied assortment of cinerary urns which look like 'stretched' versions of food vessels. They are usually interpreted as the response of food vessel users converted to in-urned cremation, but this is a gross over-simplification of what may actually have happened. The Peterborough precursors of food vessels at sites such as Meldon Bridge and Rudston included pots not only of food vessel size but also of cinerary urn size. In particular, one Meldon Bridge vessel is astonishingly like the Bipartite Urns, which are the commonest form of 'enlarged food vessel'. If these small and large sizes are not usually found together it is because the settlement evidence is so exiguous. At Kilellan Farm, Islay, one of the few settlements of the Overton period to be excavated, domestic versions of food vessels and 'enlarged food vessels' occur together. So clearly communities of this time had a range of shapes and sizes in their ceramic repertoire which they drew on as the prevailing sepulchral custom demanded. If an accessory vessel was required then small vessels – food vessels – were chosen. But when in-urned cremation was adopted, larger examples of the same vessels were available.

Most of the vase and bucket food vessel forms are found in 'enlarged' versions used as cinerary urns, but not the bowl forms, possibly because they are more difficult to handle than large, tall vessels, especially when it comes to inverting them in the grave. Enlarged food vessels are most numerous in eastern Britain from Yorkshire to the Moray Firth, where their Peterborough precursors, and food vessels themselves, are concentrated. They are also common in Wales and Ireland, but, like food vessels, are rare in southern England. The ubiquitous Bipartite Urns (Figure 3.3/13) are larger versions of bipartite food vessels, and reflect the latter's regional differences in shape and character. Ridged Urns (Figure 3.3/14,15) are larger versions of ridged food vessels, and also occur frequently in northern areas such as Yorkshire. There are also urn-sized versions of bucket-shaped food vessels, such as the Hooped

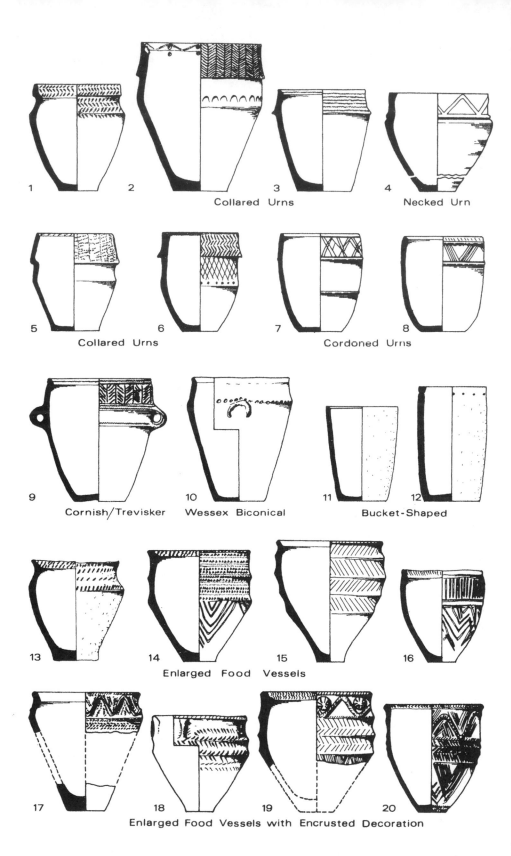

1   2   Collared Urns   3   4   Necked Urn

5   Collared Urns   6   7   Cordoned Urns   8

9   Cornish/Trevisker   10   Wessex Biconical   11   Bucket-Shaped   12

13   14   Enlarged Food Vessels   15   16

17   18   19   20
Enlarged Food Vessels with Encrusted Decoration

Buckets of Ireland. In southern Britain Ridged Buckets are sparsely decorated, in keeping with southern traditions, most often with crude impressions on the ridges (Figure 3.13/M20).

Cordoned Urns (Figure 3.3) are found mainly in Scotland and Ireland, with smaller numbers in Wales, and a thin scattering in northern England. Characteristic are two horizontal cordons which divide the body of the vessel into three zones. The most common form has an upright uppermost zone, but barrel-shaped and bucket-shaped versions are also found. Variants with one, two or even more cordons are found. Decoration is sparse and simple, confined to cord or grooved motifs on the uppermost zone and on the internal bevel.

Bucket-shaped urns (Figures 3.3, 3.16) are best known in Scotland, northern England and Ireland, but occur in most regions. It is difficult to classify such coarse and undistinguished vessels, for their plainness is relieved only by an occasional row of holes or impressions beneath the rim, or by a zone of simple decoration around the upper part of the vessel, reminiscent of Cordoned Urn decoration. They differ little from antecedent bucket-shaped vessels such as those of the Lough Gur II and Kilhoyle traditions (Figure 2.3), and are also indistinguishable from much Deverel-Rimbury material (Figure 3.13). Clearly they constitute local equivalents of Deverel-Rimbury pottery.

This leads on to the problem of 'flat-rimmed ware', an all-encompassing label applied to coarse, plain bucket- and barrel-shaped vessels, and even shouldered forms, common in Scotland and Ireland and occurring in a wide variety of contexts of different periods. A slight internal rim bevel provides the name, but this is by no means an invariable feature. 'Flat-rim' vessels were clearly used over a long period. Some of the best-dated examples are associated with metalwork of the Ewart Park phase (ninth to eighth centuries BC), for example at the Sculptor's Cave, Covesea, Moray, and at Ballinderry Crannog 2, Co. Offaly. But the 'flat-rim' pots frequently associated with stone circles, especially recumbent stone circles, in eastern Scotland, and Ireland, must be a thousand years earlier. Clearly a sub-stratum of coarse, plain barrel- and bucket-shaped pots existed in the Highland Zone throughout later prehistory and even beyond, for very similar vessels are characteristic of native Roman and even Dark Age contexts over much of north and west Britain. Bucket-shaped

---

Figure 3.3 Cinerary urns: 1. Trentham, Staffs.; 2. Wimborne St Giles G 17, Dorset; 3. Bowerchalke G 5, Wilts.; 4. Drumnakilly, Co. Tyrone; 5. Collingbourne Kingston G 8, Wilts.; 6. Kirkbean, Kirkcudbright; 7–8. Mid Gleniron, Wigtown; 9. Crig-a-mennis, Cornwall; 10. Roke Down, Dorset; 11–12. Largs, Ayr; 13. Garthbeibo, Montgom.; 14. Ferniegair, Lanark; 15. Fishguard, Pembs.; 16. Cloghskelt, Co. Down; 17. Annathill, Lanark; 18. Alvah, Banff; 19. Luce Sands, Wigtown; 20. Lyles Hill, Co. Antrim. (1. after Longworth, 1961; 2, 3, 5 after Annable and Simpson, 1964; 4. after Kavanagh. 1973; 6, 7, 8, 11, 12, 14, 17, 19 after Morrison, 1968; 9 after Christie, 1960; 10 after Calkin, 1962; 13, 15 after Savory, 1957; 16 after Waddell, 1976; 18. after Cowie, 1978; 20 after ApSimon, 1969) (various scales)

cinerary urns may well represent only a specific aspect of this 'flat-rim' tradition.

Biconical Urns, found mainly in lowland England, have a high shoulder that may be emphasized by a cordon or line of decoration. In contrast to the 'food vessel rim' of the Bipartite Urns, they have an unexpanded or outwards expanded rim, and a straight neck, angled inwards to a rim markedly smaller in diameter than the shoulder. Bipartite Urns, on the other hand are more often hollow-necked, and have rim and shoulder diameters more nearly equal. The two also differ in decoration.

Best known are the Wessex Biconical Urns, characterized by a row of finger-tip impressions on the shoulder or rim, by horse-shoe motifs on the neck, executed in cord or as applied arcs; and by plastic ornament, generally shoulder or rim cordons, less often bosses and crosses, on the neck or on the inside on the base. There is considerable variation among the Wessex Biconical Urns. Plain examples are common, and there are a few with concave, constricted necks.

Wessex Biconical Urns clearly had to fit into a complex fabric of cinerary urn burial which involved other urn types. The inevitable result was hybridization, typified by a number of bipartite vessels from Wessex, of which the South Afflington urn from Dorset is typical. This combines shoulder grooves and ridges, circular impressions, plastic horse-shoes, straight angled neck and narrow collar: apparently a mixture of Southern Bipartite, Collared and Biconical Urn influences. One of the Amesbury G71 urns is similar, though it lacks the horse-shoes (Figure 7.3).

Eastern Biconical Urns make greater use of fingernail and other rustication techniques than the Wessex variety. The equivalent of Biconical Urns in Ireland is the Necked urn (Drumnakilly urn), which made similar use of relief ornament, including internal base crosses and external finger-tipped cordons.

Cornish Urns are of bucket, barrel and bipartite shapes, and usually have prominent strap handles at the maximum diameter of the body. The zone between handles and rim is usually decorated with cord patterns, especially plaited cord.

'Encrusted urns' were, until recently, recognized as a separate category of cinerary urns, but it is now agreed that encrustation was merely a decorative device applied to enlarged food vessels (Figure 3.3). In fact it was used on whatever enlarged food vessels were typical of a region, and used in a way that fitted the decorative traditions of the region. Thus in northern England and Scotland it is found on Bipartite and Ridged urns, occurring as vertical bars, wavy lines, zig-zags and blobs, on the upper part of the pot. In Ireland, on the other hand, encrusted decoration was used on Hooped Buckets, and on Bipartite and Necked urns and used much more flamboyantly than in Britain. It is characteristically combined with complex impressed, incised and scored patterns to cover the whole body of the pot. A few encrusted Collared Urns are known, such as that from Plas Penrhyn, Anglesey, but encrustation seems to have been alien to the Collared Urn tradition.

Sepulchral pottery: relationships and chronology

For a long time cinerary urns and food vessels symbolized different cultures, which expanded and contracted in relationship to each other and to other cultures, represented by other pottery types. Given the more populous, organized landscapes and the territorial model now envisaged for the period, such a view is completely impractical. Instead of 'Food Vessel Folk' and 'Urn Folk' these pots are now seen to represent no more than alternative burial traditions. We have seen that the regional burial customs and pottery styles of the Third Millennium determined the 'how', 'why' and 'where' of burial traditions in the Second Millennium. At the simplest level they dictated the emergence of food vessels in east Yorkshire and Collared Urns in central southern England. They determined that every region could have an alternative tradition of coarse, bucket-shaped vessels. Cremation was the expanding force in the Overton period, and by its end had spread throughout these islands. In the form in which most regions became acquainted with it, in-urned cremation involved the Collared Urn, and this explains the appearance of Collared Urns throughout Britain and Ireland. But they augmented, rather than stifled local initiative, and so appear as options in a local range of cinerary urns. They inspired food vessel users to introduce enlarged food vessels, so that a single community could draw on a range of Collared Urns and enlarged food vessels for its burial rites.

In the course of time something of the 'ostentatious' tradition, represented by Collared Urns and enlarged food vessels, can be expected to have rubbed off on the coarse tradition of bucket-shaped vessels. This resulted in the relief-decorated urns of the Bedd Branwen period, the Cordoned, Biconical and Necked Urns, and the Barrel Urns of the Deverel-Rimbury tradition.

This bewildering variety of cinerary urns has to be spread over the half millennium of the Overton and Bedd Branwen periods, so it is unlikely that they were all exactly contemporary. There are many radiocarbon dates for Collared Urns, so these we can be sure remained in use throughout these periods. Bipartite Urns, too, must have had a very long life, but part of it was in domestic guise. Their emergence as enlarged food vessels varied from region to region, depending on the progress of the in-urned cremation tradition. It will have happened first in the south, and this is confirmed by the presence of a Southern Bipartite Urn in Phase III at the Amesbury G71 barrow (Figure 7.3), *c*. 1640 bc. Elsewhere it came later in the Overton period, and in the strongholds of the food vessel inhumation rite, such as east Yorkshire, perhaps only at the end of this period. In most regions the dating evidence assigns enlarged food vessels, of all kinds, to the late Overton and Bedd Branwen periods. At one end of this time span is the rich grave group from Llanddyfnan, Anglesey, comprising a decorated dagger, axe and chisel and two Bipartite Urns. The larger of these has a grooved shoulder, like the Bipartite Urn from Watch Hill, Cornwall (*c.* 1520, 1470 bc). At the other end of the scale is the encrusted Bipartite Urn from Brynford, Flintshire, associated with faience beads. The 'encrusted urn' from Mill of Marcus, Forfar, was also found with a faience bead. Since 'encrusted urns' are merely enlarged food vessels with relief decoration, their cinerary use should also have centred on the late Overton–Bedd Branwen periods. Their associations are very few, and mostly unhelpful.

Cordoned Urns were used in the Bedd Branwen period on the evidence of radiocarbon dates (*c.* 1270 bc at Grandtully, Perth, and *c.* 1375 bc and *c.* 1315 bc at Downpatrick, Co. Down) and some useful associations. Of these we may single out examples with quoit-shaped faience beads, as at Harristown, Co. Waterford (Figure 2.6), and with stone battle-axes of late forms, as at Ballintubbrid, Co. Wexford. One exceptional grave group is that from Balneil, Wigtown, comprising Cordoned Urn, quoit faience bead, bone crutch-headed pin and a shouldered bronze stake or chisel, all well documented in contexts of the Bedd Branwen period. There are several associations with Class Ib razors in Ireland, the Isle of Man and Scotland, and these are known to have been introduced in the Bedd Branwen period.

The southern Biconical urns and their Irish counterparts, the Necked Urns, have similar associations to Cordoned Urns and must also be assigned to the Bedd Branwen period. The former have several associations with Class I razors, faience and glass beads, but they may first have been used for burials at the end of the Overton period. For the example from Bircham, Norfolk, is linked by its accompanying gold cased beads to the gold graves of the Wessex Bush Barrow group. The most useful dating evidence for Necked Urns comes, strangely enough, from Wales. A classic example was deposited in a grave at Llangwm, Denbighshire, with faience beads, while some of the anomalous urns at Bedd Branwen (*c.* 1403–1274 bc) seem strongly influenced by Necked Urns. Cornish Urns may have appeared first in the Overton period, for those from Crig-a-mennis, Cornwall, have a radiocarbon date of *c.* 1565 bc. But the weight of associations is later, for example faience beads at Carn Creis in Cornwall and Winterslow in Wiltshire, in a group which also included a Class Ib razor. One from Harlyn Bay, Cornwall, takes us to the very end of the Bedd Branwen period, for it was found with a dirk of Group II, a type not introduced until *c.* 1500 BC.

Bipartite Urns were not the only urns to have had a long tradition of domestic use before being pressed into sepulchral service. We find 'encrusted urn' sherds in a domestic context of the Overton period at Kilellan Farm, and cordoned material in the lower level at the Downpatrick settlement (*c.* 1845 and *c.* 1625 bc). When specialized cinerary urns vanished around 1250–1200 bc, there is no reason why domestic versions of these vessels should not have continued in use. The pottery from the unenclosed scooped settlement at Green Knowe, Peebles (*c.* 1200–1000 bc), appears to be domestic Cordoned Urn. Cordoned Urns have much in common with Deverel-Rimbury urns in history as well as form. Deverel-Rimbury urns alone in the south continued in both sepulchral and domestic use after *c.* 1200 bc. In the north and west cremation burial undoubtedly continued into the Knighton Heath period, so it is possible that Cordoned Urns, like Deverel-Rimbury urns, survived long after other, more specialized, urns. A point to remember here is that Class Ib razors, a regular accompaniment of Cordoned Urns, remained in use throughout the Knighton Heath period. Clearly this is something only more radiocarbon dates can solve.

Pygmy cups

Pygmy cups (Figure 2.6) are miniature accessory vessels, three or four inches across and rather less in height. They were introduced in the Overton period, when they accompanied both inhumations and cremations, but later on they came to be associated entirely with cremation rites. We can only guess at their function, and whether it was always the same. Most examples have perforations at or near their girth so they were clearly not intended to hold a liquid. The alternative term 'incense cup' was coined by nineteenth century antiquaries, and the burning of a fragrant substance is certainly one possibility. Alternatively they may have held some sort of offering. Whatever the answer, Pygmy cups were prestige vessels, for an unusually high proportion have been found with grave goods other than pottery, and they are the only pottery in some of the richest grave groups found in Britain. Two examples will suffice, the Breach Farm group, Glamorgan, with bronze tools, a superb series of barbed and tanged arrowheads and stone 'arrowshaft smoothers', and the Stancomb Downs burial, Berkshire, with a Class Ib razor, stone battle-axe and an antler hammer. Pygmy cups have also accompanied rich cinerary urn burials, for example at Annaghkeen, Co. Galway, with a decorated pot-lid, a bronze dagger, an awl and a quartz pebble; and at Harlyn Bay III, Cornwall, with a Group II dirk, an awl, a whetstone and a stone bead. Another significant fact is that Pygmy cups were the only vessels regularly included in Wessex Culture graves, both in the Bush Barrow and Aldbourne-Edmondsham groups.

There are no obvious precursors of Pygmy cups and again we must think of communities dipping into their ceramic repertoires when the need for a miniature accessory vessel was felt. None pre-date the distinctive Grape Cups of the Bush Barrow graves (Figure 3.5e), whose nodulated decoration was possibly inspired by similar ornament sometimes used on Grooved ware. Bush Barrow graves occasionally have other forms of Pygmy cup, such as the slotted examples with narrow mouth in the grave groups from Wilsford G8, Wiltshire, and Ports Down, Hampshire. But in Wessex at least diversification of form and ornament came at the transition from the Bush Barrow to Aldbourne-Edmondsham phase, for that is the date of the Clandon burial in Dorset, with its fine, narrow-mouth bipartite Pygmy cup bearing incised ornament. The fine bipartite cup at Breach Farm must be broadly contemporary, but the majority of Pygmy cups probably belong to the Bedd Branwen period, certainly the finer examples, and the simple undecorated cups. Just as Bush Barrow burials had the Grape cup, so the Aldbourne-Edmondsham burials have their Aldbourne cups, with a constricted foot, internal ledge, and decoration of incised geometric patterns infilled with pricks, which may be brought out by rubbing in a white substance such as chalk. Aldbourne-Edmondsham graves have also yielded fine, bipartite, incised Pygmy cups, some with contracted mouth. Examples from Stanton Harcourt in Oxfordshire and Beedon, Berkshire, are particularly noteworthy. Many ordinary examples have also been found in Aldbourne-Edmondsham graves, as at Winterbourne Stoke G68. (Figure 3.6b.)

The story is much the same in other regions, with early examples belonging to the end of the Overton period, but with the datable majority found in the Bedd Branwen period. Among the important finds are those from Knockboy, Co. Antrim, with a faience bead; Gilchorn, Angus, with a glass bead, and Loose Howe, Yorkshire, with typical Aldbourne-Edmondsham artefacts. Dated plain cups also belong to the Bedd Branwen period, for example at Whitestanes Moor, Dumfries (*c.* 1360 bc), and Bedd Branwen (*c.* 1274 bc). Small, simple cups are also found quite often in Deverel-Rimbury graves (Figure 3.13).

Pygmy cups are widely distributed, but especially common in Wessex, western Britain from south Wales to the Clyde, and north-east Britain from Aberdeen to the Humber. In the antecedent pottery traditions of most regions there were small cups which could provide a basis for Pygmy cups. Thus there are Grooved ware cups, such as the fine example from the Unival chambered tomb on north Uist, and the straight-sided Ronaldsway cups of the Isle of Man. Whether the idea of the miniature accessory cups spread from one point or was conceived in more than one area is not clear. (Figure 2.2.)

There are innumerable Pygmy cup shapes, combined with a bewildering range of decoration. Most common are bipartite cups, with various configurations of body zones, usually combined with incised ornament. Straight-sided and round bodied cups are also widespread. Other decorative techniques include cord, openwork, and pointillée. Comprehensive classification systems and distribution patterns have not been published, but clearly regional types exist in addition to the Grape and Aldbourne cups of Wessex.

The Wessex Culture

The proportion of burials of the Overton period accompanied by or contained in a pot varies between 25–50 per cent from region to region, and only a tiny

1a   Meldon Bridge, Peebles: post-pits and holes
of the western perimeter.

1b   Meldon Bridge, Peebles: pits of post-row,
c. 1200 bc, some containing cremated burials.

11   Wedge-tomb at Island, Co. Cork, after excavation and conservation.

III   Cup-and-ring rock on Dod Law, Northumberland.

IV*a*   Stonehenge: inhumation burial found in 1978 in the ditch fill.

IV*b*   Stonehenge: barbed-and-tanged flint arrowheads and stone 'bracer' found with the 1978 burial.

v Beaker grave group from Mains of Culduthel, Inverness, comprising Step 4 Beaker, stone 'bracer' with gold-capped pins, barbed-and-tanged flint arrowheads, bone looped ring, amber bead and flint knife.

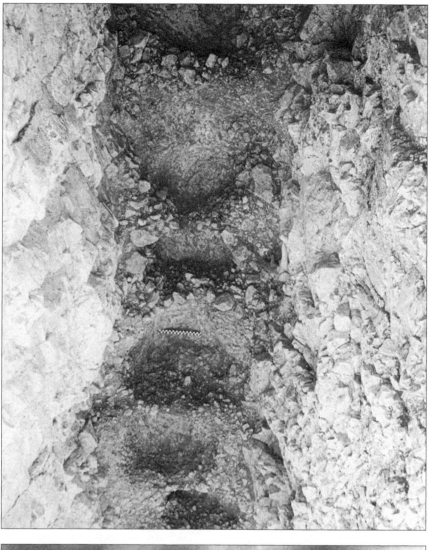

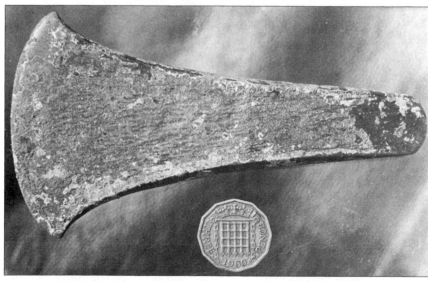

VII Turf barrow, site 45 ('Boncyn Arian'), Brenig, Denbighshire, showing the stake rings, stone ring and palisade trench of different phases of construction, and the central robbing pit of nineteenth-century excavations.

VIII Ring cairn, site 44, Brenig, Denbighshire.

percentage is accompanied by other grave goods. The notable exception to this general paucity of grave goods is the unique concentration of rich burials of the 'Wessex Culture'. As originally conceived, this arose out of an incursion by a 'dominant aristocracy' from Brittany. These newcomers achieved hegemony over the native population, and established wealthy chiefdoms which lasted for several centuries, until eventually the intrusive element was absorbed by the indigenous population. The prosperity of these Wessex chieftains was supposedly based on commerce, especially their success as middlemen in channelling trade from Ireland, various parts of Europe and the Mediterranean through their territory. Chronologically they were thought to span the 'Early Bronze Age', succeeding Beaker groups at one end, and merging into 'Middle Bronze Age' elements at the other.

The richly-furnished burials of the Wessex Culture are concentrated on the Wessex chalk, especially on the Marlborough Downs around Avebury, on Salisbury Plain, on Cranborne Chase and on the south Dorset Downs, but their distribution spills out sporadically into surrounding regions, both on and off the chalk; into Hampshire and Sussex, Berkshire and the Upper Thames gravels, the hills of Somerset and Gloucestershire, and, far-removed to the west, scattered instances on the uplands of Devon and Cornwall.

The first point to note about the Wessex Culture is that even in Wessex and the surrounding regions, these rich burials form only a small proportion of the great mass of graves. They do not usually cluster together, but are well spread out. Some come from isolated barrows as at Upton Lovell and Manton in Wiltshire, but others occur in ones and twos, in exceptional cases a half-dozen or so, in the barrow cemeteries that are such a feature of the area. In their own barrow, and in the cemetery as a whole, they stand out amidst the great number of simpler graves. Sometimes the rich burials have come from 'fancy' barrows (Figure 7.4) or from those of largest size, but equally many big barrows and 'fancy' barrows have yielded only poorly-furnished burials. Some of the richest burials have been found in quite ordinary bowl barrows, so there are no apparent rules governing the size or form of monument in which they were interred. It seems to have been more important that they should have their own specially-built barrow, for most Wessex Culture burials were primary interments, and occupied the most important position in their burial mound. This contrasts notably with the mass of poorer burials, which were frequently interred as secondaries in existing mounds.

The picture that emerges, of sporadic rich graves amidst the mass of simpler graves is very much in keeping with the concept of a structured society. In Wessex it is noticeable that these rich graves are divided amongst the several chiefdoms which have been postulated for the region, with notable gaps in the distribution between those on the Marlborough Downs, on Salisbury Plain, on Cranborne Chase, and on the south Dorset Downs. It is tempting to conclude that these were the graves of the rich and powerful in each chiefdom. The fact that within each territory they are scattered in distinct clusters perhaps indicates further division into dynastic spheres of influence. The lessers in society would have their own burial provision, according to rank. Some clearly qualified for their own mound, while others were interred in an existing one. Grave furniture would at most be a cinerary urn or accessory vessel, and perhaps a flint, one or two beads, or a simple bronze blade, but many burials have nothing. What governed the allocation of burial sites amongst these lesser ranks the evidence cannot tell us. One can postulate that those consigned to the mounds of the rich were either kin or retainers, or were deposited long afterwards when the special significance of the site was lost; and that the higher the status the greater the chance of one's own mound. But there are many other possibilities which may have governed these decisions.

The contents of Wessex Culture graves suggest both sex and wealth differences. An immediate distinction may be suggested between grave goods appropriate to males, notably stout grooved daggers, stone battle-axes and other weapons, and those suited to females, such as necklaces, beads, pendants and other trinkets, metal awls and small knives. Pottery is rare, apart from Pygmy cups, and is more a feature of female than male graves. The wealth of individual graves in Piggott's original Wessex Culture list ranges from male burials such as that in Bush Barrow, Wiltshire (Figure 3.4), with metal daggers, one with gold-studded hilt, flat axe, stone mace-head, sheet-gold mounts and bone mounts; and female burials such as that in the Upton Lovell 'Gold Barrow', Wiltshire (Figure 3.5), with gold ornaments, amber 'spacer-plate' necklace, metal knife and awl, and pottery vessels; to male burials accompanied merely by a stone battle-axe or dagger, and female burials with a few beads. Clearly the whole social and wealth spectrum is represented in this range, and many of the poorer graves are in no way different from burials with battle-axes and beads in other regions. Even burials with a large series of grave goods may include nothing that is not familiar in other parts of the country, for example the double inhumation in Upton Lovell G2 (a), with two stone battleaxes, stone axes, 'arrowshaft smoother', a large series of bone points, shale and bone ornaments and a metal awl. In this case it is the quantity, and not the quality, of grave goods which distinguishes this group from burials in other regions.

In view of the wide social spectrum implicit in the Wessex Culture graves, it seems misleading to prolong the idea of a Wessex Culture in the traditional sense. It is now clear that the graves listed by Piggott represent the wealthier and more powerful elements in Wessex Society, and as they grade so evenly down to the great mass of poorer graves, meaningful dividing lines are impossible to draw. To compare Piggott's Wessex Culture with other societies is meaningless, for the valid comparison is between Wessex society and society in east Yorkshire, northern Ireland or any other region. There were many marked regional differences, amongst them the fact that for a time in the

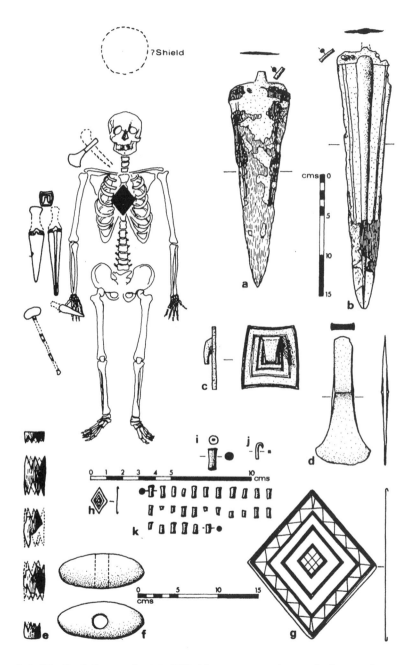

Figure 3.4 The Bush Barrow burial, Wiltshire: a. copper dagger; b. bronze dagger; c, g, h. gold ornaments; d. bronze axe; e. bone mounts; f. stone mace-head; i, k. bronze rivets; j. bronze hook (artefacts after Annable and Simpson, 1964; reconstruction after Ashbee, 1960)

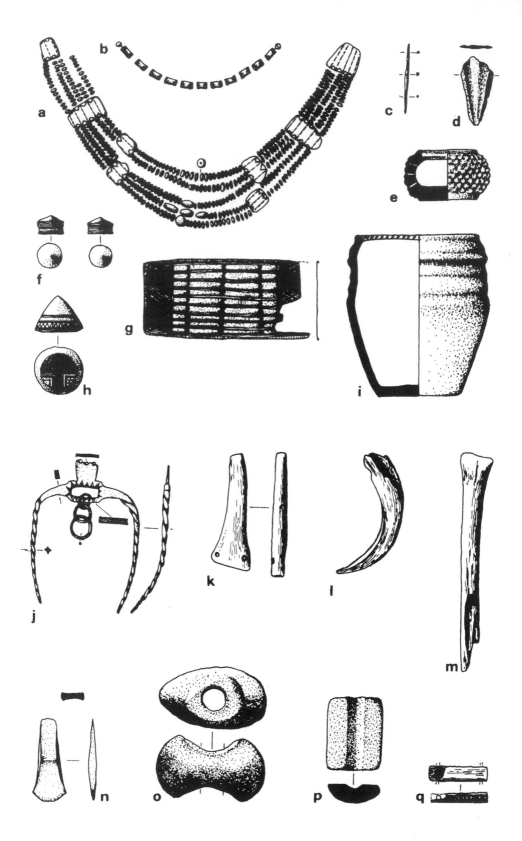

Overton and Bedd Branwen periods, Wessex hierarchies deposited much richer grave goods with the dead than the wealthy of other areas. This should not necessarily be taken to indicate that one region was richer or poorer than another, but rather that their beliefs differed. This is contrary to the normal view of Wessex Society. Other regions may for geographical reasons have been poorer in manpower and agricultural resources, and less highly organized than Wessex territories, but may well have been at least as rich in gold and bronze and other material possessions which could have filled local graves *had custom demanded*. The most difficult aspect of the problem is why in Wessex alone there arose hierarchies given to taking great wealth to the grave. And this is a question bound up with the development and nature of Wessex Society as a whole.

The various explanations of the Wessex phenomenon all have their weaknesses. The idea that Continental intruders played a significant part is attractive because what happened in Wessex was unparalleled in other regions, and because there are so many exotic items in Wessex graves. But against a foreign presence is the absence of any wide range of alien cultural evidence, the fact that there is nothing in the graves that could not have been acquired by trade or exchange, and, the contrary point, that they contain so much which is indigenous. Theories of internal development envisage a conquest of Wessex by elements originating somewhere within Britain, or see the rich graves only as the culmination in a local development, either the crystallization of local chiefdoms, or an inevitable concomitant of emerging pastoralist communities, rich in flocks and herds. The argument against internal conquest is quite simply the lack of any similar sepulchral wealth in other contemporary societies. The problem with the chiefdoms and pastoralists theory is that other regions were divided into chiefdoms and peopled by pastoralists, and these never developed any significant interest in rich graves.

In seeking an answer a logical step is surely to ask what Wessex, and no other region, had. The answer was the biggest, best and most prestigious ritual and ceremonial centres in the whole country, which may have been the result of having more manpower, more agricultural resources, better social organization and more vigorous leadership than other regions. The scale of local monuments also suggests a tendency to showiness amongst local leaders. But these great centres were at their height in the Mount Pleasant period, when, to be sure, a few rich graves, with Beakers, are known. They have often been cited as precursors of the Wessex Culture phenomenon, since they too

Figure 3.5 Two grave groups of the Bush Barrow group: a–i. Grave group from Upton Lovell G 2 (e), Wilts.: a. amber spacer-bead necklace; b. gold beads; c. bronze awl; d. bronze dagger blade; e. grape cup; f, g, h. gold ornaments; i. Collared Urn; j–q. Grave group from Wilsford G 58, Wilts.: j. bronze mystery object; k. antler handle; l. boar's tusk; m. bone tool; n. bronze axe; o. stone battle-axe; p. stone 'arrow-shaft smoother'; q. perforated bone plaque (after Annable and Simpson, 1964) (scale ¼)

contain gold objects, and are very much warrior graves. But rich Beaker graves are found in many regions, and these did not produce Wessex cultures. Many were densely populated, had considerable agricultural wealth, highly organized pastoral societies and considerable ritual centres. What, then, did they lack? The answer must be Wessex's direct and speedy access to the Continent, with all its novel ideas, in particular regular traffic with societies across the Channel which did believe in richly furnished graves. This was the catalyst which ensured that the Wessex hierarchies alone turned to sepulchral ostentation. This does not necessarily demand an incursion from Brittany, for incessant cross-Channel traffic meant that there was always a tendency for societies in southern England to mirror developments in north-west France.

Wessex Culture burials have traditionally been divided into two chronologically successive groups, Wessex I and Wessex II. This division, hotly disputed in recent years, has now been confirmed by radiocarbon dates. Attempts to determine a sequence of graves have rested on the contention that Bush Barrow daggers, with a triangular, grooved blade, six peg rivets and residual tang ('languette') are earlier than Camerton-Snowshill daggers with two or three plug rivets and an ogival blade; and that inhumation burials were early, and gave way progressively to cremation. Thus an earlier group of burials, typified by the Bush Barrow grave (Figure 3.4), has a high proportion of inhumations, and Bush Barrow daggers, which may be either flat (Armorico-British A) or have a strong midrib (Armorico-British B). The Bush Barrow inhumation, with both dagger forms, shows what else might be expected of this group: sheet gold-work, small bronze axes (Wilsford type), and stone mace-heads. The dentated bone mounts from this grave are unique in Britain but have interesting Continental parallels. By cross-referencing we can expand the content of this Bush Barrow Group to include the nodulated Pygmy cups termed Grape Cups; stone 'arrowshaft smoothers'; simple stone battle-axes with concave faces; 'fancy' beads, including pestle-shaped and ribbed examples, in a wide variety of substances; double-pointed awls; halberd pendants; and a variety of bone objects, many perforated, including the teeth and tusks of a variety of animals (Figure 3.5). In the second or Aldbourne-Edmondsham Group, the ogival, grooved Camerton-Snowshill dagger is typical, usually with three stout plug rivets, and with a thicker, more sophisticated blade. Cremation is usual, and inhumation rare. Some of the most famous burials in the group are by inhumation, but these tend to lie outside Wessex, as at Snowshill in Gloucestershire and Chippenham in Cambridgeshire. The other elements in the Aldbourne-Edmondsham Group (Figure 3.6) include bone tweezers, boat-shaped stone battle-axes, segmented faience beads, pins with spirally-twisted stems, bulb-headed pins, and Aldbourne Pygmy Cups. A particular barrow form, the disc barrow, is associated with this group, and especially with female graves.

In between the Bush Barrow and Camerton-Snowshill daggers is the

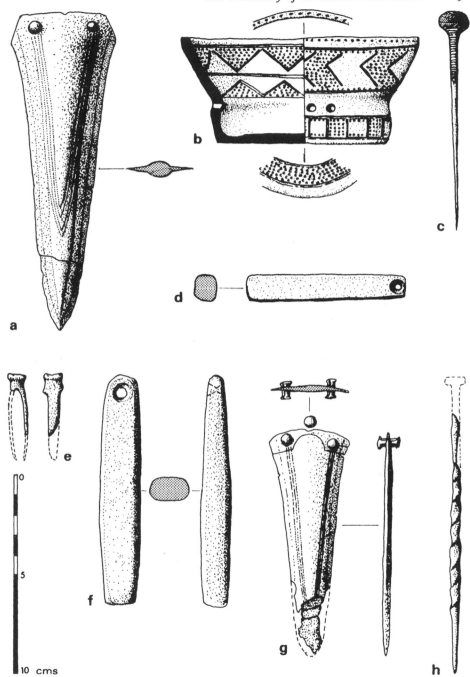

Figure 3.6 Two grave groups of the Aldbourne-Edmondsham group: a–d. Camerton, Somerset: a. bronze dagger; b. Aldbourne cup; c. bronze pin; d. perforated whetstone; e–h. Edmondsham, Dorset: e. bone tweezers; f. perforated whetstone; g. bronze dagger; h. bone pin-shaft (a–d. after Piggott, 1938; e–h. after Proudfoot, 1963)

Armorico-British C or Shave Hill form, retaining the six small rivets of the former, but having the ogival blade of the Camerton-Snowshill weapons. Shave Hill daggers are not common, but include some of the largest and finest of our grooved daggers. In view of their typological position it is not surprising that they occur with other artefacts in a number of interments which bridge the two main groups of burials. Some of these 'intermediate types' were carried over from Bush Barrow burials, notably amber spacer beads, v-perforated buttons and barbed and tanged flint arrowheads. Others were to belong mainly to the Aldbourne-Edmondsham group, such as shale rings, crutch-headed, ring-headed and lobed pins, perforated whetstones and finely-decorated Pygmy cups. Still other types are associated equally with both the earlier and the later group, such as miscellaneous amber beads, small simple knives, single point awls, and bell and bowl barrows.

A recently proposed minimal view of the Wessex Culture maintained that all these rich burials were deposited in a short period of time, insufficient for any sequence to show in the archaeological record. It was argued, for example, that all the best-quality Wessex goldwork appears to have been executed by one craftsman. This is irrelevant, because it affects only half a dozen graves out of more than a hundred. The lack of any stratigraphic evidence for subdividing the burials is equally irrelevant: since no two Wessex burials were ever placed in the same mound, there can be no stratigraphic relationship.

The third claim, that the Continental background of all the Wessex metalwork appears to lie within a single phase, Reinecke A2, raises more complex problems of Continental chronology. There is no doubt that the Bush Barrow Group, like Stage VI metallurgy, had good contacts with central Europe in its classical Únětician/Reinecke A2/Leubingen-Dieskau stage. However, the best Continental parallels for Aldbourne-Edmondsham types, especially the grooved ogival daggers and pins, are to be found in Switzerland, and in the Sögel group of north Germany in a stage alternatively described as A2/B1 or A3. This designation has been conceived to encompass material later than the classic A2 stage but not yet appropriate to full Tumulus culture.

In any case the possibility of a short Wessex chronology has now been removed by radiocarbon evidence. There are two dates for Aldbourne-Edmondsham graves with Camerton-Snowshill daggers, from Hove, Sussex (*c.* 1239 bc) and Edmondsham itself (*c.* 1119 bc), while a third grave with a Camerton-Snowshill dagger, at Earls Barton, Northamptonshire, has dates of *c.* 1219 bc and 1264 bc. These confirm that what has always been regarded as a late group of Wessex burials was indeed interred in the fifteenth century BC, some burials possibly as late as the fourteenth century. On the other hand the radiocarbon date for the Amesbury 39 burial is *c.* 1670 bc. This was associated with a large number of amber and shale or jet beads, and two conical buttons, one v-perforated, on the strength of which this burial should be assigned to the Bush Barrow group. This date agrees reasonably well with the *c.* 1650/1600 bc bracket for the emergence of the Bush Barrow group which seems appropriate with all the other evidence in mind. It also fits in with the radiocarbon dates both for the beginnings of the related Breton dagger graves, and of the Leubingen-Dieskau contexts in central Europe with which both the Bush Barrow and Breton graves were strongly connected. One other relevant date is that of *c.* 1450 bc for the phase II burial at Anner Tol III in the Netherlands, which was associated with an ogival grooved dagger with features reminiscent of both the Shave Hill and Camerton-Snowshill forms. This provides an intermediate date for an intermediate dagger.

In terms of burial rite the mixture of inhumation and cremation shown by the Bush Barrow group is appropriate to the Overton period, whilst the almost total dominance of cremation in the Aldbourne-Edmondsham group fits better with the Bedd Branwen period. This simple correlation must be qualified, however. The grave goods found with step 5 and 6 Beaker burials and those in Bush Barrow graves are almost mutually exclusive, which suggests there was little chronological overlap of the two. The Bush Barrow group, in fact was demonstrably contemporary with step 7 Beakers. Yet step 5 and 6 Beakers lasted sufficiently long in the Overton period to overlap with the earliest food vessels and cinerary urns. This is made clear both by radiocarbon dates and the stratigraphy at West Overton G6b. The Overton period must therefore be divided into two parts. Bush Barrow graves belonged to the later part, and were preceded by a phase of gestation in which burials with step 5 and 6 Beakers were mixed with novel Collared Urn and food vessel interments. But there were also burials given an assortment of grave goods but no pot, such as Amesbury 39, and these were particularly important for the development of the Bush Barrow group. Suggested dates for the first phase are *c.* 1700–1600 bc and for the Bush Barrow phase *c.* 1600–1450 bc. Closer examination of grave goods emphasizes this division. In addition to step 5 and 6 Beakers, graves of the earlier phase still had flat axes of Mount Pleasant type, double pointed awls, flat-faced battle-axes and peg-rivet knives and daggers. The Bush Barrow graves have more sophisticated daggers, flat axes and awls, and their battle-axes have concave instead of flat faces.

That the Bush Barrow group overlapped with step 7 Beakers is demonstrated by a small group of ribbed gold pommel mounts. Two of these have been found with Bush Barrow daggers, at Topped Mountain, Co. Fermanagh, and Cressingham, Norfolk, while the others come from graves with plug-rivet flat daggers, such as regularly accompany step 7 Beakers (as at Ashgrove, Fife, and Eynsham, Oxfordshire).

Thus we can dispose of another favourite source of Wessex Culture chieftains, that they were immediate descendants of those buried in rich Beaker graves. In Wessex such Beaker burials are all of steps 2 and 3; for example, Mere, Farleigh Wick, Roundway and Winterslow, all in Wiltshire, deposited in the Mount Pleasant period, centuries before the emergence of the Bush

Barrow chieftains. Intervening burials with steps 4, 5 and 6 Beakers are found frequently with tools and are much less grand, so there appears to have been no continuity on which the Bush Barrow group could have drawn. Their emergence was the result of a general social and spiritual upheaval, and contact with the grandeur of the Armorican dagger chiefs provided the extra impetus.

The famous connections between the Bush Barrow chieftains and the Mycenaean world have come under severe scrutiny following the tree-ring calibration of radiocarbon dates. For a long time classical Únětice, Breton dagger graves and Bush Barrow graves have been tied by cross dating to the Mycenaean shaft graves, and thus to the latter's historical dates of c. 1650–1500 BC. But after calibration of their radiocarbon dates of c. 1700–1450 bc, they suddenly appeared much too early to have contact with shaft grave Mycenae, and there was a flurry of activity to explain the famous connections. In the event this appears premature, for more recent historical calibration has had a much less drastic effect, and has narrowed the gap to a point where Bush Barrow and its European contemporaries could just have overlapped with the earliest shaft graves.

Certainly it is still worthwhile to review the evidence for Aegean links. The most convincing finds are the bone dentated mounts from Bush Barrow (Figure 3.4), the only parallels for which occurred in Shaft Grave Iota at Mycenae, and the amber spacer-bead necklaces, which occur in Bush Barrow burials such as the Upton Lovell 'Gold Barrow'. These were part of the British tradition of crescentic spacer-bead necklaces, and, threaded more simply, were still being deposited in Aldbourne-Edmondsham burials. Amber spacer-beads also turn up in Aegean contexts, and those in Shaft Grave Omicron at Mycenae are particularly like the Wessex examples. Most authorities would accept these as indisputable evidence for contacts between Wessex and Mycenae, although not all would agree at how many removes. Most agree, though that the beads went from Wessex to the Aegean, and not vice versa, for spacer beads at this time were peculiarly British. Undoubtedly on the continent amber spacer-beads lingered on into phases later than the Shaft Graves, so that the Mycenaean examples are no reason for tying Bush Barrow dates too closely to those for Shaft Graves. The Bush Barrow phase need only have overlapped slightly with shaft graves to make some connection possible. Iota is an early shaft grave, rather before 1600 BC on the strength of its Middle Helladic pottery, but Omicron falls within the sixteenth century BC. These contexts need only provide a *terminus ante quem* for the Bush Barrow group. If mounts and spacer-beads filtered through to the Aegean during the seventeenth century, then a date for Bush Barrow itself around 1700 BC, i.e. c. 1500 bc, would fall within the range c. 1600–1450 bc suggested above for the Bush Barrow group. A transition from Bush Barrow to Aldbourne-Edmondsham around 1450 bc, would be in keeping with the radiocarbon date of the Anner Tol intermediate dagger.

More evidence for Aegean contacts is provided by the gold cups of Wessex and Brittany, which are technologically similar to Mycenaean examples in their use of corrugation and rivet-and-washer handle attachment. The most famous of the gold cups, those from Rillaton, Cornwall, Fritzdorf in Germany and Eschenz in Switzerland, have been mistakenly linked to the classic Bell Beakers because of their S-profile, but these Beakers were centuries earlier. The Rillaton example comes from a grave of the Aldbourne-Edmondsham group, and is no more than a gold version of the shale and amber cups from other Aldbourne-Edmondsham burials like those from Hove and Farway. The latter are undoubtedly related to the handled pottery cups characteristic of much of eastern France, middle and southern Germany and especially Switzerland, in Reinecke A2 and A2/B1. It is these which provide the background for the gold cups. The striking similarity between the Eschenz and Rillaton examples is reinforced by a lost shale cup from the King's Barrow, Stowborough, Dorset, which had decoration very reminiscent of the Swiss cup. If the gold cups were in use during the Aldbourne-Edmondsham/Reinecke A2/B1 stage, then there is no chronological difficulty in associating them with Mycenaean cups. In this case it is worth considering afresh the similarities between the straight-sided, corrugated gold cup from Mycenae and the lost piece of similar shape and style from Cuxwold, Suffolk.

Other supposed Mycenaean connections are more doubtful. The gold pin hilt decoration on Wessex and Breton daggers now seems much too early to have been influenced by Aegean technology, and this is now the objection to an architectural link between sarsen Stonehenge and similar Aegean structures. The carvings on the sarsen uprights, apparently of square-shouldered Mycenaean daggers, seemed to clinch this connection, but from what is now known of the chronology of Stonehenge it is clear that they were executed long after the stones were raised. A closer date is given by the carvings of Arreton flanged axes with which they are intermingled, for these were not manufactured until the Bedd Branwen period. The identification of these carvings as Mycenaean daggers has inevitably become suspect in all of this, but it is only fair to point out that a better preserved carving of what certainly appears to be a Mycenaean dagger comes from a barrow at Badbury in Dorset.

Mediterranean connections have also been claimed in the later stages of the Wessex Culture, in the form of the beads made of the artificial glass-like material, faience. These are a common feature of Aldbourne-Edmondsham graves, particularly in segmented form, and have for long been regarded as undoubted Mediterranean imports. Faience beads of various shapes are scattered throughout Britain and Ireland, although they are concentrated in Wessex. While the segmented form is most numerous, other shapes become common outside Wessex, especially quoit-shaped and star-shaped beads. Indeed, the latter are such a feature of south-west Scotland that a good case can be made for their manufacture there.

The sophisticated technology implicit in faience beads has until recently led scholars to seek their origin in the east Mediterranean where, especially in Egypt, they were produced in vast quantities from the mid-Third, and throughout the Second, Millennium BC. In particular excellent parallels for the British beads could be found in Egyptian eighteenth dynasty contexts, dating to *c.* 1450–1375 BC.

This traditional source has recently been challenged along with all the other Mediterranean connections of the Wessex Culture. Scientific analysis of the composition of British beads has led some authorities to claim that they were manufactured locally and not imported at all. Other scientists, using the same results, have suggested exactly the opposite, that the composition of Irish-British beads did overlap with some Egyptian samples, and could not have been produced by contemporary British technology. The problem has not therefore been resolved satisfactorily. A good case for the manufacture of faience in parts of central Europe has been made out, and the rarity of the star form outside Britain supports the idea of Scottish manufacture. But the Wessex beads involve too many coincidences to accept lightly the idea that they were all made locally. We are asked to accept the proposition that British craftsmen could invent independently a segmented form of faience bead at exactly the same time that similar beads were being produced in the East Mediterranean. A compromise would be to accept that some Mediterranean beads reached Britain, and these inspired British manufacture of faience. Radiocarbon dates confirm that Aldbourne-Edmondsham burials were indeed being interred in just that period, around 1450–1400 BC, when Egyptian sites such as Abydos and Lachish provide the closest parallels for the Wessex beads. In spite of claims to the contrary, there is no evidence that faience beads were used in these islands outside a restricted period, the Bedd Branwen period. It seems strange, if there was any serious local manufacture, that a technology with such interesting potential should have disappeared so soon after a social phenomenon with such notable exotic contacts.

Other foreign connections of the Wessex Culture have proved less contentious. Links with Brittany were mainly a feature of the Bush Barrow phase, and involved an overlapping taste in grave goods. The gold nail studded hilts and some of the daggers from the Breton and Bush Barrow graves are so similar as to indicate they were supplied by the same workshops, probably in Brittany to judge from the numbers of finds. Similarly the Lannion gold 'box' incorporates tricks of workmanship suggesting the same skill that made the finest Wessex goldwork. On the other hand, Wessex dynasts did not take to the elegant Breton form of flint arrowheads, with long, drooping barbs, which are so numerous in the Breton dagger graves. But others in Wessex did, for they occur in 'non-Wessex' graves such as those at Winterbourne Came, Dorset, with inhumations and bipartite food vessel, and at Wimborne St. Giles G9, Dorset, in a typical, if unusually rich, late Beaker grave.

Other contacts between Brittany and Britain include bone models of grooved daggers, copying Armorico-British daggers at Lescongar, but the Camerton-Snowshill form at Crug-yr-Avan in Glamorgan; and dentated mounts, in gold at Kerlagat near Carnac, bone at Bush Barrow. Undoubtedly these influences were operating in both directions, for the jet spacer bead in the Kerguèvarec grave and the collared vessel from Tourony, Côte-du-Nord, suggest traffic from Britain to Brittany.

One exotic form found in Bush Barrow graves which is neither Mediterranean nor Breton in origin is the halberd pendant, as found at Wilsford G8 and Manton. These trinkets, with amber, gold-bound shaft, and bronze blade, are miniature depictions of shafted halberds, a weapon foreign to southern England. Furthermore, by this time halberds had passed out of use even in Ireland, so that the Wessex pendants must copy the central European shafted halberds of classical Únětice, as has always been supposed.

The transition from Bush Barrow to Aldbourne-Edmondsham saw a notable re-orientation of Continental connections. Links with Brittany seem to have faltered, and cross-Channel traffic shifted further north, to Picardy, Normandy, the Île de France, perhaps even to the Rhine mouth. But these were only staging posts *en route* to the Swiss-south German region, which shows remarkable connections with southern England at this time. The first indications of this realignment are the dress pins and perforated whetstones which appear in 'intermediate' graves such as Wilsford G23 and Shave Hill. Aldbourne-Edmondsham pins, bulb-headed, crutch-headed, ring-headed, multiple ring and trilobate (or trefoil), occurring in bone as well as in bronze, are widely distributed in time and space on the Continent, but, taken together, find their best parallels in the A2/B1 stage in Switzerland and in Sögel contexts in north-west Europe. The Swiss connection is emphasized by the gold cups and perforated whetstones of the two regions, while Switzerland also provides some of the best Continental parallels for Camerton-Snowshill daggers. It is not so much a question of direct imports as south English smiths being aware of these Swiss and north-west European trends. As graphic illustration of this there is the dagger from Ashford, Kent, with blade fluted in the Swiss fashion, and an intervening example, probably an actual Swiss import, from the Aisne at Rethondes in northern France. In a similar position *en route* is the hill-top settlement at Ford Harrouard west of Paris, which has the only bone tweezers known outside Aldbourne-Edmondsham contexts, a perforated whetstone, bone crutch-headed and bronze trilobate pins, and an abundance of finger-tipped cordoned vessels reminiscent of Deverel-Rimbury pots.

Settlement, farming and economics

There is no evidence for any great change in settlement and farming patterns in the Overton period. Farmsteads and hamlets of round and rectilinear timber structures, often set within stockades, were still scattered across the landscape. Examples have been excavated as far apart as Gwithian in Cornwall, Swarkeston in Derbyshire, and Kilellan Farm in the Hebrides. Ring ditch farmsteads were also widespread, some of them surviving from the Mount Pleasant period, as at Fengate, others new foundations, such as Warren Farm, Milton Keynes, in Buckinghamshire. Many of these ring ditch settlements subsequently became burial sites. The building of barrows and cairns directly on top of settlements, as at Swarkeston, Brenig 51 in Denbighshire and Arreton Down on the Isle of Wight, was clearly a widespread phenomenon.

The extension of field systems can be seen in areas as far apart as the Fens (Fengate), the south-west (Gwithian) and in Wessex and Sussex. Cross ploughing was practised even on such remote Hebridean islands as Rosinish, Benbecula, and the widespread use of a two-ox crook ard can be postulated. As before wheat and barley were both grown, in proportions dependent on local soil conditions.

Flint and stone declined in importance with the increasing availability of metal, and activity at lowland flint mines and Highland Zone stone sources was running down. Some stone axes of the old Neolithic pattern were still in circulation, for examples have been found with food vessels at sites such as Cookestown, Co. Tyrone, and Craignish, Argyll. Leaf-shaped arrowheads were also still used, as found at the Kilellan Farm settlement. A few new rock sources were developed, such as the Cwm Mawr/Hyssington picrite of the Shropshire/Montgomeryshire border, for perforated battle axes and maceheads were still prestigious warrior equipment.

Metallurgy

Some stage IV products, especially Migdale axes in Scotland, survived right through this period, but otherwise its early part was dominated by the Stage V developments, which had made a tentative start at the end of the Mount Pleasant period, giving way later to Stage VI. The most radical changes were in the design of flat axes and daggers. The transverse bevel and hammered-up face edges of the Stage V flat axes, the Ballyvalley and Aylesford types (Figure 3.7/b-d), had been designed for the novel knee-shaft handle with forked end, but this style of handle really required narrower axes, and these were introduced with Stage VI. Falkland, Greenlees, Scrabo Hill, Wilsford and other Stage VI axes are characterized by narrow butts, slender bodies and sharply expanded blades (Figure 3.7 g,k, Falkland; h, Scrabo Hill), and were clearly influenced by central European axes of Reinecke A2. The progression towards the shape of the true flanged axe of Stage VII is obvious.

Stage VI axes, like Stage V, were frequently decorated with hammered, punched and engraved designs, richer and more varied on Irish than on British specimens. Stage VI axes, too, are more common in Ireland than in Britain. Their paucity in areas such as Scotland suggests that the simple Migdale type

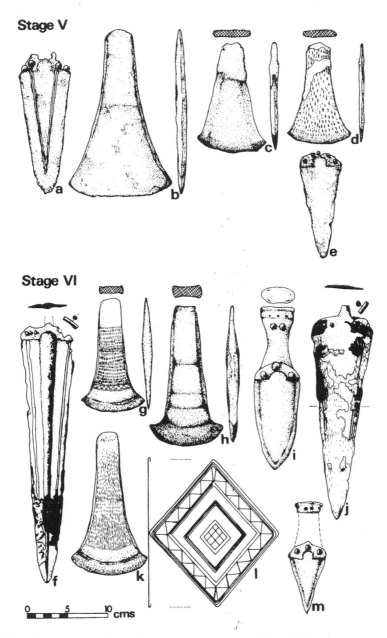

Figure 3.7 Development of early bronze-working, stages V and VI: a, b, e. grave group, Aylesford, Kent; c–d. from the Colleonard hoard, Banff; f, j, l. from the Bush Barrow grave group, Wilts.; g, k. from the Willerby Wold hoard, Yorks.; h. from the Scrabo Hill hoard, Co. Down; i. Methilhill, Fife; m. Eynsham, Oxon. (a, b. e. after Piggott, 1963; c–d. after Coles, 1968–9; f, j, l. after Annable and Simpson, 1964; g, k. after Megaw and Hardy, 1938; h. after Harbison, 1968; i, m. after Clarke, 1970)

remained in production. Any local stage VI production was slight by comparison, and in Wales and Scotland, some Stage VI axes, especially of the Scrabo Hill type with prominent blade, may have been imported from Ireland. Examples of the small, parallel-sided Wilsford type occur in several Bush Barrow graves (Figure 3.5n).

Just as Stage IV shows connections with the Reinecke A1, or early Únětician, phase in central Europe, so Stage V has links with the A2 phase, classical Únětice. This has a few radiocarbon dates between 1700–1600 bc, but probably lasted down to *c.* 1500 bc. This compares with the dates *c.* 1600–1450 bc suggested for the Bush Barrow group, whose A2 connections have already been noted. They include the halberd pendants, copies of the metal-shafted halberds which were in widespread use in A2 Europe. There is no evidence that halberds were still used, let alone made, in Britain and Ireland as late as this. Yet strangely it was at this time that halberds were enjoying their greatest popularity over much of the Continent. Supposed 'Irish' halberds found in Continental contexts of this period always prove to be of the specifically non-Irish 'International' form, which probably originated in western Europe.

The grooved Armorico-British or Bush Barrow daggers provide further evidence of central European A2 influence in Bush Barrow Wessex. As the name implies, these daggers are also characteristic of the Lannion Group ('First series') of Armorican barrow graves, with which the Bush Barrow chiefs had such close contacts. These daggers were clearly a western version of the grooved, triangular, Oder-Elbe daggers so widespread in Europe in the A2 phase, though lacking their solid cast hilt. Oder-Elbe daggers, metal-shafted halberds and an international halberd long, but mistakenly, regarded as 'Irish', form part of the great East German hoard of Dieskau II, which provides the most important evidence of a Stage VI–A2 correlation. For this hoard also includes a typical Stage VI, 'Falkland' axe, complete with 'rain-pattern' ornament, a rare Irish-British import in central Europe.

Armorico-British daggers, in the flat A and midribbed B versions, are largely confined to Wessex, with rare outliers in Kent, East Anglia, Yorkshire, Scotland and Ireland. Other Stage VI daggers were less sophisticated. The Stage V weapons of the early Overton period, such as occur with step 6 Beakers, still had multiple slender rivets. In contrast, the daggers found with step 7 Beakers have three, or in a few cases two or five, fat 'plug' rivets, set in a lower, more rounded heel. This was the standard Stage VI dagger form in most regions. Any embellishment of the flat blade is rare, but a few examples have short blade grooves, a midrib, either simple or reeded, or three wide-spaced blade ribs, as on the famous dagger from Blackwaterfoot, Arran.

Great attention was paid to ornamenting the pommels and hilts of Stage VI daggers. The Blackwaterfoot dagger, and several other Scottish examples, had ribbed gold pommel mounts similar to those which decorated Armorico-

British daggers with the Cressingham and Topped Mountain burials – the latter with an Irish Vase food vessel. Other Armorico-British daggers, in Wessex and Brittany, had their hilts and pommels decorated with myriads of gold wire pins.

The best-known gold-work of Stage VI, that found in the Bush Barrow graves, occurs as foil and sheet, and is used to cover substances such as amber, shale, and wood. This is feeble stuff compared with the spectacular gold capes of north Wales, of which the Mold example survives (Figure 4.8). Unfortunately this unique piece cannot be closely dated, but the likeliest period for a rich inhumation burial with gold, bronze and amber is the latter part of the Overton period, contemporary with Bush Barrow burials. Whether lunulae were still being made is uncertain, but their form and decoration inspired a fashion of crescentic spacer bead necklaces in jet and amber, which gained widespread popularity in the Overton period. While the amber examples were mainly the preserve of the great ladies of Wessex, the jet examples are concentrated in north Britain, and have frequently been found with food vessels.

Although double pointed awls were still used throughout the Overton period, Stage VI workshops switched increasingly to single pointed awls, with one end flattened to a tang. Collared and stopped awls are also found in graves of the Bush Barrow group. Another development late in Stage VI was the Class Ia razor with oval blade and broad riveted tang, but these belong mainly to the Bedd Branwen period, and will be dealt with under Stage VII developments.

The Bedd Branwen period: c. 1650–1400 BC (c. 1450–1250 bc)

In this period, the aftermath of a thousand year Beaker tradition, cremation, especially in-urned cremation, was the dominant form of burial throughout these islands, and inhumation practically disappeared. The latest developments at Amesbury G71 (Phase IV) illustrate this trend (Figure 7.2,3). Numerous cremations, some in-urned, were dug into the existing mound and the partially silted ditch. Some were in Deverel-Rimbury urns, and there is no reason to date these later than others in Collared and Biconical Urns. The Anglesey cemetery barrow of Bedd Branwen, with its series of in-urned cremations dated to *c.* 1403–1274 bc, belongs wholly to this period.

Re-use of existing burial mounds was exceedingly common in these centuries. This might involve simply digging new burials into a mound or more complex enlargements and modifications. The decline in barrow building is symptomatic of a more general waning of interest in formal burial monuments and ritual. The privileged could still demand their own new burial mound, witness the 'Wessex Culture' Aldbourne-Edmondsham burials which followed the Bush Barrow group. These almost invariably were primaries in a new barrow.

While barrow burial continued in southern and eastern regions, the number of flat cremation cemeteries was on the increase. These included not only the embanked 'pond barrows' of the chalk, and the ditched cemeteries of the river gravels, but also an unknown number of flat Deverel-Rimbury cemeteries. In view of the present uncertainties of Deverel-Rimbury chronology it is not known how many can be assigned to this period. There are Deverel-Rimbury cemeteries, both flat, as at Pokesdown, Hampshire, and barrows as at Latch Farm, Hampshire (Figure 7.7) and Rimbury itself, which incorporate Collared Urn burials (Figure 3.13), and must belong wholly or partly to this period.

In Yorkshire food vessel inhumation may have persisted for a time, but cremation was spreading rapidly, and was already widely practised in other former strongholds of the food vessel/inhumation rite, such as north-east England, the Pennines and south-east Scotland. In eastern regions mound burial still dominated, but in the Pennines, north-west England and over much of Scotland the emphasis is on flat cremation cemeteries of a wide variety of forms.

These enclosed cremation cemeteries may have been the ultimate expression of the henge and ring monument tradition, but seem altogether more concerned with burial as a primary function. Stone circles such as the Druid's Circle, Penmaenmawr, and henge-like monuments like that at Loanhead of Daviot, Aberdeen, have yielded in-urned cremations, but it is not clear whether these relate to the construction and primary use of such sites. At Cairnpapple, Collared Urn cremations were interred several centuries after the henge was built, and clearly show no respect for its form or function. Ring monuments at Brenig were used as ritual monuments for centuries before receiving in-urned cremations in the Bedd Branwen period. The implication is that attitudes to the ring monuments were changing. Whether they even continued to serve their former community functions, indeed what was happening at all the stone monuments littered across the landscape, is a matter for speculation.

Parts of Ireland, like east Yorkshire, may have clung to food vessels and cist burial for a time, but here too in-urned cremation was growing. Traffic between Britain and Ireland had increased in the Overton period. By the beginning of the Bedd Branwen period there was incessant movement between Ulster and western Scotland, but contacts were much more sporadic in the southern Irish Sea. Thus not only the form and decoration of Irish Collared urns but also their concentration in Ulster points to derivation from western Scotland. This was also the source of other aspects of the Irish cinerary urn tradition, including encrusted decoration and Cordoned Urns. Similarities between Irish Necked Urns and English Biconical Urns are more difficult to explain, but the presence of Necked Urns both in Wales, as at Llangwm, and in western Scotland, as at Newlands, Glasgow, provides some of the best evidence for west to east traffic. Some of the more ornate encrusted urns from Wales also show strong Irish influence.

Some Irish urn cremations were placed in cists, especially those in enlarged food vessel urns, but grave pits were much more common, especially for Collared and Cordoned Urn burials. Inevitably a mixing of traditions sometimes occurred, as at Kilskeery, Co. Tyrone, where a cist held an Irish Vase, an encrusted urn, a Cordoned Urn and a Pygmy cup.

In-urned cremations in Ireland can occur singly or in flat or mound cemeteries, sometimes in the same cemeteries as food vessel graves. In western parts of Ireland urns are as rare as cists and food vessels, and wedge tombs may still have been used for cremation burial. Chambered tombs had long since been sealed up, but their mounds and surrounds still provided convenient sites for interment. At Harristown, Co. Waterford, the entrance grave provided a site for a cremation cemetery with Cordoned Urns (Figure 2.6), while at the Mound of the Hostages, at Tara, forty burials were inserted into the mound of the passage grave. Round rather than long chambered mounds were generally chosen, possibly because the round mound was familiar to these Second Millennium societies.

The Collared Urn tradition spread to most parts of Britain and Ireland, but other cinerary urns had more restricted distributions. Thus south-west England had its Trevisker urns, and southern England its Biconical urns, while enlarged food vessel urns are concentrated in eastern regions between the Moray Firth and the Humber, but are rare in western Scotland. Here Collared, Cordoned and Bucket-shaped urns predominate. In north-west England, Collared Urns were preferred. North Wales mixed Collared Urns and enlarged food vessel urns, but the latter are rare in South Wales, where Collared Urns predominate.

Enclosures and community sites

The latest activity at the causewayed enclosures and the great southern ceremonial enclosures, was associated with pottery and radiocarbon dates of the Bedd Branwen period. Whatever the nature of this activity, it was vastly different from that for which these sites had been designed, no more significant, in fact, than the siting of a cremation cemetery in the long-abandoned centre at Meldon Bridge. At Stonehenge trouble was taken to carve flanged axes on the great sarsens at this time but the date of the final modifications to this venerable centre is uncertain. The features in question are those of Phase IIIb, comprising the Y and Z holes, a double ring of holes surrounding the main sarsen monument, and a setting of dressed bluestones; and of Phase IIIc, the present bluestone circle and horseshoe in the middle of the site. A radiocarbon date of *c*. 1240 bc from one of the Y holes suggests the Bedd Branwen period for this activity, but such a late date is so much at odds with what is known about the overall development of the site, and with the history of megalithic sites as a whole, that it is only sensible to reserve judgment on this dating. Over the country as a whole interest in stone circles and ring monuments waned in this period. In fact the great age of ritual and ceremonial monuments was almost at an end.

In the south at least a new generation of enclosures was now built, defined by a bank or wall and ditch. At Rams Hill in Berkshire and Norton Fitzwarren in Somerset, both associated with cinerary urn sherds, the perimeters can legitimately be labelled 'defences', but other sites, such as Wolstonbury in Sussex, have an internal ditch, and may hark back to henges rather than forward to new traditions. (Figures 3.8,9.)

The function of Rams Hill and similar enclosures is not yet clear, but the finds suggest they continued the 'henge role' of a community centre or gathering place, and were not simply defended settlements.

Settlements and economy

The earliest Deverel-Rimbury settlements were flourishing by the Bedd Branwen period, since this is the latest we can date the Class Ia razor in the primary ditch silt at South Lodge, Dorset (Figure 3.14). The style of settlement had changed little from earlier periods. Farmsteads consisting of a few round, and sometimes rectilinear buildings, often set within a stockade, continued to dot the landscape. Such was the pattern not only in the Deverel-Rimbury lands, where the earliest phases at some of the Sussex settlements and at Shearplace Hill in Dorset were stockaded, but elsewhere at sites as far apart as Findon, Sussex and Cullyhanna Lough, Co. Armagh. The evidence of South Lodge shows that by the Bedd Branwen period some Deverel-Rimbury settlements were enclosed within earthwork perimeters. The few Collared and Biconical Urn sherds at these sites is a reminder that these were specialist funerary wares, and that Deverel-Rimbury pottery was for everyday use.

Round buildings also predominate at those settlements where no perimeter has been located, as at Puddlehill in Bedfordshire and Downpatrick, Co. Down. In many cases, especially at East Anglian sites such as Mildenhall, Suffolk, considerable occupation deposits have been uncovered, with abundant rubbish, hearths, post-holes and pits, but neither building plan nor perimeter has been detected.

The agricultural development of the uplands of south-west England was under way in the Overton period, but it was in the Bedd Branwen and Knighton Heath periods that the exploitation of highland areas such as the Pennines and Southern Uplands reached its maximum extent. On Dartmoor a highly organized landscape emerged, with settlements of round stone houses ranging from unenclosed farmsteads to considerable enclosed villages, such as Riders Rings and Grimspound. Inevitably these were mainly pastoral settlements, but their form varied according to location and aspect, with more arable farming in the drier eastern areas, where systems of rectangular fields

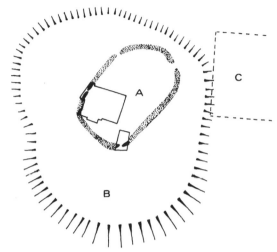

Rams Hill

A:Bronze Age enclosure B: hill-fort C:Roman enclosure

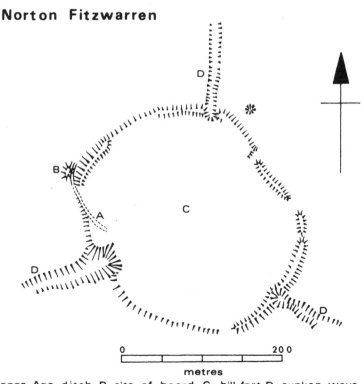

Norton Fitzwarren

```
0                    200
metres
```

A: Bronze Age ditch B: site of hoard C: hill-fort D: sunken ways

Figure 3.8 Hill-forts with underlying enclosures of the Bedd Branwen period: Rams Hill, Berkshire (after Bradley and Ellison, 1975), and Norton Fitzwarren, Somerset (after Langmaid, 1971)

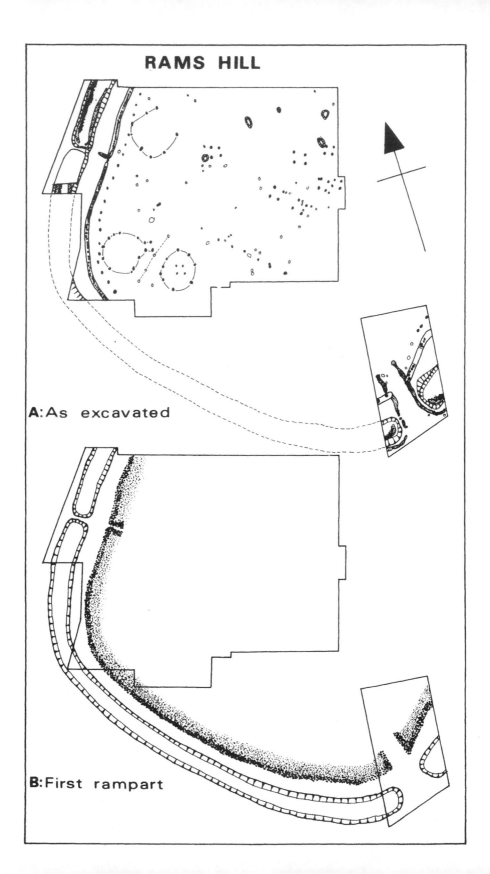

RAMS HILL

A: As excavated

B: First rampart

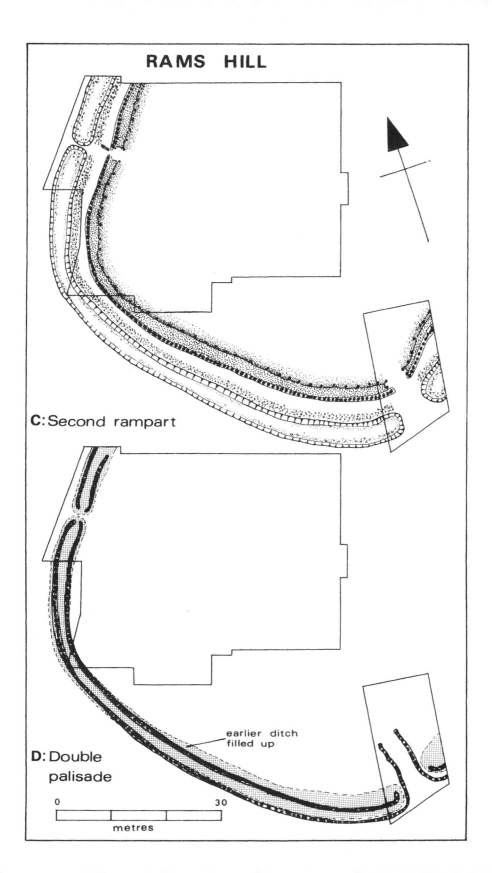

RAMS HILL

C: Second rampart

D: Double palisade

earlier ditch
filled up

0   30
metres

abound. Great tracts of Dartmoor were divided into grazing blocks by dyke or reave systems, often with pastoral settlements bonded into the reaves. Other stone-walled field systems were widespread in Ireland and in Scotland, and have been preserved beneath the blanket peat.

Metalworking

The Stage VII metalworking in the Bedd Branwen period brought major technological advances such as core casting, which allowed the manufacture of socketed and hollow forms. These innovations were sparked off by contacts with Continental industries at the stage known alternatively as Reinecke A2/B1 or A3, which marked the end of the 'Early Bronze Age' on the Continent. The material in question seems to be later than the classical Únětician contexts of Reinecke A2 (*Leubingen-Dieskau*), and earlier than the Earliest Tumulus Culture, B1 (*Lochham-Koszider*), and is particularly well represented in two areas with which Britain enjoyed close contacts: Holland/north-west Germany, and Switzerland/south Germany.

There were two rival Stage VII metalworking traditions, the Arreton tradition of southern and eastern England, and the Inch Island of Ireland (Figure 3.11). These had the same basic products, but with differences in design and emphasis. This means there are Irish and English versions of the cast-flanged axe, which was one of the main Stage VII innovations. The Inch Island products are broader, with sides more often parallel, and they have a straight or only slightly arched butt end, contrasting with the high, arched Arreton butt. This gives the Arreton axes a distinctly 'spiked' top in side view. The flanges of the Irish axes are more variable in height, but tend to be lower than Arreton flanges. The Irish transverse bevel is curved, the English bevel usually straight, and the Irish axes occasionally have a true stop ridge, even a bar-stop, which the Arreton axes never have. Decoration is more frequent and more varied on the Irish axes and usually engraved or punched, whereas simple hammered designs predominate in the Arreton tradition.

Stage VII was also characterized by new, more sophisticated dagger designs (Figures 3.6,11). The most widespread of these were grooved, ogival daggers

---

Figure 3.11 Metalwork of Stage VII, the Arreton-Inch Island traditions: 1. Three-ribbed dagger, 2. Ogival grooved dagger, 11. Socketed pegged spearhead, 12–13. Tanged spearheads, all from the Arreton Down hoard, Isle of Wight; 4. Ogival grooved dagger, 5. Crutch-headed pin, 6. Tanged and Collared spearhead, all from the Snowshill grave group, Glos.; 3. Ogival dagger with channelled blade, 7, 15. Arreton flanged axes, 19. Chisel, all from the Plymstock hoard, Devon; 8. Class Ib razor, 9. Twin-looped flanged axe, 10. Lobed pin, all from the Bryn Crug grave group, Caernarvonshire; 14. Arreton flanged axe, 16. End-looped spearhead, 17. Lugged tool, 18. Shouldered tool, all from the Ebnal hoard, Shropshire; 20–21. Hiberno-Scottish flanged axes from near Perth (20), and Dams, Balbirnie, Fife (21). (All after Gerloff, 1975, except 20–21, after Coles, 1968–9)

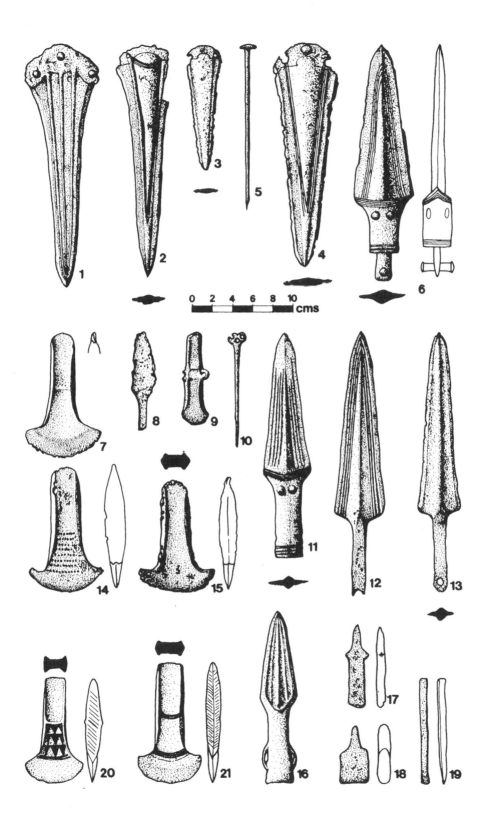

0 2 4 6 8 10
cms

with rounded or ridged mid-rib and two or three plug rivets. These are the Snowshill, Camerton and Hammersmith types, the first two of these supplied by Arreton workshops in considerable numbers to the Aldbourne-Edmondsham warriors of Wessex. Similar daggers were produced by Inch Island workshops, though fewer have been found. Daggers with three blade ribs, resembling the Stage VI Blackwaterfoot dagger, but heavier, were also produced in small numbers, mainly by Arreton craftsmen. Both tanged and socketed spearheads were developed. The tanged weapons were an Arreton product, rare in Ireland, where looped, socketed spearheads, with solid-cast head ('end-looped spearheads') predominated. The eponymous Inch Island stone mould, from Co. Donegal, includes a matrix for such spearheads. Similar socketed spearheads occur sporadically in the Arreton province, where they have peg-hole attachments instead of loops. Direct comparison between the number of British and Irish finds may not truly reflect differences in comparative production levels, for the tremendous amount of peat digging which has gone on in Ireland has artificially swelled the quantities of Irish finds of all periods. Arreton workshops were more exposed to exotic influences and novelties, so their products show greater variety, and include, for example, the experimental tang-and-collar spearheads in the Arreton hoard itself, and the Aldbourne-Edmondsham grave group from Snowshill in Gloucestershire.

The minor developments of Stage VII included lugged tools, either stakes or chisels, represented by a matrix on the Inch Island mould, and found in a number of associations of this period throughout Britain: dress pins, based on Continental crutch, bulb, ring and multiple ring-head designs, and mainly an Arreton concern; and tanged razors, both the Class Ia form, with broad, short tang and broad blade, and the more elegant Ib form, with long narrow tang and narrow leaf-shaped blade.

Stage VII products were the insular response to the flanged axes, grooved, ogival daggers and fully socketed spearheads which were in widespread use in central and western Europe at the end of the 'Early Bronze Age'. Arreton workshops, being closest to the Continent, absorbed these novelties first, but they rapidly filtered throughout Britain and on to Ireland. Local Stage VII production is attested both in Wales and Scotland, but whether sufficient to supply all the requirements of local markets is uncertain. The Ebnal industry of Wales and the Marches, represented by the Shropshire hoard (Figure 3.11), was clearly in contact both with Arreton and Inch Island workshops, and the region may have imported from both. But the distinctiveness of much of the Welsh material, the fact that local metal was used in its manufacture, and that Wales has produced a stone mould for end-looped spearheads, from Bodwrdin, Anglesey, makes it clear that there was an independent Welsh Stage VII industry. This Ebnal industry, which produced flanged axes and grooved, ogival daggers, tanged and end-looped spearheads, trunnion tools, shouldered punches and Class I razors, was initially influenced by Arreton workshops, and geography suggests that Ireland received these innovations later still, passed on via Ebnal workshops. The small number of Stage VII products from Scotland suggests limited production there, influenced more by Inch Island than Arreton practices. This Scottish industry can be named after the hoard of two flanged axes (of the Inch Island pattern) and a triple-ribbed dagger from Gavel Moss, Renfrew.

The scarcity of Stage VII products over much of Wales and Britain north of the Tees has led to speculation that these areas still relied mainly on old fashioned workshops, turning out obsolete metalwork. Some venerable implements may well have remained in production, such as awls and simple riveted knives, but there is no positive proof, from hoards or graves, of survival on a large scale. The lack of Stage VII material in these regions must in part reflect the fact that there has been much less excavation, and less human disturbance of the soil, for construction, agriculture and industry. These are the factors on which chance finds depend. There may, however, be another important explanation of the sparsity of Stage VII finds in Wales, the fact that Stage VII arrived there later than in England, and was superseded sooner by an even more advanced metallurgy.

The Continental connections of the rich Aldbourne-Edmondsham graves echo those of Stage VII metalworking, and had shifted considerably since the Bush Barrow phase. Connections with Brittany weakened considerably. Armorica has no equivalent to Stage VII metalworking, and the grave goods of the later Armorican barrows were little different from the preceding period. The main weight of traffic switched northwards, to the Low Countries and northern France, though the latter is still largely an archaeological *terra incognita* in this period. Dramatic evidence of these links is provided by the Cornish Trevisker pottery from the Pas de Calais, even more remarkably by the grave groups from Farnham, Surrey, and Pontavert in Departement Aisne. Britain, the Low Countries, northern and eastern France, south Germany and Switzerland, all had traditions of coarse, cordoned and finger-tipped pottery at this time — in Britain this is Deverel-Rimbury pottery. In the past comparisons between these regional groups, for example south English Biconical urns and Dutch Hilversum urns, have been interpreted in terms of migration, in this case of Biconical urn users to Holland. But there is little supporting cultural evidence for such movements, and these widespread similarities now make much better sense viewed in terms of normal culture contact.

Western parts of the Low Countries fall within the territory of the Sögel group, which focussed on north-west Germany. Here are many parallels for Arreton and Aldbourne-Edmondsham novelties, such as perforated whetstones and Sögel 'nicked-flanged' axes, two of which have been found in Wiltshire. But the Swiss-south German area is even more important, with gold cups so like those of southern England, and the best Continental prototypes for Arreton daggers and Aldbourne-Edmondsham pins. Connections with northern France are less well-known but were clearly crucial to judge from the few excavated sites such as Fort Harrouard, with its strong Wessex connections.

At about 1500 BC the central European community of tradition entered its 'Tumulus Culture' stage. Instead of the traditional explanations involving new arrivals, this process now seems best explained in terms of an internal upheaval. Culture contact soon spread strikingly uniform sepulchral practices and material equipment, especially metalwork, over much of Europe from eastern France to the Carpathians, and from the Baltic to the Adriatic. There may have been some territorial expansion from the German-Czech Únětician heartland, but essentially the 'Tumulus Culture' covered much the same area as Únětice had before it.

The opening Tumulus phase, Lochham or Koszider, B1 in Reinecke's terminology, saw a significant metallurgical response in Britain and Ireland, which, in traditional terms, passed from 'Early to Middle Bronze Age'. Industrial developments, the progression to Stage VIII technology, coincided with fundamental changes in society, which appear independent of Continental events. Craftsmen always in touch with European industry rapidly switched over to those products which we consider typically 'Middle Bronze Age': trapeze-butt dirks and rapiers, fully socketed spearheads with hollow-cast midrib, and the palstave, an improvement on the flanged axe in which stop and flanges were heightened and blended together to form a deep, secure seating for the forked ends of the knee-shaft handle.

The innovations of Stage VIII metallurgy were (Figure 3.12): Group I and II dirks and rapiers, the former midribbed and usually grooved, the latter, with lozenge-sectioned blade; Group I (shield-pattern) and Group II (early midribbed) palstaves; the equivalent Irish Group A and B palstaves, which, like subsequent Irish axes, were short, squat equivalents of the British forms; thin-bladed flanged 'axes' of uncertain function; improved flanged axes, at first bar-stop axes, then haft-flanged axes, with shorter, higher flanges confined to the upper part of the implement; and 'side-looped' spearheads, with leaf-shaped blade, in Britain and 'socket-looped' spearheads, with kite-shaped blade, in Ireland. In Britain Stage VIII metalworking is termed the Acton Park tradition after the important Denbighshire hoard; in Ireland, it is known as the Killymaddy tradition after the hoard of representative stone moulds from Co. Antrim. The internal contribution should not be forgotten in charting the emergence of Stage VIII metallurgy. Group II dirks and rapiers were inspired by a new Continental development, for they were local versions (though with two rivets instead of four) of the lozenge-sectioned weapons found over much of Europe in B1: Koszider weapons in central and eastern Europe, Lochham in south Germany, and Wohlde in north Germany. Continental influence in other Stage VIII products is more problematical. Socketed spearheads already existed, and the Stage VIII innovation, which was to extend

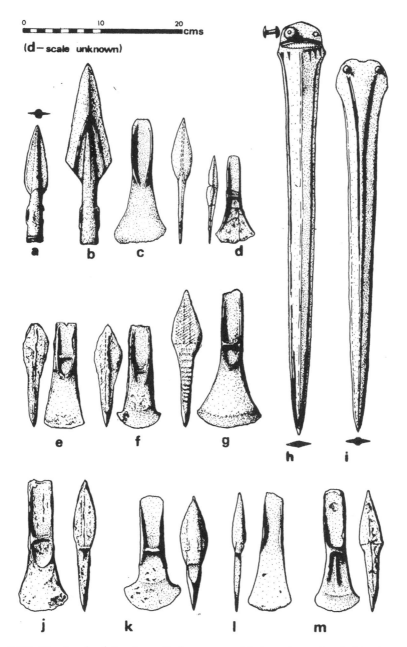

Figure 3.12 Metalwork of the Acton Park stage: a. side-looped spearhead, ?Sawdon, Yorks.; b. socket-looped spearhead, Ballyhaw, Co. Westmeath; c, d. thin-bladed flanged 'axe' and bar-stop axe from the Moelfre-uchaf hoard, Denbs.; e–f. Irish shield-pattern (Group A) palstaves from Branthwaite and Penrith, Cumb.; g, j. Anglo-Welsh shield pattern (Gr. I) palstaves from Stainton-in-Furness, Lancs., and Pately Bridge, Yorks.; h. Gr. II rapier with capped rivet, Bracknamuckley, Co. Antrim; i. Gr. I rapier, Riverstown Ford, Co. Kildare; k–l. haft-flanged axes, Tadcaster and Farndale, Yorks.; m. early midribbed (Gr. II) palstave, Handsworth, Yorks. (a, e–g, j–m. after Burgess, 1968; b. after Herity and Eogan, 1977; d. after Davies, 1949)

the socket hollow into the midrib, could have been developed in Irish and British workshops. Even palstaves are no longer a sure sign of Continental influence. The British palstave may have been invented independently, possibly in north Wales, possibly in eastern England, following experiments with bar-stop and other flanged axes. For palstaves of the British Groups I and II are found in north German hoards of the early Ilsmoor or Rülow group, which were contemporary with Tumulus B1; and the first local German palstaves only appear in the later Ilsmoor hoards, which were contemporary with B2.

The lower Thames valley, East Anglia, Hampshire, Sussex, north Wales and Ireland appear to have taken the lead in changing to the new metalworking traditions. Very similar changes were happening across the Channel throughout north-west France, where the new Tréboul tradition was intimately connected with British developments. This was the beginning of a remarkable parallelism in metalworking which became one of the most enduring and striking aspects of British and north-west French connections. It can only be explained in terms of traffic constantly criss-crossing the Channel, keeping metalworkers on both sides fully aware of what each was doing. Inevitably there were differences in emphasis to suit local markets, but these do not detract from the underlying similarities.

Although lowland English and Welsh workshops converted rapidly to palstave production, north of the Humber and in Scotland, haft-flanged axes were preferred, with a bar stop at most. Irish craftsmen developed both haft-flanged axes and their own palstaves (Groups A and B), but whether as options or in different regions is not clear. Improved flanged axes also remained in use in Atlantic France and the North Sea littoral. British, and especially north Welsh, industry influenced these regions to varying degrees. Flanged axes predominated in Tréboul contexts in Armorica. Palstaves were few, but always in the Anglo-Welsh tradition, and some were of undoubted north Welsh inspiration if not manufacture. The Normandy-Picardy area accepted Anglo-Welsh palstaves more wholeheartedly, and local production must soon have started. To the north flanged axes are again common in the Low Countries and north-west Germany, but British palstave traditions made an increasing impact in this Ilsmoor area. The most remarkable instance of British influence is the Dutch Voorhout hoard, which contains shield-pattern palstaves of the north Welsh form, made of north Welsh metal. Whether an itinerant Acton Park craftsman or trader passed this way, or whether they were acquired in the course of routine cross-Channel contacts, is not clear.

North Wales stands out amongst the leaders in Stage VIII metalworking. Two phases can be detected in the development of Acton Park metallurgy there. First there was a cautious period of experiments with flanged axes, leading to a range of bar-stop axes, near-palstaves and the first 'wide-bodied' Group I and II palstaves, still with rudimentary stop. These are the British palstaves which occur in the early Ilsmoor or Rülow group of hoards in north

Germany, which in turn provide a link with Tumulus B1 in central Europe, usually dated to the fifteenth century BC. These first Acton Park developments must therefore have occurred well before 1400 BC. We can guess that they also included Group I dirks and rapiers and the first of Group II, possibly even side-looped spearheads, but the metal used was still the old tin-bronze of Ebnal times.

Possibly still within the fifteenth century important technological advances marked a second Acton Park phase. A new alloy, lead-bronze, was introduced, with some mechanical advantages such as its free-flowing properties. Bronze moulds now appeared (Pl. XVI), for casting new, more sophisticated versions of Group I and II palstaves. Group I dirks and rapiers were rare and prestigious, the simpler Group II weapons more readily available. Side-looped spearheads were standard, and examples in French hoards of this period may have emanated from Wales. The Acton Park hoard itself belongs to this mature phase of the industry. In addition to Group I and II palstaves and a Group II dirk blade, now lost, it contains one of several thin-bladed flanged 'axes' known from the region. Whatever their function, these strange implements occur in all those regions in contact with British palstave producers: in Tréboul lands in France, and in Ilsmoor territories from the Netherlands to Pomerania.

It should be possible to extend this division of Acton Park metalworking to other areas, notably Ireland and eastern England, but there are regions, such as south-central and south-west England, where the sparsity of finds suggests the precocious emergence of even more advanced metalworking traditions.

Interest in formal burial, ritual and ceremony declined in the Bedd Branwen period. The changes appear greatest amongst those leading elements of society represented by prestigious burial. Radiocarbon dates for the 'prestige' urns, especially Collared Urns, run down to *c.* 1250 bc then stop. With them passed a tradition of formal burial stretching back for centuries. In Wessex a conservative aristocracy, represented by late Aldbourne-Edmondsham graves, may have preserved the old traditions for a while, for some of these contain Tumulus artefacts, such as that at Scratchbury with a Tumulus pin, while others have radiocarbon dates down to *c.* 1100 bc. Elsewhere in the south we find Group I and II dirks are included in cremation graves with Cornish handled urns at Mullion and Harlyn Bay III respectively, so possibly the old order vanished first in areas outside the south.

What caused this abandonment of old traditions is uncertain. Declining interest in megalithic monuments, with a consequent loss of engineering skill and geometrical and celestial knowledge, makes sense against a background of deteriorating climate, for increasing cloud cover, poorer visibility, and the insidious development of blanket peat would have made these sites increasingly difficult to use. We cannot be certain when climatic change began to have a serious impact in Britain, but it was certainly during the second half of the Second Millennium.

Conditions were also building up to an agricultural crisis, like that which had affected much of the country between *c.* 3000–2500 bc. Throughout the Overton and Bedd Branwen periods increasingly large tracts of the better farmlands had been exhausted, forcing more and more people on to difficult soils and into uplands which had hitherto been ignored. For example at Red Shore, Alton in Wiltshire, a bell barrow was raised on a clay-with-flints soil that had already been cultivated. Similar pressures are indicated by the rash of round barrows dotted over areas of poor sandy soil, lands that had been farmed but were now turned to heath, for example in the New Forest of Hampshire, and the Weald. The need to organize and make best use of the land stimulated the spread of 'Celtic' field systems on the southern chalk. There are cases of round barrows built over deserted field systems, although other fields respect barrows and seem to be part of the same stage of landscape organization. The implication is that a period of intensified enclosure began at the same time as barrow construction was petering out during the Bedd Branwen period.

The evidence from other, less fully explored, regions in general agrees with that from the south. The exploitation of south-western upland areas gathered pace in the Bedd Branwen period, and necessitated increasing attention to land division. The great age of the south-western reaves and field systems, as of the Celtic fields on the chalk, spanned the Bedd Branwen and Knighton Heath periods. The sprawling 'cairnfields' or field clearance piles of other upland areas may tell a similar story, but they have been little explored. The opening up of the Brenig valley 1200–1400 feet up in the Denbighshire hills, illustrates how farming communities were pushing into upland areas from the beginning of the Second Millennium. Cairnfields frequently incorporate genuine burial cairns of the Overton and Bedd Branwen periods, and even clearance tumps could be used to cover or contain a burial. It may well be that cairnfields will prove to be as representative of the upland farming of these times in Wales, the Pennines, north-east England and Scotland, as reaves and Celtic field systems are in southern regions.

All this shifting of settlement and agriculture can be expected to have generated social pressures, and it is this background that may have created the loss of interest in formal burial and ritual at the close of the Bedd Branwen period. The fact that Deverel-Rimbury burial survived in the south, whereas urn burial disappeared, suggests a social upheaval in which the old dynasties lost their power and were replaced by new élites. In other regions, too, cremation burial in coarse urns continued after the cessation of more prestigious cinerary urn cremations. The centres of economic power also underwent upheaval. Regions rich in the barrows and graves of the old order, such as Wessex, the Yorkshire Wolds, and the southern Pennines, became comparative backwaters. Their decline is matched by the rise of new centres of wealth, in the lower Thames Valley, the Fens, and north Wales, based on metalwork and perhaps on a new religion. Increasing quantities of the best metalwork were now discarded in wet places, such as rivers, bogs, pools and lakes. It will not have escaped notice that the lower Thames and Fen areas are dominated by water, and their new success perhaps followed their rise as centres of a novel water-based religion. For, unlike north Wales, they lacked convenient sources of raw materials to create industrial growth, and would have had to import what could not be provided from local scrap. North Wales, on the other hand, had been increasing in importance for some time, witness such rich burials as that at Mold, with its spectacular gold cape (Figure 4.8), and those at Bryn Crug, Caernarvonshire, and Llanddyfnan with their assortment of bronzes. North Wales occupied a uniquely nodal position amongst the principal metallurgical centres, and in addition had abundant ore supplies. But in north Wales, too, the eclipse of the old order coincided with the rise of Acton Park metallurgy, and a new set of economic and social circumstances.

The Knighton Heath period: c. 1400–1200 BC (c. 1250–1050 bc)

By 1400 BC (*c.* 1250 bc) little remained of a tradition of prestigious burial and complex ritual which had existed for thousands of years. The situation in southern England mirrored what was happening throughout these islands. A few conservative and declining Wessex chiefdoms, represented by late Aldbourne-Edmondsham graves such as that from Scratchbury, lingered for a short time but their days were numbered. It was the Deverel-Rimbury communities who now emerged stronger than ever before, and in the ensuing two centuries reached their apogee across the whole area from Dorset to Norfolk. The fact that cremation burial now survived only in its Deverel-Rimbury form shows how successfully these previously unspectacular groups not only survived change, but improved their position *vis à vis* the old orders.

Deverel-Rimbury and related traditions

Two Dorset sites, the Deverel barrow and the Rimbury flat cemetery have given their names to a south English tradition that is characterized above all by simple, coarse, Bucket Urns, frequently finger-tip impressed either directly on to the pot or on to raised cordons (Figure 3.13). The other two Deverel-Rimbury pot types, much less common, are the Barrel Urns, often with vertical and zig-zag cordons, and overlapping with Bucket Urns at one extreme of their morphological range; and the finer, smaller Globular Urns with a constricted neck, and very different tooled or incised ornament.

Traditionally these Bucket, Barrel and Globular Urns constitute the type fossils of a southern Deverel-Rimbury culture, which until twenty-five years ago, was regarded as wholly exotic in origin, the product of a 'Late Bronze Age'

55

Primary

M26   M27

0   20
cms

20

0
cms

27   81

46

24

17   78

29   56   M20

invasion from the Continent in the eighth century BC. This was the accepted view for so long that for many people any coarse bucket-shaped vessel found anywhere in the country is still 'Late Bronze Age' on the basis of an idea discredited over two decades ago.

In the last twenty years Deverel-Rimbury beginnings have been pushed progressively earlier, and opinions have swung round to an entirely indigenous origin. By the late 1950s it was already clear that the Deverel-Rimbury culture belonged to a mature stage of the 'Middle Bronze Age', *c.* 1200–1000 BC, although its later and earlier history remained uncertain. Recently it has become clear that Deverel-Rimbury pottery had emerged by the 'Early Bronze Age' so there is no chronological problem about its being derived from the Grooved wares which offer so many striking morphological comparisons. At the same time the work of Barrett has shown that Deverel-Rimbury traditions disappeared in the Penard period between 1200–1000 BC, amidst far-reaching social and economic changes that transformed southern Britain.

Bucket, Barrel and Globular Urns come both from burial sites and from abundant, well-preserved settlements, providing a range of evidence that is unique in our later prehistory. Deverel-Rimbury communities were not homogenous in their pottery, for the three diagnostic pottery types are unevenly distributed. Indeed, Bucket Urns were the only common denominator. Furthermore, there is considerable local variation in form and decoration, so much so that Deverel-Rimbury pottery is not uniform even within Wessex. Regional manifestations of Deverel-Rimbury have been identified as far north as the Midlands and East Anglia, but comparable coarse ware traditions existed throughout Britain and Ireland.

There are few relevant radiocarbon dates, but enough from the cemeteries at Knighton Heath and Winterbourne Kingston in Dorset; Chapel Brampton, Northamptonshire and from domestic contexts at Shearplace Hill, Dorset, Grimes Graves, Norfolk, and Itford Hill, Sussex; to confirm that Deverel-Rimbury communities flourished through the Lowland Zone in the twelfth and eleventh centuries bc. To this same period, in absolute terms the fourteenth and thirteenth centuries BC (the Taunton phase) belongs most of the metalwork found in Deverel-Rimbury contexts. This is the date of the clay moulds, including some for basal-looped spearheads, found in a deposit at Grimes Graves (*c.* 1053–986 bc). The date of *c.* 1243 bc for a settlement at Chalton, Hampshire, is earlier than the group noted above, though not statistically distinguishable from them. One of the Chalton huts produced bronzes, including a low-flanged palstave of the Taunton phase, while a pit yielded a perforated whetstone, like those found in Aldbourne-Edmondsham

Figure 3.13 Food vessels, cinerary urns and Deverel-Rimbury urns from the Latch Farm barrow, Hampshire (after C. M. Piggott, 1938, except M20, 26, 27, after Calkin, 1962)

graves. This may be a further indication that this Wessex funerary tradition lingered on into the fourteenth century BC.

There is only one radiocarbon date relevant to Deverel-Rimbury beginnings, that of *c.* 1740 bc for a cremation with a Bucket Urn at Worgret, Dorset. This fits in well with the latest dates for the putatively ancestral Grooved ware, but needs to be confirmed by many more dates. The next earliest date is one of *c.* 1380 bc for a sample some feet below Globular Urn sherds near the base of the Wilsford shaft. These two receive some support from the site evidence. The primary ditch silts of the South Lodge enclosure (Figure 3.14) produced not only Deverel-Rimbury material, including the eponymous Barrel Urn of South Lodge type, but also a tanged razor of Class Ia (Figure 3.14), dating to the Bedd Branwen period. This site has normally been dated by its famous Taunton phase bronzes, but these were in fact found high up in the ditch fill, and represent a later period of activity. The Mildenhall settlement, Suffolk, is also relevant, yielding Collared Urns, vessels with Beaker affinities and other material of the Overton and Bedd Branwen periods, in the same 'culture stratum' as local versions of Biconical Urns and Deverel-Rimbury pots. At the Deverel barrow itself, the cremation cemetery with Bucket and Globular Urns cannot have been later than a peripheral Collared Urn burial. Since Collared Urns disappeared around 1250 bc, these contexts are important for charting early Deverel-Rimbury developments. Collared Urn cremations occur at many Deverel-Rimbury cemeteries, but have usually been judged earlier than the Deverel-Rimbury burials purely for reasons of traditional dating. For example, at Pokesdown, Hampshire, two Collared Urns were found amidst Deverel-Rimbury cremation burials in a flat cemetery. There are no stratigraphic reasons why these urns should not have been part of the Deverel-Rimbury cemetery, so instead of dismissing them as strays from an earlier period, the possibility that they were the pots of the privileged dead at least deserves consideration. The fact that there are seldom more than one or two Collared Urn cremations in a cemetery of dozens of Deverel-Rimbury vessels certainly supports such a social distinction. Thus the gap between a Collared Urn primary and Deverel-Rimbury secondary burials in a cemetery barrow may be a question of status rather than date. This means that the large Deverel-Rimbury cemetery at the Latch Farm barrow, Hampshire (Figure 3.13), was secondary to Collared Urn and food vessel burials, but there was a Collared Urn amongst its array of Deverel-Rimbury vessels. Similarly, the cremation urns inserted into the ditch at Amesbury G71 included Collared, as well as Bucket and Globular, vessels.

Unfortunately, few Deverel-Rimbury burials were provided with grave goods, but a few finds suggest the Bedd Branwen period, such as the bronze beads with a Barrel Urn burial from Barton, Hampshire, and a star-shaped faience bead with a Bucket Urn in the Simons Ground cemetery, Dorset. This is also the date of a cemetery at Stainsby, Lincolnshire, where cinerary vessels

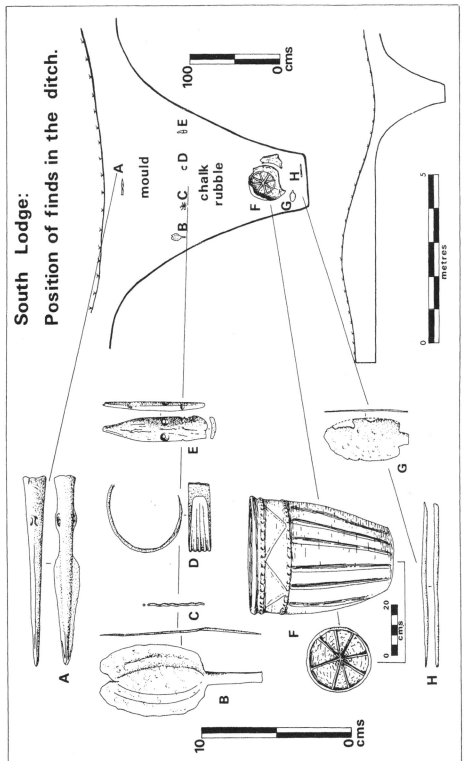

Figure 3.14 South Lodge, Dorset: stratigraphy of finds in the enclosure ditch (based on Pitt-Rivers, 1898)

belonging to the local equivalent of the Deverel-Rimbury tradition were associated with a Class Ia razor and faience beads.

The gap has thus been closed between Barrel and Globular Urns, and the Grooved wares which have always looked such obvious precursors. Some of the recent Grooved ware finds are particularly telling, notably the mass of material from Durrington Walls, which provides good antecedents not only for the bucket and barrel shapes but also for such specific Deverel-Rimbury traits as arcades and vertical and horizontal cordons. Many of these bear impressed ornament, and some are finger-tipped in the Deverel-Rimbury manner. The loss of the grooved decoration presents no problem, for the general ceramic trend in the Overton period was towards progressively less and simpler ornament.

The stumbling block to wholly indigenous origins is that pottery strikingly similar to Deverel-Rimbury vessels has long been familiar on the Continent, and this is why an exotic Deverel-Rimbury culture has always been so attractive. The Deverel-Rimbury phenomenon undoubtedly does have its international dimension, and it is here that the elusive origins of the Globular Urns lie. These have always seemed so exotic compared with the general mass of British 'Bronze Age' pottery that the search for satisfactory prototypes has repeatedly turned to Europe. They stand out as much amongst Bucket and Barrel Urns as Beakers do amongst cinerary urns, and similar differences of social status and function may well be involved. They are not only finer than Bucket and Barrel Urns, and have completely different shape and decoration, but are also smaller, generally up to the eight inches where most Bucket and Barrel Urns begin. They are also distinguished by small strap handles or perforated lugs on the shoulder, and above all by their decoration, which is confined to the shoulder and neck, and usually consists of grooved or tooled bands of horizontal lines bordering zones of zig-zags or filled triangles. This is a complete contrast to the cordons and fingertipping of the Barrel and Bucket Urns, and is a key to the origins of these distinctive vessels.

There are still no obvious indigenous prototypes for Globular Urns, though individual features can be matched among various wares of the Third and early Second Millennia. For example the globular body and hollow, incurving neck are characteristic of some Collared and Biconical Urns, though the decoration is better matched on Grooved wares. Perhaps again it was a question of local potters dipping into their repertoires in response to a specific stimulus and coming up with something which *in toto* looked not at all like anything they had produced hitherto. It is a development which makes sense only viewed in European terms, for the Deverel-Rimbury phenomenon was only part of an international tradition of coarse bucket- and barrel-shaped vessels decorated with cordons and finger-tipping, which was characteristic of the whole area from Southern Britain to Switzerland in the 'Early and Middle Bronze Age': other regional manifestations of this tradition included Hilversum and

Drakenstein pottery in the Low Countries, northern French finds at sites such as Fort Harrouard, the Retz ware of Armorica, Rhone Culture pottery in eastern France, and Morges-les-Roseaux-Goldberg vessels in Switzerland and southern Germany. The status of these coarse wares varies from region to region. In England and the Low Countries they were used both as funerary and domestic wares, but elsewhere they come mainly from settlement contexts. In Switzerland and South Germany they are common on lakeside and hill-top settlements, and the pottery from burials is very different: fine handled cups and vases of carinated and biconical forms, which are local versions of the Únětician cups in use over much of central Europe at this time. Similarly in Armorica Retz ware occurs in settlements, as at the eponymous site, and is common in the mound material of tumuli, but sepulchral vessels are superior bipartite cups and vases with handles, obviously related to the Swiss-south German vessels, and similarly decorated with grooved horizontals, hatched triangles and zig-zags. It is these finer, funerary elements in this West European tradition which explain the decoration and the bipartite handled form of Globular urns, and why indeed they were developed. In Britain, as on the Continent, there had to be finer vessels to complement the coarse cordoned pottery. Thus Globular Urns were deliberately evolved to fulfil this need, and it was natural that English potters while drawing on their own ceramic traditions, should at the same time have in their minds the Swiss, south German and Breton fine wares which they were being driven to emulate. This explains the exotic decoration, the handles, and the carinated form of Globular Urns. We may never know the precise mechanics of their development, but the handled shale, amber, and wooden cups of Wessex are clearly a local version of the Swiss-south German pottery cups, and reveal that Wessex societies were conscious of this 'finer' tradition. The derivation of Bucket and Barrel Urns from Grooved wares is not affected by these arguments, since the west European coarse-ware tradition already existed in the Third Millennium. For the Continental equivalents of Deverel-Rimbury have their own ancestral equivalents of Grooved ware, such as Goldberg III – Cham pottery in Switzerland and south Germany, and early Rhone wares in eastern France.

We have seen that both in Wessex and East Anglia Deverel-Rimbury burials have a partly complementary distribution to that of 'prestigious' urn burials, especially in Collared Urns. In Wessex, Deverel-Rimbury burials are comparatively few in the great barrow cemeteries of the chalk uplands, and, where they do occur, occupy a subordinate position. The main Deverel-Rimbury cemeteries are on the lower chalk lands, especially around the chalk margins, and off the chalk, where arable farming may have been concentrated. Similarly in southern East Anglia, Collared Urn burials dominate the chalk escarpment of Hertfordshire and Cambridgeshire, while the main Deverel-Rimbury cemeteries occur in the valleys and the coastal lowlands. This suggests that a social distinction is involved, with the prestigious burials denoting powerful pastoral groups dominating the chalk downs, and Deverel-Rimbury cremations denoting more sedentary cultivators on the lower lands. The minority of upland burials with Deverel-Rimbury urns would in this case represent lessers, and, conversely the few Collared Urn cremations in Deverel-Rimbury areas would denote social status. In both territories Deverel-Rimbury wares were in general domestic use, but in the lower lands Deverel-Rimbury wares were for everyday use and burials alike.

As might be expected of a land divided into different territories, numerous regional versions of Deverel-Rimbury can be detected. In Wessex there are four main groups, which coincide remarkably with the postulated four major chiefdoms of earlier times. In each case the Deverel-Rimbury group clusters around the downland focus of the chiefdom as if forming client communities around the hierarchical stronghold. South of the Stour the South Dorset group lacks Barrel Urns, and is characterized by cemetery barrows, Bucket Urns and Globular Urns of Type II. These are thicker and better fired than Type I, pinkish buff in colour, and finely gritted. This group clusters around the Dorset Downs 'chiefdom'. The Avon-Stour group, in the great triangle of land between the two river valleys, and away from the foci of the chiefdoms, has flat and barrow cemeteries, often of very large size, Barrel as well as Bucket Urns, and Globulars of Type I. These have a coarser, poorer fabric than Type II, and are heavily flint gritted, but their most distinctive characteristic is very lightly tooled decoration. Globular Urns of Ellison's Type III, with sparser and finer flint gritting than Type I, and distinctive formal and decorative traits such as chevron-filled triangles, are also a feature of this area, especially on the lower Stour. The Cranborne Chase group, south of the Ebble, and clustered round the Cranborne Chase chiefdom, and the Central Wessex Group, spread around the Salisbury Plain chiefdom, are in many ways similar to each other, having Type I Globulars, Bucket and Barrel Urns. They lack the Type III Globulars and large flat cemeteries of the Avon-Stour region. The main difference between the two lies in the preponderance of small cemetery barrows in the Central Wessex group, which is also characterized by Barrel Urns with finger-tip impressed ribs, a form not occurring elsewhere. Finally the North Wiltshire Group, which takes in the Berkshire downs, and is spread around the Marlborough Downs 'chiefdom', has Bucket Urns, a low proportion of Globulars, of Type I, and no true Barrel Urns.

Outside Wessex Deverel-Rimbury material has not been investigated so fully, and regional groupings must be more tentative. A Wessex-type chiefdom may have existed in the Upper Thames area, taking in the gravel lands and flanking chalk and limestone uplands of the Oxford region. Here the Upper Thames Group has mainly Bucket Urns and coarse bipartite urns, with a few Type I Globulars. Bucket Urns similarly dominate the Lower Thames Group, where the few Globulars are of a distinctive, shoulder-less local form. Both barrows and flat cemeteries are known in the Thames Valley.

Knowledge of the Sussex Group comes mainly from settlements of Itford Hill type, but cemetery barrows at Steyning and Itford Hill are now known. The overall contrast between the Sussex Group and the Wessex material is striking, Sussex having no Barrel Urns in the Wessex sense, and practically no Wessex Globulars. But local versions of the basic Deverel-Rimbury forms are all represented, although the relatively small quantity of well-preserved material, especially from burial sites, makes classification difficult. While Bucket Urns of all sizes occur, with and without cordons, there is a great mass of pottery convex in profile representing simple baggy shapes which cannot at present be easily subdivided. Amongst this material are the local versions of Barrel Urns. Local Globular Urns also exist, with more prominent handles than in Wessex. An Itford Hill Globular vessel, parts of which were found both in the barrow and the settlement, has an interesting T handle, while some of the examples from the Plumpton Plain A settlement have large vertical handles reminiscent of Swiss-south German handled vessels.

The groupings of East Anglia have yet to receive similar attention, but a coherent Ardleigh Group in Suffolk and Essex is well-known. This is represented by Bucket Urns with all-over finger-tip rustication, horizontal cordons and prominent horseshoe bands (Figure 3.15). Globular urns exist, either plain or with multiple zig-zag and cross hatched triangle decoration, more complex than in Wessex. Vertically arranged opposed triangles have a striking resemblance to Swiss-south German motifs, but the heavy rustication betrays the indigenous ancestry of this group.

Not surprisingly the interior and more northerly and westerly districts of Britain show a progressive departure from the international aspects of this tradition towards simplified local reactions. Globular Urns, for example, disappear completely beyond those regions discussed above.

In the East Midlands, the Deverel-Rimbury tradition is represented by material from several cemeteries, for the most part unpublished. One aspect is represented by urns from sites such as Stainsby, Lincolnshire; Stathern, Leicestershire; and Burton Latimer, Nottinghamshire; a mixture of bucket and bipartite shapes characterized by a cordon a few inches below the rim, or at the shoulder if there is one, defining an upper decorated zone executed in cord or impressed techniques. Some examples of this Stainsby Group are very reminiscent of southern Biconical Urns, a point reinforced by the Stainsby finds. Here the in-urned cremations lay within a penannular ditched enclosure (cf. Figure 7.8), one accompanied by a ball-shaped faience bead, one by a burnt Class Ia razor. Another burial, with a Pygmy cup in a pit, completes the picture of a cemetery of the Bedd Branwen period. A second contrasting tradition is represented by much simpler vessels from cemeteries such as Long Bennington, Lincolnshire; and Hoveringham, Nottinghamshire. These are much more in keeping with the coarse, plain essence of the Deverel-Rimbury tradition, and the differences between the two may be part social, part

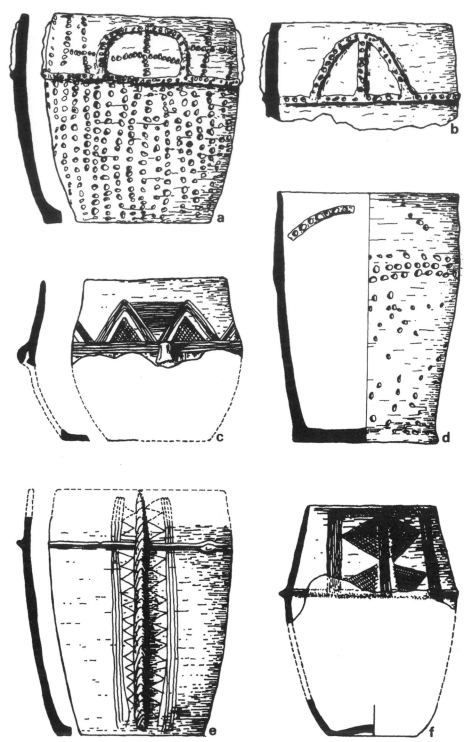

Figure 3.15 Urns from the Ardleigh cemetery, Essex; f. Brantham, Suffolk (after Erith and Longworth, 1960) (scale $\frac{1}{8}$: height of a. 42 cms)

chronological, as between the Deverel-Rimbury and the Collared/Biconical traditions in the south. This Long Bennington Group is associated with simple bucket-shaped vessels, sometimes slightly convex in outline. A cordon or line of fingertipping, if present, is set high up, just below the rim. An impressed cordon set just below an inwards-leaning rim is particularly common.

A West Midlands version of the Deverel-Rimbury tradition is represented by the cemeteries at Bromfield, Shropshire, and Ryton-on Dunsmore, Warwickshire. This far removed from the foci of Deverel-Rimbury traditions, resemblances to classic Deverel-Rimbury vessels are inevitably scant and generalized. Bucket and barrel shapes are there, including bucket-shaped urns with cordons, but there is also a lot of fingernail decoration, and ornament on the upper part of the vessel variously executed by incision, finger marking and impression. Too few sites are known to permit detailed analysis. The situation is even more difficult in Wales, where there are only a few single burials with bucket-and barrel-shaped vessels from barrows as far apart as Llanarth, Cardiganshire, and Llandegla, Denbighshire, and some finds from south Welsh caves such as Ogof-yr-esgyrn, Breconshire, and Culver Hole and Lesser Garth in Glamorgan. Deverel-Rimbury material has also been reported from recent excavations at Rhuddlan, Flintshire. The Llanarth and Culver Hole finds include examples of that very widespread phenomenon, the simple, plain bucket or slightly barrel-shaped urn with a row of perforations below the rim. Such vessels are common in southern Deverel-Rimbury groups (cf. Furzy, Hampshire, Ashford Common, Middlesex) but are also found in earlier traditions such as Lough Gur II ware. The simplicity and longevity of the form make it difficult to date and interpret its representatives scattered throughout the Highland Zone. For the north and west were open to influences both from south England and from Ireland, and the idea of rim-perforated buckets could have come from either.

It is surprising that the evidence for an equivalent of Deverel-Rimbury in Yorkshire is so slight. The Catfoss penannular ring-ditch cemetery (Figure 3.16, 7.8), and a scatter of finds, hardly constitute an appropriate follow-up to the mass of classic Grooved ware from sites such as those at Rudston. This situation may in part result from the fact that nineteenth century barrow diggers concentrated their efforts on the chalk Wolds, where they found prestigious burials, and not on the lower ground, where further finds of the Catfoss Group are most likely to occur.

The search for bucket- and barrel-shaped vessels beyond the Tees brings one up against the intractable problem of 'native' 'Votadinian' and 'flat rim' wares. Much 'flat-rim' pottery, especially that associated with stone circles, is clearly relevant to the coarse-ware traditions under discussion, but there has been insufficient work on all these northern ceramics to make sensible comment possible. The Largs Group was certainly widespread in south-west Scotland by the Bedd Branwen period. This includes bipartite, barrel and especially

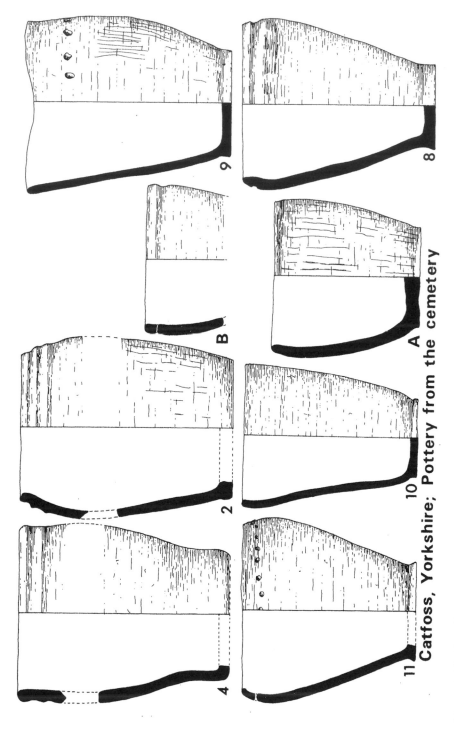

Figure 3.16 Urns from the Catfoss cemetery, Yorks. (after McInnes, 1968)

bucket-shaped vessels, including examples with a row of perforations below the rim. Some bucket-shaped and bipartite urns have a decorated zone around the upper part of the pot, usually executed in cord, and sometimes defined below by a ridge or cordon. Urns of the Largs Group are frequently found in cemeteries with other types of cinerary urns. At Misk Knowes in Ayrshire, fifteen cremations in urns of the Largs Group, were found under a small cairn with a single Cordoned Urn burial. From one of the bucket-shaped urns came traces of gold leaf, together with star and segmented faience beads. At Largs itself the seven bucket-shaped urns all huddled together in one cist, in a cemetery also containing Collared Urn burials. An opposite situation to Misk Knowes occurred at the Mid Gleniron chambered tomb, Wigtown, where most of the urns in a secondary cemetery were Cordoned, only one a plain barrel-shaped urn. This had multiple mouldings below the rim like one of the Catfoss urns (Figure 3.16). Cordoned Urns may in fact have to be brought into the Largs Group, as the equivalent, so to speak, of southern Barrel Urns. It is not yet certain whether urns of the Scottish coarse-ware groups such as Largs continued in cinerary use after *c.* 1250 bc. This is how we should perhaps interpret old finds such as that from Duff House, Banff, consisting of a cremation in a coarse bucket-shaped urn, accompanied by gold ornaments of the Taunton phase. But whatever happened on the sepulchral side, these Scottish coarse wares clearly continued in domestic use throughout the Knighton Heath period. At the Green Knowe settlement in Peeblesshire (*c.* 1200–1000 bc), the pottery consisted of bucket- and barrel-shaped vessels, including cordoned forms indistinguishable from Cordoned Urns found in cemeteries of the Bedd Branwen period. At what point Largs pots become 'flat-rim' ware is academic until this whole coarse ware problem has been investigated in depth.

Trevisker wares were the equivalent of Deverel-Rimbury wares in south-west England, and like them occur both in settlement and funerary contexts. Unfortunately practically nothing is known of antecedent pottery styles in the south-west, so that Trevisker origins are uncertain. The first glimpse of emerging Trevisker styles is seen in vessels from Layers 8 and 7 at the Gwithian settlement in Cornwall, associated with Beaker pottery. Typical are bucket-shaped tubs and jars with out-turned rim, with a broad zone of plaited cord decoration on the upper body. By Gwithian Layer 7, more squat, saucepan-shaped vessels, with an upper zone of incised decoration, had been developed. Incised Trevisker ware is thus not necessarily late Trevisker ware, but having said that, the sequences both at Gwithian and Trevisker show that incised ornament increased as handles and cord ornament decreased. Later Trevisker vessels, ApSimon's styles 3 and 4, are thus bucket- and barrel-shaped vessels, of a rougher, more gritty fabric than previously, with more incised than cord ornament, and, frequently, a distinctly angular rim treatment. Handles are absent, apart from paired finger dimples which may be separated by a pronounced pinched out 'beak'. This is the sort of pottery present in the later levels of both Gwithian and Trevisker, dating to the Knighton Heath period.

Some of the pottery from the Dartmoor settlements looks quite like Deverel-Rimbury material, such as the cordoned bucket-shaped vessels from Raddick Hill and Legis Tor. Closer in shape to Globular Urns are the pots from the entrance graves of the Scilly Isles, though these have such different decoration that the resemblance may be fortuitous. The examples from the Knackyboy tomb were associated with glass and faience beads. On the mainland a better match for the ornament of Globulars is found on some small, barrel-shaped vessels with incised zig-zags and horizontals on the upper body and paired finger-pinched depressions.

It is not surprising that the communities of this sea-girt region should have contacts with so many neighbouring maritime territories. Long sea crossings were undertaken, across the Bristol Channel to south Wales, where a late Trevisker urn with paired dimples was deposited at a barrow (Six Wells 271) in Glamorgan; across the Irish Sea to Dalkey Island near Dublin, where similar paired dimple vessels were found; and, most remarkable of all, up the Channel to Hardelot in the Pas-de-Calais, whence came a Trevisker urn made of Cornish gabbroic clay ornamented with typical plaited cord motifs. Such voyages involved conscious effort, whereas Trevisker influence in Wessex, apart from a few urns such as that from Sturminster Marshall, Dorset, is very generalized, and will have resulted from normal culture contact.

Although burials in Cornish Urns, the prestigious end of the Trevisker range, had ceased by the end of the Bedd Branwen period, Trevisker wares continued in domestic use down to the Penard period. Their latest occurrence is with early Urnfield material in layer 3 at Gwithian, but then like Deverel-Rimbury wares they vanish from the archaeological record. What replaced them has yet to be established.

To sum up: Barrel and Bucket Urns were developed from Grooved wares in the Overton period. In the Bedd Branwen period Globular Urns were developed to provide an English equivalent of the handled cups and jars of western Europe. After the Bedd Branwen period, Deverel-Rimbury traditions emerged alone from widespread social, economic and spiritual upheavals which severed other burial and ritual traditions. A number of radiocarbon dates and a few associations with metalwork, for example, a spiral finger ring at Standlake, Oxfordshire, and a fragment of a twisted torc at Berwick St. John, Wiltshire, show that Deverel-Rimbury groups as far apart as Dorset and East Anglia flourished throughout the Knighton Heath period, the fourteenth and thirteenth centuries BC. There are no unequivocal associations with Penard metalwork, but the latest radiocarbon dates, such as those of *c.* 1000 bc at Itford Hill, and *c.* 986 bc at Grimes Graves, suggest survival into the Penard period. Deverel-Rimbury pottery is not present in the re-occupation phases at Rams Hill, which have eleventh century bc radiocarbon dates, and this is only one of many sites where Deverel-Rimbury pottery was giving way to new ceramics in the Penard period, 'post Deverel-Rimbury' pottery. At Angle Ditch a transitional palstave from the bottom of the ditch indicates a Penard date. There are Deverel-Rimbury sherds present, but the most complete pot is thin-walled, and representative of the new tradition. Similarly at Eldon's Seat, Dorset, new shouldered vessels appeared alongside Deverel-Rimbury wares at this stage.

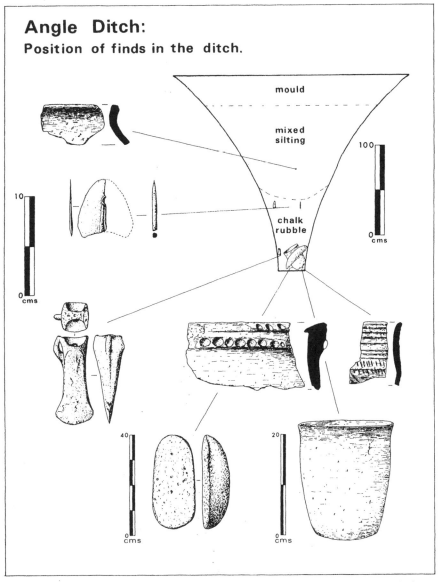

Figure 3.17 Angle Ditch: stratigraphy of finds in the ditch (after Pitt-Rivers, 1898)

The only evidence for Deverel-Rimbury survival into the First Millennium is provided by the radiocarbon dates for the Simons Ground cemetery, Dorset. But as these range right down to 71 bc and are so out of tune with all the other dating evidence they are gravely suspect. They appear, in fact, to have been contaminated by recent heath fires. In the interior, local versions of Deverel-Rimbury may have lingered later, though in increasingly unrecognizable forms. In the West Midlands the cemeteries of Bromfield and Ryton-on-Dunsmore have radiocarbon dates of *c.* 850–751 bc, while in the north and west local coarse ware traditions appear to have escaped the innovations of the Penard phase, and continued, if poorly documented, to emerge as the 'native' and 'flat-rim' wares of the First Millennium. This makes sense of the 're-appearance' of cremation in northern areas and in Ireland in the First Millennium, for example at the Rathgall hill fort, Co. Wicklow, and in Scotland in several instances accompanied by metalwork of the Ewart Park phase, *c.* ninth to eighth centuries BC.

There are no ritual or ceremonial sites which can be specifically dated to the Knighton Heath period, nor any centres to continue the tradition of causewayed camps and henges. If, as suspected, religious interest had shifted completely to rivers, lakes and bogs, this would explain the abandonment of the old centres and the absence of new ones. As a sign of this break with the past we may note that the Rams Hill enclosure seems to have lain abandoned in this period.

Settlements and economy

In the south of England the settlement pattern continued very much as before, with scattered farmsteads of circular timber buildings, sometimes with rectilinear structures, generally, but not invariably, set within an embanked or stockaded enclosure. Best known are the Deverel-Rimbury settlements on the chalk of Wessex, Hampshire and Sussex. Some had been established in the Bedd Branwen period, such as Shearplace Hill and South Lodge in Dorset, and these were modified or rebuilt on more than one occasion during the Knighton Heath period. Others were new foundations. With the need to make best use of the land, larger and larger tracts of the downs were divided into 'Celtic' field systems, taking up more and more land previously given over to pasture. Increasingly the chalk became a landscape in which settlements, new and old, stood amidst, or adjoined, neat blocks of fields.

Off the chalk, settlement remains are more tenuous, but recent discoveries on the Thames gravels have confirmed old finds such as those around Farnham in Surrey, by suggesting a similar pattern of Deverel-Rimbury palisaded farmsteads, but with ditch and bank field systems.

At many chalk sites the old palisade perimeters were replaced by bank and ditch, for example at Shearplace Hill, and at Cock Hill in Sussex. Such factors as pestilence and decay could lead to the phenomenon of 'settlement shift', as seen at Itford Hill in Sussex, although some settlements were rebuilt within the bounds of existing enclosures. Thorny Down, New Barn Down, Plumpton Plain A, Itford Hill, and other classic Deverel-Rimbury settlements clearly flourished in this period on the strength of metalwork finds or radiocarbon dates, but there are few indications of when they were founded. Still less can be said about the date of the majority of sites, which have produced Deverel-Rimbury pottery from limited excavations or surface collection, but nothing more closely datable. Unfortunately there are few sites which, like South Lodge and Angle Ditch, have produced datable bronzes from primary contexts. Deverel-Rimbury wares were developed and used over a period of several hundred years, and must have changed in this time. But until these changes have been worked out, and the pottery itself can be dated, most Deverel-Rimbury sites will defy dating except within the broadest parameters.

Deverel-Rimbury farmers practised a mixed farming economy, raising cattle, with some sheep and pigs. Wheat and barley were both grown, with the emphasis determined by the type of soil. Barley predominated on the dry chalk and gravel soils, usually the old naked barley, but Itford Hill at the end of its life had a storage pit filled with hulled barley, and this may have been an increasingly important crop in the Penard period. Damper, well-watered soils were probably more suitable for wheat, in the form of emmer.

In south-west England, low-lying settlements such as Gwithian and Trevisker still flourished in this period. At the former, the layer 5 settlement of at least three buildings adjoined a small block of cross-ploughed rectangular fields (Figure 5.10). The radiocarbon date of *c.* 1120 bc for this level of occupation matches well the date of *c.* 1110 bc at Trevisker. At these sites, and in the upland settlements, later versions of Trevisker ware continued in use. The exploitation and organization of the uplands for farming reached its maximum extent at this time, with reaves dividing the landscape into blocks, and each farmstead and village with its plots and fields. At the settlement of Horridge Common on Dartmoor, one farmer lost his palstave in a field just 60m from his farmstead. It must have been a prized possession, because it was not one of a local type but an import, a 'Bohemian' palstave which must have been made hundreds of miles away in central Europe. The date, about 1300 BC, is not significantly different from the Gwithian and Trevisker radiocarbon dates.

The great ditched and hedged field system on the fen edge gravels at Fengate remained in use throughout this period. Aerial photographs suggest that similar fields now covered much of the river gravels of England, especially the Midlands and East Anglia, so that the pressure was now on to find new land. This meant clearing less tractable soils, and moving into hill country which previously may have seen only summer graziers. The evidence for hill settlement increases markedly in this period. It comes from stray finds and from hill-fort excavations, which have revealed occupation traces, sometimes buildings, representing activity long before defences were thought of. Without radiocarbon dates such tenuous remains might have been written off as 'Iron Age', but with their help activity of this period has been revealed on hill-tops as far apart as Mam Tor in the Derbyshire Pennines, Moel-y-Gaer in Flintshire, and Kaimes Hill in Midlothian. The German term *Hohensiedlungen* is very apt for such sites, since their character is often far from clear. At Mam Tor (Pl. XV), the building platforms levelled into the hill-side strongly resemble those of the unenclosed scooped settlements of the Border hills, especially of Peebles and Lanark. On the evidence of the recently excavated Green Knowe example (Pl. XIV) (*c.* 1200–1000 bc), these sites, with their plots and clearance cairns reflect the continuing spread of settlement in the hill country of North Britain in the Knighton Heath and Penard periods.

On flatter terrain, where no scooped platforms were necessary, traces of settlement are even more tenuous, often merely slight banks, clearance tumps and haphazard plots. Little work has been done on such sites and their history is uncertain. Even excavation can help little in understanding Highland Zone settlements at this time, for they are either poor in finds, or, like Green Knowe, produce coarse, simple pottery which cannot be closely dated. For every datable Second Millennium settlement found under machair sand in the Hebrides, there are dozens of others which produce undatable coarse, plain pottery. Radiocarbon dating has been vital in identifying the settlements of the later Second Millennium, as can be seen not only from the case of the unenclosed scooped settlements, but also the 'burnt mounds' of the Northern Isles. These provide a prime example of how the application of modern scientific dating techniques to a very numerous, but previously undated, class of site can fill a period previously devoid of known settlements. Recent excavation of burnt mounds has revealed substantial stone houses adjoining heaps of burnt material, the product of innumerable boilings for cooking. The similar cooking sites of Ireland, the *fulachta fiadh*, go back even earlier to the beginning of the Second Millennium. With the encroachment of peat on more and more of the extensive field systems of Ireland, there, too, the later Second Millennium must have seen a dramatic expansion of settlement into upland areas and on to poorer soils; but this aspect of Irish prehistory has been little explored.

Flint and stone

Simple flint tools were still used extensively in this period, but it is not surprising to discover that activity at old flint mine sites such as Grimes Graves was much reduced. Here, people using a local version of Deverel-Rimbury pottery with an ample sufficiency of metal equipment clearly no longer had the need to deep-mine for top-quality flint, and were content to dig shallow pits to get at the inferior upper deposits. As if to add insult to injury, they also set up a metal workshop on the site, for quantities of clay mould fragments and other workshop debris were dumped in one of the shafts. The radiocarbon dates for this occupation range from *c.* 1053–986 bc.

Metalwork

In the latter stages of the Bedd Branwen period the metalworkers of Britain and Ireland adopted the new techniques and products which denote the Acton Park tradition. A rather experimental first phase of development was followed by a more settled second phase, epitomized by the Acton Park hoard itself. At the start of the Knighton Heath period this mature Acton Park industry, in its various regional versions, still held sway. Its Continental contemporaries, with many of whom it enjoyed close contacts, included the Tréboul workshops of north-west France, Tumulus B2 in central Europe, and the later Ilsmoor group of Montelius IIA in north-west Europe. A warrior of the early Knighton Heath period still wielded side-looped spearheads, or socket-looped ones in Ireland. For stabbing and thrusting he still used dirks and rapiers of Group II, and the ornate, but archaic, weapons of Group I may now have survived only as heirlooms, relics of a past era of more fancy workmanship. The more peaceful customer in southern England and Wales could still acquire Group I and II palstaves, now more elegant than the first clumsy experiments, but in northern Britain he had to make do with the less sophisticated haft-flanged axe (Figure 3.12). In Ireland both haft-flanged axes and the short, squat local versions of shield-pattern and midribbed palstaves were available, presumably for different purposes. We must guess at what other tools were available, for the few hoards of Acton Park metalwork contain none beyond curious thin-bladed flanged 'axes'. Trunnion tools, either lugged chisels or metalworkers' stakes were certainly available, together with single-point awls, Class Ib razors, and simple bar chisels of the pattern introduced as far back as the Overton period. But all in all the range of metal goods on offer was not great, and the lack of ornaments is especially strange.

During the fourteenth century BC, there were major changes in Irish-British metallurgy which are clearly reflected in the Continental evidence. The north European connections of Acton Park-Killymaddy metalworking were with the Ilsmoor Group, of Montelius IIa. The next group of north European hoards, the Frøjk-Ostenfeld group of Montelius IIb–c, contain a new form of British/north French palstave, the low-flanged type, indicating that on both sides of the Channel new industrial traditions had emerged. As seemingly identical palstaves were being produced in southern England and in Normandy-Picardy, the source of those in the Frøjk-Ostenfeld hoards cannot be established.

This industrial stage, IX, is termed Taunton after the famous Somerset hoard (Figures 3.18, 19). It is marked by a remarkable revival of interest in ornaments, so much so that this has been termed the 'Ornament Horizon'. Most of the new ornaments were clearly of exotic origin: twisted torcs and

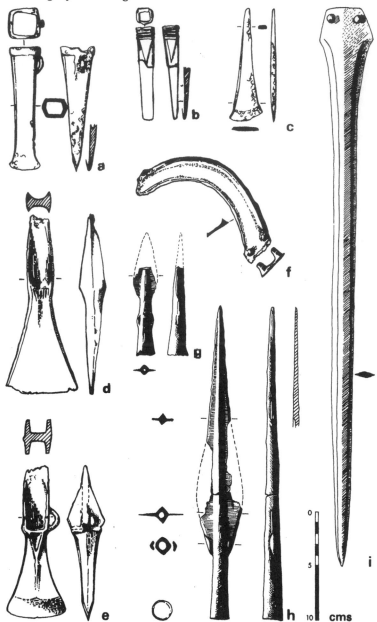

Figure 3.18 Bronze implements and weapons of the Taunton stage ('Ornament Horizon'): a. Taunton-Hademarschen socketed axe, and b. socketed punch, from the Taunton hoard, Somerset; c. chisel, Sparkford hoard, Somerset; d. low-flanged palstave, Barton Bendish hoard, Norfolk; e. South-western palstave, and f. knobbed sickle, from the Edington Burtle hoard, Somerset; g. side-looped spearhead, Stump Bottom hoard, Sussex; h. leaf basal-looped spearhead, Sherford hoard, Somerset; i. Group III rapier, Keelogue Ford, Co. Galway (after *Inventaria Archaeologica*, GB.7th set, except d., after *Inventaria Archaeologica*, GB.1st set, 7; g. after M. A. Smith, 1959; i. after Eogan, 1964)

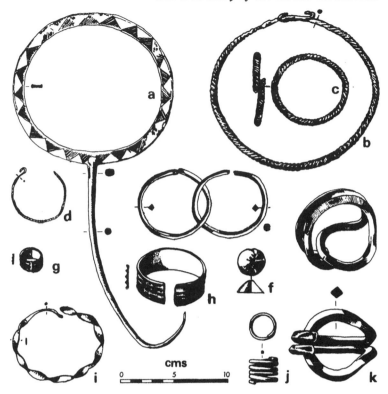

Figure 3.19 Bronze ornaments of the Taunton stage ('Ornament Horizon'): a. quoit pin, Barton Bendish hoard, Norfolk; b. twisted torc, Taunton hoard, Somerset; c, d. twisted armlets, Monkswood hoard, Somerset; e. lozenge-sectioned penannular armlets, and f. cone, Monkswood hoard; g. ribbed finger ring, h. ribbed armlet, and i. ribbon torc, from the Edington Burtle hoard, Somerset; j. spiral finger ring, and k. 'Sussex loop' ('Brighton loop') from the Stump Bottom hoard, Sussex (after *Inventaria Archaeologica* GB.7th set, except a, after *Inventaria Archaeologica* GB.1st set, 7; j, k. after M. A. Smith, 1959)

bracelets, lozenge-sectioned penannular armlets, D-sectioned plain and deco-rated armlets, spiral finger-rings, a great variety of pins and bronze cones. Others are clearly an indigenous response to this new flamboyance: Sussex loops, loosely twisted 'ribbon' torcs, and quoit pins. The greatest variety of these ornaments occurs in southern England, closest to the Continental sources of inspiration, and here they are usually found in bronze. Over the rest of Britain the range and quantity of ornaments falls away dramatically, but in Ireland local craftsmen seized on a few of the forms, especially the twisted torcs, ribbon torcs, and twisted and penannular armlets, and produced large quantities of them in gold. Whether the scattered gold examples in Wales and Scotland represent a similar local 'gold reaction', or whether they were imported from Ireland, is not clear.

The southern 'Ornament Horizon' hoards also contain novel tool forms.

Slender, square-mouthed socketed 'axes', in reality perhaps specialized wood-working tools, came in two versions, with flat collar; the Taunton-Hademarschen form, or with multiple mouth mouldings; the Bishopsland form. There were also socketed hammers, punches and chisels, saws, small anvils and knobbed sickles. Some of these innovations, as with the ornaments, were borrowed from the Continent, but it is not always easy to separate exotic imports from local inventions, nor to fix precise Continental sources.

The new metallurgy retained many old types unchanged, notably trunnion stakes, simple. bar chisels, single-pointed awls and Class Ib razors; and developed new versions of established products, notably in the areas of weapons and axes. The new palstaves of southern England and Wales had broad blades, either triangular or of 'crinoline' outline, and frequently had side-loops. They are termed 'low-flanged' palstaves, but there is also a distinctive high-flanged variant known as the south-western type, because of its concentration in that part of England. North English and Scottish communities continued to prefer flanged axes, though now with even shorter, angular flanges, often confined to the upper part of the implement. These wing-flanged or angle-flanged axes tend to be plainer and more slender than the earlier haft-flanged axes, but still frequently lack any sort of stop. The relatively few low-flanged palstaves from northern England and Scotland were clearly imported from Wales or the south, or copied from southern and Welsh forms.

As in the Acton Park phase, Ireland in this its Bishopsland phase produced both palstaves and flanged axes, the latter in the new angle-flanged version. The new palstave forms, Group C, low-flanged, and D, high-flanged, again reflect developments in Britain. Considerable numbers of Anglo-Welsh palstaves continued to reach Ireland, no doubt as part of the traffic which took the new ornaments and tools across the Irish Sea. Group C and D palstaves are short and squat in the Irish tradition, usually with the massive casting seams and deeply undercut stops typical of Irish palstaves. The example in the Bishopsland hoard, Co. Kildare, is larger, and copies more closely the Anglo-Welsh low-flanged form.

Taunton-Bishopsland craftsmen also developed new dirks and rapiers, the elegant weapons of Group III, with triple-arris or triple-ridged blades. These often attain great lengths, and were without doubt the finest achievement of the Irish-British rapier tradition. Practical considerations may have caused them to introduce Group IV weapons rather later, for these had a much simpler blade, with flattened or slightly rounded centre-section, and a smaller butt, and were easier to produce. Group I examples may still have survived as heirlooms, and Group II examples may have remained in production in some areas. As a result several rapier hoards which were deposited in the latter part of the Knighton Heath period, such as those from Talaton, Devon, Orsett, Essex and Beddgelert, Caernarvonshire, all show a thorough mixture of types, though Group III weapons predominate. Side-looped and socket-looped spearheads remained in production throughout the Knighton Heath period, but a new form was introduced in the Taunton phase, the basal-looped spearhead with leaf-shaped blade.

Northern Europe has usually been regarded as the ultimate source of most of the novelties of the Taunton-Bishopsland stage, including the twisted torcs and armlets, lozenge-sectioned penannulars, ribbed bracelets, heavy D and O sectioned armlets with ellipse-decorated examples, cones, coiled finger rings, Taunton-Hademarschen socketed axes, socketed hammers and punches, saws and knobbed sickles. Nevertheless it has always been recognized that most of these types were also widely distributed in the Tumulus Culture, and in northern France. The latter region has thus been seen as a sort of clearing house where a great variety of ornaments and tools from Tumulus and Nordic Europe were assembled before being passed onto southern England to form the basis of the Ornament Horizon. Some of these types, the ornaments in particular, are found as early as the Montelius IIa stage in northern Europe, even earlier in central Europe, but collectively they have been thought more typical of Montelius III, even IV, and some, notably the socketed axes, wholly of III and IV. Thus the Ornament Horizon, the Taunton-Bishopsland phase, has always been correlated with north European developments at the time of Montelius III and the beginning of IV, equating with Reinecke D, and Hallstatt A1 and A2 in central Europe, the period of early Urnfields there (Figure 3.20). In absolute terms this means the twelfth and eleventh centuries BC.

This long-held correlation will no longer stand scrutiny, since the Penard period which succeeded the Taunton phase in Britain, clearly correlates with these same early Urnfield stages. The Taunton phase must therefore correspond to the preceding Tumulus C stage, and in turn with Montelius IIb–c in northern Europe. Since we have already noticed the presence of Taunton-type low-flanged palstaves in Montelius IIb–c hoards, this seems perfectly reasonable; and since low-flanged palstaves are specifically absent from Montelius III contexts, there could not have been much overlap with Montelius III. We have already noticed that most of the relevant tools and ornaments were already current in northern Europe in Montelius II, or in central Europe in Tumulus C, so the fact that they were still circulating in Montelius III and even IV is irrelevant to the chronology of the Taunton phase. It has no more significance than the continued use of some Taunton types, especially the ornaments, in the Penard period.

If the Taunton phase was contemporary with Montelius IIb–c it becomes necessary to explain how in northern Europe Taunton-Hademarschen socketed axes always occur in contexts of Montelius III and IV. Some German scholars have always thought that these axes look out of place in north European metalworking, and the answer must be that far from these being a Nordic export to Britain, they must have been developed first in Britain. There are

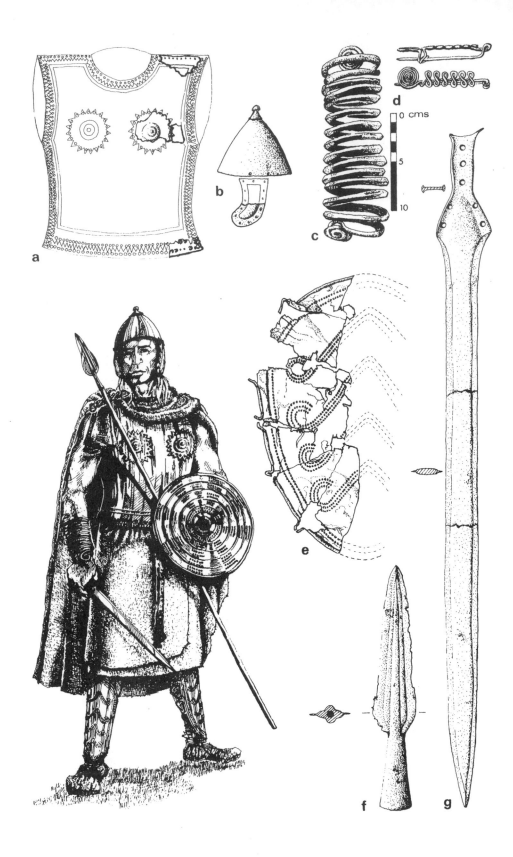

a

b

c

d

0 cms

5

10

e

f

g

now far more examples in Britain than in northern Europe, not to mention the related punches, hammers and chisels, so there is no reason why this should not have been an invention of the Taunton phase which only later reached the Nordic world.

These new correlations in no way detract from the French role in all of this, for the great quantities of 'Ornament Horizon' material in France have still to be explained, plus the fact that France has produced some Ornament Horizon bronzes, notably 'Picardy pins', which are foreign to the Nordic world. Thus France remains the collecting area for central and north European bronzes and ideas *en route* to Britain, but we must now accept that this process took place appreciably earlier than has been admitted previously.

The background of these developments is a continuing parallelism between south English and north-west French metalworking. There was a certain amount of contact with Brittany, now in its Portrieux phase, seen best in the slender Portrieux palstaves scattered through southern Britain, but traffic with Normandy and Picardy was much more important. This in turn provided links with the whole Seine basin, and beyond to the upper Loire. In the Normandy-Picardy area this was the Baux-Saint-Croix/Mont-Saint-Aignan phase, characterized by the same low-flanged palstaves and rapiers as were typical of Taunton metalworking across the Channel. This tradition block stretched as far as the Upper Loire-Cher region in the heart of France. Here the large Malassis hoard consists almost entirely of material familiar from the Taunton hoards: low-flanged palstaves, rapiers of Groups III and IV, basal-looped spearheads, knobbed sickles, D-sectioned decorated bracelets ('Bignan type'), ribbed bracelets, twisted armlets, spiral rings, and cones. But there are also a few fragments of early Urnfield median-winged axes, a sign that in western France as in Britain a time of dramatic upheaval was imminent.

In the last decade of the thirteenth century and the early part of the twelfth century BC the written sources of the great east Mediterranean civilizations are full of reports of raids, warfare and destruction, carried out by barbarians of whom the 'Sea People' are apportioned most blame. The identity of these intruders is far from clear, but references to 'all peoples of the north, coming from every country' suggests one of those periodic episodes where all the poor neighbours of privileged societies joined in the raiding and plundering. Only Egypt was able to withstand the shock; by the early twelfth century both the

Figure 3.20 Armoured warrior of Early Urnfield Europe: a. breastplate, Čaka, Slovakia; b. helmet, Gusteriţa, Transylvania, with cheekpiece from Wollersdorf, Austria; c. spiral arm-ring, Rimavska Sobota-Rimaszombat, Slovakia; d. Figure-of-eight fibula, Miejsce, Silesia; e. greave, Cannes-Écluse, Seine-et-Marne; f. 'flame-shaped' spearhead, Velatice, Moravia; g. flanged-hilt sword, ?Austria; the warrior's shield is based on one from the Nyirtura hoard, Hungary (a, b, c, d, f. after Gimbutas, 1965; e. after Gaucher and Robert, 1967; g. after Schauer, 1971; Nyitura shield after Patay, 1968)

Mycenaean and Hittite empires had collapsed, and the Aegean world entered a dark age. The parallel with the collapse of Rome fifteen hundred years later, and its aftermath, is very apt.

The background to these troubles is a story of economic collapse, of soaring population levels and of people increasingly compelled to move on to poorer lands which had hitherto been ignored. The similarity to events in Britain at this time engenders a remarkable feeling of *déja vu*, so much so that one wonders whether common factors could have been at work. Climatic deterioration is an obvious possibility, often considered as a factor in the east Mediterranean troubles but. never proved. An immediate consequence of worsening climate would have been crop failure and famine. It is tempting to see this as the cause of the famine in Anatolia mentioned in correspondence between the Pharaoh of Egypt and the Hittite king towards the end of the thirteenth century, but equally shortage always accompanies warfare, so the evidence remains inconclusive.

In barbarian Europe this was also a time of great change, and raiders and mercenaries from beyond the Balkan Mountains may well have taken a hand in the troubles further south. Central Europe now entered its Urnfield stage, again not due to sudden new arrivals from the outside world but to transformation from within. As before the changes are best seen in the emergence of a distinctive sepulchral tradition, in-urned cremation in great urnfield cemeteries. Within a matter of decades this Urnfield tradition had spread throughout the great central European community of tradition, and even beyond, from eastern France almost to the Black Sea, and from the Vistula to the Adriatic. In a world so torn by strife it makes sense to see in this great extension of Urnfield traditions some population movement: raiding, refugees, land grabbing, all are possible in the light of the disturbance and movement known to have been going on all round the east Mediterranean.

In keeping with these troubled times Urnfield armourers developed an array of new weapons, examples of which have been found as far away as Egypt. Drawing on Mediterranean ideas, they made their princes the first armoured warriors of barbarian Europe (Figure 3.20), so that a great chief like the one buried at Čaka in Czechoslovakia would have a bronze breastplate, greaves, a helmet with cheekpieces and a round shield. The warrior was now armed with a heavy sword, varying in form from region to region, but usually with solid-cast or flanged hilt, and with a long spear with flame-shaped head. He was caparisoned with a bewildering array of fittings and fastenings, especially arm-rings and fibulae. For less warlike tasks he had a tanged single-edged knife with re-curved blade, often decorated. In some areas archery, using bronze-tipped arrowheads, made a comeback.

The Urnfield traditions petered out east of Paris but inevitably Urnfield equipment and ideas were widely distributed in the lands beyond, towards the Channel and the North Sea. It is only to be expected that ripples from the unrest so widespread in the east will have been felt in these maritime territories. It was at this time that the first hill-forts were built in western France, and we can imagine an unsettled atmosphere developing which in time would have to spill across the Channel to Britain. The appearance in southern England around 1200 BC of scattered Urnfield and northern French bronzes shows that the inevitable was not too long delayed. As dramatic evidence of increased traffic from France there are now two ship-wrecks, both discovered in the last two or three years off the coast of southern England, at Dover and at Salcombe, Devon. Both have yielded French bronzes to show which way they were bound when they went down.

At this point Irish-British prehistory enters the Penard period, named after a hoard of novel bronzes from Glamorgan. This includes French and early Urnfield items, and epitomizes the transformation which now ensued. Traditions which had lasted a thousand years and more were severed, and replaced by new ones. In southern Britain scarcely anything escaped, from settlement patterns, agriculture and social organization, to burial and ritual tradition. Material culture was transformed including, most significantly, domestic pottery. There may have even been some changes in dress. So complete was the break that we may ponder the possibility of a large-scale movement of refugees from northern and western France. Inevitably the south was affected most, although the effects can be clearly traced as far north as Yorkshire, and encompassed most of England and Wales. The far north of England, Scotland and Ireland escaped all but the ripples of these upheavals. Their old traditions of cremation burial, and their coarse, plain pottery, were untouched, and survived into the First Millennium. But there was one important catastrophe even the north and Ireland could not escape, because it had nothing directly to do with upheavals on the Continent. This was an agricultural and population crisis, building up for some time, but as long as new lands could be opened up and ever larger tracts enclosed by field systems it had been kept at bay. This whole complex process now collapsed over the length and breadth of the country. Perhaps people had run out of new lands to clear and enclose, and a distinct worsening of the climate may have tipped the scales. Field systems from Achnacree in Argyll to Fengate in the Midlands and Dartmoor in the south-west were abandoned. At some of these the insidious spread of blanket peat has been revealed. Great areas of Celtic fields on the chalk were also abandoned, and the land re-organized for stock raising by division into grazing blocks with 'ranch boundaries'. These were drawn across the downland, often directly over abandoned field systems (Figure 5.14). Widespread waterlogging is indicated by the appearance on river banks from the Thames to the Trent of pile dwellings, and new trackways were laid down in all those areas, such as the Somerset Levels, prone to flooding.

The aftermath of the Age of Stonehenge is beyond the scope of the present story, but must be touched on to show how completely our prehistory changed in the twelfth century. There is no better illustration of the hiatus than the fate of the Deverel-Rimbury tradition. In a comparatively short time its ancient burial traditions were no more, and its pottery disappeared. Most significant is the appearance of radically new 'post-Deverel-Rimbury' domestic pottery traditions, involving new shapes, especially shouldered forms, and new techniques that resulted in stronger, thinner fabrics. At late Deverel-Rimbury settlements such as Eldon's Seat and Plumpton Plain B, new and old pottery exist side by side, but at new settlements it is the new pottery that dominates, and there is no sign of the old. Nowhere is this more noticeable than in the hill forts which now came to dominate the landscape of southern Britain. It is unfashionable even to consider migrations and invasions in modern prehistoric studies, but it is worth tabulating the changes which set in around 1200 BC and divide the Age of Stonehenge from the Age of Hillforts, to leave no doubts about the magnitude of the transformation which now has to be explained.

Changes in the Penard Period (mainly southern Britain)

Subject	Old (i.e. up to Penard Period)	New (appearing in Penard Period)
Domestic pottery	Deverel-Rimbury.	'Post Deverel-Rimbury' i.e. Rams Hill, Eldon's Seat I, Plumpton Plain B.
Settlements	Well marked perimeters, banks, ditches, palisades, walls, e.g. Deverel-Rimbury, south-west England.	Ill-defined, less substantial, difficult to find. Open settlements more common? Abandonment of upland settlements? Crannogs, pile dwellings. Burnt mounds.
Hill-forts	None.	Timber revetted ramparts: Rams Hill, Grimthorpe, Thwing, Breiddin etc.
Buildings	Mainly round, some rectilinear.	Rectilinear and round: 4- and 6-posters much more common.
'Town planning'	None.	Beginning, e.g. Rams Hill, Ffridd Faldwyn.
Social unit	Small, mainly farmsteads.	Larger groupings implicit in hill-forts.

Changes in the Penard Period (continued)

Subject	Old (i.e. up to Penard Period)	New (appearing in Penard Period)
Field systems	Extensive 'Celtic' blocks on chalk, south-west, river gravels (Fengate).	Largely abandoned cf. Fengate, Dartmoor, Black Moss of Achnacree.
Farming practice	Fields common, cf. on chalk, much arable.	Change depends on local situation, e.g. on chalk ranch boundaries cross old fields, swing to pastoral; abandonment of upland farms.
Crops	Mainly emmer, naked barley.	Swing to spelt and hulled barley.
Burial	Cremation: Deverel-Rimbury in all its regional manifestations.	Largely a void, but distinctive inhumations with metalwork begin, e.g. Hanley Cross.
Dress	Organic fastenings.	Dress pins.
Metal technology	1 Stone and bronze moulds. 2 Various bronze alloys.	1 Increasing use of clay moulds? 2 Standardized Penard alloy widespread.
Metal products	Stage IX Taunton-Bishopsland.	Stage X, Penard-Ballintober.
Warfare	Rapiers, looped spearheads.	Swords, peg-hole spearheads, some archery. Defended sites.

Chapter IV

People, Population and Social Organization

There is no evidence that the people of later prehistory looked very different from the present day population. Their physical characteristics, including colour of skin, hair and eyes, could no doubt be matched in Britain and Ireland today. Their stature at the extremes was no greater or less than the modern range, with individuals under five feet high to be set alongside males 'of considerable stature and strength', well over six feet tall. It is in *average* height and physique that differences can be expected, bearing in mind the changes of recent decades brought about by our welfare state. We can expect average heights for men perhaps two of three inches down on today's figures, rather less of a difference for women. But we can suppose the average physique to have been correspondingly more wiry, more lithe than our second half of the twentieth century bodies, softened as they have been by modern living.

It has long been customary to contrast a lightly built long-headed (dolichocephalic) Neolithic population, with a sturdy, robust round-headed (brachycephalic) 'Bronze Age' population, resulting from the arrival of Beaker settlers with this heavier build. It is now clear that this concept has been grossly oversimplified. Essentially it has been based on a contrast between physical remains recovered from the best-known tombs of the earlier Neolithic, long barrows and long chambered cairns, and those associated with Beakers and other typical 'Early Bronze Age' artefacts. The comparison is therefore between skeletal remains separated by the several centuries of the Meldon Bridge period, when comparatively little is known about the physical characteristics of the population. A further difficulty is the extent to which social and family status governed the type of burial. It is clear that those buried in barrows and cairns can only represent a tiny proportion of the population, and that unknown discriminatory factors were in operation then as later. Thus there may be unwitting bias in the skeletal remains chosen for comparison, a reflection of class and sex differences which could blur changes in the population as a whole. In short, it is by no means clear whether what appears to be a striking population change happened suddenly or gradually, or even whether it happened at all. There is certainly insufficient evidence to give credence to the invasion of a new physical type in the form of 'Beaker people'. It is clear that physical changes in a population can develop without external interference as a reaction to changing local conditions and environment; also, that dramatic changes can result from the arrival of a mere handful of outsiders in a strange land. There was plenty of time during the Meldon Bridge period for considerable changes to have developed gradually within the indigenous population. The parameters of the physical changes have yet to be quantified, and the transformation was not as complete as has always been claimed. We have seen that there was much more variation in the physical type of Fourth Millennium farmers than has been supposed, ranging from dolichocephaly to mesocephaly. A similar range is indicated in the Meldon Bridge period, with a shift to mesaticephaly. By the Mount Pleasant period brachycephaly had become a commonplace in burial sites at least, and it is generally true to say that individuals accompanied by Beakers and food vessels in the Mount Pleasant and Overton periods are frequently brachycephalic. But in these periods, too, a much greater variation in the physical type must be allowed than has been customary. It is curious that the great nineteenth century barrow excavator Mortimer, who dug up hundreds of burials of these periods, was in no doubt that there was *not* a single physical type, but that dolichocephalic, mesaticephalic and brachycephalic individuals were all represented. Similarly in the southern Pennines there is a thorough mixture of type in Beaker, food vessel and other graves at this time. If the published information is representative of this region, it suggests 52 per cent brachycephaly, 30 per cent mesocephaly, and 18 per cent dolichocephaly. In other areas the incidence of lighter-built dolichocephalic types may have been higher, for example on Anglesey, where those buried with Beakers were all of this type. Undoubtedly a much more scientific approach to this whole problem is urgently required, based on measurement of a whole range of skeletal variables. Little work of this nature has been attempted, and it is no help to discover that so little of the mass of skeletal material excavated in the nineteenth century has survived. Just such a broad-based survey of remains from the Yorkshire Wolds has suggested genuine physical differences between those buried with Beakers and those with food vessels, but what is not clear is the degree of chronological and social separation between these two groups. Clearly further comment would be premature without a lot more data, but it does seem safe to say that there is nothing in the skeletal record which requires a major influx of a new physical type, whether in the Beaker period or at any other time.

To judge from the bodies found in the graves of the Third and Second Millennia life expectancy of the period was considerably shorter than today. A crude death rate of about 40 per 1,000 per annum has been suggested, far higher than the 14 per 1,000 which is now the average for western Europe, but comparable with the figures still found in much of the Third World. Put another way, and not including the victims of an undoubtedly high infant mortality rate, perhaps 10 per cent of the population had a life expectancy of only 10 years, as much as 60 per cent could expect to reach only 25 years, and only 30 per cent could expect to live to 40. This would accord with what is known of Medieval age levels, which, reflecting life styles not appreciably different from those of later prehistory, are likely to provide valid comparisons. On this basis, maturity could be expected in the 30s, old age by the 40s, and an age of 50+, reached, for example, by a man buried with his dagger at Bught Park, Inverness, the equivalent of a modern centenarian. Men, not faced with the perils of childbirth, seem to have had slightly better expectations than women.

At the other end of the scale we can expect a high infant and child mortality rate. This is demonstrated with poignant clarity by several cemeteries, notably that of West Overton G6b, where the burial of an 'old' man (at least 40) was followed, in a space that may only have been months, by 11 others, 7 of them children under 7, 4 of them infants under a year old. At about the same time, of 7 burials deposited in the Amesbury G71 cemetery barrow (Phase III), 4 were children under 10, 3 of these under 4. This situation did not change with time, for late in the Knighton Heath period at Itford Hill in Sussex, the 12 cremated burials associated with a Deverel-Rimbury cemetery barrow included 4 children and 5 adults, with 3 of uncertain age. But in general children seem under-represented in the burial record, and it seems likely that some were disposed of in a less formal way.

Childbirth was hazardous for mother as well as child. Burials of young adult females with a new-born infant or foetus are all too familiar, presumably representing the death of mother and baby during or immediately after childbirth. At Nether Criggie, Dunnottar, Kincardine, a cist contained the skeletons of a 20–25 year old woman and a new-born baby. They were accompanied by no less than three Beakers, perhaps the farewell offerings of a grieving husband and family. At Warren Farm in Buckinghamshire, the primary burial within a ring ditch comprised the burnt bones of a teenage mother and new-born infant, but accompanied only by two pig's teeth. At Girvans in Ayrshire the cremated remains of a twenty-one year old female and a foetus were placed in a Cordoned urn for burial.

We can expect these deaths to have resulted from many of the illnesses and conditions which have affected us up to recent decades, and were still a major problem through much of the last century. Cause of death is seldom apparent, but condition of the skeletal remains does permit some conclusions to be drawn about general health. The population in most respects was more at the mercy of ailments than we are today, and could well succumb to conditions that present no problem to modern medicine. A very different life style would leave them fairly free of some medical conditions that are the bane of modern living, notably cancer and heart disease, but would exacerbate many others. Thus osteo-arthritis was endemic and often apparent from an early age, an inevitable consequence of a hard life style. Deficiency illnesses would also have been a major problem. Thus at Amesbury G71 we find a 25–35 year old mature male, robust, but with severe arthritic deformity of the spine, another male, of similar age, who had also suffered from this complaint, and a female, about 20, with a slightly arthritic foot. At West Overton G6b the 40 year old man in the central grave, suffered from osteo-arthritis, as did an adult of 40 or more, cremated some time afterwards. A 9 month old infant here showed cranial vault thickening due to some deficiency disease such as anaemia or rickets. A cremated individual buried at Ingleby Greenhow, in north York-shire, probably an adult male, had a strongly curved forearm, which was probably the aftermath of rickets. Osteoporosis, a pitting of the bones perhaps due to dietary insufficiency, less certainly to disease, was a common problem. Several of the children at West Overton G6b suffered from this condition, making one wonder whether famine could perhaps be held to account for the remarkable number of children buried here. One poor four year old had in addition suffered from severe facial osteitis or inflammation. Osteoporosis also affected a 20–30 year old male buried at Tickenham in Somerset. His left arm had been chopped off cleanly just above the elbow, either immediately before or after his death, perhaps the cause of his demise.

Rarer conditions included tuberculosis of the spine, possibly the reason for the vertebral abscess found on a young adult cremated at Treiorwerth in Anglesey; and spina bifida, suggested by the bony deficiencies exhibited by a mature 30–40 year old male found in a cist with a Beaker at Hatton Mill, Angus. This same much afflicted individual also suffered from osteo-arthritis and a deficiency in his left forearm muscles, perhaps disuse atrophy resulting from injury.

Lest it be thought that our 'Bronze Age' population was riddled with disease and illness, it should be stressed that these are only illustrations of some of the medical problems of the period. The health of the average individual was probably no different to that of any peasant agriculturalist in the world today. In some ways these prehistoric people were lucky, not only fitter on average than we tend to be, but also less prone to that most common of modern diseases, dental decay. With comparatively little sugar available to wreak dental havoc, the average set of teeth shows little or no sign of decay, though they are invariably extremely worn. This can be put down to a rough, often gritty diet, especially cereals and vegetables ground on rough-surfaced querns. On the other hand abscesses were common, and when dental problems did strike there were no dentists to ease the pain. Thus the old man in the central grave at West Overton G6b had four teeth with chronic abscesses and four decayed. A tall male in his late 30s buried in a cist with another female, perhaps his wife, at Buckstone Road, Edinburgh, was in a very poor dental state, showing severe periodontal disease and two abscesses. But neither was as bad as a robust male in his mid 30s, 5 feet 4 inches–5 feet 6 inches tall, buried in a cist at Mains of Daltulich, Nairn. He must have suffered severe dental pain towards the end of his life, for he had several abscesses and some caries, but worst of all was severe oral sepsis in his upper right molar, which may well have killed him.

No doubt these communities had their peasant remedies, their healers and medicine men who, with sufficient faith, may have cured many ailments. More remarkable was their ability to deal with primitive surgery. Bone-setting is a basic skill, and it comes as no surprise to find instances of broken bones well-set and well-knit. The Hatton Mill man, whatever his other afflictions, had at least managed to get a fractured right forearm to heal well enough. But broken bones were a simple matter compared with the dangerous operation of trephination which was frequently carried out. This involved removing a disc of bone, by cutting and scraping, from the skull. This is usually seen as a drastic treatment carried out on those mentally ill. In some cases, the operation, if not the cure, was a complete success. At Amesbury G71, for example, an inhumed male inserted into the barrow ditch was found to be suffering not only from periostitis of the left tibia but also had a trephination at the back of his head which had completely healed some time before his death. On the other hand an individual buried with an early Beaker at Crichel Down B14, Dorset, had been trephined at the back of the head shortly before death. In this case the trauma may well have been fatal, for the detached roundel of bone was found to have been carefully fitted back in position when the body was interred.

While double burials of mother and foetus or new-born infant are easy enough to understand, more difficult to interpret are frequent cases of females being buried with older children, and other double burials involving various combinations of sex and age. Thus at the Sant-y-nyll barrow in Glamorgan, the central cremation comprised the remains of an adult female and a child of 15–24 months, while at Goatscrag in Northumberland a Bipartite Urn contained the cremated remains of an adult female and a child of two. At Vinces Farm 3, Essex, a cremation deposit included the remains of a female, a six year old child and an infant. Whether these are instances of mother and child dying at about the same time of disease or starvation, whether one has been stored until the death of the other, or whether children were killed, for whatever reason, on the death of the mother, is impossible to say. Sometimes children accompany an adult male, as in the case of cremation C1 at West Overton G6b, an arthritic adult, perhaps a man, with a six year old child. In such cases a father-child relationship is possible, while in cases of male-female burials, for example of a double cremation in a Collared Urn at Treiorwerth, Anglesey, and a double inhumation in a cist at Buckstone Road, Edinburgh, a husband and wife relationship could be postulated. Other blood kinships may also have qualified for double burial. At Irton Moor, Yorkshire, the central grave contained the cremated remains of a robust adult male and a sixteen year old, probably male, with jaw lines sufficiently similar to suggest a blood relationship.

Double and multiple burials, both inhumation and cremation, were far more common than has always been thought, but what rules or circumstances governed them may always remain a matter for conjecture. Graves were not always covered immediately by a barrow, but might be left accessible for further burials, for only in this way can we explain cemeteries such as that at West Overton G6b, and the apparent reopening of some of the Yorkshire pit graves for new burials. Bodies could have been stored to await companions, but perhaps the most logical view to take of known double and multiple burials is that they represent cases of simultaneous or nearly contemporary death.

One other interesting clue to be drawn from skeletal remains is the frequent occurrence of a 'squatting facet' on the distal ends of the tibia, resulting from continual squatting on the haunches as is common amongst primitive peoples. It has been found on males and females alike, for example on a 25–30 year old woman with overcrowded teeth at Eriswell, Suffolk, on a fifty-five year old man buried with a late Beaker and bronze dagger in a cist at Ashgrove, Fife, and on a man of 30–40 whose cremated remains were found at Pilsgate, Lincolnshire.

The Pilsgate man epitomizes the human state of the period, spending much time squatting at his tasks, lithe, sinewy, powerfully muscled, his spine showing signs of strain perhaps due to heavy work, and apparently dying in an undernourished state. Periodic food shortage was no doubt another problem of the age, and is betrayed by the intermittent lines of arrested growth exhibited by many sets of teeth.

Population and social systems

Surviving settlements throughout Britain and Ireland suggest that for the most part the population of the Third and Second Millennia was organized in small settlements. These were farmsteads, hamlets and, at most, villages. They housed individual families, enlarged family groups, and, in the largest cases, small groups of related families, forming, perhaps, a sept of a clan. Only in the uplands of south-west England is there good evidence for village-sized settlements accommodating more than fifty people. Larger units, comprising hundreds and even thousands of people, did not appear until the needs of mutual defence led to the emergence of hill-forts in the Penard period, and even then in many areas most of the population appear to have clung to their farmsteads and hamlets.

This picture of small, regularly scattered units is entirely in keeping with what is known of the social organization, and the economic and technological level of the age. There is good reason to think that society was rigidly structured, and was firmly controlled by leading elements including both chiefs and holy men. There is also evidence that the country was divided up into territories, each with its clear boundaries, and each dominated by its leading families.

In Chapter I we have seen how misleading is the long-popular notion of an egalitarian Neolithic society. The 'collective' tombs housed a small, favoured section of the population and imply some special status. In some cases we may be dealing with the family sepulchres of the most prestigious elements in the territory, while in others it is clear that these 'tombs' in fact served a much wider range of community functions, and the identity of the few buried therein is uncertain. The majority were otherwise disposed of, not necessarily without ceremony to judge from the remains from causewayed enclosures. Hierarchical, structured and tightly organized communities may be inferred if only because of the needs of the great engineering works of the age, such as the chambered tombs and the cursūs. The building of Silbury Hill in north Wiltshire (six radiocarbon dates range from *c.* 2725–2145 bc) would have required the labours of at least fifteen hundred men for five years, and seems inconceivable without powerful leadership within a well-organized and structured social framework.

So Neolithic society no longer presents such a strong contrast to 'Bronze Age' society, where differentials in grave goods and burial speak so eloquently of princes and chiefs, of ruling dynasties and structured populations. Neolithic society, too, can now be seen to exhibit many of the traits which usually accompany social stratification and strong leadership: an increasing population, intimately bound up with developing agriculture and a growing food surplus, clearly defined territories with territorial centres serving the social, economic and spiritual needs of the population, great cooperative public works, complex and powerful spiritual beliefs and social inequality. As yet there was little sign of individual wealth and all the trappings that normally betray chiefdoms.

The best evidence that the country was divided up into territories comes, not unnaturally, from Wessex, where the field monuments have survived well, and have been intensively studied. In the Fourth Millennium the disposition of the major monuments suggests the Wessex chalk was divided into five or six territories (Figure 4.1). Each is marked by a cluster of long barrows, and a causewayed enclosure that may have served as the territorial centre. In all cases the causewayed enclosure is peripheral to the long barrows, not at their centre, and usually near the edge of the chalk, which could indicate that these territories took in areas of adjoining lower lands off the chalk, and that the causewayed sites served as foci for a geographically diverse region. This seems a more likely explanation than an alternative, provided by modern ethnographic parallels, that they stood in border locations and served adjoining territories.

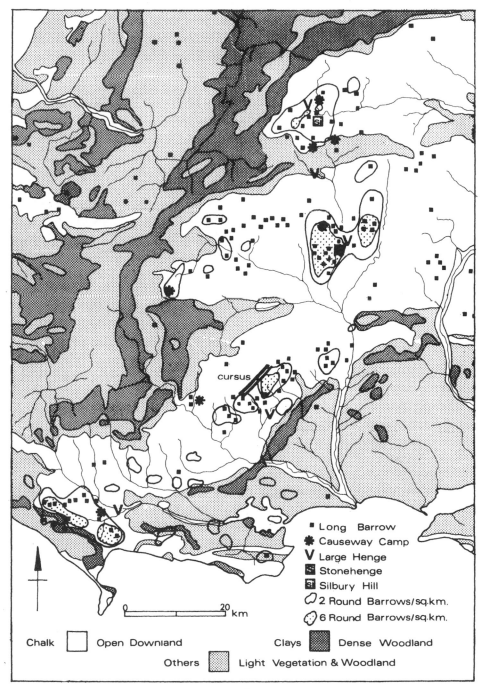

cursus

■ Long Barrow
✳ Causeway Camp
V Large Henge
S: Stonehenge
Sl Silbury Hill
⟁ 2 Round Barrows/sq.km.
⟁ 6 Round Barrows/sq.km.

0   20 km

Chalk ☐ Open Downland   Clays ▓ Dense Woodland

Others ▨ Light Vegetation & Woodland

Figure 4.1 Putative territories in Wessex, indicated by concentrations of enclosures and barrows (after Renfrew, 1973)

Proceeding from the south these territories and their causewayed enclosures were 1. The Dorset Downs/Maiden Castle; 2. Cranborne Chase/Hambledon Hill; 3. West Salisbury Plain/Whitesheet Hill; 4. East Salisbury Plain/Robin Hood's Ball; and 5. the Marlborough Downs/Windmill Hill. Between the last two territories the rich and fertile Vale of Pewsey projects like a narrow finger, dominated on its northern side by the rising chalk with two further causewayed enclosures, Rybury and Knap Hill, one of which may have replaced the other. It is possible that these arrangements denote a sixth territory, focussing on the Vale of Pewsey, and taking in the fringing chalk downland to the north and south.

In the Mount Pleasant period the functions of the causewayed enclosures seem to have passed to the great 'henge' enclosures (Figure 4.2), generally constructed not too far away. On Cranborne Chase, however, there was a shift to the east, away from Hambledon Hill on the western chalk edge to the Knowlton circles on the eastern edge. The largest of these, Knowlton South, was only half the size of the other great bank and ditch enclosures, but this territory also had the remarkable Dorset Cursus at its centre, its parallel banks and ditches running for six miles across the chalk. To the north, the whole of the Salisbury Plain area, which previously had been divided into two, now seems to have focussed on the remarkable concentration of monuments around Durrington Walls, the largest of all these new enclosures. This replaced the old Robin Hood's Ball causewayed enclosure, and the concentration of surrounding monuments included what was then the small, unspectacular henge we call Stonehenge. The viability of the Vale of Pewsey as a separate territory is confirmed by the construction of the great Marden enclosure on the fringing chalk to the south, perhaps replacing Rybury and Knap Hill on its northern edge. Finally on the Marlborough Downs the scene shifted from Windmill Hill to Avebury, which, with its enormous ditch and bank and circle stones represented the most prodigious engineering feat of all these new enclosures.

From the Meldon Bridge period onwards round barrows sprawled in ever-expanding cemeteries over the exhausted soils of the chalk. The greatest concentrations coincided with the main clusters of now-abandoned long barrows (Figure 4.1), one for each of the four main territories. The arrival of the Beaker tradition brought no outward change to this scene, but it did crystallize social distinctions, which henceforth were reflected in the richness of an individual's grave goods. Thus the same sorts of barrows were built, but might now cover richly furnished chiefs' graves which had never occurred before. For example Roundway G8 in the Marlborough Downs territory was raised over a chief of great eminence shown by the finely-decorated Beaker, large copper tanged dagger, copper pin or tanged point, stone wrist guard and barbed and tanged flint arrowhead which accompanied the body. Mere G6(a) on Salisbury Plain was raised over a similar burial, the grave goods again including a fine Beaker and tanged copper dagger, but also a gold disc with a

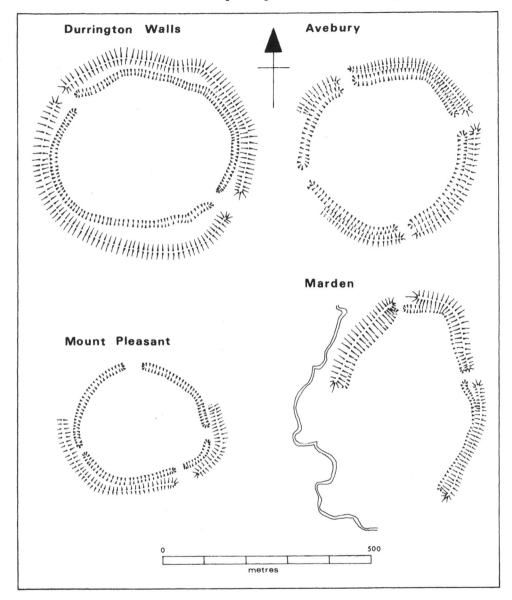

Figure 4.2 Enclosures of Durrington Walls type (after Wainwright and Longworth, 1971)

cross pattern (Figure 2.13g), perhaps a button cover, and a worked bone implement. But such burials remained exceptional down to the Overton period, and it was only in the Overton period, with the emergence of the Wessex Culture, that graves redolent of chiefs and dynasties became almost a commonplace.

While no other region has received anything like the academic attention devoted to Wessex, similar territories dominated by territorial centres and barrow clusters may be postulated in many other parts of the country, of which the rich gravel lands and flanking chalk downs of the Upper Thames valley may have constituted one. The focus passed from the Abingdon causewayed enclosure to the Dorchester Big Rings in the Mount Pleasant period. Notable barrow clusters, now surviving only as ring ditches on air photographs, have produced such rich burials as those at Dorchester XII in Oxfordshire, with fine, tall Beaker, tanged copper dagger, a copper riveted knife, and stone wrist guard; and Radley, Berkshire, with Beaker, gold basket-shaped ear-rings (Figures 2.13, 4.9b) and barbed, tanged arrowheads. A Chilterns territory would have centred first on Maiden Bower causewayed enclosure then the great Durrington-type enclosure nearby at Waulud's Bank. This is a region rich in long and round barrows, and it has now produced its own chieftain burial at Totternhoe, Bedfordshire, with Beaker, bronze double spiral-headed pin, bone belt toggle and stone wrist guard. Further north the vast field systems of the Fen Edge in eastern England imply great order and organization, and here, too, there are causewayed enclosures, henges and cursūs, and now the rich grave group from Barnack. Similar territories may be envisaged centred on areas as far apart as the Mendips, the Peak District, the Yorkshire Wolds, the North Yorkshire Moors, the mid part of Argyll between the Firth of Lorn and Loch Fyne, the Inverness area, where a richly furnished burial has recently come to light at Mains of Culduthel (Plate V), the Boyne Basin in Ireland, and many more. The types of monuments on which these suggested territories are based may vary considerably from region to region, but they all point to the same conclusion.

Major territories of the kind outlined for Wessex might measure up to thirty miles across and cover a thousand square kilometres. They would have contained many petty chiefdoms, perhaps the lands of individual septs, a few kilometres across. Lesser territories of this sort may have been detected in the Ouse Valley on the basis of the spacing of ring ditch clusters. Eighteen such community areas, each stretching for five to ten kilometres, have been suggested for the Upper and Middle Ouse in Buckinghamshire, Bedfordshire and Huntingdon. Similar blocks may possibly exist on the Wessex chalk, where linear barrow cemeteries often run at right angles to, or parallel with, the river valleys, rather like the modern parish boundaries, dividing up the land into blocks a few miles across. Around Stonehenge in particular the cemeteries tend to be evenly spaced, each dominating an area of *c.* 4.5 square kilometres, rather comparable to the Ouse units. The suggestion in both cases is that these were the 'home areas' of bands of wandering pastoralists, where the old and sick could be left in permanent settlements together with those responsible for cultivating essential crops. Here too would be the ancestral barrow cemetery. Meanwhile the rest of the sept would be away with the flocks and herds, following a well-worn pastoral circuit that would have to fit in with the movements of neighbouring groups if trouble was to be avoided.

It has been calculated that reasonable land such as could be found on downland flanks and valleys, and on the river gravels of central and eastern England, could support about ten persons per square kilometre. This is assuming pastoralists and cultivators living at the economic and technological level likely for this period. The 150 square kilometres of the Upper and Middle Ouse, which with flanking higher ground may have constituted a major territory, would on this reckoning have had a population of about 3,500 people. The known burial mounds of the area can only have accommodated a tiny favoured fraction of this figure, perhaps 1 in 44 on the basis of excavated sites. Using this figure it is possible to estimate the population of any similar territory where the approximate numbers of burial mounds are known.

In Dorset and Wiltshire, where barrows have survived well, the Ouse data suggests a population of about 16,000, based on 4,000 barrows, each producing 3 burials on average, the whole representing 30 or 40 generations spread over about a 1,000 years. The simpler population calculation of 10 per square kilometre suggests a figure twice as high for the 5 Wessex territories, about 34,000; but it is likely that large areas of the chalk uplands were now too poor to support anything like this density of population. A compromise would be to see territories with populations varying between 3,000 and 8,000. These would provide a realistic labour pool given the work implicit in the great cooperative monuments of the region. They would enable the paramount chief of each territory to reckon on a million or more annual man hours of labour from his subjects, enough to construct all the great enclosures except Avebury within the space of a year. Avebury, with all the extra work involved in its circles of great stones, would have taken half as much effort again, and even this requirement would have been dwarfed by some of the other construction feats undertaken, which would have to be spread over years. For example the Dorset Cursus would have consumed nine million man hours, which could have been spread over several seasons. But Silbury Hill is known to have been built in one go, and as it required eighteen million man hours of labour, a team of five thousand workers putting in ten hour days for a whole year without a single day off would just about have sufficed. It is doubtful that a single territory could have scraped together anything like this size of work force over such a long period, which strongly implies some arrangement with neighbouring territories. Still less could the Salisbury Plain territory have coped with the sarsen phase at Stonehenge, which required over thirty million man hours for its completion. This effort could have been managed by spreading the efforts of a two thousand strong labour force over five years, but to manage in a shorter time would have meant securing the cooperation of several other territories. Added to the Silbury Hill evidence this raises the possibility of a political situation more like that of Medieval times, with a super-chief (or king) able to secure labour from his neighbours and lessers.

Such population levels are completely at variance with Atkinson's estimate of only two thousand for the whole of England and Wales. This was based on the mistaken premise that the entire population was interred in the burial mounds, which was clearly not the case. Such a minimal population could in no way have coped with the great engineering works of the age, nor is it commensurate with the scale of land use as it is now known.

At the other end of the scale it has been calculated that by the mid First Millennium BC Herefordshire alone had a population of around 15–20,000, seven or eight per square mile, which is remarkably close to the figure of ten per square kilometre already suggested as a general guide for reasonable land settled at this socio-economic level. It was thus already approaching the Domesday population for the county of 20,534. If such figures were projected over the country as a whole it would suggest that the population of the whole of Britain at this time was somewhere between three quarters of a million and two million, for Ireland another half million or so. Allowing for natural population increase of 0.6 per cent per annum and working backwards, the figures for *c.* 2000 BC, in the Mount Pleasant period, are likely to be around half a million for Britain and perhaps 200,000 for Ireland. While such figures are very much greater than traditional estimates, they fit very well with the likely labour requirements of the great monuments of the period, and may explain why some very difficult soils were already being cultivated.

Whether it is legitimate to envisage a small but steady annual population increase in the long term is far from certain. In the short term the population may well have increased by around 0.6 per cent per annum, but there is a strong possibility of cyclical agricultural and population crises every time the carrying capacity of the land was approached and exceeded. There may have been two such collapses in our period, but others were to follow at intervals right up to the Medieval period. As the Meldon Bridge period opened, Britain and Ireland may still have been recovering from the first such calamity. With the early farming period now known to have lasted over a thousand years, not the few centuries of earlier chronologies, there was clearly plenty of time for the population to reach much higher levels than has been entertained hitherto, and for much more of the land to be cleared and exhausted. The scale of 'public works' in the Meldon Bridge and Mount Pleasant periods is a sign that population levels were recovering, in which case the great field systems such as Fengate may indicate renewed pressure on the land. The population would have risen slowly in the Overton and Bedd Branwen periods as land allotment grew ever more sophisticated, new, less tractable soils were cleared, and ever larger upland tracts were developed. Some areas formerly densely settled, such as the chalk uplands, may have suffered population decline as thin soils were exhausted, but the converse is that other areas, long thinly populated, such as clay and hill districts, now supported far more people. The next crisis, when this precarious balance broke down, came around 1200 BC, sparked off by a mixture of human and climatic factors. Everywhere existing farming patterns collapsed, and great tracts of land had to be abandoned. The population may once again have slumped, but at this point there is the possibility of new arrivals from northern France to complicate matters. After this a period of adjustment again ensued, followed probably by a gradual recovery and then increase to the near-Domesday figures which some authorities have postulated for the mid-First Millennium BC. Other crises were to follow, but they are beyond the scope of this book.

Palaeobotanical and soil studies have shown that by the Mount Pleasant period the chalk uplands that form the heart of the Wessex territories had been considerably degraded, and much former arable land had reverted to scrub, or at best open grassland. Such lands could be used only by pastoralists, and cultivation was confined to the lower flanks of the downs, to the valleys, and to the lower lands that fringed the chalk. This permits a further refinement of the political picture of the times, one familiar from some primitive parts of the world in more recent times. Bands of powerful and mobile upland pastoralists dominate a larger, more settled population of solid peasant cultivators, living in small, regularly spaced settlements in the valleys and on the lower ground. It is a possibility enhanced by the positioning of the great territorial centres between upland chalk grassland and lower arable lands. A further hint of some such population distinction is provided by the concentrations of Deverel-Rimbury burials, near the edge or off the chalk, in those lower areas likely to have been inhabited by peasant cultivators. The pattern is complementary to the concentrations of the great barrow cemeteries, and of Collared Urn and 'Wessex Culture' burials, on the high chalk grasslands. Thus Deverel-Rimbury pottery was the domestic pottery of pastoralists and cultivators alike, but only the latter, and the lower orders in society, used it for burial purposes. The pastoralists and the well-to-do had specialized funerary vessels, especially Collared Urns and Beakers with Grape, later Aldbourne Cups for the topmost level of all. Such arrangements were not confined to Wessex, for we have seen that in East Anglia local Deverel-Rimbury groups were concentrated in the coastal lowland area of Essex and Suffolk, while those with Collared Urns dominated the chalk escarpments of Cambridgeshire and Hertfordshire to the west. In the Peak District the contrast is between inhuming groups with Beakers and food vessels on the limestone, bound by cremating groups with cinerary urns, especially Collared urns, on the much poorer gritstones and sandstones. It may be significant that as yet no equivalent of Deverel-Rimbury has been found in the southern Pennines, but the lowlands to the west, south and east all have their versions of Deverel-Rimbury.

Populations of many individual territories may thus have been divided into pastoralists and cultivators inhabiting different areas. On the other hand there would have been large tracts, especially in upland areas, suited only to pastoral farming, whereas other areas, especially lowlands with rich, quickly regenerating soils, were better suited to cultivation. In many areas a pattern of small communities practising mixed farming seems most likely.

In addition to divisions between communities we must also consider stratification within the community. This clearly existed in most regions although the evidence may often-indicate no more than a family pecking order. Again pottery may provide a key, this time to status within the community and the family. First we may note the pre-eminent position of the Beaker as a funerary vessel. Although in the Overton period food vessels and cinerary urns emerged alongside late Beakers, the latter retained an important position in burial tradition. Where multiple, broadly contemporary burials occur, whether in the horizontal plane or in a dug grave, if an interment with a Beaker is present then it will occupy the most important position: either central if the relationship is a horizontal one, as at West Overton G6b (Figure 7.6), or on the floor of a grave, as at Garton Slack 75 on the Wolds (Figure 7.1). In the former case burials with food vessels or cinerary urns will be grouped around the Beaker burial, or where the relationship is in the vertical plane, will be placed higher in the grave fill. Were such differences simply a question of sex or age, for example Beakers for men, food vessels for women, then there would be no problem, but unfortunately Beakers, food vessels and cinerary urns all seem to occur with both sexes and all ages. The position is further complicated by the fact that a community could practise both cremation and inhumation. Death away from the settlement may be a partial explanation for the use of cremation by pastoral inhuming groups, but will not entirely suffice, for cremations seldom, if ever, have been found below, or central to, inhumations with Beakers. Those buried with Beakers clearly came from the leading families in the community. Food vessels and urns were for lessers, either in the family sense as seems to be the case at West Overton G6b, or in the community sense. In the Yorkshire pit graves, there are sometimes children on the grave floor, accompanied by Beakers, with adults deposited higher in the grave fill. While food vessel burials have on rare occasions enjoyed an equal position with Beaker burials, for example at Fargo Plantation in Wiltshire, food vessels never occupy a more important position than a Beaker. The fact that late Beakers, food vessels and urns can be shown by stratigraphy and radiocarbon dates to be contemporary within the same society, while never occurring together in a grave, is surely evidence of a rigidly structured family, community and territory.

The role of religion in the social organization of the period was clearly an important one. No region can boast as many great cooperative works for religious purposes as Wessex, but most areas have their share of burial and ritual monuments which would have consumed a great deal of the community's time. In Wessex much of the population must have been employed for years on end in building sites such as sarsen Stonehenge. Whether this preoccupation with religion indicates that the Wessex chiefs were also priests, or whether power was divided between chiefs and a class of priests or medicine men, the evidence cannot tell us. So specialized were the skills involved in constructing the great monuments in terms of field engineering, surveying and celestial knowledge that we may suspect a division of power between the *shaman* or priest, who would have had his hands full in these and kindred areas, and the lay chief, the warrior and leader.

With the declining interest in burial and ritual from the end of the Bedd Branwen period much of our knowledge of the people and their social organization disappears too. In particular the disappearance of 'privileged' burial, represented for instance by Collared Urns and the Wessex Culture, suggests the collapse of unequal societies with all their symbols, and their replacement by a new social order. The Deverel-Rimbury tradition in the south provides the best evidence for social upheaval, gaining ground as 'privileged' groups disappeared. The absence of rich grave groups in the Deverel-Rimbury cemeteries might suggest a relaxing of the stratification in the new society. But this is misleading, for grave goods had never been part of Deverel-Rimbury tradition, and a lowering of the social barriers is certainly not the impression to be gained from the metalwork that was the principal sign of wealth in the centuries after *c.* 1400 BC. Weapons came to dominate metalworking and society, in particular weapons which are often so large, fragile and unwieldy, or highly decorated, as to leave no doubt that display and ceremonial played an important part in the life of later Second Millennium societies. In communities where prestige and the warrior figured so prominently it hardly seems likely that chiefs, chiefdoms and class would have lessened in importance. In the Penard period pastoralism seems everywhere to have been on the increase, and a pastoral society is likely to be more martial than a society of cultivators. A warlike society, too, is more likely to need lower orders in the organization of its affairs.

We may speculate whether our five hypothetical territories in Wessex functioned separately or whether they were bound together under a superchief, perhaps septs of a clan or tribe. In view of the amount of labour required in the construction of the great monuments one may suppose some sort of confederation existed. The unique scale of sarsen Stonehenge and the concentration of monuments around it might lead us to conclude that by the Overton period power was concentrated in the hands of a paramount chief based on the area of Stonehenge. Perhaps the richly adorned man buried under Bush Barrow (Figure 3.4) was just such a leader.

It is worthwhile drawing comparisons with the type of society and the political divisions that Caesar found during his expeditions of 55 and 54 BC. He was confronted by a land divided into tribal territories, and one is entitled to ask how far back the tribal divisions of Caesar's day can be extended. If we accept the view that there were major Celtic invasions at the beginning of the 'Iron Age' then we would be able to push the tribes back only thus far. But the case for mass migration grows progressively weaker, and there seems no evidence to demand anything more than an intensification of normal cross-Channel traffic.

Going backwards in time, there is the possibility of some immigration from France at the end of our period, *c.* 1200 BC, but this appears to have affected only southern Britain. Earlier still, one has to go back as far as the first farmers to find any hard evidence for immigration on any scale, so there is every possibility that the tribal divisions, and perhaps some of the names, that the Romans found, were of very great antiquity. The pattern may have been disturbed by some 'Iron Age' incomings, especially in the south-east and in East Yorkshire, but in the west and north in particular political divisions in our period may have been similar to those of the early Roman period. The most fruitful line of inquiry would seem to be metalwork distribution patterns.

The distribution of axe types in Wales, in the ninth to eighth centuries BC, bears a marked resemblance to the tribal dispositions at the Roman Conquest. Thus the concentration of 'south Welsh' socketed axes in Glamorgan and Monmouthshire effectively delineates the territory of the Silures; the near-blank in the south-west corresponds with the lands of the Demetae; the north-west, conservative in its preference for late palstaves, was the territory of the Ordovices; while the north-east, with an unusual mixture of axes, matches the area of the Deceangli. Finally in the Marches the spear hoards of the Broadward tradition coincide in part with the lands of the Cornovii. It may even be possible to find still earlier echoes of these patterns in pottery and metalwork distributions. In the Knighton Heath period, for example, early midribbed (Group II) and late shield-pattern (Group I) palstaves are concentrated in the south-eastern lands later occupied by the Silures, contrasting with the north-west, later dominated by the Ordovices, where the midribbed implements are rare, and the heavy Acton Park palstaves predominate.

It may be possible to trace similar patterns even earlier in other regions. Thus the distribution of Trevisker ware coincides closely with the territory of the Dumnonii in Cornwall and Devon centuries later. Geographical factors are, of course, unvarying, and play a large part in the drawing of political boundaries. These may endure even though peoples come and go. It is interesting, for example, to note how many early Medieval political divisions resemble 'Iron Age' tribal territories. It would not be surprising to find the outlines of some of these territories established as early as the Second Millennium BC, but this is not the same as saying that the tribes themselves had emerged that far back. The upheavals of the Penard period must surely have had some effect on existing territories and societies, so that the political situation then is unlikely to have had more than a general resemblance to that in Caesar's day. The available evidence suggests smaller, more independent units in our period, although religion, and the urge to build great monuments, could bring groups together.

The question of language in later prehistory is very much bound up with the problem of the Celts. The arrival of the Celts in Britain and Ireland has always been linked to specific immigrations of Celtic settlers from the Continent. For a long time Hallstatt immigrants were the most favoured 'first Celts' in these islands, but with Hallstatt settlement now considered unlikely, the problem of how Britain became Celtic becomes more difficult. There is no doubt that the Romans found Britain and Ireland occupied by 'Celts' in the sense of Celtic-speaking peoples, so where did these Celts come from, and when did they arrive? If they did not appear suddenly as invaders, a solution may lie in Hawkes' principle of 'cumulative Celticity'. When Herodotus first referred to the 'Celts' in the fifth century BC he was alluding not to newcomers but to the end product of a long process of development. The idea of incessant invasions, folk movements and population displacements in central Europe, as in Britain and Ireland, now seems very much out of date, and the evidence seems instead to indicate populations that were essentially static. The answer must be that during this long period the peoples of central Europe became Celts by accretion in the due process of time. Thus it is pointless to pose the question 'When did the Celts first appear?' The Celts known to the classical writers were only the natural successors to countless generations stretching back through prehistory. In that sense the early farmers of western Europe were 'Celtic', and when some of these settled in Britain and Ireland before 4000 BC, these offshore islands, too, were brought into the realm of 'cumulative Celticity'. Thereafter the inhabitants of Britain and Ireland always kept in touch with Continental happenings, and never slipped into an alternative, wholly insular line of development. Rather than intermittent major invasions we must think of a constant dribble of refugees, traders and other adventurous folk crossing the Channel and perhaps occasionally, as in the Penard period, a larger influx.

The inhabitants of Britain and Ireland in the Age of Stonehenge may thus already have been 'Celts' in the sense that they spoke versions of Celtic languages and had already developed many of the traits and traditions which later stamped the historical Celts. In view of the known division between 'Q Celtic' and 'P Celtic' language, the former represented by Scots and Irish Gaelic, the latter by Welsh and British, it is interesting to note the archaeological evidence for strong Irish-Scottish links in our period, much closer than the connections between Ireland and Wales. Conversely it is true to say that the archaeological evidence indicates that Wales generally looked to England.

It is not hard to find evidence for this developing Celticity in the Third and Second Millennia. Now that 'Celtic fields' are known to go back at least to the Bedd Branwen period we may marvel at the unwitting clairvoyance of the term. But ritual and religion are more fruitful areas in which to find Celticity. We may note some of the most fundamental elements in the Celtic ethos were already present early in our period. In view of the interest which 'Iron Age' Celts showed in observing the heavens, especially to calculate their calendar, establish feast days and so on, it is legitimate to ask whether this was traditional knowledge handed down to the Druids from their ancestors who observed at stone circles and settings in the Meldon Bridge, Mount Pleasant and Overton periods. It is perhaps worth investigating to what extent the orientations and observations involved in these sites coincide with heavenly events significant in later Celtic ritual. Thus some stone circles, notably Castlerigg, but also the timber alignment at Meldon Bridge, embody an orientation on the sun's declination midway between the solstices and the equinoxes, in early November and early February. Is it mere coincidence that two of the principal Celtic festivals were Samain at the beginning of November, and Imbole at the beginning of February?

Perhaps, less fancifully, we may note familiar elements of Celtic religion which were already manifest by 3000 BC. Just as later Celtic religion had its subterranean as well as heavenly aspects, so we find these two elements present in the ritual practices of the Age of Stonehenge. The circles, settings and alignments which are eloquent testament to the interest of our people in the heavens are better known than their shafts and pits which betoken interests in the underworld. Wells, pits and shafts were an important element in Celtic ritual right across Europe, as seen notably in the *Viereckschanze* enclosures of Germany. In Britain they can be traced back to the Meldon Bridge period and beyond, for example to the large group at Eaton Heath in Norfolk, varying in depth from 2–8 metres, and to the ring of shafts in the henge at Maumbury Rings.

Concomitant with shafts and especially wells in Celtic religion, were springs, lakes and other waters, whose importance is vouched for both by the archaeological evidence and classical writers such as Poseidonius. Ritual offerings were regularly deposited in sacred pools and springs, for example at sites as far apart as Lake Neuchatel, Switzerland (La Tène), the source of the Seine at Saint-Germain, and Llyn Cerrig Bach on Anglesey. We have seen how in Britain and Ireland this practice seems to have developed as part of an upsurge in water-orientated religion in the Knighton Heath period, shown in the increasing amounts of fine metalwork, especially warrior equipment, deposited in rivers, bogs and other wet places. Those other, more grisly aspects of Celtic religion, human sacrifice and the cult of the head, may also have their antecedents in earlier times. There is more than a suggestion of sacrifice about the sad and often broken bodies and scattered bones recovered from the ditches of causewayed camps, and, later on, hill forts. Isolated heads and skull fragments are frequently encountered. Less explicit are the detached bones and skulls from graves of the Overton and Bedd Branwen periods, which are usually taken to signify disturbance of earlier burials in emptying the grave for fresh deposits. Similarly it is possible that the unaccompanied burials, especially cremations, frequently deposited in the fill of graves above the main burial or burials were sacrificed attendants or subordinates. Slaves loomed large in later Celtic society, indeed Strabo, writing in the first century BC, lists them as one of the main exports from Britain. In a structured society in the Age of Stonehenge, dominated by chiefs and priests, it would not be at all surprising to discover there was a significant slave class.

To sum up: the picture which emerges is of major territories perhaps covering around 1,000 square kilometres, dominated by powerful chiefs and divided into smaller units of a few square kilometres appropriate to septs or enlarged families of complex structure. Most people lived in small farmsteads and hamlets, usually consisting of not more than a few buildings and frequently only a single house. These settlements were scattered within easy reach of each other, each with its few fields and pasture, totalling perhaps a few acres. It is a settlement pattern still found in Co. Donegal and other parts of western Ireland today. One might suppose that in pastoral areas, especially where seasonal movement was involved, the size of individual communities, and thus of home settlements would have been rather greater, but, if so, this has not yet emerged from the evidence. Even in those areas such as Co. Mayo, Wessex, and on the Fen Edge, where enormous acreages were enclosed for stock farming, the associated settlements have proved to be scattered farmsteads.

Small settlements sprinkled across the countryside need a focus, and to a certain extent the local chief, his family and retainers would have provided this. But the scale of some of the great community projects undertaken implies a mechanism, and a meeting place, for bringing together the population of a considerable area, and this is where the henges and great enclosures come in. Just as market towns have varied in size and importance in recent times, so in the Age of Stonehenge it seems logical to suppose there were centres of ascending magnitude. Above all were the great territorial centres, in southern Britain the causewayed enclosures, then their successors in the Mount Pleasant period, the Durrington Walls-Waulud's Bank group of sites. These would have housed fairs, markets, ceremonies and festivals, they were also religious centres, and may well have housed the paramount chief and holy men. Lower down the scale lesser henges may have served smaller areas, and fulfilled some of the functions of the larger sites.

But in many areas such enclosures are unknown and different foci have to be sought. In Scotland the great enclosures at Meldon Bridge and Forteviot defended by massive wooden walls, may show what territorial centres looked like there around 3000 BC. But what went before and after is uncertain. In Ireland enclosures of Monknewtown type have much in common with the great south English enclosures, and no doubt served a similar function. In view of the importance of religion and ceremony in everyday life it may well be that the great chambered tombs took the place of the causewayed enclosures as the territorial centres in parts of the Highland Zone. This might explain the concentrations of apparently domestic activity around the great Irish passage graves of Newgrange and Knowth. One can picture the crowds gathering at the great tomb of Maes Howe on Orkney, and taking up position on its surrounding bank. There are many other monuments which could have served as territorial foci, for example the Stenness-Brodgar complex of rings on Orkney, the Callanish circles and alignments on Lewis, the Clava monument complex in Inverness, the Milfield group of monuments in Northumberland, Mayburgh in Cumbria, Arbor Low in the Peak District, the Rudston and Thornborough complexes in Yorkshire, the Stanton Drew circles in Somerset, the Llandegai sites in north Wales, the sprawling Beaghmore and Lough Gur complexes in Ireland, and so on. If these varied sites did serve as territorial centres, then it would be as important to dig in the areas around the monuments as within them, especially with the lessons of Newgrange and Knowth in mind.

Clothing and ornaments

There is little direct evidence for prehistoric clothing to be found in most of Europe, but in Denmark, contemporary with the Knighton Heath period, there are wonderfully preserved tree-trunk coffins under great barrows, containing a comprehensive range of male and female attire. This affords some idea of the styles of clothing worn by other societies of Second Millennium Europe.

By the Third Millennium the population of Britain and Ireland could draw on wool and linen textiles, as well as skin and leather, for making clothes. The Danish evidence suggests that inhumations were interred fully-clothed, and this is borne out by many British burials in which the fastenings and fittings of clothing are in relevant positions to the body. Thus the Kellythorpe warrior (Figure 4.3) had three v-perforated amber buttons at his throat, where they would have fastened cloak and tunic, while his magnificent gold-studded stone wrist guard was attached to the *outside* of his right wrist by a copper or bronze fastening, and his dagger lay at the small of his back as if it had slipped from his waist. Underneath him a mass of cloth, described as linen, has usually been interpreted as a shroud, but as it appears not to have covered him perhaps it was in fact a cloak, held at the neck by one of the buttons.

Bodies from graves in Britain, as in Denmark, have on occasion been reported as wrapped in shrouds, both skin, as at Gristhorpe, Yorkshire, and cloth, as at Rylston, also in Yorkshire, and Manton in Wiltshire. Perhaps some of these 'shrouds' were in fact loose-fitting clothing of the patterns found in the Danish graves. The females from Danish barrows are variously dressed, perhaps according to season and age. The famous Egtved girl (Figure 4.4), in

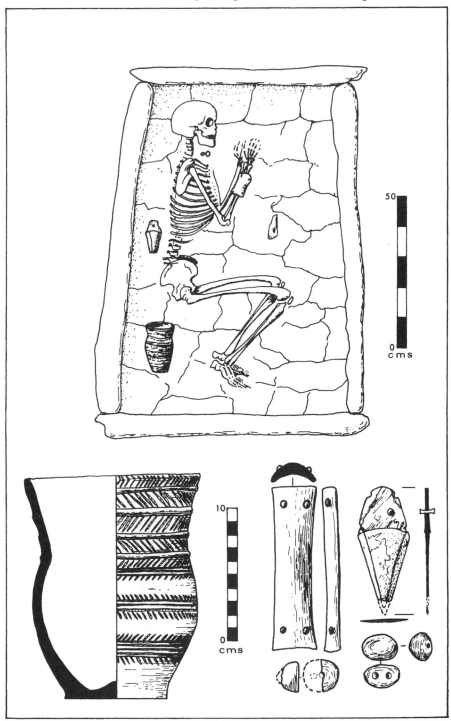

Figure 4.3 Grave at Kelleythorpe, Driffield, Yorkshire (after Mortimer, 1905)

Figure 4.4 Female 'summer' attire and male attire based on finds from Danish tree-trunk coffins (based mainly on Glob, 1974)

her late teens, was clad in an ensemble that was daring even by modern standards. Her skirt, very much a 'mini', was only 15 or 16 inches long, and made from vertically arranged woollen strands gathered at top and bottom in an elaborate edging. It was tied at the top by a knotted bow, the loops of which hung loosely at the front. The position of this skirt on the body suggests it was worn on the hips, leaving much of the stomach exposed. This bare midriff effect was heightened by the short tunic that she wore, of the brown wool which was used for all this Danish clothing. It was well-made, cut in one piece, with gussets at the arm-holes, and was hemmed around a high but wide neck. The half-length sleeves came to just below the elbow.

There was nothing unusual about the Egtved girl's skirt, for contemporary female statuettes are frequently clad in the same sort of garment. To cover her gaping midriff the Egtved girl wore a large circular ornamental disc, mounted on a woven belt with a large tassel at one end. This belt, six and a half feet long, and half an inch wide, had been taken round and round her twenty-three and a half inch waist (disc and belt have been deliberately omitted from the reconstruction (Figure 4.4), the better to appreciate the effect of these garments). Yarrow flowers in the coffin show that the Egtved girl was buried in the summer, which suggests that flimsy attire of this kind would have been worn only in the summer. Alternatively it may have been ritual or ceremonial attire, which might account for its appearance on the statuettes.

Much more sensible clothes were worn by another girl, again in her late teens, from Skrydstrup, and by a very old woman, perhaps in her fifties, from Borum Eshøj. They both wore long, voluminous skirts, reaching down to the ground and loosely gathered in folds at the waist by a long woven belt. To give an idea of size, the Skrydstrup example was made from several pieces of cloth roughly sewn together with thick thread, forming an enormous rectangle 4 feet 9 inches by over 13 feet long, without any sort of hem. The skirt of the Borum Eshøj woman was clumsily joined at the front by a seam stitch, and in both cases the skirts were of much poorer workmanship than the accompanying tunics. It is possible that such enormous skirts could have been multiple purpose garments, worn alternatively as a loose dress, fastened over the shoulders like the ancient Greek *peplos*, and belted at the waist (Figure 4.5) to make an effective summer garment. However, both the Borum Eshøj and Skrydstrup women wore them as long skirts with short tunics, like the Egtved tunic, short-sleeved, and hemmed round the high neck. The Skrydstrup tunic was embroidered at the top of the sleeves, while that worn by the Borum Eshøj woman had a long slit from the neck.

These ladies paid great attention to their hair, and complex coiffures, often held by hair-nets, were commonplace. The Egtved girl was buried with her shoulder-length hair held by a long band made of twisted black wool. But she may sometimes have used the lozenge-mesh net, made of brown wool knotted on to horse-hair, which was also found in her grave. The old woman from Borum Eshøj had much longer hair, two and a half feet long, which was held at the back of her head by a large-meshed woollen hair-net. The Skrydstrup girl had her ash-blonde hair piled high above her forehead on a false pad, possibly made from her own hair. This was held by a square-meshed hair-net of black horse-hair, and then cords were bound several times round the head from back to front to provide added stability. She must have been pleased with the effect,

Figure 4.5 Female dress options, based on finds from Danish tree-trunk coffins (based on Glob, 1974)

for an elaborately woven bonnet lay rolled up by her face, so as not to conceal her hair-do. These ladies also carried horn combs attached to their waist belts.

The men from the Danish graves wore simple, woollen wrap-around inner garments, about upper calf or knee-length, fastened over the shoulders by leather straps, and held around the waist by leather belts. The cut of the breast-line at the front varied, straight and slightly sloping towards the left armpit in the case of the Trindhøj man's costume (Figure 4.4), whereas the Muldbjerg garment was tongued upwards towards the throat. The latter was made of no less than nine pieces of cloth sewn together and over cast. A knee-length woollen cape or short cloak was worn over this inner garment, of rounded cut, oval or kidney shaped, and worn with the margin turned back to form a collar and revers. This dashing ensemble was completed by a jaunty, round woollen cap, either beehive shaped, or, in the case of the Trindhøj man, a taller, more cylindrical shape, with a hem around the rim. The Store Kongehøj cap was stitched to a wooden reinforcing ring. These caps were generally of elaborate workmanship, thick and cushiony, made up of several layers of cloth. The Muldbjerg cap was finished externally with thousands of threads with knotted ends, while the old man from Borum Eshøj had a cap with an inserted pile, creating a fur-like effect. He was more simply clothed, in a rather skimpy wrap-around woollen knee-length kilt, secured by a loosely twisted girdle cord, over which there was a round-cut cape of the usual form. Since some males from the Danish mounds were described as wearing 'shirts'; a combination of kilt and tunic, more akin to the woman's attire, may well have been an alternative to the one-piece inner garment.

These Danish men were clean-shaven, and wore their hair long and combed back. The Muldbjerg chieftain had his fair hair parted in the middle, and he and his fellows were as zealous about their hair as the ladies to judge from the frequency with which horn combs are found in their graves.

Footwear was similar for men and women. It ranged from quite sophisticated leather moccasins stitched round the edges, to cloth foot wrappings, such as seem to have survived in a dug-out coffin in the Yorkshire grave of Loose Howe. The young man from Borum Eshøj had 'traces of sandals' on his feet, whereas the old man from the same site seems to have been shod in woollen material with braided edges. Leather thongs had to be bound securely round the feet and ankles to hold such primitive footwear in place, and cloth was often bound round the ankles to prevent chafing.

The Danish graves are full of elaborate fastening devices notably ornate safety pin fibulae, looped discs and double-headed studs. But most ingenious of all was a kind of pseudo zip-fastener which secured the leather charm bag of the Hvidegard chieftain, formed by interlocking the leather eyelets on opposite sides of the opening, and passing a long pin through them to hold them together (Figure 4.9a). This could be opened instantly by pulling out the pin, but closing, by re-inserting the pin, would have been more difficult.

Over the rest of Europe the evidence for clothing is much less tangible, consisting mainly of fastenings and ornaments. There is nothing, however, to suggest any great departure from the Danish styles. In most regions graves and hoards have regularly produced fibulae, dress pins and other elaborate fastening devices, which, together with cloth fragments, confirm a widespread use of textiles for clothing. But at the beginning of the period there may have been greater use of skin and leather, for contexts of the Corded ware and Beaker phases right across Europe produce v-perforated buttons, which are supposed to be better suited to leather garments than textiles. In Britain a common association in male graves with Beakers is one, or sometimes a pair, of v-perforated buttons in jet or shale (Figure 4.9), less often in amber, together with a bone 'belt-ring'. We have seen that the buttons tend to be found near the throat or upper chest, as if securing a cape. The 'belt-ring', on the other hand, usually occurs near the waist, suggesting use as a simple belt fastening. Differential wear on these rings implies that they were sewn to one end of a leather or cloth belt, the other end of which was brought round the waist, through the ring and knotted. Two basic forms occur, 'magnifying glass' shapes with stem (Figure 4.6c-d), and annular rings, which are usually provided with v-perforations or loops to facilitate sewing to the belt end (Figure 4.9d,e). Others are simple rings, with at most a roughened area to help seat the attachment thread. Such a belt could be used either for a simple wrap around inner garment, as in the Danish graves, or for a kilt, such as seems to be represented on a fragmentary stone menhir at Sion in Switzerland (Figure 4.6g). Perhaps both cloth and leather were used, for capes as well as inner garments. The importance of leather and skins is further indicated by the numbers of metal awls found in graves, and of flint scrapers in the settlements.

But we would do well not to be dogmatic about linking buttons with skin clothing, as the Kellythorpe evidence suggests. For they seem to have been introduced into Britain only towards the end of the Mount Pleasant period, appearing first with step 4 Beakers. If they epitomize skin clothing, what was used in earlier periods? Bone pins are extremely common in some contexts in the Meldon Bridge period, notably in the passage graves of Ireland. Rather later this would be an argument for textile clothing, but as yet there is no evidence for knowledge of textiles before the Mount Pleasant period. So perhaps they were like the long bone skewer pins which were used at that time to secure the necks of cremation bags, and have been found at several cremation cemeteries.

Buttons in ones and twos, together with pulley rings, are common in late Beaker graves. In the same period perhaps a rather different kind of garment is indicated by sets of several small v-perforated buttons, twelve in a grave at Kircaldy, Fife, six with a flat axe, dagger and awl at Butterwick, Yorkshire, and five in the Migdale hoard, Sutherland. Perhaps these fastened leather jerkins or jackets. But some v-perforated buttons may not have been attached to garments at all, for at Acklam Wold Barrow 92 in Yorkshire a skeleton was found with a pair of buttons at each ankle, as if they had fastened boots at the side of the lower leg and ankle. At other sites buttons seem to have been threaded as elements in necklaces.

With the emergence of Únětician traditions in central Europe, some change in fashion is indicated by the appearance of dress pins in large numbers. Before the end of the 'Early Bronze Age' these had spread to much of western and northern Europe. At this point a contrast is usually drawn between a continuing preference for buttons, and thus leather and skin clothes, in Britain, and

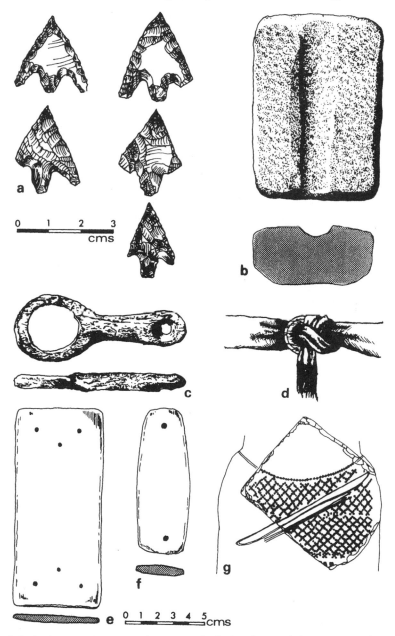

Figure 4.6 Archery equipment and attire: a. barbed-and-tanged flint arrowheads, Springwood, Kelso, Roxburgh; b. stone arrowshaft smoother, Breach Farm, Llanbleddian, Glamorgan; c. bone belt-fastener, Stanton Harcourt, Oxon.; d. suggested mode of use of bone belt ring; e–f. stone wrist plaques ('bracers', 'archers' wrist guards') from Winterslow, Wilts., and Glenforsa, Mull; g. fragment of stone menhir depicting a figure clad in kilt or cape, with bow and arrows, Sion, Switzerland (a. after Henshall and McInnes, 1967–8; b. after Grimes, 1938; c. after Grimes, 1960; d–g. after Clarke, 1970)

pinned textile clothes on the Continent, but this theory will no longer stand scrutiny. The grave evidence makes it clear that v-perforated buttons in Britain were largely a feature of the latter part of the Mount Pleasant period and the Overton period. They are very rare in the Bedd Branwen period, when dress pins of bronze and bone became quite common in graves. The Wessex evidence suggests that these pins, based on Continental forms, appeared at the transition from the Bush Barrow to Aldbourne-Edmondsham traditions. In absolute terms this is *c.* 1600 BC (*c.* 1450 bc), which is not inappropriate if this novel fashion took some time to spread from central Europe. Some of the bone pins found with urn cremations are long and skewer-like, and no doubt served, like the Third Millennium specimens, to fasten cremation bags. But the widespread and numerous examples with variously shaped heads – crutch, ring, multiple ring and lobate and bulb – may well be regarded as dress pins, like their Continental forebears. To illustrate the ubiquity of this new fashion there are pins as far apart as Wessex, Brough-on-Humber and Loose Howe in Yorkshire (both lobate), and Balneil, Wigtown (crutch-headed) (Figures 3.6, 11). The Irish evidence is similar, but v-perforated buttons were nothing like as extensive as in Britain. They are rarely found in grave groups, and such associations as there are, for example in the Mound of the Hostages at Tara, indicate that they belong mainly to the Overton period. Burials with bone pins are much more common, usually with urns or in other contexts suggesting a date in the Bedd Branwen period. Pins with expanded perforated heads or crude ring heads are most common, as at Harristown, Co. Waterford (Figure 2.6), but crutch-headed forms also occur, including a double crutch head at Caltragh, Co. Galway. Belt rings are even scarcer than v-perforated buttons.

This use of pins soon faded out, and interest did not revive until the close of the Taunton phase. Then late Tumulus and early Urnfield pins began to reach these shores, mainly from northern France. Some occur in settlements such as Gwithian, and early hill-forts such as Dinorben and Thwing. These inspired an indigenous series of ornate and often very large dress pins, most of which have been stray finds. But again the fashion was brief, for pins are conspicuous by their absence in the Wilburton-Wallington phase (tenth century BC), and in the Ewart Park phase (ninth to eighth centuries BC) they are common only in Ireland.

The sporadic finds, usually of single pins, from Britain and Ireland contrast notably with the multiple finds common all over the Continent. However they were used, the British and Irish pins cannot have functioned in the same way as the European pins. Large numbers of German Tumulus graves, especially of women, show pairs of long, wicked-looking pins, lethally arranged as if to fasten a garment at both shoulders (Figure 4.7a). We are possibly dealing with a one-piece garment belted at the waist and pinned over the shoulders, of the sort suggested as an alternative way of wearing the long Borum Eshøj and Skrydstrup 'skirts', and much like the Greek *peplos*. But other finds suggest that a long head cloth or scarf of wool was worn, and that this may have been pinned at the shoulders. The Mühltal grave (Figure 4.7) supports this interpretation, for the disposition of decorative studs here suggests a separate knee-length skirt rather than a one-piece garment. Certainly, to have worn these pins on anything other than ceremonial occasions must have been highly dangerous, and less eye-catching fastenings can be postulated for everyday wear. In central Europe as in Denmark we are probably dealing with a variety of female garments, one-piece dresses, tunics such as the Mühltal woman

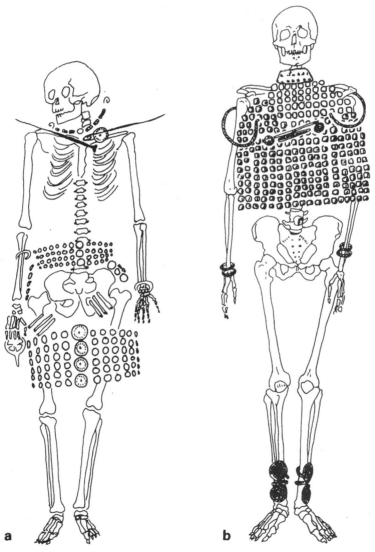

Figure 4.7 Female attire indicated by metal dress fittings: a. Mühltal, South Germany (after Piggott, 1965); b. Lübz, North Germany (after Clark and Piggott, 1970)

presumably wore with her short skirt, and skirts of varying length. East European figurines depict gaily embroidered belted skirts reaching to the floor, much more decorative than the Danish examples.

Over their inner clothes some women wore short waist-length capes. The arrangement of decorative studs on an example in a north German grave (Figure 4.7b), suggests a crew-necked, collared cape, which either slipped on over the head or fastened at the back. The unique and resplendent sheet gold cape from Mold in Flintshire (Figure 4.8), which must have been a great status symbol for the chieftain who owned it, is much shorter, and must be regarded more as an ornament than a garment.

The evidence for men's wear outside Denmark is even less than for women, but the proliferation of dress pins, and, later, fibulae as well, confirm the Danish evidence for cloaks worn over wrap-around inner garments, or kilt and tunic. The ubiquity and longevity of these basic forms of male attire is confirmed by the early First Millennium Nuraghic figurines of Sardinia, which are clad in cloaks, although square instead of round-cut, over one-piece inner garments. Some figures suggest a belted version of the same thing, or a

Figure 4.8 The gold cape from Mold, Flintshire (after Hope-Taylor in Powell, 1953)

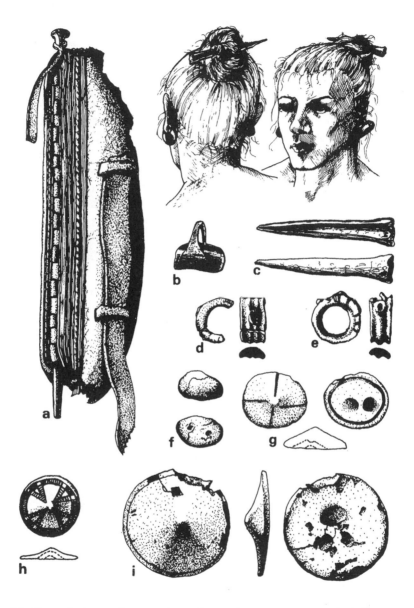

Figure 4.9 Dress fittings and accessories: a. leather bag with 'zip', Hvidegård, Denmark; b. copper or bronze basket-shaped ear-ring, Cowlam, Yorks.; c. bone hair-pin, Aldro 113, Yorks.; the head shows the manner in which ear-rings and hair-pins were worn; d–e. bone belt rings from Clinterty, Aberdeen, and Mainsriddle, Kirkcudbright; f. amber v-perforated button, Kelleythorpe, Yorks.; g, h, i. jet v-perforated buttons from Butterwick, Yorks., Rudstone, Yorks., and West Lilburn, Northumberland (a. after Glob, 1974; b. after Evans, 1881; c, f. after Mortimer, 1905; d–e. after Stevenson, 1956–7; g, h. after Piggott, 1965; i. after Tait, 1965) (scale 2/5)

tunic and kilt, but generally the garment length is shorter than in the cold north, thigh-length rather than knee-length. Cloaks in 'Bronze Age' Europe were made out of skins as well as cloth, and could be singled out for special treatment. In one central European cemetery, for example, fur cloaks had their edges embellished by cording plaited with bronze wires.

The first indication that trousers had reached Europe comes from designs incised on pots of the Hallstatt period from Sopron in Hungary, dating to the sixth century BC. These show trouser-clad men fighting, and also women dressed in full, long skirts, and in short, flaring skirts. It has usually been suggested that trousers reached Europe with knowledge of horse-riding, from the Steppes. In this case an introduction at least a century before the Sopron depictions is likely, at the beginning of the Hallstatt period, or even earlier in the Late Urnfield period, in the eighth century. Close-fitting trousers, worn with tunics, subsequently became the characteristic male clothing of Celtic Europe.

There is regrettably little evidence to indicate how closely 'Bronze Age' clothing in Britain and Ireland resembled that of Denmark and Europe as a whole. But it is clear that the abundance of elaborate fastenings and fittings, so characteristic of the Continent, was never copied. There is slight evidence that our people paid as much attention to their appearance as those in Denmark. Numerous graves of the Overton and Bedd Branwen periods from many parts of the country have produced bone points found immediately behind the skull as if to hold hair gathered into a bun (Figure 4.9). At Garton Slack Barrow 82 in Yorkshire, fragments of thread found underneath the skull of a woman might have been the remains of the hair-net Danish women were wont to wear. There is no evidence for male attitudes to hair. The Celtic male commonly wore a short beard or moustache, but the men in the Danish mound graves were clean shaven. Bronze razors of different types appear to have been in use in Britain and Ireland right through our period, so that men here may also have been clean shaven. Tweezers are also known from the Bedd Branwen period onwards, and the presence of eyebrow hair in a grave at Winterslow, Wiltshire, suggests that they may have been used to pluck out facial hair.

Chapter V

Settlements and Agriculture

For over three thousand years, from the arrival of the first farmers down to the Penard period, the pattern of settlement in these islands changed little. The population everywhere was organized into farmsteads and hamlets housing individual families and enlarged family groups, and even those field systems which covered hundreds of acres, such as Behy-Glenulra in Co. Mayo, or Fengate near Peterborough, were worked from settlements no bigger than this. The uplands of south-west England appear exceptional in that they alone have yielded larger settlement units justifying the term 'village'. These are both enclosed, as at Rider's Rings and Grimspound on Dartmoor, and unenclosed sprawls, such as Stannon Down on Bodmin Moor (Figure 5.8). The largest of these villages may comprise fifty or sixty circular buildings, implying, if only half these were houses, a population of about 150. Yet such sites are unusual even in the south-west, and here too farmsteads with less than a dozen buildings are much more the normal state of affairs.

Two caveats must be entered here. Firstly, there are still areas both of Britain and Ireland where the settlement pattern is little known. In Ireland, particularly, generalizations are dangerous, for although most of the excavated settlements have proved to be small, there are large agglomerations of round stone houses in upland areas which could belong somewhere in our period. The most famous, at Mullaghfarna on the edge of the Carrowkeel passage grave cemetery, comprises forty-seven hut circles, many covered by peat, which may have been a village of the passage grave builders. The second problem is the phenomenon of 'settlement shift'. There are settlements consisting of conjoined or neighbouring clusters of buildings, both enclosed and open, which, at first glance, appear large enough to be villages, but which on closer inspection prove to be successive farmstead units. Each phase is re-positioned slightly, along, up or down the hillside, as the existing site becomes undesirable due to disease, dirt or some similar factor. The best-known examples are some Sussex Deverel-Rimbury sites, notably Itford Hill, but the problem also arises with the unenclosed scooped settlements of the southern Uplands of Scotland. The implication is that such settlements were smaller and longer-lived than previously thought. For example, the excavators of Itford Hill were worried by the lack of evidence for house-rebuilding at their site, and thought they were dealing with a village-sized cluster of enclosed buildings which lasted perhaps a generation. The settlement shift theory sees the site as successive farmsteads, with at least three major phases, representing occupation over centuries. When, as in this case, the units abut or overlap, settlement shift is easy enough to spot, but in the case of detached clusters not even excavation will necessarily provide an answer.

Patterns of settlement

The variety of settlements in our period is remarkable, given their small size. Some are bound by a perimeter, usually a palisade, a wall or a bank and ditch, but others appear to be open. Many adjoin or are surrounded by field systems, pounds, plots or yards, yet even where these have not been found it is no guarantee that they did not exist. Indeed, given the insubstantial character of many of the sites it is no wonder that so many have been found by chance, and explored so incompletely.

Pit and post-hole settlements

The difficulty of identifying buildings at so many settlements has left a widespread impression that people must have lived in tents, or something else unlikely to leave any trace in the archaeological record. This has been linked to the popular belief that people at this time were semi-nomadic pastoralists, who would not have required substantial settlements. But when we contemplate the breathtaking scale of the public monuments of the period, and, even more, the organized landscape in which they stood, there seems to be little room for wandering herdsmen, except over comparatively short distances within defined limits.

The late David Clarke graphically described how one can stand on hundreds of Fen fields in East Anglia strewn with the relics of the intensive occupation of our period, 'sherd after sherd with grain impressions' among the thousands 'ploughed out from pits and post-holes littered with wattle-impressed daub from timber houses'. The fact remains that concentrated though settlement may have been in such areas, excavation has singularly failed to reveal coherent settlement or house plans. Occupation traces there are in plenty, including areas of intense activity, covered with pits, post-holes and hearths, and rich in domestic refuse, but seldom with identifiable structures. There has been considerable excavation at many of these sites, such as Lakenheath in Suffolk, and Chippenham in Cambridgeshire, with no better results. The problem is not peculiar to this area, as the Ballynagilly settlement shows. Here is a site intermittently occupied from the Fifth Millennium, a low hillock of glacial sand rising out of the peat bogs of Co. Tyrone, which attracted considerable activity in the Beaker period. There is the familiar pattern of holes, pits, hearths and rubbish spread over extensive areas, but despite meticulous excavations no satisfactory building plans came to light. The Ballynagilly settlement is rich in Beaker pottery, much of it of sepulchral quality, and a large series of radiocarbon dates, from *c.* 2100–1830 bc, include some of the earliest for Beakers in the British Isles. The pollen record and radiocarbon dates betray a complex sequence of abandonment and re-occupation at this site, with frequent changes of land use.

To judge from a settlement at Swarkeston in Derbyshire, which was preserved only because it was sealed beneath a round barrow, these sites had only light timber structures, unlikely to survive in normal circumstances. We can imagine farmsteads consisting of round stake-built houses, covered with wattle and daub, and perhaps enclosed by stockades. A mixed farming economy is indicated for the eastern regions, with wheat and barley cultivation suggested by grain impressions, and stock raising mainly concerned with cattle and sheep, with some goats and pigs. Deer bones from sites such as Mildenhall suggest that there was some hunting. It is in eastern England in particular that these pit and post-hole settlements are most numerous, producing many of the classic and best known assemblages of 'Beaker domestic ware'.

Two settlements which have produced more tangible structural remains are Willington, on the Trent gravels in Derbyshire, and Hunstanton in Norfolk. At Willington in addition to the usual scatter of pits and holes there were numbers of large structures, round, rectilinear and trapezoidal, employing sizeable posts. The pottery consisted mainly of coarse domestic wares, Beaker and Grooved ware, the last two occurring together in one pit. A similar mixture of structures was found in an extensive settlement complex at Hunstanton. Here large numbers of pits and post-holes were associated with fragmentary lines of post-holes, apparently representing lengths of stockade, and buildings of a variety of shapes including rectangular six-poster and nine-poster structures. Grooved ware was plentiful, together with some Beaker and Peterborough material. This phase of the settlement gave a radiocarbon date of *c.* 1736 bc.

Early enclosed settlements

The Hunstanton remains also included a rectangular palisade enclosure, measuring about 47 × 36 metres, at one end of which was a trapezoidal post-hole structure. The associated pottery was Grooved ware. Later occupation on the site is indicated by a number of pits, and a circular porched building producing Collared Urn sherds.

The Hunstanton palisade enclosure is one of a growing number of such settlements known from many parts of Britain and Ireland, enough to suggest that stockaded farmsteads were everywhere a familiar feature of the landscape. The flimsy nature of the stake-built double stockade at Swarkeston, explains why more have not survived. Both single and double stockade enclosures are known, some curvilinear, some rectilinear, some having post trenches, others having individual stake or post-holes. Of those from the Overton period, the Swarkeston example appears to be part of one side of a double, individual stake-hole, rectilinear stockade, resembling that around the Phase 8 house at Gwithian, Cornwall, which was, however, a single line. Kilellan Farm on the Isle of Islay produced a double palisade of curvilinear plan, utilizing close-set bedding trenches. Other stockades have been found as far apart as Lockerbie, Dumfries, probably associated with Grooved ware, and thus of the Meldon Bridge or Mount Pleasant periods; Cullyhanna Lough, Co. Armagh, where oak stakes gave radiocarbon dates of *c.* 1525 bc and 1355 bc; and at Findon in Sussex, where a stockaded enclosure contained a single building and yielded sherds of Collared Urn. Some early palisades are on an altogether different scale. Those at the eponymous sites of Meldon Bridge (*c.* 2330, 2150 bc) and Mount Pleasant (*c.* 1695, 1687 bc) are not strictly relevant to this discussion since they are massive defensive works on 'public' sites, employing timbers up to several tons in weight in palisades which may have stood 3–4 metres high (Plates I, VI).

At Playden in Sussex (Figure 5.1) a rectilinear ditched enclosure was defined by a ditch with a stockade on its inner margin. This site, which produced Grooved ware and a date of *c.* 1740 bc, introduces a group of enclosed settlements with bank and ditch perimeters. Both rectangular and curvilinear examples are known, mainly in southern and eastern England. The arrangement of bank and ditch varies, sometimes one on the inside, sometimes the other. They are generally of farmstead size, large enough to surround a few buildings at most. Structural remains are usually tenuous, but a second enclosure at Playden in Sussex, a ring ditch about 20 metres in diameter, had at its centre a round building *c.* 6 metres in diameter, its wall consisting partly of spaced posts, partly of lengths of foundation trench (Figure 5.1). A similar building just outside the perimeter of the Waulud's Bank enclosure, was associated with Grooved ware. A rather different structure, consisting of an oval hollow about 3 × 2.5 metres, walled round with turf, was positioned eccentrically within a large circular ditched enclosure at Streatley in Bedfordshire (Figure 5.1).

These circular ditched enclosures are indistinguishable from the ring ditches which occur in such vast numbers on English river gravels, and which have usually been interpreted as ploughed-out ditched burial mounds. It now seems that many of the ring ditches in fact began life as ditched settlements and, like that at Playden, were only subsequently converted into burial sites. One such ring-ditched farmstead at Fengate was incorporated into a system of ditched stock enclosures. Grooved ware and radiocarbon dates of *c.* 2030–1930 bc may refer to its early use. Eventually this farmstead was abandoned, and a turf burial mound was built within the ring ditch covering a Collared Urn cremation with a date of *c.* 1460 bc. Similarly occupation debris in a ring ditch

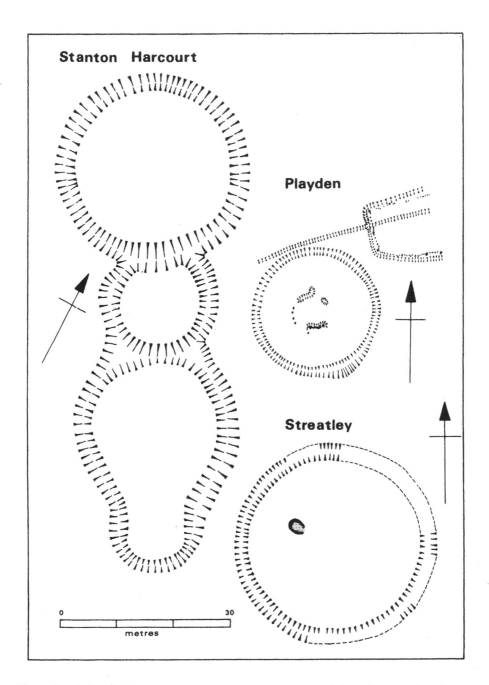

Figure 5.1 Ring-ditch settlements: Stanton Harcourt, Oxon. (after Hamlin and Case, 1963); Playden, Sussex (after Cheney, 1935); Streatley, Beds. (after McInnes, 1971)

at Warren Farm, Milton Keynes in Buckinghamshire, suggests it started out as a settlement enclosure (*c.* 1500 bc), and was much later converted to take a series of burials. A final example is the triple ring-ditch at Stanton Harcourt in Oxfordshire (Figure 5.1), which was eventually used for burial purposes, but may have been built as a house enclosure with adjoining stock pens.

There are also rectilinear bank and ditch enclosures. The one at Playden shows some had palisades, but most are plough damaged and survive only as simple, ditched rectangular enclosures, with little trace either of bank or internal structures, like those at Barford, Warwickshire, filled with a jumble of post-holes, at Fengate, and at Sonning in Berkshire. Even the comparatively well-preserved example at Belle Tout in Sussex yielded only very tenuous traces of buildings, despite meticulous excavation. Here on the edge of the cliffs west of Beachy Head (Plate XI) two overlapping enclosures were built across a small dry valley and up its sides. The earlier and smaller, measuring at least *c.* 64 × 35 metres, had dropped into the sea apart from one corner. So too has much of the superimposed enclosure, at least twice the size of the smaller site, although one complete side, 120 metres long, survives. Whereas the small enclosure had an internal bank, the larger site had an external bank, with an entrance gap on the east. The interior contained very faint traces of buildings and activity areas indicated by slots, gulleys, sporadic post-holes, pits, hearths and middens. Reconstructions suggest mainly curvilinear buildings, each with its storage pits concentrated just inside the entrance. Much of the activity here seems to have been within some sort of compound which enclosed knapping and working sites, hearths, pits and a midden, as well as the buildings. Another scatter of post holes indicated a rectilinear structure or structures. Some of the features were associated with AOC Beaker sherds and appear to pre-date the enclosure, but the main occupation was associated with a large domestic assemblage that included both comb-decorated and fingernail rusticated Beaker, and also a mass of plain, often thick sherds, from vessels of uncertain shape. Others, with horizontal and vertical ribbing, resemble Grooved ware. This is one of those typical 'Beaker domestic' assemblages, which could well benefit from re-examination in the light of new Beaker concepts.

Settlements under burial sites

The re-use of ring-ditched farmsteads as burial sites raises the wider question of the relationship between houses for the living and houses for the dead. Unknown numbers of burial mounds were built on top of abandoned settlements. Usually the remains consist of an occupation layer with scattered refuse, post-holes, pits and hearths, as under barrows at Arreton Down, West Overton, Reffley Wood in Norfolk, and Chippenham in Cambridgeshire. Structures are sometimes found, as at Swarkeston, while at Sant-y-nyll in Glamorgan and Codicote in Hertfordshire, the mounds sealed curvilinear buildings. The presence or absence of structures may indicate nothing more than the extent of the excavation, for all too often only the centres of burial mounds are removed.

The tendency has been to assume these are accidental juxtapositions of burial mound and underlying settlement, the two separated by an appreciable time-lag. However, in few cases has the relationship between occupation layer and overlying burial mound been tested in the light of modern chronologies. It is possible that some of these burial sites were raised specifically to house the dead occupants of the settlement underneath, but seldom can assumption be disentangled from fact. For example, palisades and stake rings found under many burial mounds are interpreted as part of the funerary structure, which in some cases they undoubedly are, but it is worth considering that some represent earlier settlement stockades. Many more burial mounds were raised over settlements than we now believe, for it is known that the sepulchral sites were prepared – 'purified' – by burning off or stripping off the surface deposits. In the preparatory stripping under the platform cairn Brenig 51 in Denbighshire, a small patch of the original surface was missed, and this proved to be part of an occupation layer.

This conjunction of dwellings for the living and the dead was nothing new. Some of the mortuary houses and chambers incorporated in long barrows and megalithic tombs must have resembled everyday houses, for example the large rectangular timber building under the Nutbane long barrow, Hampshire. Just such a house was found beneath the chambered tomb at Ballyglass in Co. Mayo, and later, in the Mount Pleasant period, the Bryn yr Hen Bobl chambered tomb, Anglesey, was raised over a settlement rich in pottery.

It is important to consider each of these juxtapositions on its merits, especially as it is now known that disused, exhausted land was often chosen, very sensibly, as the site for burial mounds. The biological evidence from beneath many barrows on the Wessex chalk shows they were sited in scrub, or dank grassland, land abandoned and reverting to woodland. More intensive study of superimposed barrows and occupation sites should tell us much about the abandonment of land at different periods, and the lapse of time between living house and dead house.

Deverel-Rimbury settlements

The best-known settlements of our period are the Deverel-Rimbury sites found on the chalk of Wessex and Sussex. The remains of those off the chalk tend to be much more tenuous, and have often come to light accidentally, like the sites in the Farnham district of Surrey, which were discovered in the course of gravel-digging. Extensive scatters of sherds and other refuse, pits, postholes and saddle mills point to considerable settlements, but until large-scale rescue operations became possible in recent years, there was little chance of recovering structures. Now the Thames Valley has begun to produce a scatter of Deverel-Rimbury settlements, including palisade sites. At Abingdon in Berkshire a large rectilinear palisade enclosed both round houses and four-posters, while at Muckhatch Farm, Thorpe, Surrey, curvilinear lengths of palisade were drawn round pits and holes, adjacent to a round individual post-hole structure. Similar settlements may well have been scattered all along the Thames gravels, ploughed-down versions of the better-preserved sites on the chalk.

Not all Deverel-Rimbury settlements on the chalk survive as earthworks. Many pit and post-hole sites and scatters of material on ploughed fields point to levelled and unenclosed settlements. The standard settlement unit on the chalk was an embanked farmstead, usually ditchless in Sussex, of curvilinear or sub-rectangular shape, measuring up to 50 metres across. They contained up to four or five circular timber buildings, where necessary on platforms cut back into the downland slopes. Such settlements often stand within, or adjoin, Celtic field systems, with which they may be intimately connected by tracks or lynchet ways (Figure 5.2). Some sites consist of a group of such enclosures, which may be adjacent, as at Plumpton Plain A, contiguous or overlapping, as at Itford Hill. In some cases the enclosures may be contemporary, but Itford Hill (Figure 5.3), provides a good example of settlement shift, its three overlapping enclosure groups representing three major construction phases. Each rebuilding involved a slight shift across the hillside, so as not to sit directly on the existing compounds, parts of which may have been retained for occupation, or some other specific purpose. Beaker sherds suggest that Itford Hill *may* have been founded as early as the Overton period, but it was still flourishing as late as any Deverel-Rimbury settlement to judge from its pottery, and a radiocarbon date of *c.* 1000 bc.

Even individual enclosures, too, may have had a more complex history than has usually been entertained. At Shearplace Hill in Dorset (Figure 5.4) a palisade phase preceded the main enclosure banks, and this may also have happened at Plumpton Plain A, New Barn Down and Itford Hill. The Sussex enclosures are usually embanked and without a ditch, but Cock Hill had an internal flat-bottomed ditch. This is an altogether extraordinary site, combining a henge-like ditch containing the skeleton of a baby, a bank and a palisade, all on the same circuit, food vessel and Beaker pottery, and, under the bank, a pestle-shaped bead like those in Bush Barrow graves; also a cremation cemetery, round timber buildings, Deverel-Rimbury pottery and abundant occupation material. All this suggests a multi-period site, and one which had served, successively, very different functions. Its history cannot now be certainly reconstructed from the excavation report, but it may be tentatively suggested that a henge-like, ditched ritual site of the Overton period, associated with the Beaker and food vessel material, and possibly the cremation cemetery, was followed by an embanked and palisaded settlement of conventional Deverel-Rimbury type.

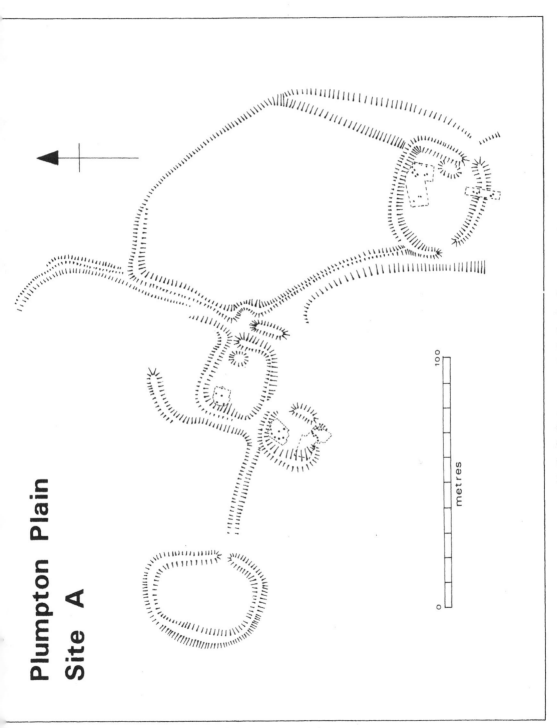

Plumpton Plain
Site A

metres

100

0

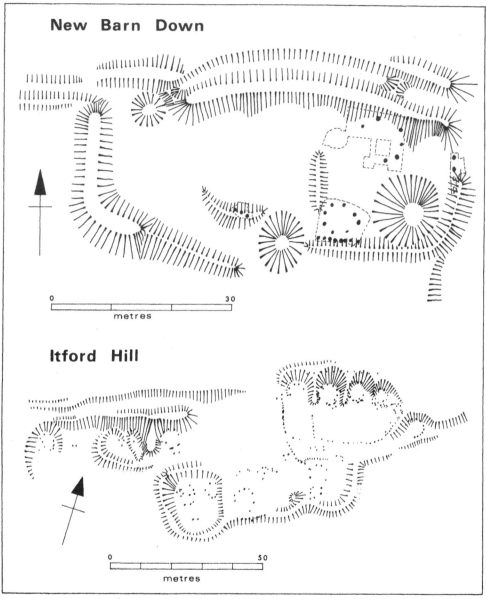

Figure 5.3 Deverel-Rimbury settlements in Sussex: New Barn Down (after Curwen, 1934), and Itford Hill (after Burstow and Holleyman, 1957, and Cunliffe, 1974)

Unlike the Sussex enclosures, those of Wessex are normally ditched. The site at Shearplace Hill shows how an apparently simple site may have had a very complex history. It began as a ditched enclosure, perhaps in the Bedd Branwen period, which was superseded by a palisade enclosure, with at least one round house. These phases were associated with Collared Urn as well as Deverel-

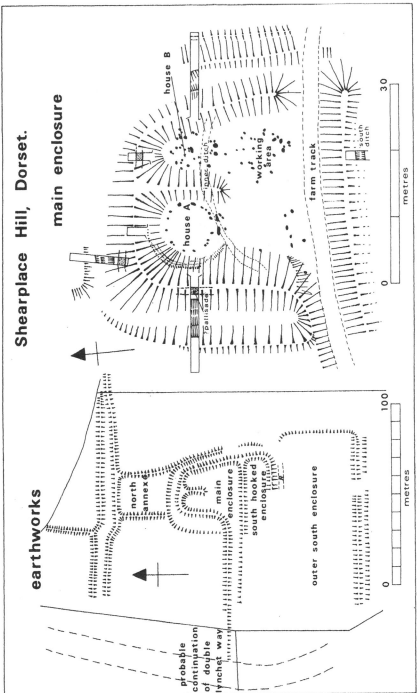

Figure 5.4 Deverel-Rimbury settlement at Shearplace Hill, Dorset (after Rahtz and ApSimon, 1962, and Avery and Close-Brooks, 1969)

Rimbury sherds, and a combined sample gave a radiocarbon date of *c.* 1180 bc. Next, in the Knighton Heath period, came a bank and ditch enclosure, subsequently subdivided, and it is at this stage of development that the settlement with its fields, pounds, and hollow ways, survived until recent times.

Similar settlements are scattered throughout Wessex, but those excavated by General Pitt-Rivers on Cranborne Chase in north Dorset and Hampshire, a group in the upper Avon basin on the south side of Salisbury Plain, and those on the Marlborough Downs in north Wiltshire, are especially well known (Figure 5.5). These Wessex enclosures overlap the Sussex ones in size at the smaller end of their range, but differ in having ditches as well as banks. Larger examples range up to 2 acres in area and over 100 metres across. Some of the Sussex enclosures have discontinuous banks, and this peculiarity is exaggerated still further in some of these Wessex sites (Figure 5.6). It is common to find one side or corner apparently completely open, as at Martin Down or Ogbourne Down west, while Angle Ditch comprises only an L-shaped length of bank and ditch. Various suggestions have been made as to how these gaps were closed, the most popular being thorn hedges or palisade lines, neither of which would leave any trace on the surface.

Doubts about the history and function of these sites sprang from General Pitt-Rivers' failure to locate structures in those he excavated. Since they produce much animal refuse, they have generally been regarded as stock pounds, especially for cattle, and this notion was strengthened by the more recent excavations of the Preshute example, the interior of which was described as having an old ground surface 'compacted through much trampling', as if by animals. But this and other recent excavations have been so slight as to be inconclusive. The only example to have been stripped in modern times, Thorny Down in Wiltshire, was full of post-holes, amidst which several structures could be identified. And now re-excavation of the South Lodge example, still proceeding, has recovered clear traces of buildings, confirming long-held doubts about Pitt-Rivers' ability to recognize post-holes. These sites are rich in finds for stock pounds (Figure 3.14), so it comes as no surprise to find that they were the equivalent in Wessex of the enclosed farmsteads of Sussex. Like the Sussex sites many examples lay within their field systems, South Lodge and Martin Down for example (Figure 5.14). In fact South Lodge proves to have been built on an existing field system. A similar mixed farming economy to that of Sussex may be postulated, but with a trend increasingly towards cattle herding. Their chronological range also seems very much the same as that of the Sussex sites. South Lodge, with a Class Ia razor and Barrel urn in its primary ditch silt, began in the Bedd Branwen period, but the finds higher up in its ditch are appropriate to the Taunton phase of the Knighton Heath period. On the other hand Angle Ditch may have started as South Lodge was finishing, for a transitional palstave of the Penard period was found in its

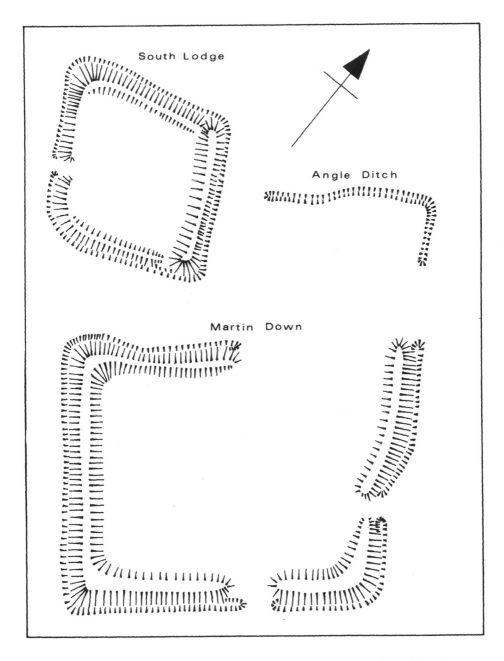

South Lodge

Angle Ditch

Martin Down

Figure 5.5 Deverel-Rimbury enclosures on Cranborne Chase dug by General Pitt-Rivers (after Pitt-Rivers, 1898, and C. M. Piggott, 1942) (various scales)

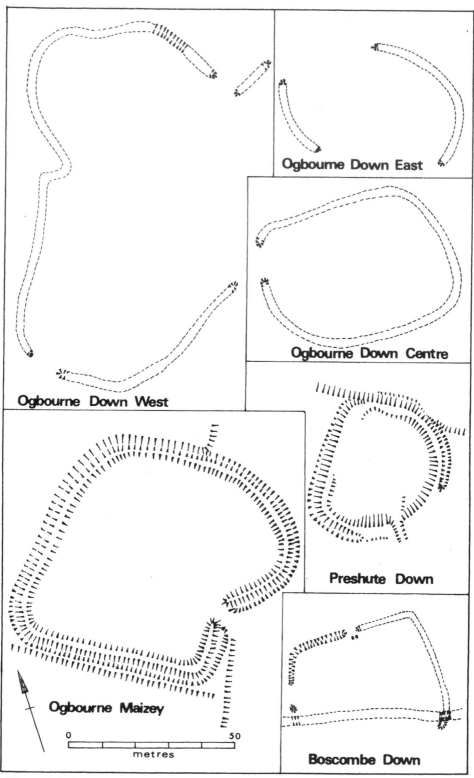

Ogbourne Down East

Ogbourne Down Centre

Ogbourne Down West

Ogbourne Maizey

Preshute Down

Boscombe Down

0   50

metres

Figure 5.6 Deverel-Rimbury enclosures in Wiltshire (after C. M. Piggott, 1942, except Boscombe Down, after Stone, 1936)

Figure 5.7 Reconstruction of a Sussex Deverel-Rimbury settlement amidst its fields (based on New Barn Down)

primary silt, together with a thin-walled 'post Deverel-Rimbury' jar indicative of new traditions (Figure 3.17).

This is not to deny the existence of specialized cattle pounds, although the evidence at present suggests most of these lie outside our period. The likeliest candidates are small enclosures adjoining the so-called ranch boundaries in north Wiltshire and Berkshire, but unfortunately none of these have been excavated. Of the superficially similar enclosures elsewhere, that at Harrow Hill, Sussex, produced between fifty and a hundred cow skulls from a small excavation, showing that whatever else was happening here cattle were being butchered in large numbers. Harrow Hill and similar enclosures, such as Bow Hill in Sussex and Portsdown Hill in Hampshire (which was built up against an existing linear boundary), were probably constructed in the First Millennium, after a far-reaching change-over to pastoralism in the Penard period. The only Deverel-Rimbury enclosure known to have been incorporated into this new farming pattern is that at Boscombe Down East in Wiltshire (Figure 5.6), where one of the new ranch boundaries was so arranged as to take in the enclosure. But the excavations were too slight to reveal whether it continued as a settlement or now became a cattle pound.

Another important class of Deverel-Rimbury settlement on the chalk is the (apparently) unenclosed farmstead. These consist of one or more round timber houses, often on platforms cut into the hillside, standing amidst or adjoining Celtic fields. Because they lack enclosing banks they are usually discovered accidentally, as happened in road-building at Chalton, or they may be revealed by surface scatters of pottery and other domestic refuse, as at Eldon's Seat, Dorset. There has been insufficient excavation to determine whether such sites really were unprotected, or whether they stood within levelled earthworks or stockades. Some of the most famous Sussex sites fall into this 'open' category, including Amberley Mount and Park Brow, and isolated house platforms were also found on the hillside 75 metres below the main settlement at Itford Hill. Clearly such 'open' sites will be visible on the surface only in ideal circumstances, and many more must lie hidden, their discovery a matter of chance or careful fieldwork.

Deverel-Rimbury settlements seem to have been based on a mixed farming economy, with the herding of cattle, some sheep, and a few pigs. Both barley and wheat were grown in Celtic fields, the emphasis no doubt varying with the type of soil. At Itford Hill the carbonized grain recovered from a storage pit consisted largely of hulled barley, with a little emmer, but naked barley may have predominated in earlier Deverel-Rimbury contexts, and wheat may have been more popular on less dry soils. The relatively small quantities of rubbish present within the settlements suggests that it was taken out with the night soil and spread on the fields. This would explain particularly why so few joining sherds are found within the farmstead area, and why so much refuse is scattered on the fields. Hunting was not important. To judge from frequent finds of spindlewhorls and loomweights each community made its own cloth from its own wool, while numerous flint scrapers suggest that the animals provided leather as well as meat and milk.

South-west England

Trevisker wares are to south-west England what Deverel-Rimbury wares are to south-central and south-east England. They are similarly associated with well-preserved settlements, which survive best, not unnaturally, on upland areas such as Dartmoor, Bodmin Moor and Penwith.

It is clear that by the Mount Pleasant period, and perhaps even earlier, farmers were clearing patches of land in the oak forest which covered much of these uplands. In the Overton and Bedd Branwen periods this clearance was stepped up until much of the land below 1,400 feet was open. On Dartmoor there may already have been extensive areas of blanket peat on the tops above this height. Increasing human interference with the soil will have reduced ever-larger areas to moorland, and the deterioration of the climate in the second half of the Second Millennium can only have hastened the spread of peat bog. Thus the great era of upland settlement in the south-west seems to have lasted through the Bedd Branwen and Knighton Heath periods, with activity declining as conditions worsened towards the end of the Millennium. The petering out of Trevisker pottery and upland settlement went hand in hand, and by the Penard period both seem to have disappeared from the archaeological record.

The upland settlements consist of circular stone buildings arranged either in enclosed or open groups, associated with yards, paddocks, stone walls and field systems. On Dartmoor, marked differences have been claimed between settlements largely devoted to pastoralism and those more concerned with arable farming, but recent work suggests these distinctions may have been exaggerated. The different environmental requirements of the arable and pastoral sites are supposed to show in their respective distributions. Two types of 'pastoral' settlements have been distinguished (Figure 5.8). Enclosed sites, which at Rider's Rings and Grimspound attain the size of considerable villages, are usually found on southwards facing slopes close to good water supplies on the south side of the moor. In the absence of attached fields cultivation is unlikely to have been important except on a garden scale, and this may have been the purpose of the small, walled plots seen at some sites. Many of these enclosed settlements consisted of different-sized enclosures appended to one another, suggesting successive phases of expansion. Rider's Rings and Yes Tor Bottom consist of two such enclosures, while Legis Tor has three.

The second type of pastoral settlement is open, and consists of a cluster of circular buildings, many of which are linked by low walls which may be so arranged as to form irregular enclosures or plots. Some houses may be

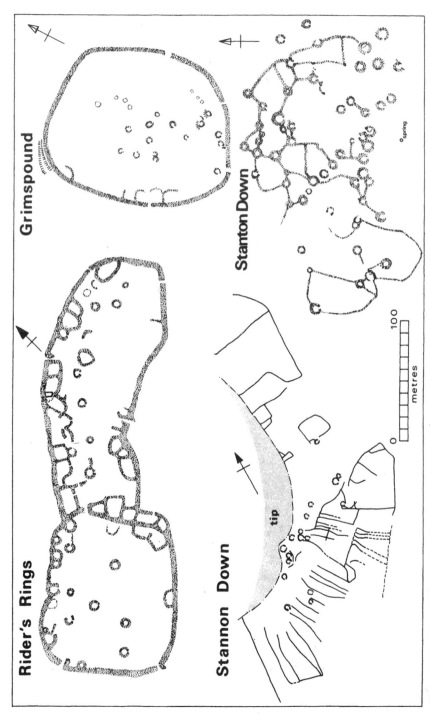

Figure 5.8   Upland 'pastoral' settlements in south-west England: Rider's Rings (after Worth, 1935 and 1953), Grimspound (after A. Fox, 1957) and Stanton Down (after Baring Gould, 1902) all on Dartmoor, Devon: Stannon Down on Bodmin Moor, Cornwall (after Mercer, 1970)

detached, however. Good examples of this type of open settlement are Watern Oke in the Upper Tavy valley, and Stannon Down, whose sixty-eight huts show that these settlements, too, can reach village proportions. They are not as common as the other settlement types of Dartmoor, and concentrate almost entirely on the wetter western fringes of the Moor. Similar settlements exist on Bodmin Moor, although these tend to be more straggly, as at Stannon Down and Rough Tor, and may be associated with more, and larger, enclosures. The walled plots and querns at Stannon Down indicate some cereal cultivation, but never more than enough to supplement a largely pastoral economy.

The so-called arable settlements, also open, tend to be smaller, consisting of a hut, at most a few huts, associated with a field system (Figure 5.9). A distinction can perhaps be made between those farmsteads which front on to a few small, square or rectangular plots or fields, and those which stand in the midst of a larger system of 'Celtic' fields. The fields associated with the first group frequently total only one or two acres, as at Blissmoor and Rippon Tor. Horridge Common, an example of the second type, is surrounded by fields covering 7.6 acres. This site has four buildings, and working on a basis of one acre to feed one man, it is clear that even here the community could not rely entirely on its crops. Stock raising must have been important to these 'arable' farmsteads as to the pastoral sites, although the greater emphasis on cultivation explains their concentration on the drier and lower eastern flanks of Dartmoor.

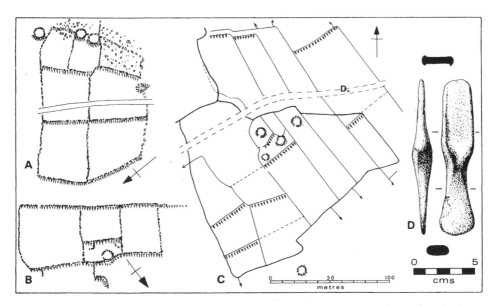

Figure 5.9 'Arable' settlements on Dartmoor: A. Blissmoor; B. Rippon Tor (after A. Fox, 1954); C. Horridge Common, and D. Bohemian palstave found in one of its fields (after A. Fox and Britton, 1969)

A profoundly significant discovery of recent years has been that the extensive reave or dyke systems of Dartmoor belong not to the medieval period but to the Second Millennium. As such they have to be incorporated into this discussion of south-western upland settlement, although they will be considered in greater detail below in the section on field systems. It is now clear that these reaves divided much of Dartmoor up into territorial blocks, and separated good land from moorland tops. Obviously all the settlements, which have usually been considered in isolation, now have to be fitted into the framework of the main reave system. The clearest illustrations of this integrated pattern are the many settlement enclosures attached to, or incorporated in, reaves (Figure 5.16), but in addition we can now see that many field systems are defined by, and sometimes connected to, reaves. For example, at the Rippon Tor settlement (Figure 5. 9), one side of the field system abuts on to a reave which extends for about one kilometre.

Recent excavations of a reave-side settlement at Holne Moor on Dartmoor (Pl. XII) have revealed that both reave and settlement had complex histories. Here the reave began as a bank and ditch system before reconstruction in the familiar dyke form, while the settlement buildings included a succession of ring-groove timber buildings and stone structures. Cultivation was carried on in plots too small to permit anything other than a man-drawn ard. There was ploughing until the bitter end, for traces of the final linear plough marks were uncovered, cut in ground that was becoming increasingly waterlogged and useless.

The economy of upland settlements in the south-west thus appears to have been based on stock raising in a highly organized landscape, combined with whatever cultivation local soils and climate, would permit. The nature of the country and of the farming suggests the possibility of transhumance, if only a simple form involving summer pasturing on the moor tops.

The Trevisker site, at only 350 feet OD, near St. Eval in Cornwall, shows that at lower levels settlements might consist of circular timber, not stone, buildings. This could give a clue to the elusiveness, throughout the south-west, of settlements from the Penard period onwards. Marginal upland areas, such as Bodmin Moor and Dartmoor, on which our stone-built settlements are best known, would have been the first to be affected by the climatic deterioration and ecological changes of the later Second Millennium. Deterioration of soil and pasture, and the spread of peat and moorland, were caused as much by deforestation and cultivation as by climatic change, and would have brought widespread abandonment of the higher farms. After Stannon Down was abandoned, at some time in the late Second Millennium, a thin band of peat was already forming on the fields before the hut walls had time to collapse. The lower areas, which had to absorb this retreat from the uplands, were probably heavily wooded, so that new settlements would involve extensive clearance, and would thus be timber built, in the Trevisker style. Yet Trevisker itself was abandoned at this time, and Gwithian soon after, and neither can help fill the settlement gap of several centuries down to traditional 'Iron Age' sites such as Bodrifty and Kestor. If there was a retreat from the uplands, this may have led to more formal transhumance, from lowlands to upland, but with the lowland settlements proving so elusive, this remains purely conjectural.

Gwithian, in its coastal setting, and deeply stratified under blown sand, at present appears unique amongst south-western mainland settlements, but compares in many respects with the stone-built, often sand-covered farmsteads of the Scillies. Some of the Scillonian sites, such as Halangy Porth and Perpitch, like Gwithian are intimately connected with field systems. Grain impressions on their pottery, a local version of Trevisker ware, confirm the cultivation of cereals. Surface observation suggests that such settlements are abundant on the islands, and that there are sites like Gwithian widespread on the mainland, but there has been little modern excavation. (Figure 5.10.)

The layer 5 settlement at Gwithian consisted of a system of small fields lying downhill from a circular ditched farmstead enclosure. The field divisions consisted of stone clearance banks, lynchets and ditches, and the fields showed extensive areas of criss-cross ard marks. Layers of blown sand above and below distinguished this phase from earlier and later levels of activity. In the lowest level that concerns us, layer 8, the house was first an irregular timber construction, then a fine circular porched building with a double stake ring wall (Figure 5.12e). The pottery from this level, and layer 7 above, included not only Beaker but also thick, coarse plain wares and flower-pot shaped jars with a decorated zone on the upper part of the body. These are early representatives of the Trevisker series, decorated with cord impressions, especially plaited, in layer 8, and with incised ornament in layer 7. The well-preserved layer 5 farmstead, following after a sand-blow, has middle Trevisker styles, and a radiocarbon date of *c*. 1320 BC (*c*. 1120 bc). This is about the same date as that of the Bohemian palstave found in one of the fields at the Horridge Common settlement on Dartmoor (Figure 5.9d). After another blow, the layer 3 occupation is more limited, but several circular stone buildings were now erected within the fields. This level was associated with late Trevisker pottery, and a fragmentary stone mould for socketed axes of an elongated form with converging ribs, while the house yielded two early Urnfield ('Mels-Rixheim') bronze pins. These finds can be securely dated to the Penard period.

Occupation at Gwithian, as at so many other sites, petered out at this point. What happened next to settlement patterns in the south-west is not clear. In part the answer must lie in a re-appraisal of the known finds, in further accidental discoveries, and in examination of local hill-forts and 'rounds'. It was, after all, underneath a 'round' that the Trevisker settlement came to light. But a solution may also lie in the pottery sequence. When the local equivalent of the 'post Deverel-Rimbury' pottery of Wessex is identified, then

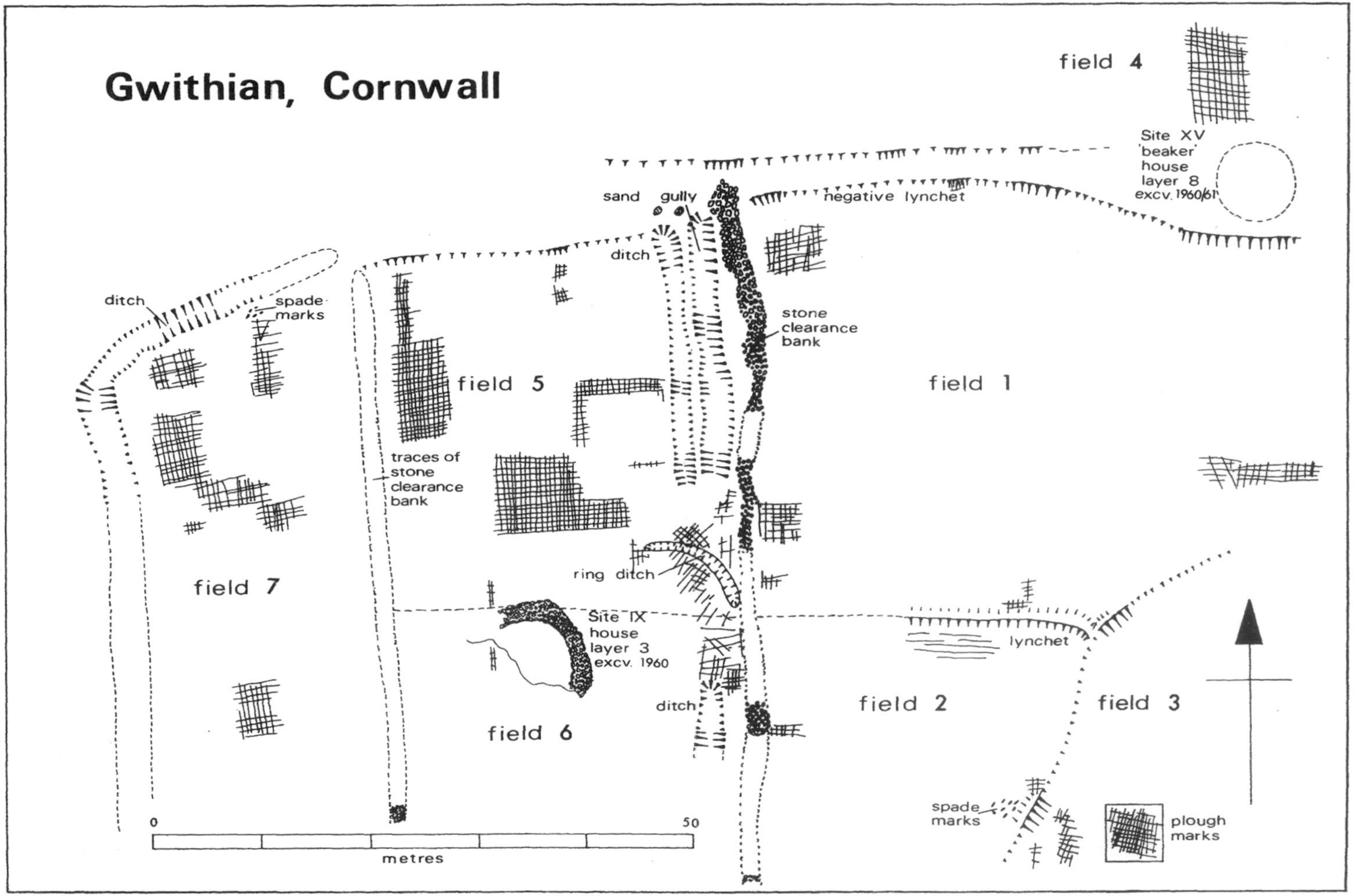

Gwithian, Cornwall

field 4

field 1

field 5

field 7

field 3

field 2

field 6

Site XV
'beaker'
house
layer 8
excv. 1960/61

negative lynchet

stone
clearance
bank

sand

gully

ditch

traces of
stone
clearance
bank

spade
marks

ditch

ring ditch

Site IX
house
layer 3
excv. 1960

ditch

lynchet

spade
marks

plough
marks

metres

0   50

ʼ) Celtic fields at Gwithian, Cornwall, plan mainly at lower 5 level (after Megaw 1976)

it may tell us something about the settlements of the late Second and early First Millennia in the south-west.

Settlements in other upland areas

The discovery of the Dartmoor reaves has sent archaeologists throughout Britain scurrying to look at their own upland dykes and field walls, and already there are signs of similar agrarian systems in other Highland Zone regions. Settlements and fields resembling the south-western examples are known from many areas, but have usually been assigned to the 'Iron Age' and Romano-British period – which many undoubtedly are. But an enclosure with a stone house at Swine Sty (Figure 5.13), so like some south-western settlements, has proved to belong to the Overton or Bedd Branwen periods, and warns against too ready acceptance of late dates. Bearing in mind the marginality of agriculture in these islands, any trace of cultivation above 800 feet, if not early Medieval has a good chance of belonging to that other period of mild climate, the Second Millennium. Thus recent discoveries in the Pennines of Upper Teesdale should come as no surprise, revealing stone-built settlements and dykes not only of the Viking period, but also of the Second Millennium BC, in some cases the two sitting one on the other.

The problem over much of upland Britain is that there has been too little landscape survey, and still less excavation. The enormous potential is revealed by recent large-scale surveys on the island of Arran, bringing to light settlements in an agrarian landscape now shown by excavation to go back at least to the Mount Pleasant period. Round stone houses lined with wickerwork (Plate XII) are associated with a domestic pottery assemblage which includes sherds of Beaker. These settlements lasted for much of the Second Millennium, but were abandoned in the Penard phase (*c.* 1009 bc).

Any modern upland excavation, even if not primarily concerned with Second Millennium settlement, is likely to reveal traces of occupation and cultivation. The Brenig excavations, 1200–1300 feet up on the Denbighshire moors, are a case in point. The only visible indication of prehistoric settlement here was a cairnfield, representative of a class of field monument found throughout upland areas of Britain and Ireland. We shall see shortly that cairnfields appear to represent field clearance, in many cases indicating Second Millennium agriculture.

The lack of survey and excavation over much of the Highland Zone is such that there are still whole classes of sites about which little or nothing is known. The excavation of the Green Knowe settlement in Peeblesshire is a good illustration (Plate XIV). This is an unenclosed scooped or platform settlement, a class which at present has a curious distribution, several dozen examples being packed into a comparatively small area of Lanark and Peebles. The fact that outliers are known as far off as Argyll and Northumberland suggests this distribution is entirely artificial, reflecting only areas of intensive fieldwork.

Equally the fact that most lie above 800 feet OD shows only the 'tide mark' of agricultural destruction. The Green Knowe excavations have revealed that at least some unenclosed scooped settlements were built and occupied in the Knighton Heath period. In the local Border context they are important, too, because hitherto practically nothing has been known about settlements there before the appearance of palisades and then hillforts from the eighth to the seventh centuries BC.

Green Knowe has produced four radiocarbon dates between 1200–1000 bc, making it contemporary with Deverel-Rimbury settlements such as Itford Hill and Chalton. This makes all the more interesting the superficial resemblance between the two, especially their use of hut platforms levelled into hill-sides. Inevitably the degree of scooping is generally much greater on the steeper Scottish slopes. Although study of the unenclosed scooped settlements is still in its infancy it is clear that two main forms are involved: linear sites, like Corbury Hill, Lanarkshire, with the scoops strung along the hillside, and cluster sites, such as Craig Law, Peebles. Pairs of scoops are common, often as elements in linear or cluster settlements, and isolated scoops frequently adjoin larger groups. In keeping with settlement sizes throughout the country the number of scoops is usually below a dozen, but occasionally many more. Single scoops are frequently encountered, but how these relate to the scooped settlements is uncertain. Cases of separated clusters or rows, as at Glenwhappen Rig, Peebles, suggest settlement shift, but this would be difficult to prove. Many of these sites adjoin small field systems, still more have adjacent cairnfields. The Green Knowe platforms were cunningly sited along the very foot of a slope, fronting on to a considerable natural terrace. This still bears traces of plots, fields and clearance, despite recent ploughing. The nearby White Meldon site adjoins a system of small lyncheted fields, some of the lynchets incorporating clearance piles. Until recently little was known about comparable sites south of the Border, but in 1979 two have been excavated in the Northumberland Cheviots, at Black Law and near Linhope Spout, showing a similar pattern of houses and fields in a Second Millennium context.

The Green Knowe scoops supported substantial round timber houses, of post-ring and double stake-wall construction, with evidence of more than one rebuilding. The pottery recovered in 1977 shows that cordoned vessels, just like the sepulchral Cordoned Urns of the Bedd Branwen period, were still in use. But to be sure when unenclosed scooped settlements as a whole began, and how long they lasted, we must await many more excavations.

With the opening up of ever larger upland tracts in the Knighton Heath period we can expect increasing evidence for occupation not only on hillsides, in the manner of the Border settlements, but also on hill-tops. Recent excavations of hill-forts in many parts of the country have located underlying occupation deposits, and sometimes structures, indicating activity in this period: at South Cadbury, Somerset (c. 985, 925 bc), Dinorben, Denbighshire

(*c*. 945 bc), Moel-y-Gaer, Flintshire (*c*. 1015 bc for a four-post timber structure), and Kaimes, Midlothian (for a hut circle, *c*. 1191 bc). When buildings
were constructed on steeply sloping hill-tops then platforms had to be
levelled, and the result can be a strong resemblance to the structural arrangements of the Green Knowe type of settlement. Broadly contemporary with
Green Knowe are the house platforms scooped into the steep summit slopes of
Mam Tor, Derbyshire, which gave dates of *c*. 1180 and 1130 bc (Pl. XV).

Coastal sand settlements

Just as blanket peat in Ireland and Scotland has buried and preserved prehistoric landscapes, so drifting sand all round the shores of Britain and Ireland has
engulfed traces of countless generations of human endeavour. These sand sites
tend to show a multi-layered occupation. Each period of activity was sealed by
wind-blown sand, to be followed by fresh occupation, and yet more blown
sand and so on, as the enduring attractions of a favoured location drew
successive communities to the same spot, century after century. Some of these
sites in fact provide the nearest thing we have in this country to the tells or
settlement mounds of the Near East. Well-preserved examples may span
thousands of years, like that at Udal on North Uist, which has occupation
levels, often of major importance, from about 2000 BC up to the post-Medieval
period. But coastal sand is also very mobile, quick to erode, and once its
protecting mantle has gone, exposed occupation deposits will soon disinte-
grate. When it is remembered that Skara Brae and Jarlshof, to name but two
examples of national importance, owe their survival to covering sand, the
potential of these sand sites, and the problems of their extraordinary fragility,
will be obvious.

   Unfortunately few sand sites were as solidly built as those in the Northern
Isles, and most are badly damaged and fragmentary. Nevertheless they tend to
be embarrassingly rich in finds, and also preserve crucial environmental
evidence. For these coastal sands, best-known of which is the calcareous
machair of the Scottish Highlands and Islands, are usually highly alkaline, and
thus kind to bone and other organic material. It is unfortunate that the
remoteness of so many of these coastal sand areas makes the task of mounting
excavations extremely difficult.

   Wales, Scotland, Ireland, south-western and northern England all have
their famous coastal sand sites, but few have been scientifically examined. The
Gwithian excavations suggest that these coastal sites reflect, to a greater or
lesser degree, settlement patterns in their hinterland. In Wales we can single
out Merthyr Mawr Warren on the Glamorgan coast, a rich source of burials
and occupation material over the years, and Newborough Warren in Anglesey.
In Ireland there are the famous 'sandhills' of the north, as round Dundrum in
Co. Down, while northern England has sites on both east and west coasts,
notably Walney Island, Furness, and Ross Links on the north Northumber-

land coast. The north Lincolnshire sand warrens, so rich in pottery of our period, should also be mentioned here, though these lie some miles inland.

But it is the coastal sands of Scotland, from Hedderwick in the south-east to Jarlshof in the Shetlands, from Rosinish on Benbecula to Glenluce in Wigtown, which are the most extensive and best known protectors of prehistoric coastal settlement. For every Jarlshof and Skara Bare there are countless others which have yielded enormous hauls of prehistoric material over the years: Glenluce, Tentsmuir in Fife, the Culbin Sands of Moray, and the Sands of Forvie on the Aberdeen coast are but some of the more famous names in this list. A midden recently excavated in the Culbin sands (*c.* 1259 bc) is one of the few mainland sites to have been scientifically investigated, yielding a wealth of evidence relating to environment and lifestyle. The associated pottery is particularly interesting, comprising coarse, plain, 'flat-rimmed' wares, for this is one of the few domestic pottery assemblages from Scotland of that period when the dead were being buried with Collared, Cordoned and other cinerary urns. It also provides interesting comparisons with the nearly contemporary Green Knowe material. The Culbin midden shows the emphasis on sea food common to these coastal sites, with clear evidence of a change in the shellfish collected. In the earlier level the common cockle, *Cerastoderma edule*, is important, but in the later, undated, midden this is virtually absent, and the mussel, *Mytilus edulis*, and common winkle, *Littorina littorea*, become more important than previously. A possible reason for the disappearance of cockles may be their susceptibility to changing environmental conditions, to storms, frost, silting and such like, and this could be another sign that the climate was deteriorating in the second half of the Second Millennium BC.

The sheer quantities of shells from these coastal middens tend to over-emphasize the dietary importance of shell-fish. In recent times in Scotland they have often been regarded as a food of hard times, and can never have more than supplemented the diet. One has only to contemplate how many shell-fish would have to be collected to equal the meat-weight of one cow. Therefore, although only a few animal bones were found in the Culbin Sands midden, mostly cattle, with some sheep or goats and pigs, these may be a more accurate indication than the shells of the subsistence economy of these people. The range of wild plants recovered from Culbin suggests that food was not as plentiful as it seems to have been at some west coast settlements. However the Culbin Sands midden may represent seasonal activity and could therefore be an inaccurate guide to the economic level of those involved.

It is the Western Isles, with their vast tracts of coastal machair, which have provided some of the most interesting evidence. A number of sites have recently been or are currently being, investigated, but most suffer from the twin excavation ills of erosion and remoteness. All have rich and extensive middens, associated with structures which are fragmentary and difficult to interpret. The three most extensively published, Northton on Harris, Rosinish on Benbecula and Kilellan on Islay, may give a somewhat biased view of coastal settlement in the islands, as they all attracted attention because of the quantities of *decorated* pottery recovered from their broken surfaces. The wares involved, including Beaker, food vessel and urn forms, are all better known in funerary contexts, and their occurrence in quantity at these three sites is puzzling. Sand sites yielding plain, coarse wares are much more common, but have not been explored to the same extent.

All three of these sites belong to the early Second Millennium. Northton, probably the earliest, is remarkable for its proportion of good quality Beaker sherds, whereas the Rosinish assemblage has a high proportion of domestic to Beaker sherds. Kilellan has only a small Beaker element, and instead combines food vessels and enlarged food vessels, unique on a domestic site, with shouldered domestic jars of a local style.

The surprising lesson learnt from Rosinish and Kilellan is how highly developed and widespread agriculture must have been in the Islands at this time. Both have produced quantities of carbonized barley, and extensive criss-cross ard marks at Rosinish show that the land was being tilled.

Middens rich in animal bones show that both communities practised mixed farming. At Kilellan, cattle were almost totally dominant, with only a small proportion of sheep or goat, and perhaps pig. Shell-fish were collected in quantity, with variations in the species found at different levels in the midden; but the absence of fish bones, and of any evidence for hunting, suggests this coastal farming community was not short of food. Unfortunately the Kilellan site was very fragmentary, but appears to have begun as a small, double stockaded farmstead. This was replaced by a strange complex of stone settings, with a paved area, a drain and pits, perhaps a specialized shell-fish preparation site. Rich midden layers accumulated over this, and then a round timber building with a clay floor was built on a platform levelled into the sloping levels of the midden.

The terrain at Kilellan permits nothing larger than a farmstead, although no doubt others lay near by. The remarkable quantity of decorated pottery from the site includes not only food vessels, and enlarged food vessels, but also decorated, shouldered vases. There is rather more plain pottery, mostly shouldered jars, often of a large size. The fact that there are so few joining sherds and that so many vessels are represented by single sherds presumably indicates that this was the residue of domestic refuse, which, along with seaweed, may have been spread on the fields.

The published structures at Rosinish include hearths and also a U-shaped stone structure above the midden, *c.* 10 metres × 3 metres, which may be similar to the main Northton 'house'. In general terms the Rosinish community may have had a similar economy to that at Kilellan, although the presence of fish bones is one major difference. In addition to the eye-catching Beaker material from the site there are, as at Kilellan, quantities of cruder domestic wares.

The relevant levels at the Northton site provide a marked contrast to Rosinish and Kilellan, for signs of agriculture are absent. There are other indications that Northton may well have had a more specialized function than the other two settlements, for abundant red deer remains suggest hunting was important, and the midden also includes not only the usual shell-fish but also seal and walrus bones. Perhaps the most surprising aspect is the prevalence of Beakers of funerary quality. The large size of many vessels and the domination of grooved decoration is understandable in a domestic context, but there is only a small proportion of the thick coarse ware that one would expect on a settlement. The main structure, an oval stone-walled enclosure that may have been roofed by a skin boat, also points to occupation of a rather different kind. Sheep and cattle bones occur in equal quantities in the midden, pointing to some interest in stock but further speculation on the nature of this unusual site must await its full publication. There are radiocarbon dates from two occupation levels of our period, *c.* 1654 bc for the lower midden, which has the stone structure, and *c.* 1531 bc for the upper midden. The Beakers from the lower level can be assigned to Steps 3 and 4, those in the later level to Step 4.

The Northern Isles

In the far north of Scotland, the Orkneys and the Shetlands, the lack of timber, an abundance of good building stone and the need to keep out the weather in a very exposed landscape led to a unique development of houses with enormously thick walls, thick enough to admit all manner of cubicles and recesses. In these lands we are up against the problem of distinguishing between secular and sacred structures, for while some are undoubtedly houses, others have been classed as 'temples', and there are also burial sites which, superficially, are very similar. In some cases we may again be dealing with houses that were subsequently given over to burials.

The most famous and amongst the earliest examples of this architectural style are the settlements at Skara Brae, Rinyo and Links of Noltland in the Orkneys. Skara Brae lies at the sea's edge, its buildings huddling together and threaded by roofed-over connecting passages. In its final form the site consisted of eight units, curved on the outside, but tending to a round-cornered square in interior plan. Walls were up to 3 metres thick, and the roofs were corbelled. The sinuous passageways were roofed over, permitting access between the units even when eventually the whole settlement was buried beneath drifting sand and accumulated rubbish. The local flagstone provided superb building material not only for the main structure of the buildings but also for the stone furniture and fittings for which Skara Brae is famous. A typical unit is entered through a narrow, low door, little more than a metre high. On either side are short beds edged by stone slabs set on edge, each with shelves let into the adjacent walls. In the centre is a large, square flagstone hearth for a peat fire, while at various points there are slab-lined 'boxes' set into the sandy floor. These have joints carefully luted with clay and thus presumably held liquids. Possibly they were for soaking shellfish. The most striking pieces of furniture are the famous two-shelved 'dressers', made of remarkably thin stone slabs, which stand against one wall. Each unit has a cubicle, or cubicles let into the thickness of the wall, some perhaps for storage but others, as they are drained, possibly toilets.

This hamlet housed perhaps thirty people at maximum. They kept mainly cattle, some sheep or goats, which became more important later in the history of the settlement, a few pigs and dogs. Their diet was supplemented by fishing, especially for cod and coalfish which were caught on a line, and they collected birds' eggs, crabs and shellfish, especially limpets, although these may have been for bait rather than eating. Skara Brae was occupied through the Meldon Bridge and into the Mount Pleasant period, being established *c*. 2500 bc and finally abandoned to the drifting sand about 2000 bc. There are two main building levels, separated by blown sand, but each involved much modification and rebuilding. The pottery used throughout was Grooved ware, but the Rinyo finds indicate that the Beaker tradition was beginning to make an impact in the final phases of these settlements.

In the Shetlands there are at least two hundred stone buildings which probably overlap in date with Skara Brae. These occur all over the islands, singly or in small detached groups, often associated with enclosures and fields, and representing a long-lasting pattern of settlement. Some buildings show many modifications, and such massive structures could have remained serviceable for centuries. Thus the 'Benie Hoose' shows three main structural phases and five modification periods. At the beginning of their development these buildings have a morphological similarity to local chambered tombs, so much so that some have been published as cairns. The other end of the tradition, in the mid-First Millennium BC, is marked by the huddle of structures forming the famous settlement at Jarlshof.

The best dated of the Shetland buildings belong to the Mount Pleasant, Overton and Bedd Branwen periods, for the pottery from Ness of Gruting and Stanydale included sherds of local Beaker, and the Standing Stones of Yoxie yielded a large vessel very much like a plain Bipartite Urn. There is a supporting C14 date from Ness of Gruting of *c*. 1564 bc, derived from a cache of barley weighing no less than 28 pounds. Here is graphic evidence of the use to which the adjoining fields were put.

The walls of these houses are of faced rubble or earth and stones, and it is suggested that the roof rested directly on the inner edge of the wall in the manner of the Hebridean 'black house'. There are three basic shapes, heel-shaped as at Punds Water II; oval, as at Ness of Gruting and Stanydale (Figure 5.12c) and figure-of-eight shaped, as at the 'Benie Hoose' and Yoxie. At least some examples of the latter result from the addition of a horned forecourt or anteroom, either to a heel-shaped original, as at 'Benie Hoose', or to an oval shape as at Yoxie. The basic oval-shaped buildings tend to have walls 1.5–5 metres thick, and measure about 14 × 11 metres, give or take a metre or two, with a main internal floor area of r. 7 × 5 metres. Internal arrangements vary so much, however, that it is difficult to give average figures, and the sites have been modified so often that a typical interior scarcely exists. Recesses and chambers opening off the main space are characteristic, especially an end chamber opposite the entrance. There is a difference between alcoves formed by projecting piers, as at Ness of Gruting, and those formed in the wall thickness, as at the 'Benie Hoose' and the Gairdie. At Stanydale and Gruting School the seclusion of the recessed end chamber is completed by drawing piers across the opening. At Yoxie the gap between a similar pair of piers leads into an inner room almost as large as the main room, with a more conventional recess at the far end.

Entrances took the form of long passages, either straight or slighly curved, as at Yoxie, 'Benie Hoose' and Gruting School, or a dog-leg, as at Ness of Gruting and Stanydale. The addition of horns in front of the entrance to provide a forecourt or ante-room provides further complications. These usually had thinner walls, though thick enough to accommodate recesses, and were normally entered via a simple break in the wall or a short, straight passage.

Usually only small areas of the interior were paved, principally those parts which saw most traffic such as entrances, connecting passages and forecourts or ante-rooms. Most sites have an internal hearth and some, a covered drain or drains. There is a notable absence of the pits and holes which cover house interiors in other regions. Many have a spread of peat ash, showing use of the local fuel both for heating and, one can imagine, spreading on the fields after burning, as is traditional in the islands.

Many of these buildings are adjacent to field clearance heaps and small systems of field plots. Fields are often terraced up to 80 metres long, and are edged by drystone dykes. The siting of these settlements sometimes singly, but more often in scattered groups near the coast, is reminiscent of more recent crofts, and they may well have functioned in much the same way.

How long these massive buildings lasted is not clear. In the Knighton Heath period changes may have been forced on the inhabitants of the Northern Isles as of other regions, for it was then that the burnt mound settlements appear, which will be described in the next section. Even then the burnt mound houses, although smaller than the Ness of Gruting type, were still within the tradition of substantial stone structures which characterized the Northern Isles throughout prehistory.

Cooking and food preparation sites

Thickly distributed in Ireland and in the Northern Isles of Scotland, and coming to light in increasing numbers in other western parts of Britain, are sites marked by great accumulations of burnt stones, earth and ash which have been regarded as cooking sites. The best known examples, the *fulacht fiadh* of Ireland and the 'burnt mounds' of the Northern Isles, are very numerous, for example over two hundred in the Orkneys and about the same in the Shetlands. In fact they are probably the most numerous field monument to be found there.

The heaps of burnt material which can make these sites so easy to locate are discovered, when excavated, to adjoin an activity area, the focus of which is a large trough with associated pits and hearths (Figure 5.11). In Ireland these troughs are made of wood, in the Northern Isles, of stone. They appear to have been filled with water and used for boiling meat, the masses of burnt material, pot-boilers in effect, being the product of many boilings. At most sites there is evidence for some sort of structure either adjacent to or incorporating the cooking area. The Irish sites have produced light circular stake structures, but the recently excavated Liddle I and Beaquoy sites on Orkney involve very substantial stone buildings. At Liddle I (Figure 5.11A) the large stone trough, measuring about 1.6 × 0.62 metres deep, was incorporated in a complex oval stone building *c.* 6 × 4 metres. This still retained many of its stone fittings, including a large hearth, slab-built boxes and compartments, some of which may be beds. The Liddle burnt mound, about 20 metres across and 1.5 metres high, contained approximately 200 cubic metres of burnt material, but individual sites can be larger or very much smaller, presumably depending on their length of use.

These sites, both in Scotland and Ireland, represent a practice carried on over a very long period. The C14 dates from the Drombeg site, Co. Cork (*c.* ad 430, ad 560) suggest they were in use as late as the early Medieval period in Ireland, while thermoluminescent dating of several Orcadian examples show they were still a common feature in the 'Iron Age'. But radiocarbon dates and rare datable finds both from Ireland and Orkney reveal a tradition which already existed in the Second Millennium. The two sites at Killeens, Co. Cork, have dates of *c.* 1763 and 1550 bc, broadly confirmed by the pollen evidence from Ballyvourney I, Co. Cork. The site at Millstreet, Co. Cork, produced a short flanged axe, suggesting the Knighton Heath period, and this may have been when the burnt mounds emerged in the Northern Isles. The Liddle site has dates of 958 bc and 876 bc, but there is a range of thermoluminscent dates from other Orcadian examples suggesting the tradition began in the Knighton Heath period and continued down to the later First Millennium BC.

These sites have usually been regarded as specialized cooking places, but the recent Orkney excavations give the impression that in the Northern Isles at least they were the normal form of settlement in the later Second and First Millennia, and that boiling was only one of their functions. The substantial nature of the Liddle building, the fact that no settlements are known for this

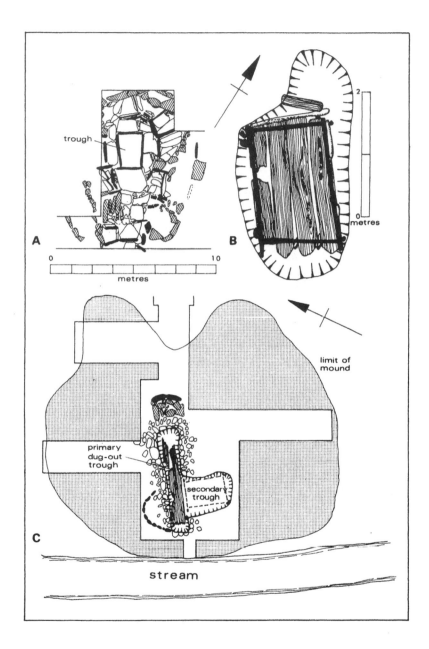

Figure 5.11 A. Stone building associated with burnt mound at Liddle Farm I, Orkney (after Hedges in Huxtable et al., 1976; B. Wooden boiling trough in a *fulacht fiadh* at Killeens, Co. Cork; C. *Fulacht fiadh*, Ballyvourney II, Co. Cork (B. and C. after O'Kelly, 1954)

period, the large number of sites and the fact that they concentrate on the best land, all point to this conclusion. It may well be that cooking by boiling was necessitated by the northern environment, for the islands appear to have been largely deforested by the Second Millennium and wood was in short supply. The alternative fuel, peat, is not suitable for direct roasting of meat, and as pottery appears to have been in short supply, the boiling tank may have been the logical solution. The situation was possibly different in Ireland, where there were not the same pressures of space and resources. But as Irish sites have not yet yielded substantial buildings, and have not been studied to the same extent, their status must remain in doubt.

The preparation and cooking of the great range of foods used by prehistoric populations may often have involved structures which make little sense to the modern mind. Thus the stone slab tanks in the Skara Brae houses may have been used for soaking limpets to prepare them for use as bait and something similar may have occurred at Kilellan, where a massive heap of winkles lay on one side of a strange complex comprising stone settings, a paved area, and a stone slab trough. The implication is that these features played a part in the preparation of sea food, but one can only guess how this may have worked.

Another specialized type of cooking site has been claimed at the Downpatrick settlement in Ireland, consisting of oval pits rimmed by stakeholes, each pit *c.* 1.75 × 0.9 × 0.4 metres in depth, with a smaller hole at one end, the whole lot filled with burnt stones and soil. These have been interpreted as cooking pits shielded by stake screens.

Crannogs and waterside sites

The remarkable amount of bronze implements and weapons from rivers in many parts of these islands, notably the Shannon and Bann in Ireland, the Trent and Witham in England, and above all the Thames, indicate a dense occupation along their banks. Generally settlements have been noticed only where the presence of piles has attracted attention. Museum records and early reports frequently describe 'pile dwellings' found on river banks, notably the Thames and Trent, but where finds have survived these usually belong to the Penard period or later. The rich collection of bronzes from the famous pile settlement on the banks of the Trent at Clifton is best assigned to the Penard period, like many of the surviving bronzes from the Thames pile sites. This suggests a major increase in the use of piles to consolidate riverside settlements in this period, another pointer to increased waterlogging in the late Second Millennium. There may, nevertheless have been a growth of riverside settlements in the Penard period, for the known settlements of the Knighton Heath period, for example the Deverel-Rimbury sites at Mucking, Essex, at Egham and at Abingdon, are all set back from the Thames banks.

This is a convenient point to introduce the subject of crannogs, small artificial islands of peat, stones, layers of brushwood and other debris, held together by piles and built in lakes in many western parts of Britain and especially in Ireland. Most belong to the First Millennium and later, but some of the so-called 'crannogs' of Holderness, in Yorkshire, are at least as early as the Penard period. How many of these sites were true crannogs is not clear. Old reports of sites such as West Furze mention piles and brushwood, which suggest some sort of consolidated settlement in what was obviously a water-logged location. The only example recently excavated, at Barmston, produced no evidence of piles or platforms, but resembled instead a settlement established in a marshy hollow. Jumbled beams and planks, betraying the hands of skilful carpenters, were probably used for rectangular framed buildings, 5.5 × 3.5 × 2.5 metres high, with gabled ends, associated with hearths. In view of the radiocarbon dates, *c.* 1010 and *c.* 950 bc, it is tempting to make comparisons with early Urnfield island and lake-side settlements such as the Wasserburg in southern Germany, which consisted of well-made rectangular wooden houses.

Barmston appears not to have been a long lived site, and was eventually inundated and abandoned probably still within the Penard period when there is so much other evidence for increasing wetness. Flooding due to changing land configurations around the mouth of the Humber was a possible cause, although whether this was due to worsening climate or some other disaster is not clear. This flooding may certainly have caused the waterlogging of a site at Thorne Moor, north-east of Doncaster, ending cereal cultivation in a small temporary clearance in the mixed oak forest. A date of *c.* 1040 bc was obtained from a trackway constructed in response to the flooding.

Some waterside settlements in Ireland show less evidence of their watery environment. The Downpatrick site in Co. Down, consisting of at least two round timber houses, appears to have been established on the shore of a tidal marsh off the River Quoile. A settlement at Sheepland, Co. Down, with similar Cordoned Urn pottery to Downpatrick, was established on the edge of a shallow peat-filled valley, and there are indications of rock-cut steps leading down to the water's edge. The Coney Island settlement in Lough Neagh, with traces of a rectangular structure, may be broadly contemporary, but is associated with Irish Bowl sherds and a radiocarbon date of *c.* 1400 bc.

Caves

Caves were used for a variety of purposes in our period, but were not a normal form of settlement. Temporary shelter, storage, burial and ritual are all attested, though it may be difficult to be certain of the nature of the activity in individual cases.

The use of caves and rock shelters for burials has already been discussed, with the Church Dale, Elbolton and Gop inhumations, and the rock shelter cremation cemetery at Goatscrag in Northumberland, representing the ritual and chronological extremes of this tradition. A few caves may have been used for burials as late as the Knighton Heath period, for example at Llanarthney, Carmarthenshire, where ashes and bones were found in a limestone cave with a side-looped spearhead. Caves may also have been used for ritual purposes, as has been suggested in the case of the 'windypits' of north Yorkshire. The best-known is the Antofts Windypit where the remains of eight skeletons were found, some of them mixed with animal bones. At one point a fire had been lit on a limestone block, and around it were animal bones, including ox bones split for marrow, flints and an AOC Beaker. The fire gave a radiocarbon date of *c.* 1800 bc.

There are several examples of metalwork hoards from caves, so they may frequently have been used as hiding places. The bronzes from the Monkton cave, Pembrokeshire saw, chisel, transitional palstave and twisted ring, deposited in the Penard period, may have been hidden and never recovered. But a less simple solution is demanded by those caves which produce a wider range of material. The Ogof-yr-esgyrn cave in Breconshire produced both pottery and metalwork, including Group IV rapier, bifid razor, awl and biconical gold bead. The difficulty of separating stratigraphically prehistoric and later finds at this site is a common one, and it is not known whether all the material is contemporary. Some at least of the pottery may be earlier than the bronzes, and could indicate two phases of activity. The pottery from two Glamorgan caves, Culver Hole and Lesser Garth, presents the same problem, for it is usually regarded as a local equivalent of Deverel-Rimbury pottery, which hardly admits close dating. Many south Welsh caves seem to have been used as intermittent refuges, for burials and other purposes, and in areas in which caves abound, as in the Mendips, the Peak District and the central Pennines, there are many similar deposits.

In some caves occupation of sorts is indicated, even if only by those seeking temporary refuge, but the deposits seldom indicate more than short-lived squatting, and it will be clear from some of the sites mentioned above that interest in caves may have taken many, less obvious, guises.

Houses and buildings

Wherever the buildings of the early farming communities have been discovered, from Devon to Perthshire and from Mayo to the Fens, they have invariably proved to be rectangular and timber-built. From the Fifth Millennium through the Fourth and into the Third this was the pattern. The first hint of a change comes in the Meldon Bridge period, with the appearance of round timber buildings at sites such as Meldon Bridge itself and Thirlings in Northumberland. Unfortunately neither of these examples is closely dated, and for more certain evidence of round structures we have to wait until the Mount Pleasant period. Then they became commonplace, especially in the large enclosures of Durrington Walls type. It is by no means certain that all of the circular timber structures in these sites were roofed buildings, although the most severe critics appear to accept the smaller examples as such. The origins of this circular tradition, when, where and how it began, are still very obscure, not helped by the gaps in the settlement archaeology of the Meldon Bridge period. Nevertheless from the Mount Pleasant period onwards, right through to the Roman conquest, round, or at least curvilinear, buildings were characteristic of these islands. This is not to say that rectangular buildings disappeared with the advent of circular traditions. In the Mount Pleasant period many sites combine rectangular or trapezoidal and round structures, for example Willington in Derbyshire and Hunstanton in Norfolk. At both sites there are also examples of 'six-posters', rectangular structures based on three paired post-holes, while Hunstanton has in addition a nine-poster, with the two outer holes in each trio containing two posts, the central one a single post. A substantial ridge-roofed structure is indicated here. Of the circular buildings, the one at Willington was associated with a corded Beaker sherd, while the Hunstanton example, with projecting porch, produced Collared Urn sherds.

In the case of long-lived sites like these it is difficult to prove that differently-shaped buildings are contemporary. Nevertheless examples of rectangular and trapezoidal buildings occur sporadically throughout our period, although chronology and relationships to other structures are not always clear. This is the problem for example at Cock Hill, where there are square four-posters and circular structures. At Swarkeston, the settlement of the Overton period had two small, flimsy, stake-built rectangular structures, and no sign of circular buildings, although only a fragment of the site was exposed. Circular structures dominate in the two best-known settlement groups, Trevisker and Deverel-Rimbury, though rectilinear structures can occasionally be detected. At Thorny Down, for example, the mass of post-holes clearly represents both curvilinear and rectilinear structures, but here as on so many Deverel-Rimbury sites the likelihood of long occupation makes it difficult to relate the various features. At Itford Hill, too, some of the buildings seem more rectilinear than circular, notably in enclosure IV, where round building F appears to be adjoined by a rectangular structure (Figure 5.3).

It seems true to say, however, that until the Penard period rectilinear structures were in a minority, and not usually used for houses. One of the many important changes of the Penard period was the increasing popularity of rectilinear structures. They were characteristic especially of the defended sites which sprang up in this period, for example Rams Hill, Grimthorpe in Yorkshire and Ffridd Faldwyn in Montgomeryshire, normally in four-poster form. At many of these sites there is a strong hint of 'town planning', with four-posters laid out in rows. But generally circular buildings are there, too, and the differences between the two are not clear. This combination of round and square buildings remained a feature of hill-fort interiors in many regions throughout the First Millennium, culminating in the remarkable 'streets' of four-posters which filled the interiors of hill-forts in the Welsh Marches.

The reconstruction of multiple post-hole rectilinear structures as ridge-roof, gable-ended buildings, with timber frame and wattle fill, seems reasonable enough, but the four-posters, and perhaps some of the six-posters, deserve extra comment. The four-posters, ranging in size from *c*. 1.5–5 metres square, though mostly 2.7–4 metres square, were first recognized by Bersu at the Little Woodbury excavations in the late 1930s, where they were thought to be granaries on stilts. The granary interpretation survived until the 1960s, when whole streets of four-posters began to turn up in large-scale hill-fort excavations. The smaller examples may have been granaries on stilts, or served similar functions – in South African kraals, for example, chicken-houses on stilts have this post-hole plan. The widespread 3 or 4 metres square variety especially when arranged in rows, have been interpreted as dwellings in recent years, but of late opinion has been swinging back to a storage function. It must be admitted, therefore, that four-posters are still a problem. Usually it is not even certain whether they represent structures with floors at ground level or whether they were on stilts. Clearly in the rather soggy, dirty interiors of prehistoric settlements it must have been an advantage to raise floors off the ground.

The circular buildings which in most areas dominated later prehistoric settlement show a remarkable diversity of structure. For the most part they are smaller and simpler than in the late First Millennium. Diameters are usually between 4 and 10 metres. The most widespread plan is a simple ring of posts, with or without a central support post for the conical roof. Doorways may be marked by the placing of larger posts, or doubled posts, either side of the door, or by the presence of an out-turned porch. Porches were common at Deverel-Rimbury sites such as Itford Hill and Shearplace Hill (Figure 5.12), but the simple post ring without doorway features is also found, for example at Eldon's Seat I. At Trevisker the post rings lay within slightly sunken house floors.

There has perhaps been a tendency to underestimate the size and form of many of these post-ring houses. The main ring has usually been taken to mark the position of the outer wall of the house, but recent discoveries have given rise to alternative interpretations. At sites such as Shearplace Hill, slight ring grooves or a ring of small stake-holes were found outside and concentric with the main post ring. These features are so slight that on many sites they will have been removed by ploughing or erosion. The suggestion in such cases is that the main post ring in fact supported the roof, while the outer ring marks the house wall, of much slighter construction. This may affect the appearance as well as the size of the house represented. On sloping sites such as Amberley Mount, and Itford Hill, where a level platform has been cut into the slope for the house, it has been customary to see the building nestling within this prepared scoop. But it has also been pointed out that run-off water would have poured into such an emplacement. If the visible post rings were merely the roof supports, an outer wall ring rimming the scoop would have diverted water and resulted in a much drier site. The problem of drainage was frequently tackled with an encircling drip trench, as at Fengate (Figure 5.12b).

Variations on the simple post-ring can be found from early on in our period. At sites such as Waulud's Bank and Downpatrick the main house-ring consists partly of spaced posts, partly of construction trench. This is also seen at Playden, but here the ring included a foundation trench for a stretch of low stone walling (Figure 5.1). The houses within the ramparts at Mam Tor in Derbyshire also employed post holes and gullies. At Kilellan the upper house ring, on a floor cut back into the sloping midden layers, had both post-holes and smaller stake-holes.

Round houses with stake-built 'cavity' walls were also widespread. The rather irregular first phase of the layer 8 'Beaker house' at Gwithian was cleared away to make room for just such a building (Figure 5.12e). Towards the front the structure is strengthened by introducing lengths of bedding trench on the line of the inner stake ring, so that the outer ring forms a horned porch. Circular houses at Lough Gur, site C, were also based on double stake rings and lengths of slot, reputedly associated with Beaker pottery. A double stake-ring house has also been described at the Green Knowe platform settlement, differing from earlier examples in having its stake rings set in a slight, rather straggly stony footing. The interior was partitioned into 'rooms' by lines of stake-holes, and there was a fine oval stone hearth.

These stake-rings may have formed a cavity wall which was filled with turf, daub or some similar material, although no evidence for this was found at Gwithian where it might have been expected. Alternatively the stakes may have provided a framework for a wattle or wicker-work filling.

Reconstructions of circular buildings have almost invariably envisaged a low outer wall, with projecting eaves, and a conical roof supported by internal post or posts, or tie beams. This classic reconstruction may not always be correct, for various alternatives are possible, ranging from an asymmetric roof apex to a tepee-like structure. The latter can be indicated by angled post-holes or casts as in the case of a structure at Totternhoe in Bedfordshire (Figure 5.12d). That the lighter stake-built buildings formed a 'bird-cage' structure, rather like North American wigwams is possible but difficult to prove.

An alternative to the ring of posts is the 'ring-groove', a continuous bedding trench. This permits a much stronger wall of close-set upright timbers, so it is perhaps no coincidence that ring-groove construction began to increase in the Knighton Heath period as settlement pushed higher and higher into hill country. For example, a fine ring-groove building was found at the Holne Moor settlement on Dartmoor. At present ring-groove buildings seem to occur mainly later, in the First Millennium. They are particularly common in the last four centuries before the Roman Conquest, when very large and

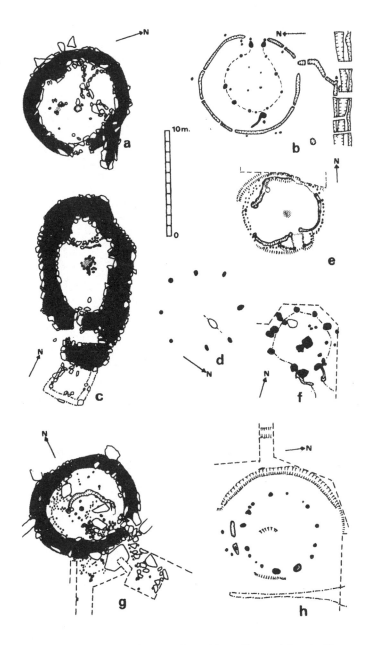

Figure 5.12 Representative house plans: a. Dean Moor, Devon (after A. Fox, 1957); b. Fengate, Peterborough (after Pryor, 1977); c. Stanydale, Shetland (after Calder, 1960–1); d. near Totternhoe Knolls, Bedfordshire (after Matthews, 1976); e. Gwithian, Cornwall (after Thomas in Megaw, 1976); f. Itford Hill, Sussex (after Burstow and Holleyman, 1957); g. Stannon Down, Cornwall (after Mercer, 1970); h. Shearplace Hill, Dorset (after Avery and Close-Brooks, 1969)

complex examples were built. Simple post-ring houses may have predominated in most areas down to the Llynfawr period.

Oval, egg-shaped and pear-shaped buildings while not as numerous as
circular structures were widespread. In Ireland in particular egg-shaped buildings seem fairly common, for example at Knockadoon, Lough Gur, especially
on site D, where the associated pottery included Beaker. A fine example, also
with Beaker, occurs in the Monknewtown enclosure. This had a sunken oval
floor, rimmed by a scatter of stones which may have weighted the bottom of
the eaves. There were roof support posts in the interior, a hearth and a paved
area. Curvilinear buildings may have started early in Ireland, for an oval
structure was found just outside the entrance of Newgrange. This had a sunken
floor and a wall outlined by post-holes, post-slots and patchy stone footings,
and is thought to relate to the chambered tomb, and thus to the Meldon
Bridge period, rather than the intense activity of the Mount Pleasant period.

An unusual oval or boat-shaped structure was found in the lower Beaker
level at Northton, consisting of an area about 9 metres long and 4.25 metres
wide, defined by a stone wall, still standing nearly 1.0 metres high in places,
and perhaps no more than 1.5 metres high originally. The end facing the sea
had collapsed, and here, perhaps, was the way in. In the interior was an oval
setting of stake-holes, insufficient to support anything more than a flimsy
covering. This stone structure must therefore be thought of as reveting the
sides of a hollow scooped in the sand, with the interior stakes indicating a light
shelter. Alternatively a skin-covered sea-going boat of the type to be discussed
in Chapter VI could have been inverted over the stone structure to form a roof,
as seen amongst recent maritime communities on the Atlantic seaboard of
Europe. The site certainly provided shelter on at least two occasions, for in
addition to a hearth and a peat ash spread there were two thin occupation layers
separated by a sterile layer of wind-blown sand.

It is surprising that so few areas, even stony uplands, have yielded evidence
of building in stone. Circular stone structures abound over much of Wales,
northern England and Scotland, but usually prove to belong to the centuries
immediately before and during the Roman occupation. But although the
wealth of stone-built settlements on the uplands of south-west England appear
unique at present, we have seen that recent fieldwork, for example in the
Pennines and on Arran, is redressing the balance. In areas such as Dartmoor
and Bodmin Moor, the accidents of history and geography have allowed stone
buildings to survive in vast numbers, often in a remarkable state of preservation. The 'hut circle' of those parts consists of a low rubble ring-wall, faced
inside and out, on which rested the conical roof, supported usually by a ring of
interior posts. While the shape is usually roughly circular, pear- or egg-shaped
examples are quite common, and two joined together, like a pair of semi-
detached houses, are frequently encountered. External diameters range from *c.*
9–17 metres, but, because of the thick walls, internal space is considerably

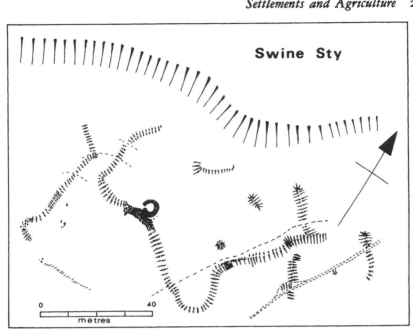

Swine Sty

0   40

metres

Figure 5.13 Enclosure with stone-walled house, Swine Sty, Derbyshire (after Machin, 1971, 1975)

less, with 6–8 metres a common size. It is unusual to find a projecting porch like those characteristic of timber houses, but instead a curved length of walling may be built out on one side of the doorway to form a lobby, and this may be almost completely enclosed where the projecting wall is hooked round. Stake-holes in the entrance indicate some sort of door or screen. Entrances are frequently paved, and this paving may extend in a curve round the centre of the building, covering an interior drain. At some sites, and Stannon Down is a notable example, the paving may lead away from the doorway for several metres. At Stannon Down hut circle 8, this paved approach was edged by stake-holes running right up to the doorway, a distance of *c.* 6 metres, suggesting a long approach passage (Figure 5.12, a,g).

Floors tend to be only partially paved, and beaten earth, perhaps covered with rushes or mats, sufficed for much of the interior. The fact that the paving is usually restricted to the area by the doorway, and perhaps on one side of the building, with hearth and pits sited here too, suggests that this was the working area of the house. In some cases the other portion of the interior may be walled or partitioned off, logically to screen the sleeping quarters. This area is usually cleaner than the rest of the building. Dean Moor Hut 5A shows an improvement of this separate chamber principle, for it was built in a pear-shape to provide an inner 'room', rather smaller than a modern double bed, at the far end from the door. The Stannon Down houses were filled with stake-holes suggesting internal fittings. Some, following the curve of the wall at a distance of 30 to 40 centimetres, could be benches or shelves, while rectangular settings against the wall suggest a table, dresser or bed, depending on location. Hut circle 4 had alcoves let into the wall thickness, perhaps for storage.

Recent discoveries suggest we should look for similar settlements and stone houses in other upland areas. The possibility has already been mentioned that the extensive stone house settlement at Mullaghfarna, Co. Sligo, was a village of the passage grave builders. In northern Britain many stone structures resembling hut circles have proved to be ring cairns, but it would be a mistake to dismiss all circular stone structures in this way. The problem is epitomized by the site of Woodhead in Cumberland, which was superficially similar to many Dartmoor houses. Just inside its entrance there was a pit full of occupation debris and charcoal, but because there is no background of stone hut circles in the north, because of the great numbers and variety of ring-cairns, and because the finds included a v-perforated jet button and pulley ring like those so often found in graves, this has usually been classed as a burial site. Unfortunately the absence of a burial is not conclusive, as an inhumation would decay quickly in such acid soil. Another northern hut-circle, in the Swine Sty enclosure (Figure 5.13), is more certainly domestic, and the stone hut circles of our period now coming to light in the Pennines of Upper Teesdale, in the Cheviots, on Arran and in the Hebrides suggest that the south-western settlements are far from unique.

Patterns of farming and land use

By the beginning of our period, around 2700/2500 bc, there had already been a thousand years of farming in these islands. This sort of time scale makes nonsense of traditional concepts of early farmers and their world. In a thousand years it is unlikely that they would still be few in number, scratching a bare living in small clearings in the most favourable parts of the country. There are after all well established equations between agricultural development, improved nutrition and increased population. In a thousand years, given the crude annual population growth rate of 0.5–1.0 per cent applicable to peasant farming societies, 500 original immigrant farmers would have multiplied to a population of anything up to 10,500,000, had nothing intervened to keep numbers down to a level which the land could support. The starting figure could well have been higher. In fact it is well known that agricultural population limits are self adjusting, that when numbers rise beyond the carrying capacity of the land catastrophes ensue which bring the population back below the critical level. War, famine and plagues have been notable agents in maintaining the crucial balance, and history is full of recurrent population disasters, in which anything up to fifty per cent of the people were wiped out both at the local and international level.

Prehistory is not different, and the development of prehistoric as well as historic agricultural societies in these islands must be viewed against a pattern of recurrent agricultural crises and population collapses. Given the much longer time scales now afforded to prehistory, we have to contemplate the possibility that population and agricultural levels previously accorded only to historic societies were attained and even surpassed at various times in later prehistory, each time the upwards curve being checked by a catastrophe forcing numbers back below the critical limit.

One way of staving off if not avoiding such catastrophes is recourse to territoriality, and this is seen in human society as it is in the social life of many animals. It is against this background that we must view on the one hand the development of major territories with defined boundaries, and on the other, organization of the land into field systems and pastoral units by boundaries of one sort or another.

Before applying these concepts to our period some further general observations must be made. First, we must remember that the physical controls which govern the state of these islands today are not the same as those which prevailed through much of our period. In particular our present marginality for crop ripening was then much less, thanks to a much milder climate. Vast tracts which are now suitable only for rough grazing, in the Third and Second Millennia were cultivable. Similarly great areas which now are useless heath or moorland could then grow crops. It is prolonged agriculture, during our period and later in prehistory, which has helped reduce these barren lands to their present state. No better example of this loss exists than the vast acreages of blanket peat in Ireland and Scotland. For every known example of an extensive field system, in Co. Mayo, around the Sperrins in Co. Tyrone and in the mosses of the Scottish Highlands and Islands, there will be dozens more lying buried beneath the uncleared peat.

The possibility that even a few hundred immigrant farmers could have grown to hundreds of thousands in a thousand years makes it clear that long before this time elapsed, drastic agricultural collapse must have intervened. It is in this light that we must view the evidence recently assembled for widespread forest regeneration on cleared land between *c.* 2900–2500 bc. With evidence for clearance, if only small-scale, and cultivation from the south coast to northern Scotland and from western Ireland to East Anglia between *c.* 3500–3000 bc, it is clear that the extent and scale of the early agricultural exploitation of the islands, and the size of population attained, was very much greater than previously entertained. In the centuries down to *c.* 2900 bc there was plenty of time for the emergence of an excess of people over resources. Many of the most tractable soils chosen by the agricultural colonizers were also the most fragile and easily ruined. In the pioneering centuries supplies of new land must often have seemed inexhaustible, and quite likely land did not receive the careful husbandry it merited, and received, in later periods when pressures were greater.

The collapse when it came was widespread, with a consistent picture from many sites in northern Ireland, in north-west England, in Wales, East Anglia and the Somerset Levels. Between *c.* 2900–2500 bc scrub and forest regenerated on cleared and cultivated areas in all these regions as the delicate soil balance broke down. The loss of productive land forced people to open up new lands, in valleys for example, but the extent of these new clearances has yet to be established. In some cases an attempt was made to maintain permanent grassland by grazing previously cultivated land, to help stave off complete disaster. At Ballynagilly this eventually failed, and a grassland phase was followed by regeneration from *c.* 2600 bc. Over much of the southern chalk permanent grassland was maintained, and it was in this grassland setting that many of the round barrows of our period were built. The Dorset Cursus was laid out over no less than 10.4 kilometres of the downs, and the fact that it was laid out in straight stretches between points that were not intervisible shows that this whole great swathe of country was clear of trees before work could begin. But even on the chalk there was extensive regeneration of scrub and woodland, for example on the Berkshire Downs around Rams Hill.

Increased territoriality may have been one product of these pressures. The possibility has already been discussed that the Wessex chalk was divided up into four or five major territories in these difficult times, each with its causewayed enclosure and group of long barrows. Division and organization at the local level is implied by the enclosing of great blocks of land by field systems, most notably at Behy-Glenulra.

Thus farmland in many areas was abandoned, but whether there were still sufficient virgin lands in valleys and on heavier soils to make up this loss is not yet clear and we cannot be certain that agricultural disaster was accompanied at this stage by population collapse. One indication that society was able to weather the storm without appreciable loss of numbers is the scale of public monuments undertaken in the Meldon Bridge period. With sites such as Silbury Hill and the Dorset Cursus requiring millions of man hours of labour it seems inconceivable that there could have been any major loss of population. It seems unlikely, too, that sufficient time had elapsed since the arrival of the immigrant farmers for population figures to reach dangerous levels.

There is an interesting correspondence between the end of this collapse episode and of forest regeneration around *c.* 2500 bc, and the cultural hiatus that marks the onset of the Meldon Bridge period. This can hardly be coincidence, especially as the next agricultural collapse, around 1200 BC, was also marked by profound social change. But what the innovations and upheavals of the Meldon Bridge period mean in human terms has yet to be established.

In the Meldon Bridge period some of the lost lands were cleared again, from

Ballyscullion in Co. Antrim (*c.* 2250 bc), to Nant Ffrancon in Caernarvonshire (*c.* 2306 bc), but others were not brought back under cultivation until early in the Mount Pleasant period. The clearing of new land must have gone on all through this period. Meldon Bridge itself stood in a substantial cleared area, and this was a region which hitherto had seen little farming activity. Adjustment to new circumstances is also reflected in still further territorialization. The territories of Wessex were consolidated in this period, and there is growing evidence for the emergence of new blocks on very similar lines from the Fens of eastern England to the Orkneys. Lessons about care of the land may by now have sunk in, for it was at the turn of the Meldon Bridge and Mount Pleasant periods that the great field system at Fengate was established, and presumably also the many similar systems now known from aerial photographs of southern river gravels. Complex pit alignment boundaries on the Milfield plain of Northumberland may also belong to this time.

By the early part of the Mount Pleasant period another problem was beginning to make itself felt in Ireland, the formation of blanket peat. To what extent this was caused by the onset of a damper climate, or by human disturbance of natural drainage patterns, is not clear. How early the peat formed depended very much on the local geography. At Goodland, Co. Antrim, in undulating chalk country, the area around an abandoned ritual enclosure appears to have been hand-tilled during the Mount Pleasant period. But this was a hollow in which water would naturally collect and peat would form early. By *c.* 2000 bc the centre of the hollow was already showing a growth of damp *Juncus* sward, which soon gave way to blanket bog. The area then lay abandoned until the massive agricultural clearances of the early Medieval period, whereas surrounding hillocks, being drier, continued to provide grazing throughout our period. Blanket peat may have been an even bigger problem in the more oceanic west of Ireland, where some of the most remarkable early field systems have been recorded. At Belderg Beg in Co. Mayo, blanket bog had already begun to encroach on the fields by the Mount Pleasant period. On the other hand at Ballynagilly the regenerated forest was cleared around 2000 bc, and a mixed farming settlement of people using early Beakers was established, growing cereals and grazing stock. Later in the Mount Pleasant period the forest re-asserted itself yet again. At *c.* 1650 bc there was yet another clearance episode, but this time by pastoralists using Irish Bowls, late Beakers and plain, coarse, domestic wares. The lack of interest in cultivation indicates that a damper climate and inception of peat growth had already set in. Throughout the rest of our period and into the First Millennium the story at Ballynagilly is one of continuing deforestation for grazing in the face of spreading blanket bog. By the later First Millennium this glacial, sandy hillock was surrounded by peat moorland, suitable only for rough grazing.

Throughout the Meldon Bridge and Mount Pleasant periods the population continued to rise, and it was no doubt the need to feed more and more mouths which drove pioneers to clear ever larger tracts of upland. There seems to have been a big expansion of activity in the Overton period, reflected for example in the cultivation of the Denbighshire uplands at Brenig, and extensive clearances on Dartmoor. It must not be forgotten that the chalk downs of Wessex had long been open grassland, and cultivation was concentrated on the slopes, the valleys and on the lands around the chalk. By the Overton period 'Celtic' field systems already existed on the southern chalk, but it was in the subsequent Bedd Branwen period that these began to spread all over the downland slopes and valleys. This marks the beginning of a peak period of upland agricultural activity throughout the country. For example on Dartmoor the major episode of reave and field system construction now began, and far away to the north the dyke system at the Black Moss of Achnacree may also have been established. On the other hand some traditional lowland farming areas now lay abandoned and presumably exhausted, such as the Milfield Plain, all perhaps signs that the carrying capacity of the land was again threatened. For the time being the problem could be contained by dividing up ever larger areas by dykes and field walls and by clearing increasing areas of difficult soils and upland. In the Knighton Heath period these processes reached their zenith, with field systems at their maximum extent on the chalk and on the south-western uplands, and with more and more hill country opened up in areas such as the southern uplands of Scotland, where unenclosed scooped settlements of Greene Knowe type now sprang up on hillsides up to 1,200 feet OD.

But already disaster was threatening. In the south Deverel-Rimbury cemeteries were being established on sandy soils in Dorset, Hampshire and Surrey that for a while had been usable, but were now turned increasingly to heathland, and in Ireland many of the great field systems had been engulfed by blanket peat. Signs of imminent collapse can be detected at many sites, particularly in south-west England. At Holne Moor, on Dartmoor, the last ploughing had to contend with ground that was already waterlogged, while at Stannon Down on Bodmin Moor a thin deposit of peat may have built up before the settlement was abandoned, and certainly before its buildings had time to collapse. Far away to the north, long-established settlements on the uplands of Arran were also abandoned now.

The end of the Knighton Heath period and the early part of the Penard period saw a repeat of the agricultural disaster of two thousand years before, but this time the effects may have been far more dramatic. For there was no longer the room for manoeuvre which Fourth Millennium farmers had enjoyed, neither new lands which could easily be opened up, nor much opportunity for further enclosure. This time population levels may have been severely affected, for numbers had been rising gradually for centuries, perhaps for two thousand years or more, and on any count must have been coming perilously close to the danger limit. What followed in the Penard period makes sense in terms both of an agricultural and population disaster.

An added problem this time may have been a sudden worsening of the climate. Evidence for waterlogging comes not just from upland farms but from a variety of settlement contexts. Pile dwellings are now recorded on the banks of a number of rivers such as the Thames and Trent, and some of the Holderness 'crannogs' may reflect measures taken in the face of rising water levels. There is evidence from many low-lying regions of a flooding episode at this time, implicit in a renewed burst of timber trackway construction. The Somerset Levels, the Lancashire Mosses and the Humber basin have all yielded examples of tracks built in this period. While localized instances of peat formation and the abandonment of upland fields might be put down to waterlogging caused by human mismanagement of the land, it is the extent of the evidence for damper conditions which points to climatic deterioration as a major contributory factor in the Penard period. Evidence for the collapse of existing agricultural systems comes from one end of the country to another, and not just in upland areas such as Dartmoor. Numerous radiocarbon dates show that the, by now, ancient field system at Fengate was finally abandoned in the face of flooding at this time, an indication, no doubt, of what was happening to the established order all up and down the Fen Edge. What happened next to this land is not clear. By the later First Millennium the familiar mixed farming economy epitomized by 'Iron Age' storage pits prevailed here as through so much of lowland England. Reassessment of this phase of activity at Fengate suggests its beginnings may go back to the ninth or eighth century BC, but this still leaves a century or two to fill after the abandonment of the ditched fields. Two and a half thousand years later a similar combination of deteriorating climate and population pressure led to the collapse of another well-established pastoral system on the Fen Edge, and the demands of hungry mouths saw the land turned over increasingly to arable. This is perhaps what happened in the Penard period, for cultivation would not have demanded such careful maintenance of field boundaries as stock raising.

The Black Moss of Achnacree field system was also given up at this time (*c.* 980 bc), and there was wholesale abandonment of the 'Celtic' field systems which covered much of the southern chalk. These disappeared with the Deverel-Rimbury societies with which they had been so closely connected. The downs were now reorganized for pastoralism, and this involved carving up the land into great grazing blocks by the linear earthworks known as 'ranch boundaries'. These frequently ignore the abandoned Deverel-Rimbury settlements, and cut right across the old fields (Figure 5.14). If anything they relate to the new pattern of hill-top settlement which was now emerging including those examples, such as Rams Hill, which were provided with defences.

It is not only the disappearance of Deverel-Rimbury society in lowland

England and of Trevisker society in the south-west, but also the blanks which now appear in the settlement archaeology in so many regions, which suggest the complete breakdown of the existing social order and a serious population disaster. As on the Fen Edge and in south-west England so in the Scottish Border country it is difficult to know what came next. This region has a very familiar sequence of defended settlements in later prehistory, beginning with palisades in the Ewart Park phase, but did the unenclosed scooped settlements persist down to this point, or did the Border hills, too, see a disaster in the Penard period?

A population collapse would have created a vacuum which migrants from across the Channel could progressively have filled. It is against this sort of background that we may have to view the disappearance of the established order right across southern Britain, the appearance of novel cultural traditions, some of undoubted French origin, and the wreck of French boats at Dover and Salcombe.

Field systems and land division

The best-known and most extensive field systems of prehistoric Britain are the 'Celtic' fields, vestiges of which can still be traced over much of the chalk downland of southern England. Unfortunately 'Celtic' fields remained typical throughout the prehistoric and Roman periods and into Saxon times, so that individual groups may have been established at different times, may have been used over centuries, and are difficult to date unless there is some explicit connection with a datable monument or artefact.

'Celtic' fields are rectangular in shape, though varying from approximately square to a 6 : 1 rectangle, they are from 20–150 metres in length, and range in size from about ¼ acre to 1½ acres. Fields of different sizes and proportions are generally grouped into blocks which may extend for hundreds of acres over downland slopes. Although one hesitates to suggest any average size for those systems which belong to our period, examples of 15–20 acres seem fairly common, although some may attain a hundred acres or more. Deverel-Rimbury farmsteads such as Plumpton Plain A, Martin Down and New Barn Down (Figures 5.14, 6.3) stand next to their 15–20 acre systems, which are usually separated by a belt of open country, perhaps common grazing, from adjoining field groups.

'Celtic' fields were carefully and skilfully laid out, the limits being marked out by a scraped up bank, a turf bank, or a small bank and adjoining ditch, all of which may be augmented by clearance stones. In some systems the fields seem to have been marked out individually, but in others, fields were laid off very accurately surveyed base lines. Many systems, the smaller farmstead groups in particular, have a layout respecting the lie of the land, so that the axes of the fields will tend to conform with the slope of the ground. This facilitates the formation of lynchet banks, which result when plough soil drifts downhill and piles up over the field banks. Thus lynchets are most prone to form over field margins which run along the slope of the land. In contrast to these positive lynchets, the constant ploughing and drifting of soil away from the top end of a field will lead to denudation, creating a negative lynchet.

Lynchets are therefore not strictly speaking a primary feature of 'Celtic' fields so much as a by-product of the system, and one which tended to heighten the original field margins. They would have formed much less coherently on those field systems, especially some of the larger examples, which were laid out on axes unrelated to the lie of the land, angling across spurs, slopes and valleys irrespective of the contours.

Looking at 'Celtic' fields one has the impression of double standards, as so often happens when we look at society in the Age of Stonehenge. Most of the smaller farmstead systems could easily have been set out by anyone, but the larger, more regularly laid-out blocks, such as those which extend over hundreds of acres around Cheselbourne in central Dorset, imply much greater surveying skill, and a much larger, well-organized labour force. Were these the fields of the more powerful elements in local society?

The greatest concentrations of barrows naturally tended to occur above or outside the field systems, in the upland pasture and scrub areas, often on land which may once have been cultivated but by now was degraded. Comparatively few are found amongst field systems, even allowing that some may have been ploughed out, for by-and-large field systems respect barrows, incorporating them where necessary in corners, at junctions, or even in the field banks. In an area like Cheselbourne it is noticeable that the field systems do not extend on to the tops of the downs and on to the higher spurs, and it is here that the majority of barrows survive. This carefully observed relationship suggests that in some sense barrows and fields were contemporary features in the landscape, although not necessarily contemporary in conception and construction. Because they tend to respect each other there are comparatively few sites offering a direct relationship of barrow and field. In most of these cases the barrow seems to have been there first, but at Winterbourne Abbas, Dorset (Figure 5.14), a triple bell-barrow seems to have been built over the corner of an existing 'Celtic' field. Similarly at Pentridge Hill, Dorset, a large barrow stands within a 'Celtic' field in such a position that it must have been raised when the field was already there. Had the barrow come first it would have been sensible to incorporate it in the field margin, but, a more important point, the impressive lynchets which define the field could not have formed with the barrow standing in their midst.

To generalize, it seems that a majority of 'Celtic' field systems are later than a majority of round barrows, but that the two traditions run on together in the latter part of our period. Translated into absolute chronology, the suggestion is that the main phase of 'Celtic' field construction did not begin before the latter part of the Overton period, by which time the chalk was already thickly

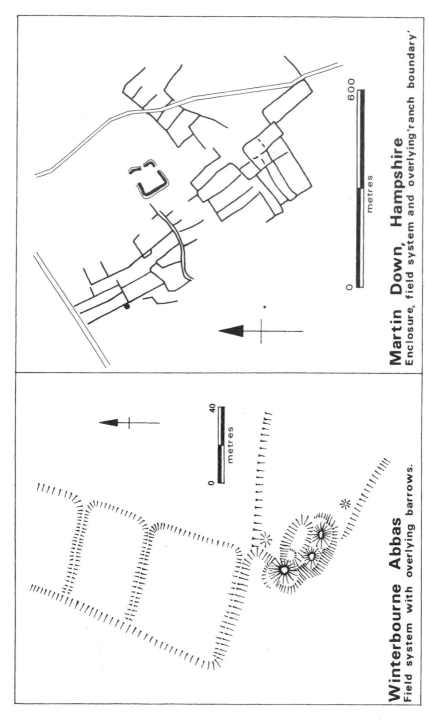

Winterbourne Abbas
Field system with overlying barrows.

Martin Down, Hampshire
Enclosure, field system and overlying 'ranch boundary'

Figure 5.14 Round barrows overlying a field system, Winterbourne Abbas, Dorset (after Bowen, 1961); Martin Down, Hants.: ranch boundary overlying a field system (after *RCHM Dorset*, by permission); Martin Down, Hants.: enclosure, field system and overlying 'ranch boundary' (after *RCHM Dorset*, by permission)

studded with barrows. Most of the field systems will then have been laid out in the Bedd Branwen and Knighton Heath periods, with round barrow construction continuing, albeit on a reduced scale. In support of this is the fact that so many Deverel-Rimbury farms incorporated a field system; that some, such as Itford Hill, can now definitely be associated with nearby barrows; and these settlements belonged mainly to the period between Overton and Penard. Further valuable dating evidence comes from bronzes found in the banks or lynchets of field systems, for example the 'Ornament Horizon' hoard of armlets and a twisted torc from Ebbesbourne Wake in Wiltshire. This lynchet, and the field system of which it formed a part must therefore have been in existence by the Knighton Heath period.

The development of 'Celtic' field systems on the chalk was perhaps a response to rising population levels and the need to make the best use of land, large areas of which had already been ruined. Given the likely level of agricultural skills at this time no amount of careful husbandry could have kept the thin downland soils fertile for ever. The fact that at Winterbourne Abbas and Pentridge round barrows were built over field systems indicates that by the Knighton Heath period arable fields were already being abandoned and given over to pasture. The culmination of this trend, in the Penard period, saw the wholesale abandonment of the field systems, and their replacement by the 'ranch boundaries' and a new pastoral economy. By this time the downs may well have become better-watered pasture due to increased precipitation, and thus a much more attractive prospect for organized stock raising.

Before leaving the subject of fields and boundaries on the chalk, mention must be made of the hollow or sunken ways, made by the incessant passage of cattle, and the double lynchet trackways that often form an integral part of 'Celtic' field systems and farms. At Plumpton Plain A examples of the double lynchet ways link the farmstead enclosures with each other and with the fields (Figure 5.2), while at Shearplace they extend from the farm out between the fields (Figure 5.4). These have often been laid out as part of the original field plan, between banks which in time will become lynchets like the surrounding field banks. Uphill they will be defined by a positive lynchet, whereas a negative lynchet will tend to form below the downhill bank.

'Celtic' fields resembling in general shape and size those on the southern chalk, have survived widely throughout Britain on marginal land and upland where subsequent ploughing has not been too savage. They differ from the southern systems mainly in the method of constructing the field boundaries. Many of the systems in south-west England belong to our period (Figures 5.8, 5.9), not so the many systems in northern England, notably the Pennines, where they are generally assigned to the centuries immediately before and during the Roman occupation. They are often intimately related to settlements of those periods, for example the famous systems around Grassington in

Yorkshire, and the fields clustering around the Crosby Garrett settlement in Westmorland.

Since they are invariably in areas where stone is readily available, field boundaries in the Highland Zone tend to be of stone, either lines of boulders and slabs on edge, as often on Dartmoor and in parts of Wales; or stony banks, formed either from field clearance material, from stones assembled for the purpose, or, very often, a combination of the two. Lynchet formation depends on local conditions.

Not all the well-documented fields of south-west England can be classed as 'Celtic' fields. Fields and plots attached to the Dartmoor settlements are often irregular, even curvilinear areas, girt by stone walls (Figure 5.8). Another pattern could be seen at Stannon Down on the edge of Bodmin Moor (Figure 5.8), where long strip fields 5–20 metres wide and up to 70 metres long were delineated by rough stone walls formed of field clearance stones. The total area of these plots is under two acres, although this may have been doubled if similar strips extended northwards under the encroaching china clay tip. Clearly these amounted to no more than garden plots for a community which must have numbered up to a hundred people. Nevertheless they provided a source of vegetable food for a predominantly pastoral settlement. To the north of the main cluster of houses, well away from the arable plots, were irregular enclosures of very different shape and construction, much more square in proportion, and bound by carefully built stone walls. These can reasonably be interpreted as the stock pounds which would have been much more central to the life of this community.

The so called 'arable' settlements on the drier northern and eastern sides of Dartmoor are characteristically integrated with a group of a few stone-walled rectangular and square fields which seldom cover more than two acres altogether. As at Stannon Down a heavy dependence on stock-raising must be assumed. Some larger systems are known. Of the extensive systems on Horridge Common, fields totalling about 7.6 acres appear to belong to one settlement (Figure 5.9C) theoretically enough to feed the twenty or so people in this community. In a completely different coastal environment at Gwithian, the total extent of fields is unknown, but they perhaps covered about a half of the Horridge area.

At Horridge Common the field systems of adjoining farmsteads appear to abut on to each other, but their boundaries can be detected by discontinuities in alignment. More significant land divisions are provided by the Dartmoor reaves, linear stone dykes, occasionally faced on one or both sides, which can extend for up to 2.3 kilometres, and divide the moorland into large blocks. Some run along the contours between 1100–1350 feet, dividing the moor tops from the lower slopes, but others run directly up the slopes to meet the along-the-contour reaves at right angles, then sometimes continue on to the moor top. In some cases reaves are utilized as field system boundaries, as at

Rippon Tor (Figure 5.9B). Clearly reaves were major land divisions, equivalent in some respects to the ranch boundaries of the southern chalk. They may well have served several functions. Those running along the contours still separate the exposed tops from gentler slopes today, and may thus have separated winter from summer pastures. On the other hand, those running up the slopes would have served better as territorial boundaries between the lands of one community and the next.

That these reave systems were fundamental to the land management of Dartmoor in our period is illustrated by the well-explored systems near Cholwich Town (Figures 5.15, 16). The reaves are clearly earlier than peat growth, and are intimately connected with several enclosed pastoral settlements. In this area the Willings Walls and Cholwich Town reaves seem best interpreted as boundaries between upper and lower pasture, but the cross dyke, Rook reave, Shell Top reave and, in this case the along-the-contour Penn Moore reave, make more sense as territorial boundaries. The positioning of the entrances into the various settlements supports this theory.

Similar complex functions may have been served by the linear banks and dykes now coming to light beneath the blanket bogs of Scotland, best explored at the Black Moss of Achnacree in Argyll. Here several hundred metres of banks have been traced beneath the peat, clearly only part of a much larger system. They consist of a gravel and earth core derived from a fronting ditch on the north side, with a battered north face reveted with large stones, and a top and sloping southern side capped with smaller stones. There are two radiocarbon dates, one of *c.* 1359 bc from the old land surface beneath the bank, and another of *c.* 980 bc for the inception of the peat growth which covers the site. This suggests the system was constructed and used in the Bedd Branwen period, and became unusable, following waterlogging and podsolization, in the Penard period.

The Black Moss system appears to face north towards the high ground, and seems best interpreted as a head dyke, a cattle barrier and drain dividing rough grazing on heathland to the north from cultivable land on the south. The present land use shows a very similar division, for the modern crofts extend roughly up to this line, and it was in cutting back the peat bog to extend the croftlands northwards that the banks came to light. There is a hint of other dykes angling southwards, so that the system may have included boundary dykes running up to the head-dyke, dividing one farm from the next.

The impression given here, as so often in south-west England, is that some crops were grown, but that stock-raising was all-important. Surface observation elsewhere in the Highlands and Islands, for example around the Callanish complex on Lewis, suggests that such field systems will prove to be common in Scotland, and indeed in many other upland regions, once work like that on the Dartmoor reaves gets underway. Fields have been reported dating from the beginning of our period at the deeply stratified Udal site on North Uist, and

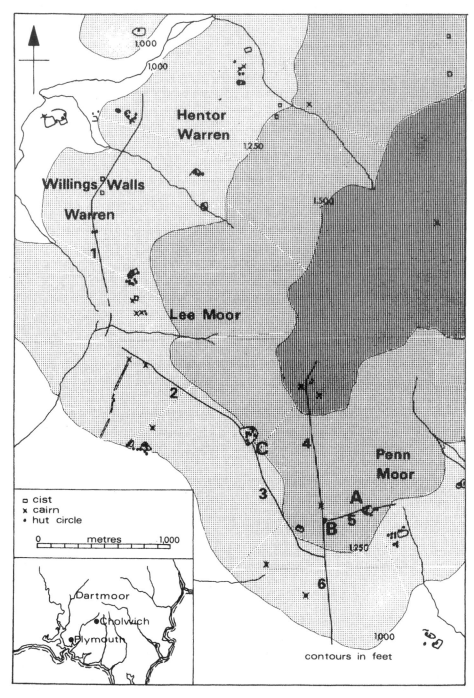

Figure 5.15 Reaves on Dartmoor, near Cholwich Town, Devon (after Fleming, Collis and Jones, 1973)

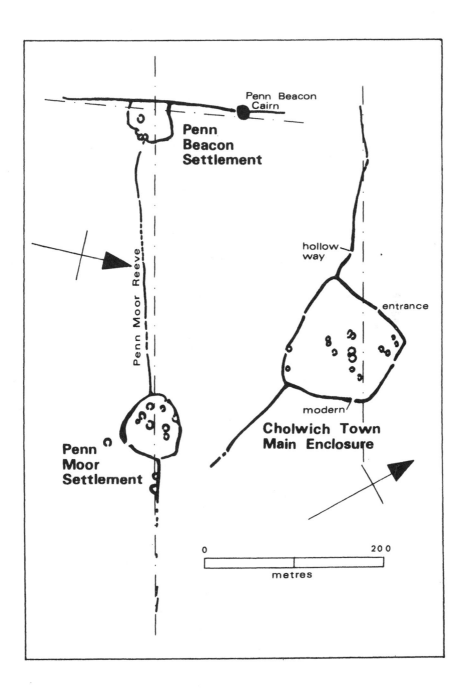

Figure 5.16 Dartmoor reaves: the relationship of reaves and enclosed settlements (after Fleming, Collis and Jones, 1973)

the evidence for Second Millennium cultivation in the Hebrides and Northern Isles is now mounting so rapidly as to suggest that many field systems which are at present undated will prove to belong to that period. In the Shetlands the massive stone walled houses often stand adjacent to, or within, a group of irregular curvilinear fields defined by stone dykes. These may be terraced when on sloping ground, and they are generally dotted with the neat stone piles of clearance heaps. Individual plots range from 0.1–1.5 acres, but a figure of half an acre is common.

The field systems of Ireland are second only to the Celtic fields of southern England in extent, owing their survival to the blanket bog which cloaked and sealed the prehistoric landscape almost as effectively as volcanic ash buried Pompeii. Considerable field systems, with associated farmsteads and burial sites, have now been discovered beneath the peat in Tyrone, Kerry and especially Mayo, although these are merely the areas where fieldwork has been most intense. The distribution must be very much wider. The remarkable Beaghmore ritual complex in Co. Tyrone illustrates how extensive are the landscapes preserved by the peat. Here the past has been peeled back, so to speak, to reveal 1½ acres of stone circles, cairns and rows, some of which, together with three earlier field dykes, run on under the undug peat.

The most extensive and best explored field system under the bog is the Behy-Glenulra system (Figure 5.17), investigated over an area of 1.3 × 0.9 kilometres (117 hectares, 290 acres) in Co. Mayo, but still running on under undug peat. This fine example of a running block system consists of long,

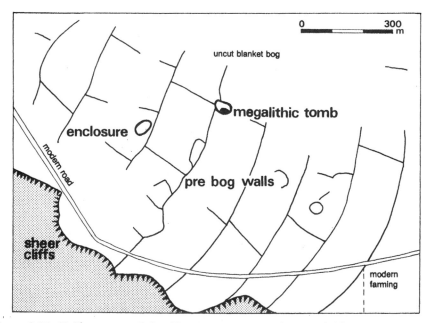

Figure 5.17 Field system at Behy-Glenulra, Co. Mayo (after Caulfield, 1978)

slightly curved stone dykes, 150–250 metres apart, extending from unexplored peat for about 1 kilometre down to the edge of a steep cliff edge, forming long strip fields. These are divided by off-set cross dykes at intervals of 200–300 metres, forming large fields of 5 acres and more. This system was designed for stock, but on the most fertile parts of the hillside there are small enclosures set within the larger fields, which can be interpreted as arable plots.

The Behy-Glenulra system incorporates a court cairn, and its finds, and a radiocarbon date of *c.* 2510 bc, suggest that the whole complex was laid out and in use just before our period began. Whether it continued to be worked in the Meldon Bridge period is uncertain, but the inception of peat growth in the Mount Pleasant period may have brought its usefulness to an end, and that of many other Irish field systems. The site at Belderg Beg in Co. Mayo illustrates the problem which some farming communities had to face in Ireland by this time. Here an earth and stone wall enclosed a circular structure, which, to judge from the number of saddle mills and grinding stones found, may have been a granary rather than a house. Adjacent were several contiguous tillage plots of irregular shape, which at first had been cross-ploughed. But signs of lazy bed cultivation were superimposed on the criss-cross ard marks, a sign that the ground was becoming increasingly damp and difficult to work. After up to 30 centimetres of peat had formed a long dyke was built using material robbed from the earlier enclosure, and suggesting, together with cow horns trampled into the peat, that local farmers had now to give the area over to stock. A barbed and tanged flint arrowhead suggests this later activity occurred in the Mount Pleasant or Overton periods.

But local conditions, especially the lie of the land and the soil, will have dictated land use, and better-drained soils will have remained cultivable throughout our period. The evidence at the crucial Lough Gur complex in Co. Limerick is sadly fragmentary, but by the Mount Pleasant period fields had been formed on the hillside by running cross-walls between gullies running downhill. Soil drifting downhill and piling up at these cross-walls gives these fields a terraced effect. Little is known of their extent and size, but there is evidence for cereal cultivation both before and during our period. Individual fields are difficult to date, but on site D, for example, the terraces are later than houses producing Beaker pottery but earlier than a structure from which came mould fragments for spearheads and palstaves of the Penard period.

In a completely different environment, a pastoral field system of similar extent to that at Behy-Glenulra, but of completely different structure, has in recent years been excavated at Fengate near Peterborough (Figure 5.18). Here the fields are on the gravel of the Fen Edge. As excavated they are defined by ditches, but originally there must have been banks too, and probably hedge-banks, for these fields were designed for cattle. The largest system, covering *c.* 288 acres, is partly laid out on 'running block' lines, extending away from the fen margin at right angles. Its main linear elements are formed by paired

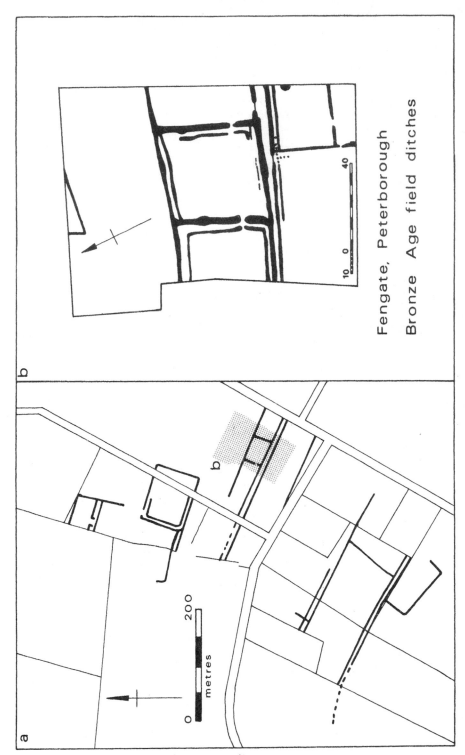

Fengate, Peterborough

Bronze Age field ditches

Figure 5.18 The field system at Fengate, Peterborough: a. general plan, b. detail of northern part of site (after Pryor, 1976)

ditches, each pair 75–100 metres apart, and ditches divide these strips into smaller units. To judge from the positioning of causeways through the ditches, each strip may have been an individual land holding, the paired ditches forming farm boundaries. To the north and south these large divisions give way to groups of smaller multiple-ditched fields. On the north there is a major boundary between two field blocks, each having access to a trackway between the dividing ditches (Figure 5.18). System A to the south of the main field block appears to represent a separate pastoral unit. Here a large ring-ditch farmstead adjoins a few, small, rectangular ditched enclosures. Cattle bones and flint tools for butchering are evocative of the principal activity at this complex, while several radiocarbon dates, ranging from 2030–1860 bc, together with much Grooved ware, assign it firmly to the Mount Pleasant period. The laying out of the main field blocks, also for stock farming, must have occurred at about the same time, for c14 dates range from 2030–1833 bc. But this main system remained in use until the Penard phase, for the terminal dates range from *c.* 1040–940 bc.

It is unlikely that the Fengate fields are unique, for air photography suggests that other systems cover the gravels of much of the Midlands and eastern England. In particular they can be traced northwards from Fengate for a distance of twenty miles or more along the Fen Edge, to a site at Billingborough Fen in south Lincolnshire, where a rectilinear enclosed settlement associated with a local equivalent of Deverel-Rimbury pottery adjoins another field complex. It is also in the north-east Midlands that aerial survey has brought to light much more extensive, much larger ditch and dyke systems, although these appear to be major territorial boundaries.

The Fengate fields take one stage further the evidence for pastoral activity in the Overton period that Green has deduced from a study of ring ditches in the Ouse Valley. In the Lowland as in the Highland Zone it seems easier to identify evidence for pastoral activity than for the cultivation that is known to have been widespread. This is perhaps because stock need more substantial, and therefore more durable, boundaries than arable plots.

One other important indication of prehistoric cultivation is provided by the 'cairnfields' which are so numerous and widespread in the Highland Zone. These consist of scatters of up to several hundred small, stony tumps, each up to a few metres across and half a metre or less high which may stretch over many acres. They are littered over upland areas on moorland, heaths and rough grazing up to *c.* 1,200–1,300 feet. There is a marked resemblance to the random pattern of field clearance still practised not only by peasant farmers in countries such as Turkey, but still occasionally in Scotland today. Excavation of individual heaps has often shown that they are just that: loose piles of stones with no sign of structure or function. On the other hand cairnfields do incorporate larger mounds which are genuine burial cairns, High Knowes, Alnham and Chatton Sandyford in Northumberland being notable examples.

At the same time some of the smaller heaps have been found to cover pits and other traces of burials, or have had burials inserted into them, so that some cairnfields undoubtedly had a sepulchral function. But to cairn-burying communities engaged in field clearance it would surely be a natural process to combine the two activities, to inter their dead under or in clearance piles in the process of being formed, and to build the occasional larger, more formal cairns for those of higher rank.

The study of cairnfields is very much in its infancy, and has been limited to field survey, and excavation usually of a few individual heaps. Not unnaturally the largest, and most prominent, examples have usually been chosen, and not surprisingly these have sometimes yielded burials. What is clearly required, if this manifestation of upland agriculture is to be fully understood, is the total excavation of a cairnfield, not just the heaps but all the ground between and around them.

At many sites low banks and lynchets exist or have been claimed, zig-zagging in amongst the heaps, joining up some and surrounding others, forming small plots. Unfortunately the heather, bracken and other usually dense ground cover, makes the extent of these boundaries difficult to estimate.

Like so many vestiges of ancient agriculture, cairnfields are difficult to date, but they were probably assembled throughout prehistory and up to fairly recent times. However, those which have produced burials have a good claim to be considered relics of Second Millennium field clearance. Many lie well above the present limits of cultivation, and must thus represent cultivation when a kinder climate would have permitted it at such altitudes. This means the Second Millennium BC or the early Medieval period. If opinion so often favours the former it is because of the burials, and because so many are cloaked by the peat which formed in later prehistory. Some examples, as on the Fell Sandstone moorlands in Northumberland, are probably prehistoric because they are on soils which were ruined for cultivation, and turned to acid moorland, by the Roman period. Some cairnfields adjoin or include buildings which offer some chance of dating. Those around the massive stone houses of Shetland combine with irregular plots and enclosures to suggest genuine Second Millennium field systems. But in southern Scotland and northern England those overlying or adjoining settlements and buildings can often be assigned to periods much later than the cairnfields.

Ploughs, tillage and crops

Evidence for cereal crops has been recovered in so many different parts of Britain and Ireland that there can have been few communities which did not cultivate at least a few small plots to supplement their diet. The evidence takes the form of seed and grain impressions on pottery, plant remains preserved by carbonization or waterlogging, and the presence of the pollen of cereals or weeds of cultivation in pollen samples. Indirect evidence comes from querns or mills for grinding grain and other plant food, from rubbing stones and storage pits.

Cereals appear to have been the only crops grown in these islands down to the late First Millennium BC, when legumes such as the Celtic bean were introduced. There has been considerable confusion over the different cereals preferred in different periods in prehistory. It has long been axiomatic that wheat was preferred to barley in the Neolithic, but that the 'Beaker folk' instituted a massive swing to barley, no doubt to cater for the alcoholic beverages that filled their Beakers. This view appears to have arisen from a misreading of the evidence, which was based largely on the considerable body of material recovered from the Windmill Hill causewayed enclosure. The many grain impressions from this site showed a dramatic preponderance of wheat over barley, and this was taken to indicate a general preference for wheat at this time. Only recently has it been appreciated that the Windmill Hill figures reflect a local, not a national trend. A factor not previously taken into account is the relationship between soils and crops. The light calcareous soils, such as these on the chalk, are equally suitable for the cultivation of wheat and barley, whereas heavy clay soils are better suited to wheat. The significance of this point at Windmill Hill is that much of the pottery bearing wheat impressions was brought in from the Bath-Frome district of Somerset, which is characterized by heavy soils. Thus the heavy emphasis on wheat at Windmill Hill reflects a local situation twenty miles away, not even the situation in the immediate neighbourhood, let alone over the country as a whole. The supposed preponderance of barley in the 'Bronze Age' also rests on biased evidence. Most grain impressions then come from Beakers, and as these were specialized drinking vessels it is hardly surprising that they bear mostly barley impressions.

So the relative importance of wheat and barley did not change with time but varied from region to region according to local conditions. Furthermore it is important not to translate this southern evidence into Highland Zone settings, where the evidence for crops is regrettably slight. Northern and western regions, with their very different environments, were better suited to pastoralism than cultivation, and this is reflected in the much greater incidence of grain impressions on southern pottery than on pottery from the Highland Zone.

The principal strains of cereals grown throughout our period were naked barley and emmer wheat, though hulled barley and einkorn were both cultivated in smaller quantities. By the later First Millennium a changeover to hulled barley and spelt had taken place, but exactly when this happened is not clear.

The important point about spelt and hulled barley is that they are autumn-sown varieties, whereas emmer and naked barley are winter-sown. This means that the former could be sown in the slack season after the harvest, and would ripen ahead of the emmer and naked barley. By planting seed of one sort in the autumn and the other in the spring it would be possible to effect a more even distribution of work through the farming year, extending both the sowing and the harvest considerably. To an outsider it might appear that there were two harvests, and it is in this context that the reference of Diodorus Siculus to two annual harvests in Britain at about 500 BC may perhaps be seen. It is tempting to place these changes in the Penard period, when so much in Britain was transformed. The evidence for this conclusion rests on the preponderance of hulled barley at the Blackpatch and Itford Hill settlements. At the latter a cache of hulled barley gave a radiocarbon date of *c.* 1000 bc, confirming the pottery evidence that this was late Deverel-Rimbury activity, in the Penard period. It may be no coincidence that a change from naked to hulled barley has been observed in the Netherlands at this time. Unfortunately the situation in the crucial area of north-west France is unknown.

There is no evidence that the cultivation of other cereals, such as oats, rye, club and bread wheat, reached these islands before the late First Millennium. This is surprising in view of the sporadic evidence for the cultivation, certainly of oats and bread wheat, in the Netherlands from the Third Millennium onwards. The absence of oats is particularly puzzling since this crop is so well-suited to many of our Highland Zone environments. Reports of oats from the settlement of the Overton period at Rosinish on Benbecula have proved to be premature, but it must be stressed that comparatively little work has been done on plant remains from Highland Zone settlements.

No doubt the farmers of our period were as adaptable in their methods of tillage as in everything else. The marks left by their ploughs or ards are now known from many parts of Britain and Ireland, and suggest that a light ard was generally used, one which scratched a groove-like furrow in the ground but was not provided with a mould-board to turn a furrow. 'Bronze Age' engravings of ploughing scenes have been found widely in Europe, from Sweden to the Alpes Maritimes and Val Camonica in Liguria, and they consistently show a similar light ard, almost invariably drawn by two oxen (Figure 5.19). If the terrain demanded it could also be drawn by humans. Many upland fields were too small for ox-drawn ploughs and could only have been ploughed using human traction, for example at Holne Moor on Dartmoor, where the plough run was only 38 metres long. Two forms of ard are represented in the engravings, the more primitive crook-ard or sole-ard, which resembles a giant hoe, with beam and horizontal sole in one acutely angled piece, and an attached stilt (Figure 5.19); and the more complex spade-ard or beam-ard, which has the stilt and share as an entity, attached near the bottom of a separate beam. Examples of both have been found in Danish and Dutch bogs, usually dated to the last few centuries BC or even later, but the Hvorslev crook-ard from Denmark has recently been C14 dated to *c.* 1490 bc. In view of the typological simplicity of this form, this is the one likely to have been pulled by

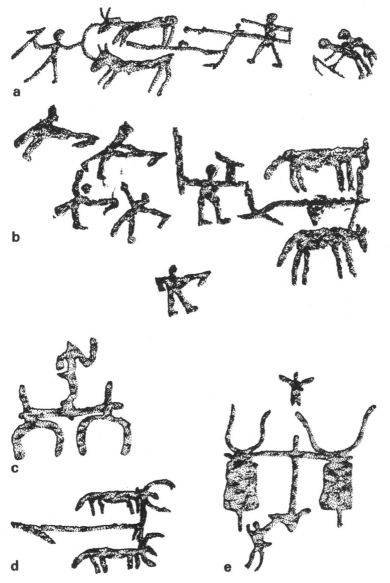

Figure 5.19 Ploughing scenes in European rock art: all in the Val Camonica, Italy, except e. Monte Bego, Alpes Maritimes (a–d. after Anati, 1965; e. after Clark, 1952)

two oxen, and sometimes human labour, over the fields of Britain and Ireland in the Third and Second Millennia. The spade-ard was probably not introduced until towards the mid-First Millennium, which is the likely date of the combined stilt and plough-head of a spade-ard incorporated in the foundations of the crannog at Milton Loch, Kirkcudbright (*c.* 490 bc, 400 bc).

No bronze shares for ards are known from these islands, but attachable stone bar shares, which probably fitted into a frame in the wooden share, have frequently been found in Scotland, especially in the massive stone-house settlements of Shetland. Usually these stone shares are represented only by the broken tip, such as was found lodged in a furrow in one of the Gwithian fields. Amongst the ard fittings, that were probably common but have seldom been recognized, are the pebbles which were fitted into plough soles as an anti-wear device. Some Danish crook-ards from bogs, such as the Andbjerg ard, actually have pebble-studded soles, though these examples are probably of fairly recent date. Plough pebbles, with one side worn to a convex face, are best known from Roman sites such as Newstead, but there are probably examples languishing in collections up and down the country as 'polishers' or 'rubbers', and they are worth looking out for in prehistoric contexts.

The ubiquity of crook-ards in our period is attested by discoveries of plough marks in many parts of Britain and Ireland. Best known are the criss-cross ard marks, from sites as far apart as Rosinish on Benbecula, Sumburgh in Shetland, Skaill in Orkney – where a cross-ploughed field produced over 150 bar share tips – South Street in Wiltshire, possibly under barrow Amesbury G71 in Wiltshire, in two layers at Gwithian in Cornwall, and Belderg Beg in Co. Mayo. Sometimes these may indicate genuine cross-ploughing both across and up the slope, as recommended by Pliny many centuries later. In other cases one may be dealing with superimposed layers of one-way ploughing at right angles. Criss-cross ard marks are known long before our period under the long barrow at South Street, Wiltshire (before *c.* 2810 bc). They were still common in the Romano-British period to judge from examples as far apart as Walker, Newcastle upon Tyne, and Overton Down, Wiltshire. The reasons for cross-ploughing are imperfectly understood, but it was easy enough to do in the 'Celtic' fields of prehistory. It may certainly have been advantageous in breaking new ground. Undisputed cases of one direction ploughing are hard to find before the late First Millennium. But at the Sumburgh settlement on Shetland, two levels of criss-cross marks were followed by a layer which showed ploughing in one direction only, while the recent Holne Moor excavations on Dartmoor have produced signs of one-way ploughing in plots adjoining a reave.

Not all land was suitable for ploughing, and even in recent times there have been those, such as Scottish crofters and Irish small-holders, who have been compelled to prepare their plots for sowing by means other than the plough. Hoe agriculture is a common recourse of peasant cultivators, and the spade is still the standby of gardener and allotment holder alike. No doubt both these tools were familiar to prehistoric farmers. Some of the European rock engravings of cultivation scenes show the hoe being used, in Figure 5.19a by a woman with a baby on her back. She is following a typical two-ox crook-ard, led by a man apparently with another hoe. Many so-called 'axes' of bronze may have been hoe-heads, especially the smaller socketed 'axes' of the Ewart Park phase. Rock engravings such as that just described show that spades and hoes must have had their uses even where ploughs were in use. This is further illustrated by some of the ploughed fields at Gwithian, where spade marks are frequently encountered around the borders of the fields, suggesting hand digging of those areas where it was difficult to take the plough. Casts of these spade impressions suggest a wooden implement with an asymmetric D-shaped blade. Spade marks have been reported at several other sand sites, notably at Rosinish and at Kilellan Farm.

In many areas spade and hoe would have had to suffice for tilling the ground, especially in stony hill country. At Stannon Down in Cornwall it would have been impossible to use a plough in the small strip fields, which in any case were so littered with boulders that they could only have been worked with hand tools. Spade marks found here were very similar to those preserved at Gwithian. The upland plots associated with cairnfields, littered with stone heaps and with thin uneven soil cover, would also have demanded hand-working. The spade would also have become increasingly necessary with the onset of waterlogging and a wetter climate. One answer to this problem, at least on a small scale, is to hand dig trenched cultivation ridges, the 'lazy beds' so familiar in recent times in Scotland and Ireland. The early onset of peat growth in Ireland meant that this sort of system was developed there by the Mount Pleasant period. Thus at Belderg Beg in Co. Mayo, criss-cross ard marks are overlaid by vestiges of a 'lazy bed' system, and at Carrownaglogh in Co. Mayo patches of lazy bed ridges were found in irregular plots within an enclosure.

Milling, grinding and reaping

Both saucer and saddle mills ('querns') were known to early farmers, but the former seems to have lost some of its popularity by the Mount Pleasant period, when the saddle mill became the standard cereal grinding device. Saddle mills occur consistently on Deverel-Rimbury settlements in southern England, and in the south-western settlements such as Gwithian and Stannon Down. Another, rarer form of mill is the flat-faced oval type as found in the primary silt of the Angle ditch (Figure 3.17), and in the Kilellan Farm settlement. The purpose of this form is uncertain. A word of caution about the function of all these mills is necessary, for they can be used to grind not only plants other than cereals but also other substances. For example, in the 1920s saddle mills were observed in use in Algeria for grinding gypsum.

Reaping implements of both flint and bronze are known. For the earlier part of our period there are one piece flint sickles, both curved and straight, their purpose indicated by the characteristic lustre of 'corn gloss' which many bear. It was a long time before the first bronze sickles appeared, the knobbed form found in Ornament Horizon hoards of the Knighton Heath period. In the Penard period the cylinder-socket sickle was a notable British invention, instituting an indigenous tradition of socketed sickles, which lasted through the first half of the First Millennium. Doubt has been cast on the efficacy of at least some bronze sickles for reaping grain, but this is a problem which only experiment can resolve.

Domesticated animals

Cattle were the principal domesticated animal of our period, and many communities seem to have kept cattle almost exclusively. At many settlements over 90 per cent of the animal bones have proved to be cattle. Bones from the Wessex 'Deverel-Rimbury' enclosures consisted of 50–70 per cent cattle, while the proportion of cattle at Rams Hill ranged from 90 per cent in the early phase to 79 per cent in the rebuilt site of the Penard period. Animal bones are unfortunately comparatively few on the Deverel-Rimbury settlements of Sussex. At Itford Hill and Shearplace Hill cattle predominated, but at most sites cattle, sheep/goat and pig are all present, usually in too small a quantity to indicate relative importance.

Unfortunately because of harsh soil conditions, few Highland Zone sites have produced bones so that the surviving evidence could be biased, and not representative of the true situation in upland areas. One might have expected differences of emphasis compared with lowland sites, for example that sheep might have been a better proposition than cattle. Much of the Scottish evidence comes from coastal sites under calcareous sand, purely because bone survives exceedingly well in such an environment. Preferences on these sites need not reflect the situation in Scottish upland areas, indeed, there are considerable differences in the proportions of animals even among the coastal sites. Thus at Northton on Harris cattle and sheep occurred in equal numbers and abundant red deer suggest hunting was important. But at Kilellan cattle were overwhelmingly dominant, representing over 90 per cent of the bones recovered, sheep and pig were very few, and wild animals practically absent. Another complete contrast is provided by the Culbin Sands midden, where practically all of the bones recovered were sheep and/or goats.

The Irish material is rather scanty, but at Lough Gur cattle were reported as totally dominant, comprising 90–99 per cent of the bones in the various levels. Of the bones recovered from the 'domestic' levels which accumulated around the Newgrange passage grave in the Mount Pleasant period, 56.5 per cent were cattle, 30.9 per cent pig, only 5.3 per cent sheep or goat, and 1.6 per cent horse. Cattle continued to predominate in Ireland well into the First Millennium, for at Ballinderry II crannog, Co. Offaly, in the occupation level of the Ewart Park phase, cattle were again described as the most important animal, but sheep/goat and pig were also present.

The prevalence of pig at Newgrange raises another problem, that special types of site involving special activities might demand some animals rather than others, for example for sacrifice or ceremonies, creating a situation in no way representative of the state of affairs in everyday life. Thus the emphasis on pig was even greater at another 'public' monument, Durrington Walls, with over twice as many pig as cattle, both from the enclosure itself and from the occupation outside the monument. Other animals, notably sheep or goats, were scarcely represented. Another potential source of distortion, affecting the importance of sheep or goats, is the question of the uses to which different animals were put. Cattle, as primary sources of meat and leather, may have been butchered with greater regularity than sheep or goats if the latter were being kept primarily for their wool. They could well be kept in large flocks for this purpose, in which case their true numbers would not be revealed in bone counts, which mainly reflect animals butchered for food and skins.

Nevertheless there is some evidence that the importance of sheep and goats increased from the end of our period onwards. At Fengate, where the fields were abandoned in the Penard period, cattle consistently made up 70 per cent of the animal bones. There is some evidence that at the outset pig, with 25 per cent of the bones, came next in importance, but that sheep or goats overtook pigs as time went on. At about the same time as the Fengate fields were being abandoned, the late Deverel-Rimbury settlement at Eldon's Seat on the Dorset coast appears to have had almost as much concern for sheep or goat (40.7 per cent) as cattle (50.6 per cent). Pig here was down to 3.5 per cent. But when the site was re-occupied around the eighth century BC, sheep or goats (61.7 per cent) were much more important than cattle (28.3 per cent) in the economy of the settlement. Similarly at the Grimthorpe hill-fort in Yorkshire, again built in the Penard period, sheep or goats have a figure of 25 per cent against 54.9 per cent for cattle and only 7.8 per cent for pig. Horse, with 7.3 per cent, was almost as important. And in the pre-hill-fort settlement at Ivinghoe, Buckinghamshire, dating to the Ewart Park phase, sheep or goats show 31 per cent against 59 per cent cattle and 7 per cent pig. The trend to sheep or goat husbandry continued to increase into the late First Millennium, as indicated by the evidence from the later levels at Eldon's Seat. Compare, too, the figures from later hill-fort levels, as at Rainsborough, Northamptonshire, with cattle 34.2 per cent and sheep or goats 45.2 per cent.

Importance in bone count must not be confused with importance in the diet. The significant figures are average carcass weights: 900 pounds for a cow, 800 pounds for a horse, 200 pounds for a pig and only 125 pounds for a sheep. Thus at the Grimthorpe hill-fort, although the bone count figures were 54.9 per cent cattle and 25 per cent sheep or goats, the comparative meat weight counts were 82.4 per cent cattle and only 5.3 per cent sheep or goats. Horse, with a bone count of only 7.3 per cent, had a greater meat weight count with 9.8 per cent. Even with the increased importance of sheep or goats in the later First Millennium, beef clearly remained the principal meat for most people.

The main breed of cattle kept by Bronze Age herdsmen was the small *Bos longifrons*, the Celtic short-horn, which stood only 4 feet high at the shoulder, and was about the size of the modern Dexter. However larger breeds have been detected on some sites, for example at Boscombe Down East most of the cattle were *Bos longifrons*, but one horn-core, larger, coarser and fluted, belonged to another type. At both Mildenhall in Suffolk and Ogbourne Down in Wiltshire, in addition to bones of *Bos longifrons* there were larger horn cores and bones attesting small numbers of another breed.

It has been customary to distinguish between the *Bos longifrons* of the Second and First Millennia BC and the earlier *Bos frontosus*, of the first farmers, which with its larger size and longer horns, stood closer to the wild *Bos primigenius*. It was convenient to explain this change by supposing that *Bos longifrons* was introduced from the Continent by Beaker immigrants. Without Beaker migrants a much more complex solution must be contemplated, recognizing that changes in animals as in people, could emerge gradually by indigenous genetic processes. The evidence for the existence of larger breeds alongside *Bos longifrons*, and the undoubted skills of early farmers in animal husbandry provide clues to the workings of such a process. So few large assemblages of bones are known that it would be unwise to be dogmatic about the range of breeds and sizes of animals present over Britain and Ireland as a whole both before and during our period.

Certainly herds of the larger *Bos frontosus* still existed in the Mount Pleasant period, for the Durrington Walls cattle are of this form. On the other hand bones from a contemporary pit site at Puddlehill, Bedfordshire, already included a small breed of cattle, suggesting that *Bos longifrons* had emerged by this stage. It should not be forgotten that Durrington Walls is a specialized site, and the animals brought to the site might be selected specially, perhaps for size.

Study of the Durrington Walls cattle suggests that castration was practised, another indication of the skilled husbandry of early herdsmen. It has often been claimed that prehistoric farmers were unable to carry all their stock over the winter and thus killed off yearlings to alleviate the problem of winter feed. More recent studies have disputed this, showing that for most communities overwintering of stock was no problem. At Newgrange, for example, only 10 per cent of cattle were killed before $1\frac{1}{2}$ years of age, 55 per cent reached $2\frac{1}{2}$ years, and 20 per cent $3\frac{1}{2}$–4 years. It was estimated that most of the cattle on this site had been slaughtered between 2 and 3 years old, at the end of immaturity, and that this would indicate beasts reared primarily for meat rather than milk or traction. But this would be expected of a 'special' site like Newgrange. By comparison at Ram's Hill, cattle had a quite high life expectation, suggesting that dairy products were important and that living animals, i.e. the size of herds, was important as an indication of wealth. Local conditions no doubt controlled husbandry practice, and there may well have been areas where food, fodder and over-wintering were a more difficult problem. Thus at the Kilellan settlement the cattle which provided much of the meat were all young when killed. On the other hand at Eldon's Seat, on the south coast of England, meat supply seems to have been no problem, since only 22 per cent of the total of available joints of beef were taken from the carcass (and only 24 per cent from sheep carcasses).

Sheep and goats (*Ovis aries/Capra hircus*) have so often to be bracketed together because of the problem of distinguishing between their bones. Both were clearly kept by prehistoric farmers, and it would be a mistake to assume that sheep were necessarily more numerous than goats in most regions. The breed of sheep seems to have been a rather small scrawny animal something like the modern Soay sheep. The evidence from Ram's Hill suggests that in some areas at least the ewes may have been horn-less.

With pig remains there is often the problem of deciding whether one is dealing with the domesticated animal (*Sus domesticus*) or the wild boar (*Sus scrofa*), since the two overlap at the extremes of their size ranges. The situation may have been further complicated by domesticated pigs being left to forage for themselves in local woods and crossing with wild boars. There may also have been deliberate crossing of domestic pigs with wild males to improve the breed, as Homer describes so much later. The Durrington Walls remains suggest an animal standing 28 inches high at the shoulder, while the New-grange pigs 'were among the largest domestic breeds of prehistoric Europe', possibly remote ancestors of the Irish 'greyhound' pig with a long face and long legs.

The horse (*Equus caballus*) presents the most severe problem of detecting domestication, as, unlike most other animals, domestication does not appear to have caused skeletal changes and adaptations. Horses from pre-First Millennium contexts in Britain and Ireland have usually been described as wild breeds, but mainly because it has for long been a maxim that the domesticated horse did not reach western Europe before the First Millennium. Even when domestication is proved, the food value of horse should not lead to automatic assumptions about riding and traction.

Recent work has upset the traditional horse theories. Domesticated horses have now been claimed from various parts of Beaker Europe, with the discovery of horses in larger than usual numbers at Chalcolithic Beaker sites in Hungary and Spain. Even if domestication is proved, there is no evidence for the horse-riding that has been claimed. Early domestication may now have to be considered for Britain and Ireland, too, for it has been argued that the Newgrange horses belonged to a domestic breed.

Whether domesticated or not, the horses which ranged over Britain and Ireland in our period appear to have been a small breed, a pony rather than a horse, of twelve to thirteen hands, with larger animals reaching fourteen hands. This would indicate an animal rather like a modern Exmoor pony.

Horse bones are rare on sites of our period, although this might merely reflect that horses normally were too valuable to be butchered for food. At

Grimthorpe, however, no less than 7.3 per cent of the animal bones were horse, and as some were less than two years of age these may have been killed for consumption.

While the domestic dog was known in Britain from the early Mesolithic period, domestic cat has not usually been accepted before the later First Millennium. Cat bones from earlier contexts, as at Newgrange, and some of the Knockadoon, Lough Gur, sites, have usually been referred to the wild species (*Felis silvestris*) which undoubtedly existed, though the fact that domestic cat has been claimed at the Ivinghoe Beacon hill-fort in the Ewart Park phase urges caution.

With domestic dog we are on firmer ground, for two sizes of domestic dog were already present at the Mesolithic settlement of Star Carr, Yorkshire, around 8000 BC. Clearly a variety of breeds can be expected on later prehistoric sites. In our period there are records of a large animal, of Labrador or large Retriever size, standing 50 centimetres high at the shoulder and represented by a complete skeleton at Ram's Hill, and by some of the canid bones at Durrington Walls; and of a smaller breed, of terrier size, known from several other sites. Even dogs may have been eaten to judge from the state of some of the canid bones at Newgrange, but the same site has also produced evidence for old dogs, suggesting that their importance in hunting and herding, as guard dogs and as pets, may have preserved most from the pot.

Hunting and gathering

Now that we can see how much of these islands had been cleared for agriculture by the early Second Millennium the potential of the countryside for hunting and gathering must be reviewed. Enough sites have yielded well-preserved plant remains to suggest that it was easier in our period to gather wild plants, as food, for medicinal purposes and for raw materials, than to find game. Since wild plants have been extensively used right up to modern times, we should expect prehistoric communities to have made full use of whatever was available.

The famous bog people of Denmark provide a wealth of evidence for the plants exploited by prehistoric communities. Analysis of the contents of the stomach of Tollund Man shows just how many plants in some form or another found their way into the prehistoric diet. His last meal appears to have been a not very appetizing gruel made up not only of barley but of less familiar ingredients such as linseed (*Linum usitatissimum*), 'gold of pleasure' (*Camelinasativa*) and one of the 'knotweeds', pale persicaria (*Polygonum lapathifolium*), not to mention a variety of other seeds from weeds such as blue and green bristle grass, dock, black bindweed and camomile. The knotweed occurred in such quantity that it must have been deliberately gathered, but most of the others will have been included accidentally. The gruel eaten by Grauballe man was even more mixed, containing no less than sixty-three varieties of seeds including those present in the Tollund gruel.

The Grauballe and Tollund evidence shows that the exploitation of wild plant resources was scarcely less intense in later prehistory than at the Star Carr settlement several thousand years before. The local environment affected the range of plants available, but old favourites occur time and time again. Thus 'fat hen' or 'goose foot' (*Chenopodium album*), a nutritious green plant with more iron, protein, calcium and vitamin B1 than cabbage or spinach, occurs widely not only in our period, but throughout later prehistory. It occurs by the pot-full in late First Millennium contexts. It can be used as a vegetable, and its seeds in gruel and in cakes. Its value to early man is indicated by its strong representation at sites as far removed as the Culbin Sands midden (sixty-three out of ninety-five seeds), and at the Ram's Hill hill-fort on the Berkshire chalk. The Culbin Sands seed list included several others which could be used in gruels, notably corn spurrey (*Spergula arvensis*, twenty seeds), persicaria (*Polygonum c.f. persicaria L.*), chalkweed (*Stellaria media (L.) Vill.*), sheep's sorrel (*Rumex acetosella L. Sensu lato*) and black bindweed (*Polygonum convolvulus*). These plants have a variety of other uses, for example chickweed can be cooked as a vegetable or used raw like cress, or, in medicine, fresh chickweed leaves when bruised can be used as a poultice on ulcers, or it can be made into a cooling ointment for skin irritations and chilblains. The Ram's Hill list also includes the shrub crache, *Cf Atriplex sp*, the leaves and seeds of which can both be used; violet, *Viola sp*, a source of oil, an antiseptic, an ingredient in cosmetics, and the basis of various drinks and cough medicines; knotgrass, *Polygonum aviculare*, with medicinal uses, and the wild cabbage *Brassica sp*, which can be used as a vegetable. On water-logged sites the catalogue of plants can reach enormous proportions.

Some plants, notably fungi, survive badly even in the most favourable environments. We can assume that many varieties of fungi were gathered and used for all manner of purposes, as they have been right up to modern times. Rare survivals emphasize this point, such as the puff-balls, *Bovista nigrescens*, collected at Skara Brae. Their cottony inner tissue has a variety of uses from staunching wounds to stopping up holes.

These lists will illustrate how wild plants could be important in practically every aspect of life. In addition to foods, dyes, and medicines they would provide fibres for ropes; material for withies; covering materials, as in thatch or bark for canoes; the raw material for mats and basketry; the wattle used in construction; and bedding and floor covering for animals and humans.

There may have been far fewer wild animals to exploit than wild plants, thanks to the large-scale clearances and highly organized landscapes achieved by our period. In spite of the ubiquitous barbed and tanged arrowheads, few settlements produce significant evidence for hunting. It may seem reasonable that a site such as Ram's Hill in the highly developed and thickly populated south should produce so few wild animal bones (only three per cent of the total in the early phase, all red deer), but it is more surprising that the Kilellan site on a remote Hebridean island should produce scarcely any wild animal remains. Wild animals are rare on Deverel-Rimbury settlements, where the few red deer bones from sites such as Amberley Mount and Cock Hill are typical. Eldon's Seat I, produced one of the highest figures of red deer, 3.2 per cent of the total bone count, but important sites such as Itford Hill and Shearplace Hill produced none at all.

This scarcity of wild animals was not new in our period. The bone counts from causewayed enclosures and settlements as early as the Fourth Millennium show no greater proportions of deer or other wild animals. Nor are wild animals better represented at the special centres of the Third Millennium, such as Newgrange and Durrington Walls, except that the wild ox, *Bos primigenius*, was still present at Durrington Walls. This had been common for thousands of years, but was shortly to disappear. The hunting of such large and fearsome beasts, bulls standing six feet high at the shoulder, was not a task to be undertaken lightly, especially when other food was so easily obtained. Perhaps hunting the aurochs was the prehistoric equivalent of the lion hunt among recent African societies, a way of proving manhood.

There are rare exceptions to this dearth of wild animal remains. At Northton red deer bones were common, a notable contrast to the situation at other island settlements such as Skara Brae, and Kilellan. But these three sites clearly had very different economies and, the last two were perhaps more formal settlements than Northton.

It will not have escaped notice that most of the sites mentioned above are either in specialized habitats, as on coastal strips, or in the highly developed lowland zone, where the demands of farming had drastically reduced the importance of hunting as early as the Fourth Millennium. It is hardly surprising that farmers busy with their land and stock should have had little opportunity for, or interest in, hunting, or that the extensive clearances in lowland areas would have left little cover for game animals. What is missing is evidence from upland sites, where more extensive forests could mean more cover for game, and poorer agricultural potential mean greater incentive to catch it. Unfortunately it is these upland sites, with harsh soil conditions, which so seldom have surviving bone evidence.

The Kilellan site, with scarcely any wild animal bones, but with both leaf-shaped and barbed and tanged arrowheads, epitomizes a problem that applies to north and south alike. With archery so prominent and hunting so unimportant does it imply that archers were usually shooting at men rather than animals? Or is it just a reminder that the forests of Britain and Ireland could be dangerous places, with brown bear and wolf lurking, a constant threat to flocks and herds.

Chapter VI

Crafts, Industry and Communications

In many other periods, and many other countries, this chapter might have been headed 'Arts and Crafts', but if there was any artistic spirit in these islands in the Age of Stonehenge then little evidence of it has survived. In many prehistoric communities an aesthetic sense, even if unconscious, is frequently expressed in clay, both in ceramics and in figurine art. In Britain and Ireland in the Third and Second Millennia there is no trace of figurine art, in clay or any other materials, while pottery shapes were functional rather than pleasing, ceramic techniques were of the simplest kind, and decoration, if present at all, basic and repetitive. Only in rock carving was there anything that might conventionally be described as art, but both passage grave and cup and ring carvings appear to have been purely for ritual/religious purposes, and were entirely abstract and repetitive. Similarly metalworkers were capable of the most aesthetically pleasing work, especially in weapon production, but their feelings were expressed in refining the functional form and scarcely ever in ornament or embellishment. The notable rarity in these islands of ornaments and decorative fittings, in direct contrast to the vast quantities possessed by most Continental societies, is itself eloquent testimony that people on this side of the Channel had little interest in the decorative arts.

It could be argued that any artistic spirit might have been expressed in perishable materials such as bone, antler and wood. But again the surviving evidence shows how severely practical most societies were. Consider, for example, the bone dagger pommels of the Overton period, which were made to be functional, not decorative. Surviving artefacts of bone, horn and similar substances, for example from the Hebridean sand sites such as Northton and Kilellan are of the simplest functional form, and seldom ornamented. The same can be said wherever artefacts in these materials survive in Britain and Ireland. There are exceptions, such as the pig bone with a crudely outlined fish from North Carnaby Temple, Rudston in Yorkshire, found in a pit with Grooved ware; and the fragments of antler and deer-rib bearing incised chevrons in-filled with red paint, from a hengi-form enclosure at Maxey, Northamptonshire. But these are rare.

Thus the end products of the many crafts practised in our period were very much utilitarian. When considering crafts we must bear in mind the way in which society was organized: in many family and enlarged family-sized communities, rather than in villages and towns. Most skills would have been within the capabilities of the family and the community, such as domestic pottery, wood-working, stone and flint-working, textiles and basketry, bone, horn and antler-working and leather-working. A few would have required a greater specialization, such as prestige potting and metallurgy. But on the whole there is little evidence for industrialization in the normally accepted sense, although there are indications of community specialization. This involved communities, perhaps a group of communities, concentrating on a raw material abundant in or peculiar to their particular area. Examples are those groups who exploited sources of stone and flint, such as the flint of Grimes Graves, or the picrite of Cwm Mawr/Hyssington on the Shropshire-Montgomeryshire border.

However, we cannot dismiss our prehistoric forefathers as completely unartistic without remembering the long-held enthusiasm in these islands for the aural arts: for the spoken word and music. We would also do well to remember those societies whose artistic ethics are expressed in dance. These are, of course, intangibles, and difficult to demonstrate in prehistoric contexts. The peoples of our period may have been musical, but the only evidence comes from a simple pipe, made from a swan's ulna, found in a grave group dating to the turn of the Overton and Bedd Branwen periods from Wilsford in Wiltshire. Later Celts had their great poets, singers and tale-tellers, and it may have been into these arts that the societies of our period put all their energy.

Crafts and industry

Potting

There is no evidence for industrialized potting in our period, or for a trade in pottery such as is known, in the Severn Basin for example, in the later First Millennium. There is no reason why much of the pottery of the Third and Second Millennia should not have been produced by the individual community. The technology is generally simple, involving ring-building, moulding or pressing techniques. No certain pottery kiln has been found from our period, so clamp firing in a bonfire was probably employed, which would be within the capabilities of any group, and would leave little trace in the archaeological record. In the Penard period completely different pottery traditions were introduced, involving slab building and much thinner and finer products, but that was part and parcel of the sweeping changes which brought our period of interest to an end, and is beyond the scope of this book.

Beakers, and possibly other fine funerary vessels, constitute a notable exception to this picture of community potting. Beakers, highly-decorated food vessels and perhaps some Pygmy cups, were prestige vessels, requiring greater effort and skill in their manufacture. The finest may have taken up to six working hours to complete, so that a specialist potter working on his own would produce perhaps twelve a week. The Beakers certainly, and sometimes other burial pots, required finer clays than domestic pots, and suitable supplies would have been of limited distribution. These prestige wares were probably made by a limited number of potters, working close to suitable clay deposits. The specialists or their products, may have circulated over a considerable area, perhaps even across territorial boundaries, into places where the appropriate skills and clay were lacking. This could explain the presence of isolated Beakers in remote areas and their similarity to a group of Beakers in another region. For example the fine step 5 Beaker from Glenforsa looks rather out of place on the island of Mull, but is very similar to Beakers from eastern Scotland. Generally, however, Beakers form regionally compatible groups, and may not have travelled further than immediately adjoining territories. The same can be said of food vessels. Those sufficiently similar to suggest the work of the same potter or workshop are not usually found so far apart that they could not fall within the same major territory. For example, the food vessels from Bowsden and Bolton House in Northumberland, so similar in their form and unusual decoration as to suggest the same hand, were found about twenty miles apart.

Woodworking

Woodworking techniques were applied to stone in a remarkable way in the construction of sarsen Stonehenge. Not only were the lintel stones seated firmly on the uprights by mortice and tenon joints pounded from the solid rock, but the lintels in the great ring were interlocked, by tongue and groove jointing. Clearly people who could use such skills on stone blocks weighing many tons must have been formidable wood-workers. Unfortunately little evidence of the carpenter's craft has survived from our period. The scale of timber structures, ranging from the ubiquitous round buildings of so many settlements up to the massive post-ring constructions of Durrington Walls, hint at great skills in carpentry and joinery, but only rarely have water-logged environments preserved wooden artefacts. There are for example actual bows from a number of sites, here and on the Continent, to complement the flint arrowheads which are such a widespread indication of archery (Figure 6.1). Some exceptional sites have preserved a range of artefacts: the lower fill of the Wilsford shaft, Wiltshire (*c.* 1380 bc) produced a range of wooden containers, including fragments of stave-built tubs, a monoxylous hod-like container, a thin-walled, turned bowl, and composite vessels which had employed stitching or binding. At the other end of the scale are the dug-out canoes which were used throughout our period, often skilfully shaped. Evidence of the use of

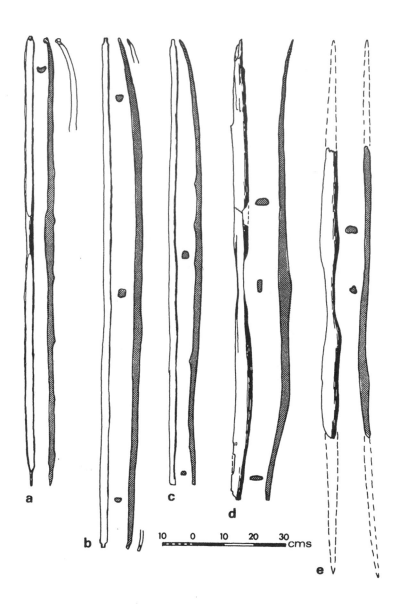

Figure 6.1 Bows from Britain and Holland: a. Edington Burtle, Somerset (1320 bc ± 110: Q 669); b. Onstwedde, Holland (2020 bc ± 65: GrN 4069); c. near Cambridge (1730 bc ± 110; Q684); d. Noordwijkerhout, Holland (1550 bc ± 100: GrN 4070); e. Denny, Stirling (1300 bc ± 85: Q1196) (After Clark, 1963, except e., after Feachem in Switsur, 1974)

planks, beams and of jointing comes from waterlogged structures as disparate as the trackways of the Somerset Levels and the collapsed timber houses at the Barmston crannog. Planks frequently survive in carbonized form under burial mounds, and the boats from North Ferriby, Yorkshire, made of planks sewn together, show what skilful hands could do with simple equipment.

It is easy to forget that the artefacts recovered from excavations represent only the indestructible elements in the total range of material culture. Thus we invariably find pottery vessels and containers, but seldom those of wood or basketry or bark. There are sometimes clues to things which have not survived, for example, the decorative treatment of many handled Beakers, suggests that there must have been very similar wooden beakers.

The remarkable fact about the wood-workers of our period is that they had so few metal tools and mechanical aids. For the most part they made do with a combination of stone and organic tools. For example, there were no saws to produce planks, these had to be split, using wedges and wooden mallets like that found recently in the Somerset Levels. Flint and stone could be used for hammers, pounders, chisels and scrapers, both convex and hollow, as well as for axes and adzes which were the mainstays of the wood-worker's tool-kit. Metal axes and adzes became increasingly available from the Mount Pleasant period onwards, but the stone versions were still being used in the Overton period, and shaft-hole stone axe-hammers were still in use in the Bedd Branwen period. The only other metal tools to appear as early as this were chisels, punches and lugged stakes ('trunnion tools'). Small bronze saws were introduced in the latter part of the Knighton Heath period, along with socketed axes, chisels, hammers and punches, as innovations of the 'Ornament Horizon', but bronze gouges did not appear until the end of the Wilburton phase, *c*. 900 BC.

Of the mechanical aids, the bow-drill was certainly used, but evidence for the lathe, most likely a simple pole-lathe, is ambiguous. It is usually held that the lathe was introduced in the late First Millennium, but it has been claimed that the amber and shale cups of the 'Wessex Culture' are partially lathe-turned. With so little wood-work surviving no definite answer is possible, but we should note that a wooden vessel from the Wilsford shaft has been described as 'finely turned'.

Leather working

There is no unequivocal evidence for textiles before an advanced stage in the Mount Pleasant period, and before that time skins and leather must have taken the place of cloth. The evidence for leather and leather-working comes mainly from the craft tools, especially flint scrapers and metal awls. A few items of leather have survived, for example a dagger sheath made of two qualities of animal skin, sewn and with horn strip mounts, from a cist burial at Kirkcaldy,

Fife; a sheath containing a slightly flanged axe of Derryniggin type from Brockagh, Co. Kildare, belonging to the Bedd Branwen period; and the hide shield from Clonbrin, Co. Longford, a more practical version of the familiar sheet metal shields known from the Penard period onwards. This was probably formed in a wooden mould like that from Churchfield, Co. Mayo.

It is perhaps significant that awls, probably for leather-working, were amongst the earliest metal artefacts produced in these islands. Early forms, of copper and bronze, were double-pointed, and closely resemble modern leather-working awls. A bronze example is included in what has been interpreted as a leather-worker's tool kit which accompanied the primary inhumation with a Beaker at West Overton G6b. Also present were a flint flake and knife, which could be used for cutting, skinning and scraping, a flint strike-a-light and marcasite lump for kindling curing fires, and an antler spatula and stone 'sponge finger'-shaped implements, which were essential for such purposes as rubbing in fat and burnishing. Similar tools have frequently been found in Beaker graves, especially in late Beaker graves of the Overton period. Many of the bone tools from Skara Brae have also been interpreted as for skin-dressing, but by far the most familiar leather-working tools are the flint scrapers found in such vast numbers throughout these islands.

Bone, horn and antler

Many crucial tools made from bone, horn and antler required little or no shaping. Amongst the most familiar artefacts of prehistory are the digging implements termed 'antler picks' and 'ox scapulae shovels', used in flint mines, in excavating ditches, and wherever digging was necessary. These, and the less familiar antler wedges and rakes, could be made with a minimum of alteration to the raw material.

Bone, antler, horn and similar materials were of course basic raw materials everywhere, but generally they were used only for a limited range of simple implements, with no attempt to embellish or decorate. The range of uses was greatest in the Meldon Bridge period, when the passage grave builders of Ireland and the Orkneys, as at Skara Brae, had a rich bone and antler industry. Both these societies produced great quantities of pins, beads and pendants in these materials, the Irish pins typically with mushroom heads, the Orcadian pins usually with simpler swollen heads, but frequently with side-loops. The inhabitants of Skara Brae produced a great variety of artefacts, in antler, ivory and bone, including whalebone, ranging from chisel-ended bone tools, some of which were possibly skin scrapers, adzes, perforated sleeves or handles and polished bone blades, to a great range of pins, needles, points and awls.

After this time bone and antler artefacts are generally of the simplest form, and mostly points, awls and similar types. For example, all of the bone artefacts from Durrington Walls fall into this category. The Deverel-Rimbury communities of southern England appear to have made little use of these materials, and the few surviving implements are mostly points and awls. Bone weaving combs have been reported at two Deverel-Rimbury sites, Shearplace Hill and Eldon's Seat in Dorset, at the latter site as part of a larger than usual range of bone artefacts. These included rib knives, gouges, the usual variety of points and awls, and flat, highly-polished bone objects with one end finely toothed.

Acid soil conditions have left little trace of these materials over much of the Highland Zone. The calcareous machair of the Scottish Highlands and Islands is kind to bone, and from sites such as Kilellan and Northton have come the familiar range of points, awls and gouges. The Northton assemblage is wider than usual, with spatulae and flat bone fragments, polished at one end, which, like the West Overton pieces, may have been used in skin dressing. Four finely toothed combs are just like those which must have been used to form the dentated ornament on Beakers.

Much more effort and skill was required to make the bone pommels fitted to so many daggers in the Overton period. The hilts of these daggers, and of the dirks and rapiers of the Knighton Heath period, were of course fashioned from organic materials, and riveted to the bronze butt. Several Scottish daggers of the late Overton period have surviving horn hilts. That from Auchterhouse, Angus, has a shaped pommel, but examples from Wasbister, Orkney, and Ashgrove, Fife, have flat, projecting tongues perforated to take a separate bone pommel. The famous lost dagger from Roke Down, Dorset, was described as having a hilt and hat-shaped pommel, carved in one piece from ivory.

The Irish bogs have preserved several dirk and rapier hilts, and in most cases they seem to be of horn. The most famous one, on the fine Group I rapier from Galbally, Co. Tyrone, has a simple shaped pommel, and is fairly representative of the series. This weapon was probably made at the end of the Bedd Branwen period, but similar horn hilts were used with dirks and rapiers right through the Knighton Heath period.

Other artefacts of osseous materials which deserve special mention are the 'sceptre mounts', cylindrical at Knockast burial 6, Co. Westmeath, and dentated in the case of the famous Bush Barrow examples. The Wilsford pipe, complete with finger holes and made from a swan's ulna, has already been mentioned. Similar pipes must have accompanied a range of instruments, all of perishable substances, reflecting the musical side of prehistoric life which, because of its dependence on organic raw materials, has been almost completely lost to us.

Most of the bone-work of our period could be made by simple cutting, splitting and rubbing methods. Basic techniques such as 'groove-and-splinter' could be used to obtain blanks for working into spatulae. At some sites working debris has survived to illustrate the methods used. For example at Skara Brae, and the contemporary Links of Noltland site on Westray, bones were notched round at intervals and snapped to provide blanks for beads.

These simple techniques can all be used on dry bone without preparation, but more complex shaping, for example by whittling, carving and incision, is best carried out on material which has been wetted. To force the material into unnatural shapes, steaming would have been necessary.

Flint and stone

Primary deposits of flint in these islands are strictly limited to the areas of cretaceous rocks, in lowland England as far north as the Yorkshire Wolds, in Antrim, and in Aberdeen. Secondary or redeposited flint, which inevitably is of poorer quality, occurs in glacial drift, or in tertiary conglomerates such as that on the south coast of Mull. The implication is that the inhabitants of much of the Highland Zone and Ireland had no direct access to good-quality flint, although secondary sources, notably beach-pebble flints, were widely available. Scrutiny of flint-work from settlements remote from good flint, such as Kilellan, shows the surprisingly high standards that could be achieved with scarce, poor-quality material by competent knappers. But this assemblage also reveals the limitations of such material. It sufficed for small artefacts like scrapers, knives and arrowheads, but for larger items, such as axes and the fine daggers found in Beaker graves, mined flint is desirable. It is in chalk country that the best quality flint and the largest nodules occur, in seams often deep underground. These seams tend to lie in beds of varying quality at varying depths, and upper levels might be ignored by sinking shafts down to the coveted 'floorstone' flint. At the Grime's Graves flint mines in Norfolk, the miners ignored the 'topstone' and 'wallstone' seams in digging down to the floorstone, over 8 metres from the surface.

Strict rules of economics governed flint mining. If the desired seam was less than 5 metres down then tunnelling was not economic, and it was cheaper to sink new shafts. Below 5 metres it was worth tunnelling, and consequently intricate networks of mined galleries characterized such famous flint mine sites as Grimes Graves and Harrow Hill in Sussex. Flint mining is almost as old as the earliest farming communities to judge from radiocarbon dates from sites such as Church Hill, Findon (*c.* 3390 bc) and Blackpatch (*c.* 3140 bc) in Sussex. Some of the most intensive mining seems to have been carried out in the Mount Pleasant period, possibly in response to the threat posed by metal. The mines at Grime's Graves (*c.* 2340–2154 bc) and at Easton Down, Wiltshire (*c.* 2530 bc) appear to have been started in the Meldon Bridge period. A maze of structures built around the Easton Down shafts has produced Beaker pottery, suggesting intensified activity in the later Third Millennium, while a large series of dates from the shaft excavated at Grime's Graves in 1971 averaged out at *c.* 1820 bc. The pottery associated with the sinking and exploitation of this mine was Grooved ware.

The recent excavations at Grime's Graves make it clear that as increasing quantities of metal became available for large tools, so the demand for good quality flint fell. Mining at Grime's Graves may not have outlasted the Mount Pleasant period. After a period of abandonment there was renewed activity in the Knighton Heath period. By this time the 'topstone' and 'wallstone' dumped by earlier miners sufficed for the limited needs of metal-using communities. But some flint tools, such as scrapers, seem never to have been replaced, and remained in use at least until the Roman conquest.

In most regions people could get hold of sufficient flint to fill basic needs, but there were some areas remote from flint sources where other stones usually had to make do. Here we can include much of the Outer Hebrides and the Northern Isles. For example the Rosinish settlement on Benbecula produced few flint tools but considerable quantities of quartz flakes and cores. Similarly Orcadian settlements such as Skara Brae have comparatively impoverished flint assemblages, and make correspondingly greater use of local stones such as quartz and flagstone. There were also inland regions in the Highland Zone where flint was not readily available, and local substitutes had to be found. For example, in the Border country of Northumberland and southern Scotland, and especially in the Tweed basin, cherts and agates were extensively used, having some of the mechanical properties of flint. The comparatively small stone industry from Meldon Bridge consists largely of these materials, with little flint.

Some mined flint filtered through to non-flint areas, for example Wales, either in the form of raw material or as finished products. But over most of the Highland Zone local fine-grained rocks were exploited as raw material for larger tools. Like the flint mines, some of these rock sources were developed by very early farming communities before 3000 bc, especially those in Cornwall. Some of the most famous stones were still being worked in the earlier part of our period, such as the Great Langdale sites in Cumbria, and Graig Lwyd in Caernarvonshire, along with less well-known rocks like the hornfels of Creag na Caillich, Killin, in Perthshire. Peat under an axe production floor at this site has given dates of *c.* 2510 and 2250 bc.

Some of the most famous rocks, including many of the Cornish groups and both Great Langdale and Graig Lwyd, seem to have been little used once metal tools became available. Others were used both for the new-style perforated implements as well as for the old style unperforated tools, and must therefore have continued to be exploited into the Overton period. Preselite, the spotted dolerite of the Stonehenge bluestones, is a case in point. Other rocks, such as Cwm Mawr/Hyssington picrite, appear to have been exploited little, or not at all, before the introduction of perforated tools. Their period of use must have been centred on the Mount Pleasant and Overton periods, lasting in some cases into the Bedd Branwen period, when the most sophisticated and elegant forms of stone battle-axes were produced.

Just as good quality flint found its way into northern and western Britain, so implements of a wide range of Highland Zone rocks are scattered in great quantities throughout lowland England. Traditional explanations are couched in terms of trade in the raw materials and finished products, and it is tempting to think of reciprocal exchange of flint for stones, but the situation is not as simple as it seems at first glance. An unknown proportion of the lowland stone axes may have been made locally, not from directly imported material but from glacial erratics. This challenge to traditional concepts of stone axe production and distribution is currently a subject of hot dispute.

Metallurgy

At first glance it might seem that the metalworker in copper, bronze and gold would require a lot of tools, equipment and workshop furniture, and therefore fairly permanent and substantial premises. A hearth, a furnace, an anvil and a casting pit were just some of the most obvious essentials. It is surprising that not one reconstructible workshop of our period has ever been found in these islands, though many sites have produced traces of metalworking in one form or another. In practice workshop fittings could be simple and assembled almost anywhere. Afterwards much could have been used for other purposes, such as the hearth, anvil stone and casting pit, and the furnace was only a simple bowl a foot wide and the same deep. Such slight traces would easily be eroded by the passage of time. Not surprisingly the most familiar traces of metallurgy are discarded mould fragments, which can tell us only so much about the methods and organization of metalworking in our period.

In part this lack of workshops must be due to the generally scanty knowledge of settlements. Even in the best-known settlement areas, such as the southern Deverel-Rimbury lands and south-west England, excavations have been few and small-scale, and for the most part were carried out before the advent of modern methods. But even recent excavations of workshop debris, for example at Dainton in Devon and at Grime's Graves, have failed to locate the workshop itself, or at least a range of features appropriate to metal-working activity. If such negative evidence means anything then the conclusion must be that permanent workshops with substantial fixtures and fittings were not a part of metallurgical practice in our period. Before we can follow this implication further, we must look more generally at the organization of primitive metalworking in more recent times.

Prehistoric metalworkers have long been thought of as itinerant, and their wanderings have been regarded as a major factor in the diffusion of ideas and goods in prehistory. Yet, outside the Middle East, there are few ethnographic parallels for detribalized, travelling smiths. At most they may have travelled around villages within a restricted locality, but would have a base workshop in their home village, and a fixed position within their own community. The degree of specialization of the smith may also have been over-estimated. In many peasant societies the smith is only a part-time specialist, perhaps operating for only a few months in the year when not taken up with the tasks of an otherwise ordinary farmer and member of the community. It may be necessary to distinguish between such village smiths and more highly-skilled men who might be employed by chiefs, whether full-time or in passing, to concentrate on weapon production. The structured society of our period, the evidence for chiefs, and the emphasis on warrior equipment, all suggest that such patronage may have existed.

Thus the organization of metalworking was probably complex. Looking overall at the distribution patterns, and mindful of the lack of evidence for major workshops and industrialization, a combination of operations seems likely. Village craftsmen, perhaps part-timers, would have concerned themselves with simple, functional items, especially tools and perhaps cheap trinkets, and with repairs; status craftsmen, more skilled, perhaps supplied weapons and prestige ornaments to those in authority; and itinerants, operating within the territory, would have met the demand for specialities and served those communities without their own metalworker.

Such divisions of responsibility are familiar from many modern primitive societies: one pointer to such a system in our period is the fact that multiple mould finds tend to consist of moulds either for tools or for weapons. It is not necessary to assume that any category of smith enjoyed special privileges or status, for in many societies, especially amongst pastoral and nomadic groups, the smith is held in contempt because his calling sets him apart.

The existence of the specialist involves exchange, of services for goods or other services. If each major settlement had its own smith, then whether the customer went to the smith, or he travelled round those local communities without smiths, the range of his influence would probably not have been great. Novelties apart, ordinary tools are unlikely to have been distributed long distances given village or regionalized smiths. And implement types mostly have coherent regional distribution patterns. Weapons should be different, as prestige equipment in demand over much wider areas. But even here there is little explicit evidence for long-range distribution. For example, out of the thousand or so dirks and rapiers from Britain and Ireland, there are only three undoubtedly from the same mould. With axes and tools there are more mould pairs and multiples, but these do tend to occur within the twenty to thirty mile radius which could indicate the bounds of a major territory. Even when much greater distances are involved, and there are mould pairs over a hundred miles apart, there are several possible explanations, apart from the itinerant craftsman or trader. Repeated exchange, with moulds or castings passing from hand to hand, fits the facts at least as well.

Until recently it seemed that analysis of trace elements would enable metalwork to be assigned to an ore source and area of origin, but the latest work has largely dashed these hopes. The trace elements sought are too widespread, and re-used scrap too often a principal source of raw metal (leading to an inextricable mix of metals) to give much hope of success with present methods. The old idea that Ireland provided much of Britain's metalwork, and that wandering Irish smiths criss-crossed not only Britain but large parts of the Continent, is now seen to be completely erroneous. Metallurgy was practised on a local basis from a very early stage, for small but usable ore sources were very widely scattered in the Highland Zone, and these were exploited wherever possible. As a result most were completely worked out, and only the major deposits survived into later periods.

Four thousand years of mining has left little trace of prehistoric mines. Some workings survived up to recent times, for example, the old tin mine re-opened in the late eighteenth century near the River Fowey, where miners found a splendid Ornament Horizon dress pin of the Knighton Heath period. Copper mines on the slopes of Mount Gabriel, Co. Cork, have also been dated to our period (*c.* 1500 bc). They do not approach in scale the famous Austrian copper mines, but are nevertheless impressive testament to the efforts of miners nearly four thousand years ago. Dumps of waste around the entrances to the workings show where the ores were brought out and broken up with stone mauls. The mines themselves consist of low, narrow approach galleries which slope down and open out into the chambers from which the ores were removed by fire setting and pounding.

For much of the west and north metal supply would have been no problem, but the south-east has no local ores. The remarkable thing is that metallurgy seems to have started in the south-east apparently as early as anywhere in Britain. From the outset it must have been an industry which used large amounts of scrap, although one would expect some importation of ores from Highland Zone mines. The demands of the scrap trade would have led to a misleading flow of metalwork within the region and attracted undue amounts of exotica from the outside world. Scrap was acquired not only from other parts of Britain and Ireland but also from the Continent. The Dover hoard, containing many fragments, seems to represent scrap shipped in from France.

In all regions the earliest metalworkers used one-piece stone moulds, which are the only surviving moulds known from the Mount Pleasant and Overton periods, but thereafter Irish and south British producers often differed in their choice of mould materials. Stone moulds continued to dominate in Ireland and Scotland, but the craftsmen of southern Britain preferred bronze and clay moulds. Stone moulds belonging to these later phases are unknown in lowland England, and in Wales there is only one, from Bodwrdin, Anglesey, to be set against three bronze moulds. In north and south-west England a few stone moulds are known, but clay and bronze moulds were used as well.

The products of the Mount Pleasant and Overton periods were for the most part simple castings which could be produced in one-piece stone moulds. Rudimentary flanges on flat axes, and simple midribs on daggers, were representative of surface relief that could be worked up in the finishing stages. But a few products demand more sophisticated methods, notably some halberds, where the complex relief on *both* faces points to bivalve moulds. As none have been found, these were probably of clay.

The Arreton and Inch Island industries of the Bedd Branwen period represented a major technological leap. Practically all of their products indicate bivalve moulds, and the presence of socketed forms shows that core-casting techniques had been introduced. Irish Inch Island craftsmen persisted with stone for their mould technology, but the lack of stone moulds for the English Arreton products suggests the use of clay.

The bronze bivalve mould appeared in the next stage, at the time of the Acton Park and Killymaddy traditions. The only example of this period is one for shield-pattern palstaves of the north Welsh Acton Park type which was found long ago in Ireland (Plate XVI). This must have been brought from Wales, for all other Irish moulds of this period are of stone, including the eponymous Killymaddy examples, and it is known that Welsh Acton Park smiths were sending their palstaves to Ireland.

With the Taunton industry of the Knighton Heath period bronze moulds became common in England and Wales. Experiment has shown that these could have been, and perhaps sometimes were, used for direct bronze castings, but it makes more sense if they were for casting wax or lead patterns, to be used in conjunction with clay moulds. For direct casting they would need to be much more carefully heated, and prepared, than for wax or lead casting, and they would have a much shorter life. The fact that several bronze moulds have yielded traces of lead castings seems to clinch the matter. The clay moulds surviving from the Knighton Heath period could have made use of patterns from the bronze moulds, although wooden patterns were also used.

Textiles

Seldom can it be said with complete certainty that a small stone weight was used on the bottom of a spindle and not on the bottom of a fishing net, or a heavier weight on the loom rather than the thatch
Henshall, 1950, 42.

These words from a pioneering survey of ancient textiles sum up one of the difficulties in interpreting the evidence for spinning and weaving. Although textiles were known in the Near East at least as early as the Seventh Millennium BC, and in eastern Europe not much later, they were not introduced to much of western Europe until the Fourth and Third Millennia. In Britain and Ireland there is no evidence for spinning and weaving before the Mount Pleasant period, and then probably only at an advanced stage. One of the earliest clues is a lone baked clay spindlewhorl from Durrington Walls, which, in view of Miss Henshall's warning, can hardly be conclusive. The earliest undoubted evidence comes from the step 4 Beaker grave at Kelleythorpe, Driffield (Figure 4.3), where the skeleton lay on a mass of cloth. From the beginning of the Overton period the evidence is increasingly abundant, and takes the form both of cloth and cloth impressions, and the indirect evidence of spinning and weaving equipment.

It is very difficult to deduce the material of these early fabrics from the scanty evidence which survives, but it appears that both wool and linen were being produced. The famous Rylston (Yorkshire) shroud was of wool, enveloping a body in a tree-trunk coffin from head to foot. This probably dates to the Overton period, like the boat burials at Loose Howe, where fragments of finer fabrics suggested linen. In general the finer of these early cloths may be regarded as linen, and the coarser weaves wool. There is evidence only for plain weaves, patterned weaves, such as herring-bone twills, appearing in the First Millennium.

In addition to finds of cloth, there are cloth impressions, such as occur on bronzes in Wessex Culture graves at Ridgeway, Dorset, and Bush Barrow, but most of the evidence is indirect, and comes from the equipment used in textile manufacture. First and foremost are the spindlewhorls and loomweights which are always tell-tale signs of spinning and weaving respectively. But there are also at least two weaving combs, from the Deverel-Rimbury sites at Shearplace Hill and Eldon's Seat, toothed devices for packing the wefts on the loom. These are known in much greater numbers from First Millennium settlements.

The simple upright loom was the type used. At best this would survive as a pair of post-holes, representing the loom uprights, with loomweights scattered between and around. At the Cock Hill Deverel-Rimbury settlement, a large oval pit in one of the buildings yielded ten loom weights in a line along the axis of the pit. Fragments of burnt wood were interpreted as parts of the loom frame, perforated flints as toggles to prevent the threads from slipping through the holes in the weights, and a perforated sheep metapodial as a shuttle or bobbin. At the Trevisker settlement in Cornwall pairs of post holes 60–90 centimetres apart were associated with loomweights and interpreted as loom emplacements. But such explicit pointers are rare, and the evidence normally consists merely of discarded loomweights and spindlewhorls. The standard form of loomweight in our period was a cylinder of baked clay, and is well represented on Deverel-Rimbury settlements, as at Itford Hill, Shearplace Hill, and Thorny Down, and on the Trevisker settlements of the south-west, as at Trevisker itself. On the few occasions loomweights have been found in other regions, as at Fengate, they are also of this pattern.

Spindlewhorls come in two main forms and materials. Flat, disc-shaped examples tend to be of stone, whereas biconical examples are usually of baked clay. Stone disc-shaped whorls are more widely distributed in time and space than the biconical ones. They are found both on Deverel-Rimbury settlements such as Amberley Mount, Sussex, and on Trevisker sites, as at Dean Moor. The Durrington Walls 'spindlewhorl' is of the biconical clay form which is more familiar from First Millennium contexts. From the end of our period onwards spindlewhorl forms became more varied. For example, the Plumpton Plain B settlement produced no less than nine clay 'whorls', mostly biconical, but also drum-shaped and bun-shaped.

How far textiles had spread by the Overton period is uncertain, so uneven is the settlement evidence. In some Highland Zone regions there is nothing to indicate the manufacture of cloth before the First Millennium. In the Scottish islands, for example, there are many settlements of the late Third-early Second Millennia which are rich in cultural material but are notably deficient in evidence for spinning and weaving. There are scattered 'spindlewhorls' from Irish, Scottish and Welsh contexts, but it is only with the fuller settlement record of the Isleham and Llynfawr periods, and actual finds of cloth from hoards such as Pyotdykes, Angus (linen) and Cromaghs, Co. Antrim (wool), that the question is placed beyond doubt.

Basketry and fibres

The use of plants and fibres, interwoven, plaited and twisted to make baskets, mats, ropes and so on, is one of the most basic crafts, known even to very primitive societies. Little material has survived from our period, but there is enough to make it clear that such skills were widely practised. Ropes have been preserved at several sites, for example two thicknesses at Skara Brae, made of twisted heather, and well-finished lengths from the Wilsford shaft, made from lime bast or wild clematis. String, in a wide range of qualities, is attested by the cord impressions which decorate so many pots, and it has survived on occasion. One of the best known finds is the string 'hair-net' of vegetable fibre found in a grave at Garton Slack in Yorkshire. Remains of basketry and matting are much more tenuous, and usually take the form of negative impressions. The imprint of a mat was found on a sherd at Rinyo, a settlement of Skara Brae type in Orkney, and of a coarse basketwork lining on the sides of a Collared Urn cremation pit at Blanch on the Yorkshire Wolds. Traces of baskets have been reported with cremation burials at Winterbourne Steepleton, Dorset, and Throwley, Staffordshire, while a child cremation found in a cinerary urn at Martindown, Dorset, appears to have been contained in a grass bag. Cist burials at Mount Vernon, Glasgow, and Stromness, Orkney, produced traces of a fabric made by threading together hanks of moss, possibly for use as a shroud or mat. Finally we may note the abundant use of hurdle techniques to produce loosely woven panels for trackways in the Somerset Levels. It is in such waterlogged contexts that a fuller understanding of so many of the crafts of our period will be found.

Other crafts

In addition to the crafts which most communities will have practised, such as potting and basketry, there were local specializations, determined, for example, by proximity to special raw materials. Flint and stone are obvious examples, including shales and similar materials. Kimmeridge shale was worked into rings and armlets at Dorset sites such as Eldon's Seat, and 'cannel coals' at Highland Zone sites such as the Swine Sty settlement in Derbyshire. Similarly Whitby jet must have been worked at local settlements, but these have yet to be located.

Of the manufactured materials, faience was produced in Scotland in the Bedd Branwen period, with concentrations of the distinctive star-shaped faience beads pointing to the Culbin sands area of Moray, and the Glenluce sands of Wigtown as the likeliest production areas. Glass beads may also have been made in the latter part of our period. Specialist potting no doubt developed near particularly fine clay sources, and smelting workshops in ore-bearing areas. The surplus of such activities implies complex exchange systems, but it remains to be seen how these operated, and over what range.

Communications

Traditional concepts of prehistory involve simple mechanisms of movement, contact and exchange. There are traders, prospectors, raiders, missionaries and migrants, who travel through a primitive world, spreading new ideas. While all these categories may have existed in our period, the picture of organized landscape and societies which is now emerging demands more complex mechanisms of movement and contact. Communities were much more static than has been traditionally entertained, although still receptive, and able both to absorb and pass on ideas to neighbouring groups. In many ways the picture of society is closer to Medieval Britain than to recent Africa, as regards social organization, economic development and limited mobility. Within the territory there would have been movement to markets, fairs and festivals, but contacts with the outside world would have taken place mainly along territorial boundaries, and may have been both informal and formal, including, perhaps, specially organized inter-territorial gatherings held near the border. To what extent independent purveyors of change could operate outside such a framework, whether traders, prospectors, craftsmen or holy men, is difficult to estimate. Distribution patterns, for example of metal goods, suggest they operated mainly within the territory, and not usually outside it. In maritime areas, along the Mediterranean and Atlantic sea routes, long distance movement by such travellers would have been comparatively easy, but the evidence for regular long distance traffic overland is equivocal to say the least. European distributions tend to be regionally coherent, and there are few intrusions which cannot be accounted for by normal contacts at frontiers. There is no doubt that this can lead to rapid dissemination over considerable areas. For example amongst Australian aborigines, artefacts can be carried a thousand miles from source in a few years, merely by being handed on from group to group.

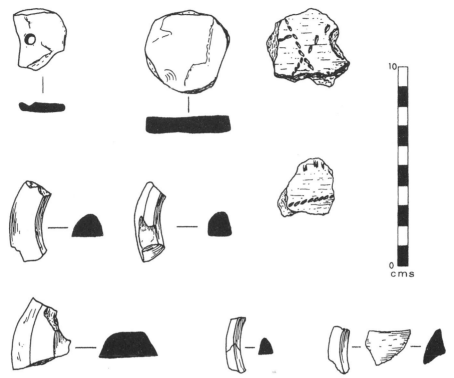

Figure 6.2 Worked shale and pottery fragments from Swine Sty, Derbyshire (after Machin, 1975)

Land transport

The only means of movement available to every person in prehistory was his or her own two feet. There is no evidence in Britain and Ireland for use of the horse, either for riding or traction, or of any other traction animal, wheeled vehicle or beast of burden, before the First Millennium. From the end of the Wilburton-Wallington phase, *c.* 900 BC, articles of harness equipment, in bronze, bone and antler, and bronze fittings from wheeled vehicles, appear widely in these islands. But it must be made absolutely clear that this is not to deny the earlier presence of horses and vehicles, traction and pack animals, merely that positive evidence for their use only dates from this point. Before there can be any extensive use of wheeled vehicles, roads must be adequate. As late as the eighteenth century wheeled traffic was rare over much of the country, and the packhorse was king because roads were still so woeful.

Nevertheless it would be most surprising if horses and wheeled transport were unknown in our period, for wooden disc wheels, implying vehicles of some sort, were used in Holland in the Third Millennium, and have radiocarbon dates of *c.* 2100–2000 bc. At Nieuwe Dordrecht one was associated with a heavy duty wooden trackway suitable for vehicular traffic. Danish wheels are at least as early. Wheeled vehicles, with solid disc and block or jointed plank wheels, had appeared in east and central Europe by the early Third Millennium if not before, and were widespread in north Europe before *c.* 2500 BC. By the later Second Millennium, spoked wheels were known in north Europe on the evidence of the two-horse chariot carved on a grave slab at Kivik in Sweden. Given the extent to which the societies of Britain and Ireland kept in contact with European happenings, it seems inconceivable that they could remain ignorant of wheeled vehicles until the First Millennium.

Although the Kivik chariot is pulled by horses, the ox was an alternative and perhaps more likely draught animal for everyday use, and can still be found pulling carts and waggons in parts of Europe today. It is not clear when the horse was domesticated north of the Alps. Horse-riding is not definitely attested until the seventh century BC when models and representations in Hallstatt contexts suggest this skill had at last been learnt, probably from steppe dwellers to the east. But high proportions of horse bones in contexts with Beakers, both in eastern Europe and Iberia, suggest horses may have been domesticated for some purposes as early as the Third Millennium, though there seems no reason why such finds should be considered proof of horse riding as has sometimes been claimed.

We are on much firmer ground in suggesting the use of oxen as draught animals. It is important to remember that unless speed is essential the ox has many advantages over the horse as a traction animal, being more durable and notably more steady, especially over rough ground. Furthermore, until the horse collar first appeared in Medieval Europe, the horse could not be harnessed efficiently as a draught animal. Right across Europe from Sweden to Italy there are rock carvings of ploughing scenes (Figure 5.19), with ploughs invariably drawn by two oxen. With so many instances of plough marks known in our period, from sites as far apart as Rosinish on Benbecula, Gwithian in Cornwall, and South Street, Wiltshire, clearly a light ard was widely used, drawn, to judge from the Continental evidence, by paired oxen. If oxen were pulling ploughs, and wheeled vehicles were in use just across the North Sea, then it seems likely that ox-drawn waggons and carts were also familiar by the Mount Pleasant period. The vehicle and its fittings, and the harness for the oxen, could quite easily be made entirely from perishable materials, so that definite proof of their existence would only come from an exceptionally fortunate accident of preservation.

Wheeled waggons and carts were not the only vehicles, for amongst peasant societies drawn sleds and *travois*-type vehicles are often a more practical proposition than wheeled vehicles. Certainly they are better suited to rough terrain. Indeed, simple sliding devices of one sort or another have been used in upland areas of Europe until modern times. Unfortunately these are unlikely to have survived from the 'Bronze Age' except under exceptional conditions, as in the case of a possible sled found with a Beaker burial at Dorchester, Oxfordshire.

Even if ox-drawn vehicles were known in our period they were probably used only locally and for special purposes, because of the lack of suitable roads. Pack animals must have been in widespread use, but these, too, are difficult to identify in the archaeological record, since they require only a rope halter. Our earliest record of pack animals comes only in the late First Millennium, when the Greek Diodorus Sicilus tells us that the Cornish tin was carried in waggons over the causeway to Ictis (St. Michael's Mount) for shipment to Gaul, but that for the long journey through Gaul to markets in the south, pack horses were used. In Britain and Ireland down to the eighteenth century road conditions ensured that packhorses remained the chief way of transporting goods, as reflected in countless 'Pack-horse' inns up and down the country. Wheeled vehicles were practically unknown in most areas until the eighteenth century, there being scarcely any roads which could take them.

Thus pack animals were almost certainly used from the beginning of our period, but perhaps oxen rather than horses. Oxen are suitable for the purpose, as can be seen from the use of yaks as pack animals in modern Tibet. The rolling gait of the ox does tend to shift its load, but this only requires that care is taken to seat it securely. In view of the important role of cattle in the life of our prehistoric communities, their use as pack animals, as for draught purposes, seems quite reasonable.

It is important to know whether draught and pack animals were known in the Age of Stonehenge, because this could have had a profound effect on the effort required to construct the great monuments such as sarsen Stonehenge. A job which might take several hundred men ten years on their own could be finished in a much shorter time using animal power. The degree of time-saving would depend on the extent to which animals could be used. In the case of Stonehenge there is some doubt whether oxen could be used to pull the sarsens, because of the difficulty of controlling ox teams of the required size, but they could have been used effectively to shift heavy equipment such as rollers, and in the transport of supplies and workers. All of this would have meant marked reductions in the size of the human labour force, and would reduce man-hour calculations. As so many conclusions about population and social organization have been based on the labour requirements of these sites, the availability of animal help is a crucial question.

Routes and tracks

The problem of prehistoric routeways is full of pitfalls. The temptation is to assume that a cross-country route well-used in recent centuries was also used in prehistory. Leaving aside the fact that our knowledge of the prehistoric landscape and political organization makes such an automatic assumption foolhardy, we would do well to remember how many Roman roads, following conveniently practical lines, are not, for various reasons, shadowed by modern roads. A modern routeway may in prehistory have been impractical because of natural hazards such as dense forest or bogs, or for political reasons. Because of the nature of unmetalled tracks their course cannot be fixed. They may shift over a considerable belt of country as wear or waterlogging makes one line unusable and a new one necessary. Unless defined by artificial features, as in the case of the sunken ways running between lynchets across Deverel-Rimbury farms (Figure 6.3), they are unlikely to leave any traces in the archaeological record. We would do well to remember the deplorable state of our roads as late as the eighteenth century. When General Wade, for example, was confronted with the problem of moving military traffic around Scotland in 1723, he found scarcely a road outside the main towns which could take a wheeled vehicle.

Some natural cross-country routes have better claims than most to be considered as prehistoric lines of communication. The best known long-distance examples include the Jurassic Way, linking the Cotswolds with the Yorkshire Wolds, the Ridgeway/Icknield Way running all the way from Avebury in north Wiltshire to the Wash; and the Harroway/Pilgrims' Way, from Salisbury Plain to Folkestone. Some are much shorter, such as the track which runs from the Conway Valley near Bodnant, ascends via Roewen to the ridge below Tal-y-fan, and extends westwards along the watershed, dropping down to the Menai straits near Llanfairfechan. On the way it passes countless prehistoric find spots and monuments, and was the line of the Roman road. We can be fairly sure that such obvious and natural lines of communication as this, and the High Street down the length of the Lincolnshire Wolds, were used by travellers in our period. Many old routeways, such as those which criss-cross the Cheviots and the Pennines, are not recorded until Medieval times, but because they are the most obvious and easiest lines of movement, they have almost certainly been used since earliest times. The validity of such routes is suggested by the numbers of prehistoric monuments and finds which mark their course. For the most part they make use of natural lines which can easily be followed, such as ridges, scarp edges, and belts of light, well-drained soils threading through areas of heavier ground likely to have been heavily forested, and cross rivers at convenient and well-known fords.

Timber trackways

One of the easiest and most obvious ways to move over wet ground is to lay down a timber and brushwood trackway. Tracks of this sort have been used throughout the ages, and may still be laid down today when conditions demand it, for example in warfare. The modern duck-board is merely a prefabricated device designed for the same purpose.

It is thus not surprising that timber trackways are the only prepared tracks to survive from prehistory, for by their very nature they are preserved by the

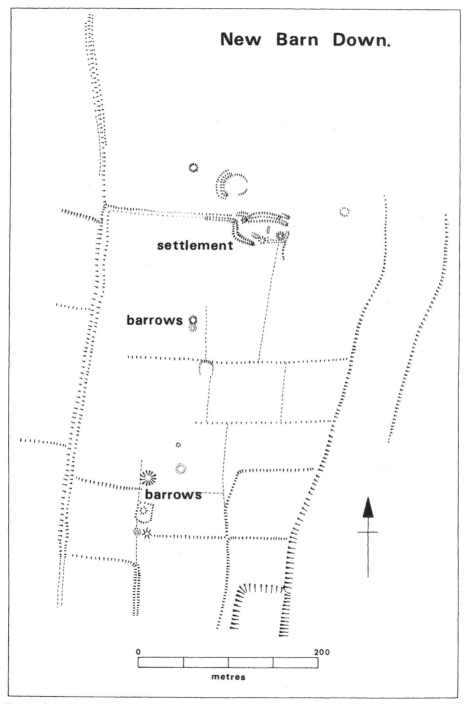

New Barn Down.

settlement

barrows

barrows

0   200

metres

Figure 6.3 New Barn Down, Sussex: settlement, fields, and double lynchet ways (after Curwen, 1934)

waterlogged environment in which they are laid down. The distribution of timber trackways as might be expected reflects the location of the principal boggy areas of the country. The most numerous and best explored examples have been found on the Somerset Levels, but others are known as far apart as the Cambridgeshire Fens (Fordy), the Humber flats (Thorne Moor, Brigg and North Ferriby), the Lancashire mosses (Danes Pad, Kate's Pad, Pilling) and the bogs of Ireland (Corlona, Co. Leitrim).

Several methods of track construction are found, width and solidity depending on the intended use. Most are light trackways for foot traffic, in which the timbers are usually laid longitudinally along the line of the track. There are also stouter constructions formed of heavy timbers, involving baulks or split logs, laid edge to edge transversely across the axis of the track. Longitudinal stringers, long lengths of shaped timber, or straight branches, are placed along both edges of the track and the whole edifice is held in place by long wooden pegs outside the stringers, driven down into the peat either through mortise holes in the ends of the cross timbers, or in the gaps between their ends. A foundation of brushwood is sometimes present, giving added stability. This type of 'corduroy road' is found at Nieuwe Dordrecht in Holland, with an associated vehicle wheel, dated to *c.* 1890 bc. But a similar, broadly contemporary track in Somerset, the Abbot's Way (*c.* 2090–1984 bc) has a width of only 1.0–1.2 metres, too narrow to take anything other than a light sledge or *travois* at the most.

Of the purely foot tracks of longitudinal construction, the simplest include the Tinney's tracks (*c.* 1090–1070 bc) and Westhay track (*c.* 850 bc) in Somerset, which consist of bundles of light timbers laid longitudinally, usually on a brushwood foundation, the end of one bundle overlapping the next, and the margins pinned by pegs driven obliquely into the peat. Transverse timbers are rare. The width of such tracks varies from *c.* 0.60–2 metres. A more solid, but narrower, mode of construction is represented by the Sweet track, in which 'rails', timbers of telegraph pole proportions, are laid end to end, pinned between pegs driven obliquely into the peat, along a line marked by vertical posts spaced at *c.* 3 metre intervals. Turves are piled over the rails, and planks are then laid along the top of this packing, secured by long, thin pins driven through holes or notches in the planks into the turves beneath. The result is a very narrow plank walk suitable only for one-way traffic. A similar effect, again using great quantities of prepared timber, is achieved by the Meare Heath track, where transverse timbers, laid like railway sleepers and pinned at their ends, supported a walkway of planks laid longitudinally, two planks wide (*c.* 1030, 890 bc).

A much more complex form of construction involves weaving brushwood either in and out of vertical pegs, as in the case of Viper's track (*c.* 680–570 bc), or under and over transverse rods laid at intervals of 0.30–0.4 metres. A variation is found at the Eclipse track (*c.* 1510 bc), where woven hurdles *c.* 2

metres long were prefabricated elsewhere so they could be brought in and laid straight down on to the peat.

The extensive work in progress on the trackways of the Somerset Levels has shown that they were built to maintain communications between the occupied 'islands' rising above the general level of the peat. They extended up to several kilometres, often ran in series, and formed a very complex network over these marshes. Some of them represent major human achievements, the Abbot's Way, for example, consuming 20,000 metres of 20 × 12 centimetres alderwood, not to mention thousands of metres of birch stringers and 50,000 birch pegs. The earliest examples, such as the Sweet track (*c.* 3274–2937 bc), must have been laid down by the first farmers in the region, but thereafter we find tracks being laid down at intervals right through prehistory. Some at least seem to have been short-lived, but whether this was because they were soon inundated, or were made redundant by the return of drier conditions, is not always clear. The multiple Tinney's tracks were continually replaced as successive lines were inundated over perhaps two centuries. They are usually seen as a response to intermittent flooding of the levels, but whether caused by climatic deterioration, coastal changes leading to inundation, or human interference with natural drainage, is uncertain in individual cases. A large number belong to the Meldon Bridge and Mount Pleasant periods: Bell A, Baker, Honeycat, Blakeway, and the Abbot's Way, with dates ranging from *c.* 2500–1904 bc. Increased precipitation towards the end of our period eventually waterlogged the levels again, for another group of tracks, including Meare Lake, Tinney's, Meare Heath and Westhay, are dated between *c.* 1090–850 bc. The possibility of further climatic deterioration in the Llynfawr period is supported by a group of tracks with dates between *c.* 680–460 bc: Toll Gate House, Skinner's Wood, Viper's, Nidon's, Shapwick Heath and Platform.

There are too few dated tracks from other regions to be sure whether these periods of track building apply right across the country. The one Irish date, from Corlona, Co. Leitrim (*c.* 1445 bc) does not fit well, but the dates for Kate's Pad, Lancashire (*c.* 810 bc), and Thorne Moor, Yorkshire (*c.* 1140, 1040 bc) support the Somerset evidence for major track building activity in the Penard period. The later burst of construction in the Llynfawr period, *c.* seventh century BC, is supported by the dates from Fordy, Cambridgeshire (*c.* 610 bc) and Brigg, Lincolnshire (*c.* 602 bc).

Water transport

Wherever overland travel is difficult for either natural or political reasons, water transport will be important. Although we no longer believe that our prehistoric landscape was covered by a sea of virgin forest, nevertheless the difficulties of overland travel, even through regions extensively farmed and de-forested, would have turned travellers towards waterways when they existed. Boats in any case would have been vital in a maritime setting, and seamanship and navigation would have been well-developed skills among coastal communities. Different sorts of craft must have been constructed for different purposes, and those vessels which have survived in waterlogged contexts from our period can only represent part of the story.

It is significant that the earliest historical mention of Britain and Ireland, in the *Massiliote Periplus*, refers to seaborne trade. It records a voyage made in the sixth century BC from Massilia (Marseilles) down the eastern coast of Spain, through the Pillars of Hercules to the lost city of Tartessos on the Iberian Atlantic coast. It also mentions the fact that the traders of Tartessos were active as far north as the Oestrymnides, usually taken to be the islands and peninsula of Brittany, and that the inhabitants of the Oestrymnides traded with two large islands, *Ierne* and *Albion*. Archaeological evidence for this trade is provided by the distinctive Armorican socketed axes which were being shipped to Britain in large numbers around the seventh and sixth centuries BC. One commodity that may have been sent to the Oestrymnides in return was Cornish tin, which was certainly famous enough to be mentioned by later classical writers, such as Diodorus Siculus. Strabo, writing in the first century BC, records the principal exports of Britain at that time as corn, cattle, gold, silver, iron, slaves and hunting dogs, which gives some guide to the trade goods of earlier periods. Clearly boats plied a regular traffic across the Channel from at least the Overton period, for there is no other conclusion to be drawn from the remarkable similarities in the material culture of the lands facing each other across the narrow seas. An even more dramatic illustration of this maritime activity has now been provided by the cargoes of French bronzes recently recovered from the sea off Dover and off Salcombe, implying foundered boats.

We can only guess at the form of the craft involved in this traffic, but certainly they were not the dug-out canoes known in such numbers from prehistoric times. The dug-out canoe is the oldest form of boat known, one of the simplest and most basic types of craft, and one that is still used in some parts of the world today. Essentially a hollowed-out half of a tree-trunk, the boats were in use by the early post-Glacial period, for example at Pesse in Holland, in a Maglemosian context. The vast majority of dug-outs recorded from Britain and Ireland, as well as Europe, have been made from oak trunks.

Dug-out canoes vary greatly in size and in the shape of their ends. At least seventy are known from England and Wales, so the number from the whole of Britain and Ireland must be considerably greater. Only a handful have radiocarbon dates, but it is clear that they must represent use over the whole period from the Mesolithic to the Medieval, and perhaps even later in Ireland. Sizes vary from as little as 8 feet to the $48\frac{1}{2}$ feet of the example from Brigg in Lincolnshire, dated to *c.* 834 bc. The crudest examples have simple cut ends, but usually some sort of shaping has been attempted. This may be a simple squaring or rounding-off, a more elegant tapering to a point at both ends, or a pointed prow and squared stern. Some have a shaped beak thrusting out at the prow. One complex stern arrangement involved fitting a separate stern board into a groove cut into the end of the trunk. Two canoes with inserted stern boards came from the Trent at the Clifton pile site, and this may have been a popular feature of the boat-builders craft in the Penard period, for it is also present on the Brigg canoe (*c.* 834 bc) and the one from Short Ferry, Lincolnshire (*c.* 846 bc) (Figure 6.4d).

Dug-out canoes were sometimes used as coffins for the dead, most notably the group of three found under a barrow at Loose Howe on the North Yorkshire Moors. Two, one inverted over the other, formed the coffin for the extended body, while the third lay on its side close by. All three were about 9 feet long and a few inches over 2 feet in the beam, having a carefully shaped, upswept prow, with a short projecting 'beak'. The third canoe and the lid canoe both had rather square, vertical sterns, but the coffin canoe had an upswept stern. Whether these short canoes from sepulchral contexts were actual craft, or whether they were specially made ritual boats, is not clear. It is fruitless to argue that the similarity of the paired vessels used on such occasions indicates special manufacture, as an effective coffin would require that two similar canoes were selected. To put these burials in context we should note that boat symbolism was part of contemporary burial tradition, as boat-shaped graves confirm. On the other hand some tree trunk coffins were not boat shaped and were shorter than those discussed here, which could indicate that the dug-outs in graves were actual craft.

Without doubt dug-out canoes, particularly the long examples, were unwieldy craft, and, although safe and manoeuvrable enough in the hands of skilled boatmen, they could be used only in calm inland waterways, and had limited load-bearing capacity, both in size and weight. Quite clearly something else was needed for sea traffic, and for transporting large loads, which, in the case of animals, might be unwilling voyagers.

The problem of large loads could have been solved by the use of 'composite boats'. For the transport of the 'foreign stones' up-river to Stonehenge, each weighing several tons, the most practical craft would consist of dug-out canoes lashed side by side, the transverse tie beams forming a platform for a heavy load. Theoretically only two canoes, each 55 feet long and 4 feet in the beam, would need to be fastened together to support the largest of the 'foreign stones', the Altar Stone, weighing nearly 7 tons, but the safety margin would be insufficient, and the weight would probably cause the sides of the canoe to buckle and spread, and eventually the whole craft to break up. Experiment has shown that three canoes, of the same beam and draught, but with length reduced to 24 feet, could do the job far more effectively and safely.

But prehistoric boatmen would not regularly have been confronted with loads of this magnitude, and for most purposes two canoes tied together would have sufficed. It is therefore interesting to note that dug-outs have sometimes been found in pairs, as near the River Mersey at Warrington. The Clifton find from the banks of the Trent comprised three side by side, and, if tied together, these would have formed just such a craft as has been suggested for the transport of the Stonehenge 'foreign' stones. Where boats have been found in groups, as here and at North Ferriby, we may well be dealing with river ferries which might be called on to transport heavy loads.

There is no certain evidence that dug-out canoes in Britain and Ireland were ever used with outriggers, although this would have made them more feasible as sea craft. Indeed, there seems to have been no outrigger tradition anywhere in Europe. The North Ferriby boats, already referred to, show one attempt to improve on the dug-out canoe, though the result was no more seaworthy. Here on the northern bank of the Humber, within a space of some 30 metres, the remains of three keeled boats with upswept pointed prows and narrow flat sterns were found (Figure 6.4). They were made of oak planks jointed edge to edge and stitched together with yew withies, the joints being caulked with moss. The resulting structure was braced on the inside with cross-bars found passing through cleats to link the keel plank and adjoining bottom planks. Bow-shaped frames fitting into slotted projections on the keel plank provided extra bracing. One or more double lashing passed transversely round the whole exterior of the boat would have helped to hold the whole thing together, and could have been tightened by twisting as necessary.

The results were three large, if flimsy, flat-bottomed boats of U section, prone to leaking and liable to ship water at bow and stern. They would have been perfectly adequate in normal river conditions but were likely to be swamped even by small waves. In view of their obvious shortcomings they might seem a short-lived experiment, but a similar stitched plank boat found across the Humber at Brigg in Lincolnshire (*c.* 680 bc, 593 bc), is much later than the Ferriby examples (boat 1, *c.* 1430, 1362 bc; boat 2, *c.* 1556, 1443 bc). These plank boats look like imitations of carvel-built boats by craftsmen versed in dug-out construction. However unseaworthy the result, plank boats could at least be made broader in the beam, more capacious and more stable than the ordinary dug-out. For river ferry work, and both at North Ferriby and Brigg this function is implied, plank boats would have been very useful.

But neither stitched plank boats nor dug-outs would have lasted long in the stormy waters around the shores of Britain and Ireland, and the most probable sea-going craft of the period is likely to have belonged to the family of

---

Figure 6.4 a, b. Double-prowed boats depicted in South Swedish rock art: (after Clark, 1952); c. Reconstruction of a double-prowed boat as a craft with hide cover over timber framework: based on a trial boat built in 1971 (after Johnstone, 1972); d. dug-out canoe with inserted stern-board: based on example from the Trent at Clifton (after Phillips, 1941); e. Sewn plank-built boat, North Ferriby, Yorks. (after Wright, 1976)

IX   The central grave pit at Rudston barrow LXII, Yorkshire.

X   Triple cairn on Beeley Moor, Derbyshire.

XI Siting of the rectangular enclosed settlement at Belle Tout, Beachy Head, Sussex.

XII Burnt wicker lining on the inside of a hut wall, Tormore, Arran.

XIII Excavation of reave and adjoining settlement at Holne Moor, Dartmoor, Devon, England.

XIV Unenclosed platform settlement at Green Knowe, Peeblesshire: house platform in course of excavation.

xv   Hill-fort at Mam Tor, Derbyshire. An unknown number of the visible hut platforms were occupied in the Second Millennium in a pre-defence phase of occupation.

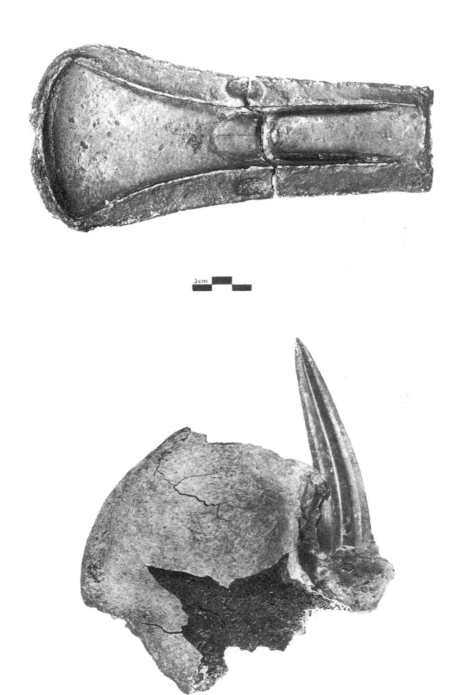

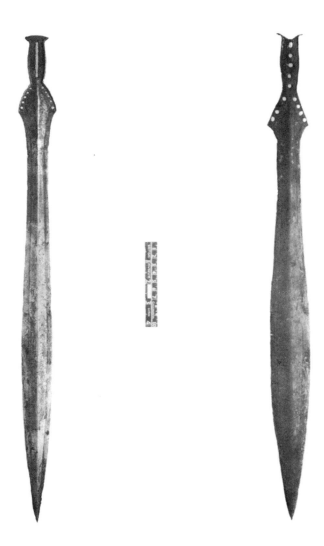

XVIII   The new weapons of the Penard phase: *a*. straight-based basal-looped spearhead, Enfield, Middlesex;   *b*. Two rod-tanged swords (*Griffangelschwerter*) from the Salcombe 'wreck', Devon.   *c*. Hemigkofen sword, River Thames at London;   *d*. Erbenheim-derived sword, Barrow, Suffolk.

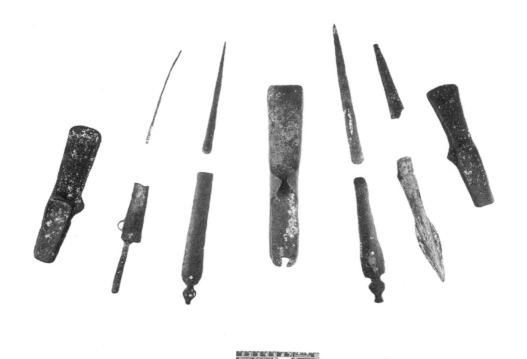

XIX   Bronzes from the sea-bed off Dover, Kent: a median-winged axe, palstaves, a Taunton-Hademarschen socketed axe, pin, Rosnoën swords, pegged spearhead and pointed ferrule, part of the Dover 'wreck' find.

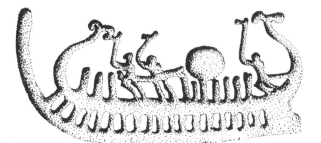

a

b

c

d

e

skin-covered frame boats. These exist in a variety of sizes and designs, from the one-man coracles, still paddled on quiet Welsh rivers, to the great sea-going curraghs which to this day ply the treacherous Atlantic waters off western Ireland. The structure of these craft, involving a skin cover stretched over a wicker or light timber framework, is such that they are only likely to survive in the archaeological record in exceptional conditions. Thus the oval basket-like structure containing a skeleton found at Brigg on the Ancholme estuary around 1926 may have been a coracle preserved by waterlogging.

Coracles, in view of their light and economical structure, and the ease with which they can be carried around portages, are likely to have been at least as important as dug-outs on inland waterways. For rougher waters keeled boats would have been required, though not necessarily of more substantial size. The light *kayak* of the Eskimoes is a notably sea-worthy craft, as we may deduce from the example paddled into Aberdeen in the eighteenth century after being blown off course during a journey off Greenland. But for general purposes a larger keeled craft, on the lines of the modern Eskimo *umiak* or the Irish curragh, would have been required. Such boats are described by Caesar as plying along the southern shores of Britain, and the third century AD writer Colinus describes 'small boats formed of pliant twigs, covered with the skins of oxen' navigating the 'rough and stormy' seas separating Ireland and Britain. The early Irish sources are full of references to the excellence and seaworthiness of such craft, and it is in such boats that St. Brendan supposedly carried out his remarkable voyages into the North Atlantic.

Yet in the time of Caesar it was the Veneti of Brittany who ruled the Channel seas and controlled its trade, presumably because they had much more robust plank-built boats. These are described as having 'broad bottoms and high poops and prows, on account of the tides', the latter reminiscent of the ships depicted in Scandinavian 'Bronze Age' rock art. Some of the simpler Scandinavian designs appear to represent ordinary *umiaks*, but much more eye-catching are large craft with extraordinary double prows rearing up at the stem, and with an equally prominent stern piece towering up at the other end, both crowned by figureheads (Figure 6.4). Various interpretations of these carvings have been proposed, notably that the outer keel and prow represent an outrigger, joined by multiple tie-bars to a dug-out, but the absence of any outrigger tradition in European culture makes this doubtful. A more likely solution, made all the more appealing by sea trials with an actual replica, is that these carvings depict large, double-prowed, keeled, skin-covered boats. The multiple bars shown on so many engravings would then be the light timber ribs which show through the thin hide covering of any skin-covered boat. The double prow would then be a device to protect the light frame when beaching, the leading member taking the shock. The inner, up-thrust prow and the stern piece could have their ends carved into figureheads as the rock-carvings depict.

The trial boat referred to above, 6.68 metres long and 1.25 metres in the beam, was built with a light alder framework covered by eight cowskins sewn together. The result was an extremely sea-worthy vessel which could reach nearly three knots with a crew of six paddling. It was found that the waves lifted the keel extension of the double bow, so that the whole vessel rode easily over the waves, and was as stable and dry as a curragh. A load of more than a ton, including a six man crew, could be safely accommodated in most seas, assuming careful planking of the bottom, and the carriage of domestic animals would thus have been no problem.

Many of the boats depicted in the Scandinavian carvings are considerably longer and larger than this experimental craft, and some have an uncanny resemblance to the galleys, propelled by up to thirty oars, which were plying the eastern Mediterranean from the Third Millennium. One vessel engraved on a Danish sword blade of the mid-Second Millennium, with a high up-swept prow and stern but not the double bow, shows this resemblance to a marked degree, though it is not thought that oars, or sails, reached temperate Europe before the First Millennium BC. Whatever their form, craft of this period were probably propelled by paddles. The world's earliest known item of navigational equipment is a wooden paddle recovered from the early Mesolithic site at Starr Carr near Scarborough (*c.* 7607 and 7358 bc). Several other paddles are known from Maglemosian contexts in northern Europe, and they occur sporadically throughout prehistory in many parts of Europe. Although the surviving boats of our period from Britain, Ireland and north-west Europe lack provision for oars or sails, in some cases paddles have survived, for example with the North Ferriby boats. Sails had certainly reached the waters of temperate Europe by the late First Millennium, when Caesar describes the Venetic boats with their leather sails. Sailing vessels were used by the Egyptians as early as the Third Millennium, and carried the commerce on which so much Minoan and Mycenaean success depended in the Second Millennium, but sail technology was so primitive (and remained so until recent centuries) that oars were vital even in the Mediterranean. Another form of propulsion, a sort of sail substitute, may have been used in our period. Many of the Scandinavian representations show a curious vertical bar amidships, surmounted by a blob. This has been interpreted as a leafy branch or bush mounted to act as a sail. There is abundant ethnographic evidence for such a practice, for example among the Micmac Indians of Canada, who mount a leafy bush in the bows of their canoes. Experiments with the trial double-prowed boat showed that even a very modest branch, *c.* 1.5 metres high and 0.5 of a metre across, produced some steerage way.

Unfortunately such experiments cannot prove conclusively that the type of craft depicted in Scandinavian art was a double-bowed skin boat, nor that they were propelled by paddles and assisted on their way by bushes mounted amidships. But they demonstrate the properties and capabilities of craft which seem the likeliest deep-water boats of the period. In the same way coracle-type skin boats may have figured prominently on inland waterways, although it is dug-out canoes, being more durable, which have usually survived, possibly exaggerating their importance in the period. The concentrations of dug-out canoes and plank boats at North Ferriby and Brigg, approached by timber trackways laid across muddy river banks, suggest ferries, where these more robust craft may have had advantages over fragile skin boats.

Chapter VII

Burial, Ritual and Ceremony

The number and variety of burial monuments surviving from our period is so great as to suggest a population totally pre-occupied with death. It must be remembered, however, that these sites accommodated only a small proportion of the population, and it is not clear what happened to the majority.

Nevertheless the fact that burial and ritual were so important to the social élite ensured that society as a whole spent an inordinate amount of time and resources in building appropriate monuments. For this reason changing attitudes to burial remain a legitimate basis for subdividing the Age of Stonehenge.

Burial, ritual and religion were so interwoven in prehistory that it is often difficult to categorize individual sites and even classes of sites. Many 'burial monuments' were not merely for burial but were used for a range of ceremonial activities perhaps not directly connected with interring the dead. Chambered tombs and early henges illustrate this point particularly well. Thus when investigating burial and ritual sites it must be remembered that they may have served a variety of functions throughout history. Just as old churches bear tell-tale signs of alteration and additions over the centuries, so Stonehenge was transformed from a modest Class I henge to the great edifice we see today. Even the simplest burial mound can conceal a long history of modification and enlargement, and just as a church may have its cemetery and cater for a variety of social needs, from worship to meetings and bazaars, so prehistoric 'burial' sites may have been used for much more than meets the eye.

A basic distinction has to be made, both before and during our period, between formal burials in formal burial sites, and interments, often token deposits, at sites which were not of primary or original sepulchral intent. In some cases there is insufficient evidence to ascertain whether formal burial has been accompanied by complex ritual, or complex ritual has included interment as one of its many elements. The problem arises with chambered tombs, which cannot simply have been charnel houses, for none contain anything like enough bodies. Many, indeed, have yielded strikingly few bodies given their size and complexity, and there is now overwhelming evidence that they were the centres of a very complex ceremonial and ritual pattern, in which storage of the dead played a role of varying significance. There are tantalizing glimpses of some of the activities that may have focussed on chambered tombs; the regular parading of the bones of the ancestors, the 'oracle boxes' of Newgrange and other passage graves; the celestial observations implicit in the careful arrangement of the Newgrange passage, so that the midwinter sun could strike fleetingly down its full length; the great spreads of 'domestic' features and material around the great passage graves; and the activity in forecourts and surrounds implied by hearths and deposits of artefacts and human and animal bones. The great range of ring monuments – ring cairns, stone circles, henges and the like – seems also to have served a broad spectrum of ritual, ceremonial and public functions in which interments played only an incidental part.

The principal changes in the burial customs of the Third and Second Millennia have already been outlined, and the intention here is to scrutinize some of the general principles which arise, and to look in greater detail at some of the major types of sepulchral monuments. Practically all the generalizations made about the burial practices of the period prove, on closer examination, to be hopelessly misleading: supposedly this was an age of individual burial; cremation and inhumation were culturally and chronologically discrete; and round barrows, individual crouched inhumation and grave goods were introduced by 'Beaker Folk'. All these, like the Beaker-food vessel-urn sequence, are now known to be fallacies.

The changing burial traditions of our period especially the ebb and flow of cremation and inhumation, and of individual types of funerary pottery, have customarily been interpreted in terms of the changing fortunes of different cultures. But now we must see these changes as a part of the continuously evolving traditions of societies developing in sympathy with each other. The mix of ideas filtering in from adjoining territories with those developing locally governed the way in which a society developed its attitudes to life and death. Innovations, whether material or ideological, could be accepted either in part or in full, by only some members of society or by all of them, and might also be adapted to suit local circumstances. Within one territory the situation was no doubt further complicated by individual community preference: any community might accept a new idea sooner or later than its neighbours, use it differently, accept different innovations, develop its own novelties, or cling to old ideas longer than its neighbours. With so many variables it is difficult to make generalizations even at a regional level, let alone on a national scale.

These concepts do, however, make sense of the infinite variety of sepulchral traditions, monuments and pottery. They help to explain how inhumation and cremation could be in use at the same time in the same community, and how late Beakers, and the various food vessel and cinerary urn forms, could all be contemporaneous in a national sense, but be in part successive at the regional level. They make it possible to understand how a community in Wessex could practice both inhumation and cremation and use both Beakers and cinerary urns; while at the same time on the Yorkshire Wolds, another group of people could also practise inhumation and cremation, but with food vessels and Beakers, with no sign of cinerary urns.

This contradicts another proposition, that some societies inhumed their dead while others went in for cremation. In fact, until the Bedd Branwen period, the two were often options in the same community, as is shown by the frequency with which burnt and unburnt bodies went into the same grave or cemetery. There are three possible explanations for their use together: individual preference, family custom, or the conventions of the community. Quite clearly there was no single answer, for the evidence at different sites suggests various solutions.

The fact that Beaker-accompanied burials usually occupy the prime position in burial sites has traditionally been interpreted as stratigraphic evidence that Beakers were earlier than food vessels and cinerary urns. But radiocarbon dates and careful study of the associated finds now leaves no doubt that late Beakers and early food vessels and cinerary urns were all contemporary. The suggestion now is that the different vessels involved social, not chronological distinctions. In the case of a site like West Overton G6b (Figure 7.6), where the inhumed adult with Beaker was central to a number of burials, mostly of children; family status, perhaps a patriarchal system, may be involved. But the situation was even more complex, for some of these satellite burials were inhumations, some cremations, and two of the latter were in cinerary urns, while the others were simple cremations. Unlike the central burial none was provided with grave goods, nor did any merit a Beaker. Compare the situation at Acklam Wold 204 on the Yorkshire Wolds where the central adult (?) was unaccompanied, and one of the surrounding children had the Beaker. As at West Overton both cremation and inhumation were used here, though the single cremation was with a Yorkshire Food Vase, not a Collared Urn. There are abundant ethnographic parallels for such differences in burial rites within the family and community, determined by such factors as sex, age, wealth, prowess as a warrior, and even whether the deceased is married or unmarried.

At Garton Slack 75 the crouched skeleton of a mature male with a Beaker lay on the floor of the deep primary grave (Figure 7.1). Higher up in the grave fill was a double burial, an inhumed female and cremated adult, accompanied by a food vessel, while in the top of the grave fill there was a cremation with another food vessel. On the lip of the grave rested an inhumed female with a further food vessel. This sort of arrangement confirms the impression of a male dominated society and some sort of pecking order, either in the family or the community. But it is not so patently a family tomb as the West Overton and Acklam Wold sites seem to be. The separation of adults and children at these two sites contrasts with some other graves, like Corston, Somerset, and Towthorpe 21, Yorkshire, where an adult (or adults) and a child were buried in the same grave. It was not always the mature male who occupied the primary position. At Hanging Grimston 55 in Yorkshire a 'youth' accompanied by a

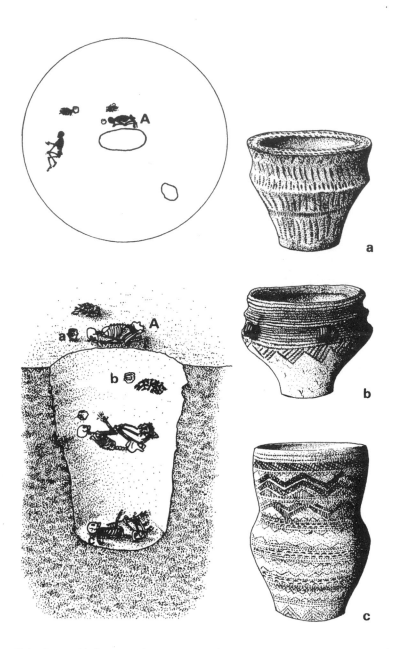

Figure 7.1 Garton Slack 75, Yorkshire: plan and section through central grave. Beaker from floor of grave; Yorkshire Vase one of two 'almost similar' accompanying the burials higher in the grave fill; Bipartite Vase with burials on grave edge (after Mortimer, 1905)

Beaker lay on the floor of a grave pit, while a more mature individual, also with a Beaker, was deposited higher up in the grave fill.

We can conclude from all this that if there were rules in burial practice, they were probably made by the individual community, perhaps even by the family. One general observation that seems valid is that while inhumations and cremations frequently occurred together, cremations were seldom placed in a primary or superior position relative to inhumations.

Multiple and single burials, like cremation and inhumation, are known from most areas. This is supposed to have been a period dominated by individual burial, whether by inhumation or cremation, but the situation was everywhere more complex. For example, in Yorkshire, the Pennines, and in southern England multiple inhumations, sometimes with cremations added for good measure, were all placed in the same grave. Petersen has counted no less than a hundred graves on the Yorkshire Wolds containing two or more inhumations. In some cases these multiple interments may have involved opening up a grave on one or more occasions to insert new bodies, which hardly tallies with the accepted view that the individual was all-important. There seems little difference between successive openings and interments at these pit graves – up to fifteen individuals at Aldro 54 on the Yorkshire Wolds – and the repeated use of the 'collective' long barrows and megalithic tombs of earlier times. Furthermore, there are cases of genuine simultaneous multiple burials to judge from sites such as Painsthorpe Wold 4, where there were three Beaker-accompanied inhumations on the floor of a grave, with the possibility that several more may have been contemporary in adjoining graves. Even more frequent are double burials, such as Huggate and Warter Wold 254, where the two inhumations each had a Beaker, and Painsthorpe 83, where one was accompanied by a 'drinking-cup'.

Such instances were not confined to Yorkshire. To take examples at random, at Mere, Wiltshire, there were two skeletons 'embracing each other,' accompanied by rich grave goods, including a Beaker and gold discs; there were three bodies with Beakers at Corston, Somerset, and with food vessels at Badbury Barrow, Dorset. The frequent cases of adults buried with children have already been noted.

There are innumerable instances of inhumation and cremation together in the same grave. Petersen has listed a large number of such sites on the Yorkshire Wolds, and we may note typical examples at Painsthorpe 83, where a cremation with 'food vase' lay under the knees of a skeleton, and Garton Slack 75, where a skeleton accompanied by a food vessel and jet necklace had its feet resting on a cremation (Figure 7.1). At the Great Barrow, Bishop's Waltham in Hampshire, the primary grave contained a tree trunk coffin in which were a cremation and an inhumation, both accompanied by bronze daggers. We have already noted examples of inhumation and cremation in the same grave from the Mount Pleasant period, as under the Stockbridge Down cairn, Hampshire.

Nor were cremations always of individuals. Modern study of cremations has frequently revealed the presence of two or three bodies and sometimes more, with female adult, presumably mother, and child a particularly common combination. For example, an enlarged food vessel in the Goatscrag rock shelter cemetery in Northumberland contained the remains of a woman over twenty and a child of two or three, while a simple grave pit in the centre of the Warren Farm ring ditch, Milton Keynes, Buckinghamshire, contained the burnt bones of a female aged fifteen to twenty, and a foetus or new born infant. Multiple cremations include that at Gazely, Suffolk, where a pit contained the burnt remains of male and female adults.

To these illustrations from southern and eastern England we can add others in those upland areas where cist burial is common. There are double and multiple interments in cists, with mother and child burials again common (e.g. Dunnottar, Kincardine, with three Beakers). There are also multiple burial cists where the disordered bones suggest successive deposits in the manner of the Yorkshire grave pits, as at Bee Low, Derbyshire (Figure 2.9). Mixed cremation and inhumation is not unknown. At Horsbrugh Castle Farm, Peebles, a cist contained the bones of a probable male aged about eighteen, but in the packing of the cist were the cremated remains of three people, two buried together while the pit was being filled.

The difference between the cemeteries of our period and the collective burials of earlier times has been overstated. There are many sites throughout Britain and Ireland where burials may not have been placed in the same grave, but were clearly deposited under the same mound or within the confines of the same cemetery, all at broadly the same time, as at West Overton G6b, or Bedd Branwen. Whether successive burials were added in the horizontal plane, or vertically at different levels, in the grave pits, the contrast with 'Neolithic' practice is a question of degree rather than kind, involving perhaps greater spatial separation of bodies and more regular deposition of grave goods, but not necessarily a radical change in ideology.

Although inhumation and cremation were practised in most regions, there are differences of emphasis depending partly on pre-existing traditions. In Ireland and Scotland cremation had always been comparatively popular, and continued to dominate, whereas in Yorkshire and the Pennines there had long been interest in inhumation as well as cremation, and this interest survived into our period. There is also a general correlation between the strength of inhumation burial in a region, and of the Beaker tradition there. Thus in east Yorkshire, the southern Pennines and north-east Britain, Beakers are numerous, and so too are food vessels and inhumation burials. Contrast the situation in Wales, with Beakers poorly represented, and a very weak inhumation tradition. In lowland England Beakers are as numerous as anywhere, but cremation always persisted, and gained ground as the Beaker tradition petered out.

The principal changes in the burial customs of our period have already been outlined. A site which illustrates all the main stages of development is Amesbury G71 on Salisbury Plain (Figure 7.2). This began as a small, ditched burial enclosure, within which a stake circle with central inhumation was possibly covered by a low mound. These primary features may have belonged to the Meldon Bridge period, for the next stage has a radiocarbon date of *c.* 2010 bc. A new inhumation grave was dug into the existing site, and a large bell barrow, incorporating three rings of stakes, was then raised over the site. Centuries later the site was extensively modified for a further series of burials (*c.* 1640 bc). The mixture of cremations (at least two) and inhumations (four), is characteristic of the Overton period, as are the novel funerary vessels which accompanied some of the interments. With one inhumation there was a southern Bipartite vase food vessel (Figure 7.3), a form normally found with cremations, and often met with in the enlarged version for use as a cinerary urn. Just such an enlarged example was found in fragments, scattered over the flattened mound which had been prepared for the new burials. One of the cremations was in an inverted cinerary urn owing something both to this tradition and to Collared Urns (Figure 7.3, top left).

After these burials a new ditch was dug just outside the existing one to provide spoil for an enlarged barrow. Further burials took place subsequently, and as two were inhumations, dug into the outer ditch, at least some of this activity could still have been within the Overton period. But thirteen or more cremations which were deposited in the mound and the ditch, must constitute a cemetery of the Bedd Branwen period. Many were in urns, including Collared, Biconical, and enlarged food vessel examples, and also Deverel-Rimbury urns.

Few sites were used over quite as long a period as this, but many can match large parts of the sequence. At Chatton Sandyford in Northumberland the original inhumations were in dug graves, one a deep pit of the form familiar from Yorkshire and southern England, but hardly to be expected north of the Tees in cist country. The accompanying step 3/4 Beakers suggest deposition in the latter part of the Mount Pleasant period, so that the radiocarbon date of *c.* 1670 bc seems too young. These first burials were covered only by a low mound, of surplus upcast, but the site was subsequently converted into a platform cairn, delimited by a fine kerb of contiguous dressed slabs fitting beautifully together. This work may have been carried out in connection with a third interment also in a pit. This was accompanied by a late incised Beaker, pointing to deposition in the latter part of the Overton period. Subsequently, in the Bedd Branwen period, two cremations were inserted into the cairn material, one in a Ridged Urn enlarged food vessel.

It is not just the formal burial monuments which betray this sequence of funerary traditions, for the ring monuments, where burials are incidental to the primary function, tell a similar story. At Cairnpapple activity began with

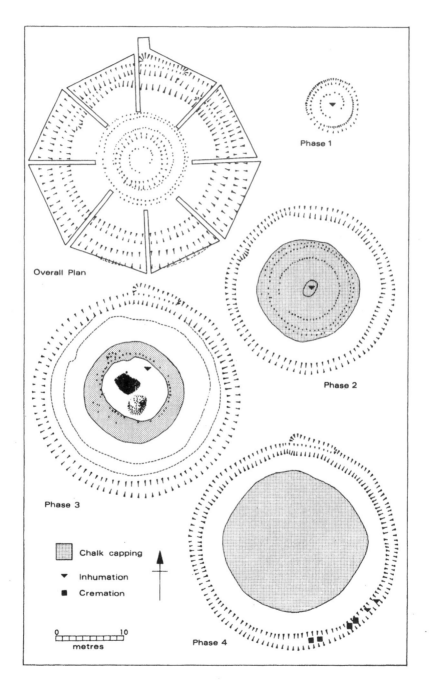

Overall Plan

Phase 1

Phase 2

Phase 3

Phase 4

Chalk capping

▼ Inhumation

■ Cremation

0 ⌶⌶⌶⌶⌶⌶⌶⌶⌶ 10
metres

Figure 7.2 Amesbury G 71, Wiltshire: stages in the development of the cemetery barrow (after Christie, 1967)

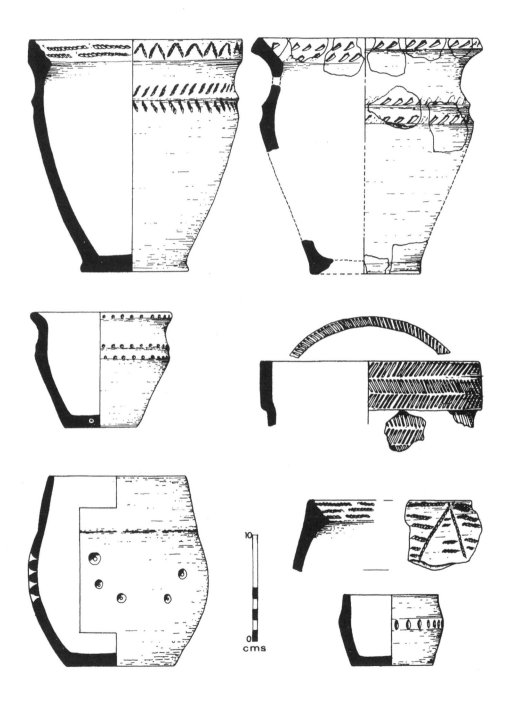

Figure 7.3 Amesbury G 71, Wiltshire: pottery (after Christie, 1967)

the erection of a setting of standing stones and the establishment of a cremation cemetery, probably in the Meldon Bridge period. The bone deposits were found both in the stone-hole fills, and on the old ground surface. Some were associated with the bone skewer pins typical of such burials. In the Mount Pleasant period a Class II henge was built around the original features, and the existing stone setting was removed to make way for a stone circle extending round inside the henge. Circle and henge may have been built at different times for the two are not on the same axis, but eventually they formed a unitary monument. A pit complex of uncertain function was dug in the centre at this stage and an inhumation, accompanied by a step 3 Beaker, was interred at the foot of one of the circle stones. In the Overton period a large grave pit with a standing stone at one end was excavated to one side of the centre of the site and surrounded by a stone kerb. The inhumation in this grave was accompanied by two Beakers of steps 5/6. Just outside the kerb a well-built cist with a large capstone was constructed to accommodate another inhumation, accompanied by a Globular Bowl food vessel. A few metres to the east a more irregular cist was built for a cremation. There is no reason to think that any great lapse of time separated these burials, and the mixture of rites is in keeping with the trend in this period. Subsequently all three were buried beneath a cairn with a kerb of large stones, the limits of which overlapped the circuit of the stone circle. Clearly the circle was dismantled to make way for the new work, and its stones were used to form the massive kerb of the new cairn, and to build the cists underneath. Some time elapsed after this activity before, in the Bedd Branwen period, the cairn was enlarged to cover two cremations in Collared Urns, and a new outer kerb was added overlapping the silted up henge ditch.

The site at Balbirnie, Fife, also charts the decline in stone circle traditions. First, in the Meldon Bridge or Mount Pleasant periods, a free-standing circle of stones was constructed, with cremated bones in some of the stone holes. This circle surrounded a square setting of stones sunk into the ground, associated with further scraps of burnt bone. Finds were few but included two sherds of Grooved ware. The next stage, in the Overton period, saw the construction of several cists within the circle, probably for cremations. One contained a food vessel, another a v-perforated jet button. A disturbed deposit with a late incised Beaker may represent an inhumation burial of this phase. Most of these burials were disturbed when, in the Bedd Branwen period, a cairn was finally piled over the space within the circle stones. This was a complex process, in which at least sixteen cremations were interred, in pockets inserted into the cairn material, and as scatters, along with sherds of Cordoned and Collared Urn, in and on the surface of the cairn.

Barrows, cairns and cists

The best-known and most widespread type of burial monument of our period was the round mound, termed a barrow if built mainly of earth, and a cairn if composed largely of stones. The structure of burial mounds depended usually on the building materials most easily available. The simplest way to make a round barrow was to dig a circular ditch and pile the spoil into a heap. In upland areas, with tough stony subsoils but no convenient outcrops or sources of stone at hand, both ditch digging and cairn building might be out of the question, so a large area was stripped of turf to pile up a turf barrow (Plate VII). In many areas where ditches could have been dug easily, the mound builders preferred to cut turf or bring in gravel, sand or earth from any convenient nearby source. Generally speaking where stone was readily available, and this applied to most hilly areas, it was gathered and piled up into a cairn.

Round barrows and cairns vary enormously in their exterior appearance (Figure 7.4), even more so in their internal construction. The simplest form of burial mound is the low tump left over a grave when the upcast is shovelled back, but unless protected beneath later monuments, or conditions for preservation are exceptional, low heaps of this kind are unlikely to survive. The simplest form of augmented burial mound is the bowl-shaped barrow or cairn, with or without ditch, consisting of material piled into a domed heap. Numerous more complex forms, 'fancy barrows', occur in Wessex. Here most examples are ditched, and the shape and relative size of the mound, combined with the width of the flat berm between mound and ditch, lead to many different forms (Figure 7.4).

But even in Wessex round mounds are only part of the story. Most regions also have sepulchral ring monuments (Figure 7.5), where the perimeter may be an earthen or stone bank, a stone-faced wall, a stone kerb or ring, or composite bank and ring. In the south, disc and pond barrows fall into this category, but ring ditches also exist in vast numbers, scattered especially on the river gravels and usually visible only as crop marks from the air. Many of these are undoubtedly ploughed-out ditched barrows with all trace of the mound removed, but others appear to have been ring barrows, with the ditch defined only by an internal or external bank. In upland areas of the north or west equivalent sites may have a ring bank of earth, stone or the two mixed together, but most ring cairn banks have facing stones at least on the inside and sometimes on the outer face as well. A whole range of inter-related and often superficially similar monuments is found in many upland areas such as north Wales, the Pennines and many parts of Scotland, but not all were primarily sepulchral sites. Ring cairns with a small, infilled central space are termed platform cairns, while embanked stone circles have a ring of stones set into, or more usually at the inner edge of a bank, usually provided with an entrance gap. Erosion of mounds may make it difficult to distinguish between these true ring monuments and round cairns incorporating similar ring features. Thus a cairn may cover a cairn ring or a circle of stones, or may have its margin edged by a circle or kerb of stones (cairn circle, kerb circle). Also

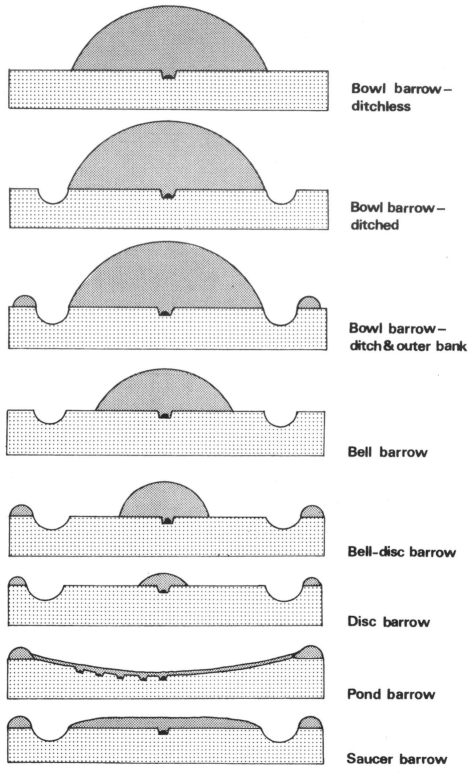

Bowl barrow – ditchless

Bowl barrow – ditched

Bowl barrow – ditch & outer bank

Bell barrow

Bell-disc barrow

Disc barrow

Pond barrow

Saucer barrow

Figure 7.4 Principal forms of round barrow (after Grinsell, 1953, and Ashbee, 1960)

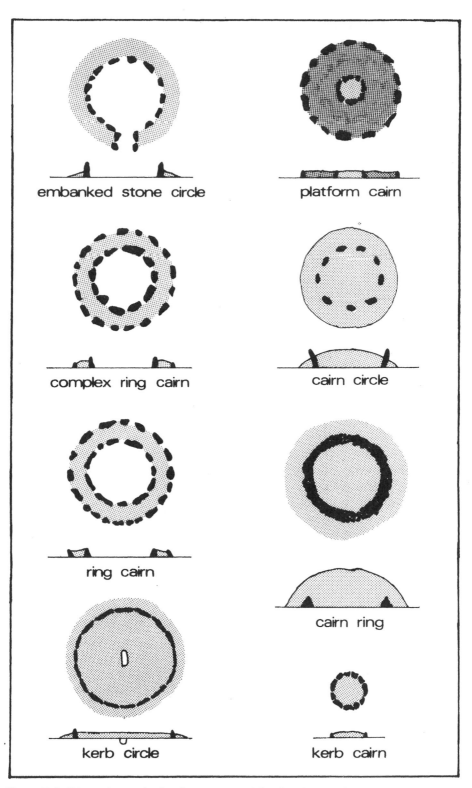

Figure 7.5 Ring cairns and related monuments (after Lynch, 1972)

distinctive are small, low cairns with a massive boulder kerb, known as kerb cairns.

The smooth turf-clad dome of a barrow may also conceal what was originally a very different shaped monument. Thus in south-west England and south Wales many barrows may once have been drum-shaped, or annular turf stacks with open or filled centres, rather like the platform cairns and drum-shaped cairns of the north and west. Many barrow mounds also conceal a ring or multiple rings of stakes or posts, set in continuous bedding trenches or individual post-holes.

Most regions also have 'flat' graves of one kind or another, unmarked when discovered, though perhaps covered originally by low mounds or girt by perimeters which have been removed by ploughing. The flat cist graves, which are such a striking feature of regions north of the Tees, epitomize this problem. These consist of box-like compartments formed from stone slabs and roofed over with cap-stones, sunk into pits in the ground and packed round and covered over with the upcast. Most are short cists, designed to take a crouched or contracted body, on the side with knees drawn right up. The siting of these cist graves, on easily-cultivable soils, leads to a steady stream of accidental discoveries in ploughing or building operations. The circumstances of discovery are themselves grounds for querying whether these were genuinely flat and unmarked burials. Constant ploughing will soon remove all traces of a covering mound, and the surplus upcast from a cist pit will have formed a sizeable tump when replaced. The coincidence of flat cist burials and agricultural land, and the presence of similar cists under cairns and barrows and within ring monuments in unploughed areas, leaves a niggling doubt that cist graves really were unmarked. Careful examination of some recently ploughed-up examples has revealed traces of a covering mound, as at Reaverhill Farm, Northumberland. Field names may also give a clue to the former existence of a barrow or cairn, as at Sprouston, Roxburgh, where a 'flat' cist grave, containing an inhumation accompanied by a food vessel, was ploughed up in a field with the suggestive name of 'Horse Knowe Cairns'.

The simple, apparently 'flat' graves so common on agricultural land in southern Britain present a similar difficulty. These also frequently contain crouched inhumations, often accompanied by Beakers, and were presumably the equivalent of the cist grave in areas without stone. We may speculate that they were covered at least by low tumps of upcast. Some uncovered in large scale land stripping operations have proved to cluster in cemeteries, as at Cassington and Eynsham in Oxfordshire, which raises doubts about those apparently isolated flat graves, be they pits or cists, uncovered by more modest disturbances such as ploughing. The circumstances of discovery make it impossible to know the ratio of single graves to cemeteries.

Burial mounds may cover inhumations and cremations, and short cists and dug graves usually yield inhumations; but ring monuments, small pits and small irregular cists made of numerous stones piled into a rough chamber, usually produce cremations. Round mounds appear to have been used from the Fourth Millennium right through our period, but ring monuments appeared only in the Meldon Bridge period and achieved their greatest popularity in the Overton and Bedd Branwen periods. The simplest form of round barrow or cairn was one of uniform construction covering a single burial. Many Beaker burials were thus covered by small, low mounds, for example some of those in the Crichel Down cemetery in Dorset. But strikingly few of even the simplest and smallest barrows escaped subsequent use. For example Crichel Down Barrow 14, only 17 feet in diameter and 6 inches high, covered a large deep grave pit, on the bottom of which was a crouched inhumation accompanied by an early Beaker. Subsequently a pit had been dug for a cremation through the small covering barrow, and into one corner of the original grave.

The Crichel Down barrows form a barrow cemetery, which, like the equivalent cairn cemetery in stone country, consists of a grouping of burial mounds, usually in a cluster, but occasionally, especially in Wessex, in a line. We can speculate that these served one community or sept over a period. They have often been confused with a cemetery barrow or cemetery cairn, an individual mound containing a number of burials interred either at one go or on more than one occasion. A barrow or cairn cemetery might include several cemetery barrows or cairns. These cemetery mounds may have been the tombs of individual families, but so little is known about the qualifications for different forms of burial that this is entirely guesswork. But it is clear that cemeteries were commonplace throughout our period, and that many accidentally discovered 'single' burials may have belonged to cemeteries.

Many cemeteries represent activity over enormous lengths of time. The most extensively explored cairn and barrow cemetery is that at Brenig in Denbighshire, founded in the Overton period. The range of monuments is remarkable, and includes several barrows of clay-capped turf covering multiple stake rings, and, sometimes, stouter post rings. Central burnt timber structures may have been mortuary houses, and burials, surprisingly few, were by cremation. The few pots found were mostly Collared Urns, and radiocarbon dates of *c.* 1660 bc (Brenig 42), *c.* 1670 bc and *c.* 1620 bc (Brenig 45) (Pl. VII) show that these two were built in the Overton period. Brenig 51, a typical platform cairn, was constructed at about the same time (*c.* 1560 bc) on top of an occupation site which produced Beaker and other domestic sherds (*c.* 1550 bc). Brenig 44, a fine ring cairn with several dates between *c.* 1680–1520 bc, was built for ritual activity, which involved the deposition of charcoal in elaborate pits dug against the inner face of the ring (Pl. VIII). Two Collared Urn cremations were not inserted until *c.* 1280 bc. Clearly the Brenig complex was in use right down to the end of the Bedd Branwen period, but its monuments served a range of purposes, and these may have changed in the course of time. Some of the sites, notably 44, were designed mainly for ritual and only incidentally for burial. This site warns us against jumping to the conclusion that the burials within a monument necessarily date its construction and indicate its primary function. In the Bedd Branwen period cremations were inserted into all manner of existing monuments, many of which may have been built for quite different purposes in earlier periods. Very similar problems arise in eastern Scotland, where there is also a mixture of ring monuments and round mounds. There are wide and narrow ring cairns, platform and kerb cairns, and the specialized Clava ring cairns, which occur in cemeteries with the morphologically similar Clava passage graves. The two were clearly complementary parts of the local sepulchral/ritual set-up, certainly by the Overton period if not before. The burials associated with most of these ring monuments raise the same doubts about function as Brenig 44. Cremated bone occurs in small token deposits, sometimes scattered in a dark, charcoal-rich layer over the centre of the site. All this is in marked contrast to the more formal cist and mound burials with Beakers and food vessels that must belong to the same period.

A large proportion, perhaps a majority, of barrows and cairns underwent successive modifications to accommodate new burials or fresh ceremonial demands. Clearly many sites were left open for a period of months, perhaps years, after the deposition of the initial burial or burials before a covering mound was raised. This is often encountered on the Yorkshire Wolds, for example at Willerby 235 and Garton Slack 141, but also occurs in southern England at sites such as Rockbourne Down, Hampshire and Frampton G4 in Dorset. In these cases graves were shovelled out at least once to take new burials, all before they were covered by a mound. Recent excavations have given a better idea of the length of time a burial site could be left open before barrow building commenced. At the eponymous West Overton G6b the site was prepared by stripping off the turf and a large grave pit was dug to take the crouched body of a mature man accompanied by a late necked Beaker and a set of leather-working tools (Figure 7.6). While this grave was being filled the cremated remains of an adult and a child of six, were deposited just above the inhumation, perhaps in a leather or cloth bag. At about the same time two young children were interred in pits a few feet away, and these were then covered by a ring bank of flints and sarsens built round the central grave. Subsequently a whole series of inhumations and cremations, two in Collared Urns, and mostly children, were interred in small pits in the space between the central grave and the stony bank, all in the north-west sector, which seems to have held some special significance. Large numbers of frog bones, snail shells and worm castings were present in most of the graves, suggesting they were only partly filled when these animals tumbled in and were unable to escape. These burials must therefore have taken place over at least one autumn, for frogs would only have been active this far from water in the autumn. The last two burials, an inhumation and an in-urned cremation, did not contain these

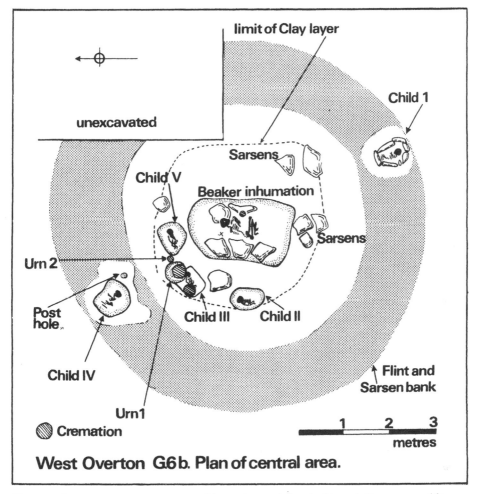

Figure 7.6 West Overton Barrow G 6 b, Wiltshire (after Smith and Simpson, 1966)

animal remains, and must have followed some time later, for they cut into one of the original inhumations, the exact position of which had presumably been forgotten or lost. This could easily have happened in a single winter, so if the original burials had been deposited one summer or autumn, the last two could have been interred and the mound built by the following spring.

How usual it was for burial sites to pass through this initial open phase is uncertain, but it was clearly a widespread practice, and the comparison with the initial open phases at many long barrow sites is self evident. Some re-openings certainly took place after a mound had been piled over the original grave, requiring the intruders to dig through the covering barrow to reach the shaft underneath. For example at Aldro 52 and 54 on the Yorkshire Wolds they dug through the original chalk mound and completely emptied the grave pits they found underneath, probably enlarging them. At Aldro 52 their secondary burials were deposited at various levels in the re-filling, from the grave floor upwards, but at Aldro 54, although the intruders disturbed the whole pit, they refilled part of it before placing burials in the upper fill. Subsequently this refilled pit was dug into yet again. At Rudston 63 the re-opening involved an enormous enlargement of the original shaft, so that only its very base, with an inhumation burial, survived. At all three of these sites outer earthen mantles were thrown over the original chalk mounds to cover the intrusion and probably the new burials.

At least some dug graves south of the Tees held wooden coffins, which could be regarded as the equivalent of the northern cists. Both monoxylous examples, hollowed from tree trunks, and composite structures made from several pieces of wood have been recorded, the latter nearer to the conventional idea of a coffin and to the concept of the stone cist. Being flimsier, the composite examples have survived much less often than the monoxylous type, so it is uncertain how representative are the 'wooden boxes' recorded by early excavators from several graves, and plank-built coffins such as the one found under a barrow at Pewit Farm in Berkshire.

Cist graves were as familiar a feature in Ireland as they were in north Britain. Between six and seven hundred have been recorded, mostly short cists, some flat, some under round mounds. Only about half are known to have produced datable grave goods, predominantly food vessels of local forms. On this basis the whole series has been assigned to the 'Early Bronze Age', but strictly speaking those without grave goods are undated, and some could conceivably belong to an earlier period when grave goods were not customary. Exactly the same problem surrounds the origin of the North British cist grave.

The proportion of cremation to inhumation in the Irish cists is about two to one. Almost half have been grouped in cemeteries of three or more, and both flat cist cemeteries and cist cemeteries in mounds ('multiple cist cairns') are known. The flat cemeteries, such as those at Coolmore, Co. Kilkenny (four cists) and Woodend, Co. Tyrone (five cists), are usually small, under a dozen cists, and the mound cemeteries are seldom much larger. The famous Mount Stewart cemetery cairn in Co. Down had fifteen cists, but larger cemeteries tend to mix cists and dug graves. For example, of the forty graves inserted into the mound covering the Mound of the Hostages passage grave at Tara, Co. Meath, only a minority were in cists. As in Britain burial mounds are both simple and complex. At some sites the burials all appear to be covered by the same mound and are broadly contemporary, for example Corrower, Co. Mayo, and Knockast, Co. Westmeath. Other mounds produce evidence of a complex history with successive phases of enlargement or alteration, such as Moneen, Co. Cork. Very often cemeteries were inserted into existing passage grave mounds, as at the Mound of the Hostages, and at Harristown, or in mounds of Linkardstown type, as at Baunogenasraid (Figure 2.10). Sometimes the sealed chambers of the megalithic tombs were broken into and burials deposited there, as at Carrowkeel K and in some of the Carrowmore sites in Co. Sligo.

Many smaller cemeteries combine cists and dug graves, as at Edmondstown, Co. Dublin, and Keenogue, Co. Meath, where most of the burials were in small pits or scoops. In some cases there are no cists at all, as at Harristown, Co. Waterford, where the burials were in pits sunk into and around a chambered tomb of entrance grave type (Figure 2.5). It will not have escaped notice that the pots accompanying some of the Harristown burials were all cinerary urns, and as a general rule pits seem more closely associated with cinerary urns, cists with food vessels. Thus in the Bedd Branwen period, cemeteries of in-urned cremations, more often flat than in mounds, tend to consist wholly or largely of pits and scoops. Strangely, very few enclosed cemeteries have been recorded, though the two cremations in Cordoned Urns found within a penannular ring ditch at Urbalreagh, Co. Antrim, suggest that some await discovery.

The later cremation traditions

As early as the Meldon Bridge period cremations were associated both with round mounds and with flat, sometimes enclosed, cemeteries. Use of both types of monument continued to the end of our period, but by the Bedd Branwen period, with cremation dominant everywhere, fewer new sites were being constructed. Instead cremations were frequently dug into existing monuments, not only round barrows, cairns, chambered tombs and other burial sites but also monuments such as stone circles and ring cairns which had not been designed as sepulchral monuments. The deposition of new burials in an old mound might involve little or no modification to its form, as at Rhoscrowther in Pembrokeshire, though frequently a new capping was put over the site, as at Amesbury G71. At some sites new burials involved more complex enlargements and modifications, which happened at Sutton 268, Glamorgan. That fewer new sites were built could partly reflect a desire not to waste further valuable land, but more likely it characterizes the declining interest in formal burial and ritual of the Bedd Branwen period. The privileged could still expect their own burial mound, to judge from the 'Wessex Culture' Aldbourne-Edmondsham burials, for these are usually primaries in a new barrow.

There appears to have been increasing use of flat cremation cemeteries in many parts of the country at this time. Hitherto the so called 'pond barrows' have appeared to be the sole representatives of this class of monument in the south. These are concentrated on the Wessex chalk, but it is now clear that other types of enclosed cemetery were constructed in the south-east, on river gravels in particular. In addition some of the often extensive flat Deverel-Rimbury cemeteries can be assigned to, or at least began in, this period. Those Deverel-Rimbury cemeteries, both flat and in mounds, which include Collared Urn burials, are obvious candidates here. This includes examples in new mounds, as at Deverel itself, and others added to existing barrows, like Latch Farm, Hampshire (Figure 3.13). Flat cemeteries with Collared Urn burials include those at Pokesdown, Hampshire, and Steyning, Sussex.

The Latch Farm site (Figure 3.13) highlights another great problem of sepulchral practice, the extent to which unmarked burials may have been interred in 'consecrated' ground around a burial monument. The original bell barrow at Latch Farm covered three central primary pits, one containing an oak trunk coffin with a cremation, one a Collared Urn with the cremated remains of two children, while the third was sterile. Subsequent quarrying discovered two bipartite food vessels (M26, M27), one, possibly both, with cremations which were probably also part of this primary cemetery. After the ditch had silted up to about half of its depth, which need not have taken many years in such friable gravel, turf grew over it. The site was then used for a large Deverel-Rimbury cremation cemetery, large numbers of burials being deposited in pits dug into the gravel fringe of the south side of the mound, and into the turf-covered ditch (Figure 7.7). The particular interest of this secondary cemetery is the presence, amidst all the Deverel-Rimbury urns, of a Collared Urn (81). About 10 metres north-north-west of the barrow the enlarged food vessel M20, a typical Southern Ridged Bucket containing a cremation, was found in quarrying. How many more burials may have existed around this mound is unknown, but it is a fact that barrow excavations have always concentrated on the visible monument, and have seldom tested the surrounding area. The possibility that burials may have been deposited as much around as within burial monuments is suggested even more strongly by General Pitt-Rivers' excavation at Handley Hill 24, Dorset, where the whole of a large cremation cemetery lay outside a penannular barrow ditch (Figure 7.8). All the urns here were Deverel-Rimbury types apart from one Collared Urn (42) which contained a cremation and a pair of bone tweezers of Aldbourne-Edmondsham type (Figure 7.9). Penannular ditched barrows are frequently associated with cremation cemeteries. An example very similar to Handley 24, at Catfoss, east Yorkshire, again had some of its cremations outside the barrow ditch (Figure 7.8).

In east Yorkshire, stronghold of food vessels and inhumation burial, the rising tide of cremation was resisted more successfully than in any other region. Mortimer and Greenwell uncovered a preponderance of inhumations unmatched elsewhere, with only a few barrows, such as Calais Wold 24 and 114, covering primary in-urned cremations. Usually cremations are secondary, and inserted into existing inhumation barrows, as at Huggate Wold 216 and Garrowby Wold C69. There are seldom more than five or six of these intrusions in one mound, and there are few Wolds examples of the larger cemeteries of up to twenty burials so familiar in other areas. The fact that the Catfoss cemetery is off the chalk perhaps points to where the larger cemeteries lie.

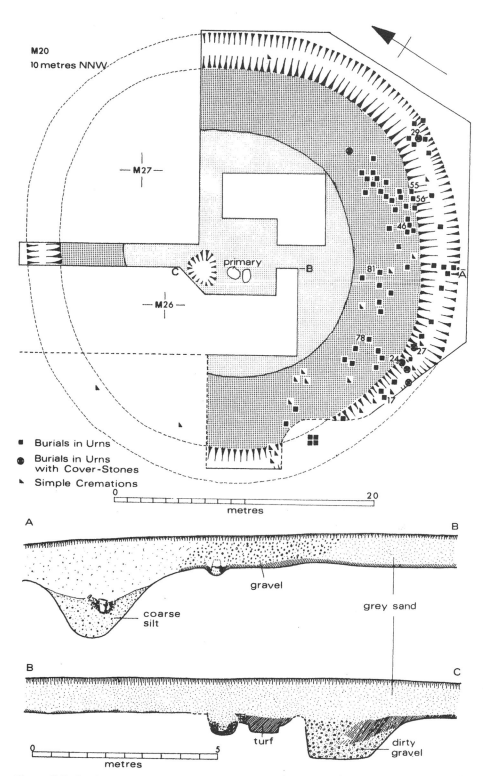

Figure 7.7 Latch Farm Barrow, Hampshire: plan and section (after C. M. Piggott, 1938)

Barrow 24, Handley Hill, Dorset

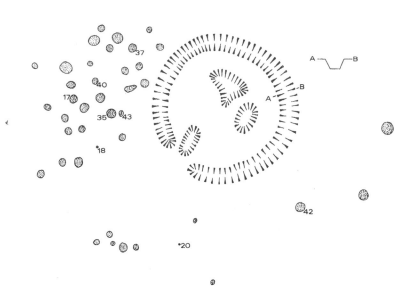

Catfoss Cemetery, Yorkshire

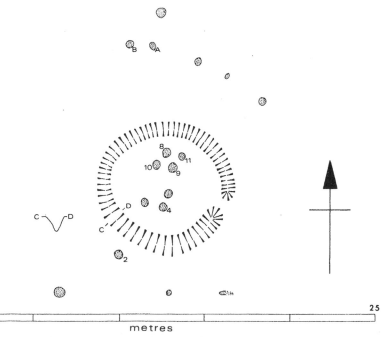

0   25

metres

In other areas where Beaker and food vessel inhumation had been entrenched, such as the southern Pennines, the north-east of England and eastern Scotland, in-urned cremation gained ground much more quickly. Both new and old cairns were utilized, but the Pennines, and much of the north and west, are especially characterized by flat cremation cemeteries of a wide variety of forms.

In the southern Pennines there are considerable numbers of ring-cairns and other enclosed burial sites. These are mostly on the grits and sandstones, avoiding the limestone areas which for long had been the preserve of Beaker and food vessel users. The south Pennine ring-works are very variable in form, including simple ring cairns, ring cairns with one or two opposed entrances, and some with an interior cairn; also multiple cairns (Plate X) embanked stone circles and free-standing stone circles. At Totley a ring cairn surrounding a small central mound of stones, produced five cremations, three with Collared Urns. Embanked stone circles are common: the one at Barbrook II has a single entrance and again produced Collared Urn cremations, one with a radiocarbon date of 1500 bc ± 150. The nearby Stoke Flat circle had opposed entrances and yielded an in-urned cremation in the last century. The Nine Ladies site on Stanton Moor was very similar, except that it enclosed a mound. Doll Tor, on the same moor, apparently combined stone circle and partly contiguous ring cairn, suggesting various building stages. It produced numbers of cremations, including one with a segmented faience bead which confirms activity in the Bedd Branwen period. Many of the burial mounds on Stanton Moor have been excavated and shown to have kerbs or buried cairn rings. Cremations were almost invariable, sometimes one in a mound, but more often two to five, and as many as thirteen. Collared Urns predominate, as is usual in the region.

Enclosed cemeteries are an even more prominent feature in the central Pennines and north-west England. In addition to ring cairns there are embanked cemeteries such as that at Blackheath, Todmorden, Yorkshire (Figure 7.10), where a low annular bank of earth nearly 30 metres across enclosed more than a dozen cremations in pits and cists, some in-urned. These were sealed beneath a clay floor laid across the interior. Many of these north-western enclosed cemeteries have 'pavements' covering the burials. At Mosley Heights near Burnley an embanked stone circle had a stone-paved interior below which were numerous 'ritual pits' and cremations. The Sun-brick embanked and paved cemetery at Birkrigg, Cumberland, yielded no less than eighteen cremations. The nearby Druid's Temple, a concentric stone circle, had its inner ring just within the margin of a circular cobbled area covering several cremations, one in a Collared Urn. Most famous of all these

---

Figure 7.8 Pennanular ditched barrows with cremation cemeteries in Dorset and Yorkshire: the numbered graves have their urns illustrated in Figures 7.9 and 3.16 (Handley Hill after Pitt-Rivers, 1898; Catfoss after McInnes, 1968)

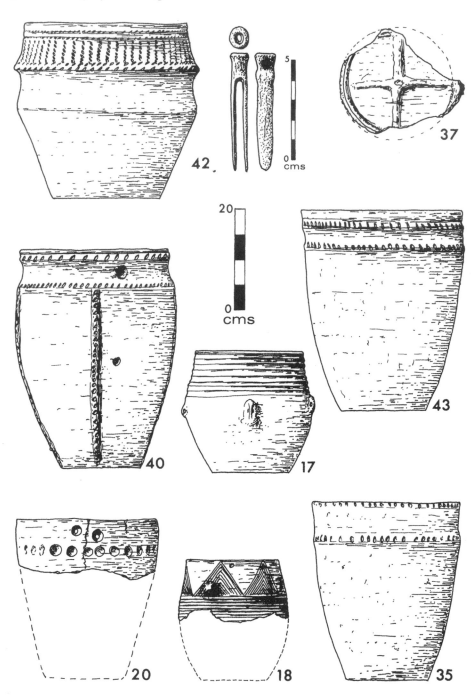

Figure 7.9 Urns from Handley Hill 24, Dorset, including 42. Collared Urn with bone tweezers (after Pitt-Rivers, 1898)

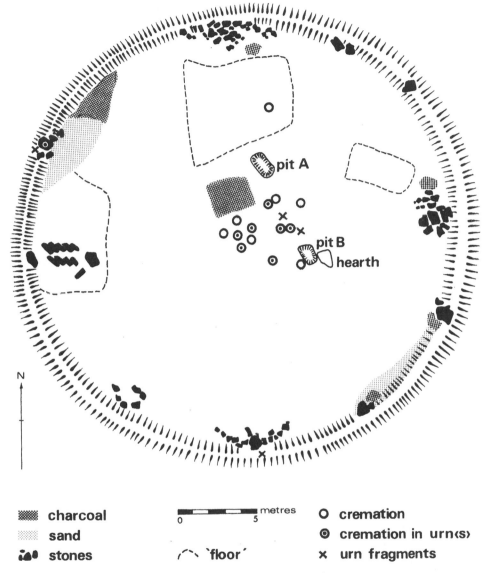

pit A

pit B
hearth

N

		metres
charcoal	0 5	O cremation
sand		◎ cremation in urn⟨s⟩
stones	⌒ `floor´	✕ urn fragments

Figure 7.10 Enclosed cremation cemetery at Blackheath, Todmorden, Yorkshire (after Bu'Lock, 1961)

enclosed cremation sites, and very different in character, is Bleasdale in Lancashire. This complex site consisted of a penannular, henge-like ditch of U-profile, its flat bottom lined with birch poles. This enclosed a ring of oak uprights, with an entrance 'porch' at the causeway formed by other posts. At the centre was a pit with two cremations in Collared Urns, and the whole space inside the ditch had been covered with a low mound. This monument stood within a large palisade enclosure, but placed so eccentrically as to suggest the palisade was pre-existing.

A number of flat cemeteries in the north-west had no recorded enclosing or marking feature. These include Garlands, Aglionby and Urswick in Cumbria, and sites on Lancaster Moor, where the burials occurred in rows or arcs. In such cases some sort of destroyed marker seems likely at the very least.

The Druid's Temple is one of several north-western stone circles with associated burials. Comment on such sites is risky, because some of the smaller examples may well be merely the stone kerbs of robbed cairns, and not true stone circles at all. Such, possibly, was Broomrigg C, Cumberland, which produced several cremations, one in a Collared Urn. At Oddendale, Westmorland, the inner ring of a double circle edged a mound covering a cremation. In some cases a cairn appears to stand within a stone circle, as at Moor Divock (with a food vessel burial) and Grey Croft, Seascale, both in Cumberland. Some stone circles surrounded one or more cists: Shap Centre, Gunnerkeld, Westmorland, is a good example. Finally we should note the mixture of features in the Lacra group of stone circles in Cumberland. One surrounded a low cairn, which covered a burnt area with traces of cremated bone; another also produced charcoal, while circle D produced a cremation in a Collared Urn from the foot of one of its stones. One of the difficulties with this sepulchral use of stone circles is to know whether it was primary to the monument or represents the conversion of essentially non-sepulchral monuments to serve as burial sites. So few examples have been scientifically and extensively excavated that this problem cannot be solved at present. There are henges and stone circles, notably Cairnpapple, where cremation burials of the Bedd Branwen period were interred with scant regard for the original form of the site, suggesting a change in ethos had taken place by this time.

Flat cemeteries also abound in Scotland, including cemeteries of mixed cists and pits which may have been in use over long periods. Sites such as Aberdour Road, Dunfermline, and Dalmore, Easter Ross, include burials of the Overton period but also cremations of the Bedd Branwen period. At Aberdour Road, inhumations in cists, one with a Tripartite Vase food vessel and a date of *c.* 1631 bc, were deposited considerably earlier than a series of cremations, one in a Bipartite Urn. At Dalmore an en-cisted crouched inhumation with a fine stone wrist guard could have been deposited centuries before a cremation with a Class Ib razor. At Kinneil Mill, Stirling, 50 metres separated a cist cemetery from an appreciably later ring ditch cremation cemetery. Here the burials were in Collared and Cordoned Urns, some *outside* the enclosure, reinforcing the point about burials in venerated ground surrounding burial monuments.

Scotland has many notable cremation cemeteries likely to belong entirely to the Bedd Branwen period. Some have no known perimeter, such as that at Lawpark, Fife, where there were up to twenty in-urned cremations. Most were in Cordoned Urns, one with a Class Ib razor, but there were also two in

Bipartite Urns at the foot of a large stone which may have marked the site. In some cases the burials in a cemetery have come to light over many years, as at Brackmont Mill, Fife, where the slow advance of a sand pit has uncovered dozens of in-urned and simple cremations spread over a considerable area. The range of enclosed cemeteries includes Loanhead of Daviot, Aberdeen, much like a Class II henge, but having within a large number of in-urned cremations, mostly in Bipartite Urns and Collared Urns. This raises afresh the problem of re-use of an originally ritual site. Also widely-distributed in Scotland are 'enclosed cremation cemeteries', consisting of an unfaced ring bank, surrounding a rough low cairn piled over simple cremations in pits. Pots and grave goods are rare. Excavated examples with radiocarbon dates are Weird Law, Peebles (*c.* 1490 bc), and Whitestanes, Dumfries, where the date of *c.* 1360 bc came from a cremation in a pit accompanied by a single Pygmy cup.

North Wales also had both mound and flat cemeteries in the Bedd Branwen period. At Brenig, the existing mounds continued to receive new burials, while the ring-cairn, 44, which had been built for ritual purposes, was dug into for some burials with Collared Urns. Anglesey has a number of notable cemetery mounds. At the eponymous Bedd Branwen, in-urned cremations were deposited in two main groups, one in an enlargement of the mound not too long after the other. Radiocarbon dates of *c.* 1403–1274 bc suggest that the burials here all took place over a few generations. These were contained in a mixture of enlarged food vessels and Collared Urns which is typical of the mixed ceramic traditions favoured by north Welsh communities. Not surprisingly the region has produced many hybrid Urns. Another notable cemetery barrow at Llandyfnan, Anglesey, had most of its cremations in Cordoned Urns, but one, detached from all the others, was a very rich grave group consisting of a cremation in a Bipartite Urn, accompanied by a fine decorated bronze dagger, a bronze chisel, a small flat axe of Wilsford type, and a small Bipartite Urn which served as an accessory vessel.

Cemetery mounds abound throughout north Wales and extend into the norther marches, where there are such notable examples as found in Houndslow, Cheshire. At the most famous of the flat cemeteries, at Cae Mickney, Anglesey, twenty-five out of thirty-two cremations were in-urned, mostly in Collared Urns, South Wales, on the other hand is best known for its complex barrows and cairns. In this region the deposition of cremations in existing mounds frequently involved enlargement and alteration of the site. For example, a small barrow of the Mount Pleasant period at Talbenny, Pembrokeshire, was enlarged with material from a newly dug ditch, and given a new stone revetment ring. At Sutton 268 in Glamorgan a very similar enlargement of an early Beaker barrow was carried out in connection with the addition of four cremated burials, one in a Collared Urn. Cemetery mounds, purpose built in this period, are also known. That at Colwinston, Glamorgan, covered an oval platform on which were fourteen cremations, eleven in Urns. This area was rimmed by a low stone wall. At least four other cremations were inserted in the covering mound. The Urns comprised a mixture of Cordoned Urns, very rare in south Wales, and Collared Urns, which are typical in the region. Another cemetery mound, at Mynydd Carn Goch near Swansea, covered a large number of burials, mostly in Collared Urns.

Burials in caves and rock shelters

Cave and rock shelter burials were a familiar phenomenon at least from the Meldon Bridge period, and notable early examples such as Caherguillamore in Co. Limerick, Gop Cave in Flintshire and Church Dale Cave in Derbyshire have already been discussed. Burials were still being deposited in caves, fissures and rock shelters as late as the Bedd Branwen period. At Elbolton Cave in Wharfedale (Figure 7.11), the earliest burials in a deeply stratified sequence were inhumations, some in rough cists, but higher up were more inhumations and a cremation, accompanied by Collared Urns. Collared Urns have also been found with disarticulated inhumations in south Welsh caves, as at the Tooth Cave, Gower. A very different approach, more in keeping with the prevalent sepulchral attitudes of the period, is seen in two rock shelter burial sites in north Northumberland. Underneath a sandstone overhang at Goatscrag near Ford were four cremations, two in fine relief-decorated enlarged food vessels, amidst a complex of pits and post-holes. Another sandstone overhang at Corby's Crags, near Alnwick, produced a similar in-urned cremation, suggesting that many burial sites of this pattern await discovery along the extensive Fell Sandstone crag lines of the region.

Grave goods

Despite the enormous quantities of sepulchral pottery from the Overton and Bedd Branwen periods, by no means all burials were provided with a pot, and still less received other grave goods. Unfortunately no accurate figures have been calculated, but clearly only a few per cent of known graves have accompaniments other than pottery. The proportion of burials with pottery is higher. The figures obtained by Mortimer and Greenwell, on the basis of the hundreds of interments they excavated in the nineteenth century, mostly on the Yorkshire Wolds, coincide remarkably: 28.5 per cent of Greenwell's burials were accompanied by pottery, 28.9 per cent of Mortimer's. A spot check on two burial mounds often mentioned in this book confirms these figures: 30 per cent at West Overton G6b, and 28.6 per cent in Phase III at Amesbury G71, where damage to later burials makes it impossible to give an overall figure. Nevertheless a lot of work would be needed before one could state firmly that about a third of burials were accompanied by pots, and there may have been considerable regional variation, and differences between one period and another. For example, 52 per cent of Irish cist burials had vessels of

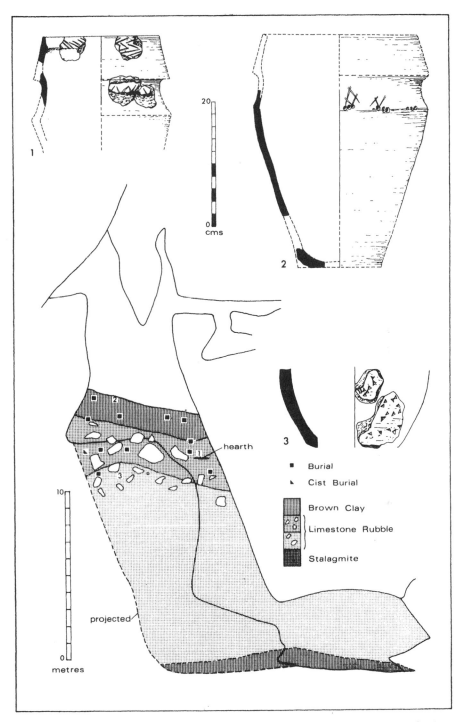

Figure 7.11 Elbolton Cave, Yorkshire: section showing stratigraphy of burials and other finds. 1–2. Collared Urns, and 3. Peterborough bowl, from the burial layers (after Gilks, 1973)

some kind, while the proportion of burials with pots may have increased as cremation ousted inhumation.

Thus it was quite common for the dead to be provided with an accessory vessel or placed inside a pot, but it was unusual amongst most communities to deposit other sorts of grave goods. Certain artefacts were rarely, sometimes never placed in graves, particularly some types of metal equipment. The list includes halberds, flat axes, and, in the Bedd Branwen period, flanged axes and tanged and socketed spearheads. Perhaps these were very practical people who did not believe in wasting valued possessions on the dead. Flint and bone items, the most frequent accompaniment, could be fairly easily replaced, but even these occur only with a tiny minority of graves. For those rare individuals interred with more ostentatious articles, such as ornaments of metal, amber, jet and stone, or with weapons, perhaps some special status is indicated, or some eccentricity on the part of the bereaved. Where rich grave goods and a prime position in the burial monument go together then we are likely to be dealing with the burials of the wealthy and powerful. But it frequently happens that a central burial has nothing with it, whereas burials in subordinate positions may have pots, sometimes trinkets or tools. This suggests that the attitude to grave goods may have varied considerably not only from area to area but within the community, and even the family.

The big imponderable, and one which might turn this whole problem upside down, is the question of grave goods made of organic substances, which would not normally survive the passage of time. Where exceptional conditions for preservation exist, as in the case of water-logged boat and coffin burials, a range of organic artefacts have sometimes been found.

At Gristhorpe they included a wooden pin which held the shroud, a wooden 'miniature spatula', a double ring of horn, and a dish made of pieces of bark sewn together with animal sinews, containing a quantity of 'decomposed matter', presumably a food offering; also a 'singular ornament' of unknown substance on the lower breast, 'in the form of a double rose or riband with two loose ends'. The remarkable Loose Howe dug-out burial contained 'the remains of hazel branches and three or four hazel husks . . . rotted rushes, reeds or straw . . . fragments of a pillow made of grass or straw', and fragments of foot-wrapping and a laced shoe on one of the deceased's feet. Such discoveries remind us of the remarkable wealth of clothing, organic grave goods, fittings and even furniture that have come from the Danish tree-trunk coffin graves. A further warning is provided by wooden grave goods which have been preserved by carbonization. The individual in the rock-cut grave at Cairnpapple had a long oaken object at his right side, possibly a club, while another oaken object, perhaps the remains of a mask or a cup, lay over his mouth. At Amesbury G71 a child aged three was accompanied by a carbonized object of oak which may have been a toy.

These discoveries have disturbing implications, for inferences about the relative wealth or poverty of a grave are usually based on the presence, absence and variety of associated inorganic grave goods, of pottery, flint, metal and so on. Organic grave goods could completely alter our ideas about rich and poor graves. They must certainly be borne in mind when making generalizations about 'unaccompanied burial', and whether or not grave goods were normal practice. It may have been exceptional to place inorganic artefacts in the grave, but there is no way of telling how often organic grave goods were included.

Henges, enclosures and cursus monuments

The public monuments conceived and built in our period include some of the most remarkable engineering feats of the prehistoric world, designed on such a grandiose scale that little wonder later ages ascribed them to the hands of giants. We are concerned with two main categories of monuments in this section, ditch and bank enclosures, most of them lumped together under the catch-all heading of 'henges', and the type of linear bank and ditch monument known as the cursus (plural cursūs). Many henges incorporate stone circles, but stone circles as a whole will be dealt with in the next section. The role of all these sites as territorial centres, of varying degrees of importance, has already been touched on (Figure 7.16.).

The term 'henge' is used here in its most general sense to encompass all those circular or oval bank and ditch enclosure sites of the Meldon Bridge to Overton periods, having at least one entrance and a variety of internal features. In its purest form a henge was an enclosure defined by a single bank with an *internal* ditch, Class I having a single entrance, Class II two opposed entrances. In practice there are so many variations that most authorities have fought shy of strict definitions. Thus also included here as 'henges' are the few examples with external ditches, mostly of Class I, which includes Stonehenge itself; those with median bank and internal and external ditches (Class IIa in Atkinson's original definition); sites with one or more segmented ditches; those with one or more uninterrupted outer ditches, like Arminghall in Norfolk; and embanked sites without ditches, such as Mayburgh in Westmorland and some of the Irish sites. A few examples, such as Dorchester XI in Oxfordshire, consist of continuous ditches without entrances, but otherwise they have much in common with henges. Taking all such sites together, well over one hundred are now known scattered all over Britain and Ireland, and more are discovered by aerial photography every year. Clearly they are capable of endless subdivision into types according to form, internal features and function, but that exercise cannot be entered into here. The range of internal features includes (a) a ring of stones running concentrically around just inside the ditch (e.g. Arbor Low in Derbyshire, Stripple Stones in Cornwall); (b) a ring of posts (e.g. Arminghall); (c) a ring of pits (e.g. Stonehenge I, Dorchester I and XI); (d) a ring of deep shafts (Maumbury Rings, Dorset); (e) multiple post rings (e.g. Woodhenge, Mount Pleasant, Durrington Walls);

(f) simple post rings not concentric with the perimeter, possibly buildings (e.g. Marden); (g) inner stone circles not concentric with the perimeter (e.g. Avebury); (h) a stone setting or 'cove' (e.g. Mount Pleasant, Avebury). In addition, there is frequently a pit, standing stone or post just outside the entrance and sometimes a pair.

The range of sizes is enormous, from a diameter of 8.5 metres at High Knowes, Alnham in Northumberland and just under 9.5 metres at Fargo Plantation in Wiltshire, to *c.* 480 metres at Durrington Walls, and an internal measurement of *c.* 518 × 315 metres for the unusually irregular example at Marden, Wiltshire. This encloses 14 hectares, the largest area of all these sites. Five main groups can be distinguished: (1) over 300 metres in diameter, which takes in the great Wessex enclosures of Durrington Walls, Marden, Avebury and Mount Pleasant; (2) from 140 metres (Ring of Brodgar in the Orkneys) to 185 metres (Thornborough Central in Yorkshire); (3) from 55 metres (Eggardon, Dorset and Normangill, Lanarkshire) to 98 metres (Stonehenge I); (4) from 25 metres (Dorchester II) to 48 metres (Corsey Bigbury); and (5) under 15 metres. There are a few sites which fall outside these limits, but generally there is a break between one group and the next.

Clearly sites of such wildly differing sizes and internal arrangements must have varied enormously in function. The smallest sites, under 15 metres, have for the most part produced burials, though how important a part of their function this was is not certain. At the other end of the scale the great southern enclosures indicate a great variety of functions such as would imply major territorial centres. Middens and circular timber buildings suggest some sort of permanent population, if only caretakers, but the possibility that they housed a corps of holy men, or the greatest chief of the territory, perhaps both, is much more in keeping with the general aura of these sites. Rings of pits, posts and stones attest an important ceremonial and ritual function, and some sites clearly had an astronomical significance which will be touched on below. Sporadic inhumation burials are best viewed as part of the ritual that went on in these sites, like those in the causewayed enclosures before them. Most enigmatic of all are the great multiple rings of posts best known at Woodhenge, Durrington Walls and Mount Pleasant. These have generally been restored as vast timber buildings, in which case they may have served as temples or assembly halls rather like those of certain North American Indian tribes. The northern structure at Durrington Walls is comparatively simple, and has a better claim than most to be regarded as a large building. As for the more complex rings, some prefer to see them merely as multiple rings of upright posts of different sizes, for ceremonies of an uncertain nature. Such grandiose sites must inevitably have attracted people from far and wide, like the causewayed enclosures of earlier times, and it is their role as centres for markets, fairs and festivals that in many ways is the most interesting. To demonstrate such activities in concrete terms is not easy. The resemblance of the vast surrounding banks to grandstands has often attracted comment, and now that pits, rubbish and buildings have been discovered in the areas immediately outside the perimeters of Waulud's Bank and Durrington Walls, it takes little imagination to picture the milling throng, the entertainments, stalls and animal pens that would be part and parcel of such public occasions. A priority must obviously be to excavate extensively outside, as well as inside, not only these great enclosures but also the smaller sites.

The functions of the great mass of henges between 25 and 185 metres in diameter must clearly have mirrored some of the activities at the major centres, but on a far less grand scale. It is difficult to see beyond the ceremonial and ritual role, which may well have dominated what went on inside the actual enclosures. They have produced little evidence of the timber buildings, post rings and rubbish which would point to a wide range of activities, although few have been extensively excavated. Still less excavation has taken place outside their perimeters, where more secular activities, and settlement, may have occurred if only for reasons of space. Their internal arrangements could potentially cater both for the celestial and subterranean aspects of the contemporary ethos, but the astronomical and mathematical implications of their structure will be considered in greater detail later. Interest in the heavens was balanced by an awareness of the underworld, if this is the inference to be drawn from the ring of deep shafts, up to 11.7 metres deep, around the interior of Maumbury Rings in Dorset. A number of sites have yielded cremation cemeteries, including Stonehenge, Llandegai A and several of the Dorchester sites, but in at least some of these cases the cemetery appears to be an afterthought, a later development and perhaps not a primary part of the site's function. At Cairnpapple in Midlothian a cremation cemetery preceded the building of the henge.

The only Irish 'henge' which has been extensively excavated, that at Monknewtown in Co. Meath (Figure 7.12), has facilities for a mixture of activities, very reminiscent of the major British sites, but with a diameter of 96 metres it is very much smaller. Like some other Irish sites, it has a large bank but no ditch. Its interior produced great quantities of occupation debris, including Beaker and domestic wares, much of it from the area of a pear-shaped house with sunken floor and hearth (*c.* 1860 bc). Burials in pits, cists and, in one case, enclosed by a ring-ditch, were scattered widely in the interior.

The title of this book demands some more detailed consideration of Stonehenge itself. Set amidst the rolling downland of Salisbury Plain, close to the River Avon, Stonehenge began modestly as a Class I henge, provided, like many early examples, with an external ditch. At this stage, in the Meldon Bridge period, the much larger site of Durrington Walls, only 1¾ miles away to the north-east, had yet to be built. Similarly at least one of the two cursūs which lie even closer to the north, may not have existed at this time. Clearly

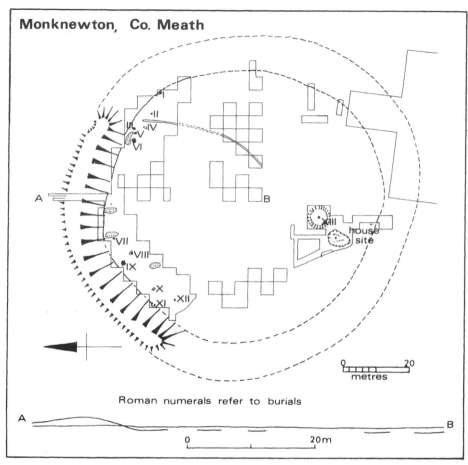

Figure 7.12 Embanked enclosure at Monknewtown, Co. Meath: plan, showing positions of principal excavated features (after Sweetman, 1976)

this area, and Stonehenge itself, had not yet acquired the special significance of later years. (Figure 7.13.)

The first Stonehenge (Figure 7.14) had a circular bank constructed from spoil dug from an irregular external ditch, and is dated by a C14 assay of *c.* 2180 bc from the ditch bottom. The bank stood about 2 metres high and enclosed an area about 90 metres in diameter. Access to the interior was provided by a 10 metres gap on the north-east, and here numerous structures were erected. Originally a pair of sarsen portal stones stood between the ends of the bank in holes D and E. Alongside them only the fallen 'Slaughter Stone' survives today, but whether this was one of the original portals or was erected in a later phase is uncertain. On the causeway there is a jumble of 53 stake-holes, which makes best sense as an indication of some earlier activity. Outside the entrance, stones C and B were possibly raised at this time, and 4

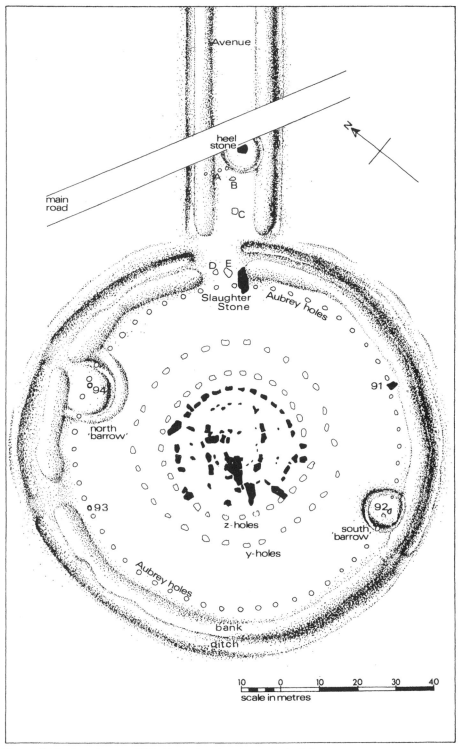

Figure 7.13 Stonehenge, Wiltshire: plan showing principal features

post-holes in a line mark the position of timber structure A. A little to one side and just beyond this a great sarsen block was raised, the Heel Stone, weighing 35 tons, though possibly a post stood here first. In the interior 56 holes, called the Aubrey Holes after the famous seventeenth century antiquary John Aubrey who discovered them, were dug in a ring extending around the inside of the bank, forming an accurate circle 288 feet (87.78 metres) in diameter. Up to 1.8 metres across and 1.14 metres deep, these holes may have been intended to take posts or stones, but whatever the intent they were immediately filled up again. It is possible that a timber structure was erected in the central area, perhaps a building, a ring or rings, but subsequent developments make it difficult to make sense of numerous post-holes found in this area. The exact place in the sequence of the 4 Station points, 91, 92, 93, 94 is uncertain. In the later phases they were apparently marked by sarsens, one of which (91) survives, but it is possible that originally they held posts and were markers for the layout of the site. They form the corners of a remarkably accurate rectangle of 79.3 × 33.5 metres, whose diagonals cross at the centre of the site at approximately 45°. Furthermore, these diagonals are symmetrical to the main axis of the site, while the short sides of the rectangle are parallel to the axis, the long sides at right angles.

One undoubted activity at this first Stonehenge, extending over a considerable time into the Mount Pleasant period, is reflected in the deposition of at least fifty-five cremation burials, some in the ditch, some dug into the bank, and others in holes dug into and around the filled-up Aubrey Holes. The first were deposited soon after the site was completed, for one lay on the bottom of the ditch, but others were found right through the various levels of ditch fill, and one, inserted into an Aubrey Hole, was dated to *c.* 1848 bc. Clearly burial was an important activity at this first Stonehenge, but hardly the main function of the site.

The inhumation burial recently discovered in the ditch provides a complete contrast to the cremations. It was accompanied by barbed and tanged flint arrowheads and a stone wrist-guard. These usually accompany Beaker burials, but no Beaker was present. This interment was clearly deposited late in phase I or even in phase II, because it was in a pit dug right down through the silted-up ditch (Plate IV).

The scanty finds confirm that the site was built in the Meldon Bridge period and continued in its original simple form into the Mount Pleasant period, for the primary ditch silts have produced Grooved ware but not Beaker, which comes in only at secondary levels in the ditch fill, at the same horizon as the first chips of bluestone.

Stonehenge may have continued in its original form for centuries, during which time the great enclosure at Durrington Walls and the two cursūs were constructed. Whether they detracted temporarily from the importance of Stonehenge, or were built to enhance Stonehenge is not clear. Eventually the

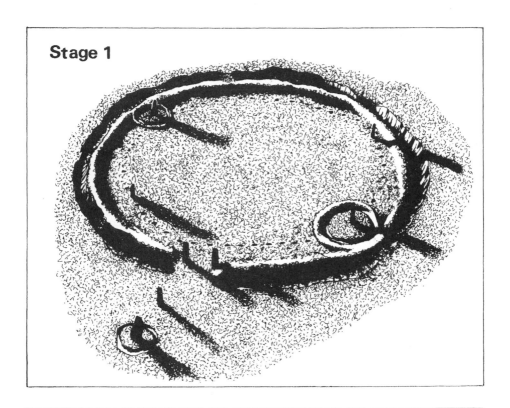

Stage 1

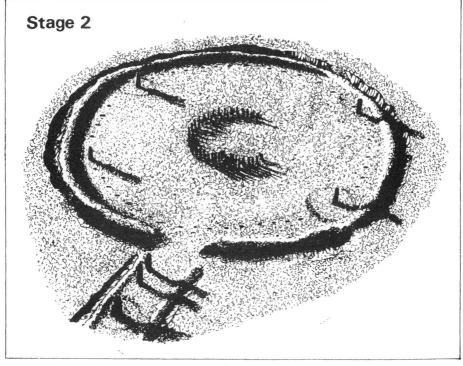

Stage 2

Figure 7.14 Stonehenge: reconstructions of phases 1 and 2

decision was taken to remodel the site. The centre-piece of the new work was to be a double circle of eighty blocks of Prescelly bluestone, or preselite, from Pembrokeshire, weighing up to four tons apiece. These circles were given an entrance on the north-east, marked by extra stones, and on the opposite side, a large pit was dug, possibly to take an extra large stone. The axis of these circles through this pit and between the entrance stones pointed roughly towards midsummer sunrise, and differed somewhat from the axis of the earlier henge. Accordingly some 8 metres of bank on the eastern side of the original entrance had to be levelled and an appropriate stretch of ditch filled in to make a new entrance corresponding to the orientation of the stone circles. Modifications at the entrance did not stop there. Two of the original portal stones, D and E were dismantled. What happened to the Slaughter Stone and its vanished twin is not clear. Timber structure A was removed, and a symbolic ditch was dug round the Heel Stone and immediately filled in. The fate of Stones B and C is not certain, but the Avenue, defined by low banks with external ditches, and measuring 23 metres between ditch centres, was constructed at this time. Eventually it followed a circuitous course of two miles, from the new entrance, to the River Avon. It has not been established that the whole length was built in one go, but the Avenue looks like a narrower, smaller and more devious version of the cursūs, two of which by this time stood on the downs just to the north of Stonehenge. There is no context for such linear monuments in later periods, so it seems best interpreted as a unitary construction of phase II. The function of the Avenue is as obscure as that of the cursūs, and although it looks very much like a processional way, it would be very difficult to prove this.

A long-favoured explanation of the Avenue was that it marked the final route of the bluestones up to the site from the River Avon at the end of their long journey from Wales. Unfortunately the *immediate* source of the bluestones is now very much in doubt. There is no doubt that they came at some time from the Prescelly Mountains, but what is at issue is when and how these great blocks reached Salisbury Plain. The long-accepted belief was that the builders of the new Stonehenge had the blocks quarried in Pembrokeshire and transported to Wiltshire. Supposedly they were shipped by raft along the coast of south Wales, then across the lower Severn, finishing their journey by composite boat up the Bristol Avon and other convenient Wessex rivers, being dragged on sleds and rollers from one river to the next. Eventually they finished up on the bank of the Wiltshire Avon two miles from the site, and were dragged in triumph up the Avenue.

Unfortunately this epic feat, though it may have happened, now seems less likely to have taken place at this time. The presence of a bluestone block in a neighbouring long barrow, Bole's Barrow, shows that bluestones were already present on Salisbury Plain before the beginning of the Meldon Bridge period, centuries before Stonehenge was conceived. Thus there may already have existed a stock of bluestones in the area that the builders of Phase II could utilize. An alternative and in many ways more credible theory, is that some glacier in a distant Ice Age littered bluestones as erratics all over Salisbury Plain, so that they were lying around for the use of prehistoric builders. However, there is still disagreement among scientists as to whether any glacier behaved in just this way, while the absence of preselite in any glacial debris in the area argues against such a solution. In favour of human transport there is a comment by the Medieval historian Geoffrey of Monmouth, who claimed that Stonehenge was built of stones brought from Ireland. It would be a remarkable coincidence if this did not preserve a genuine folk memory of the bluestones being brought from the west. If so, it still leaves the possibility that whenever and however the bluestones reached Salisbury Plain, the eighty blocks used in Stonehenge II were transported specially all the way from Pembrokeshire. Certainly the rulers of the Salisbury Plain territory were reaching their apogee at this time, and it would have been within their capabilities, politically and technologically.

Before the bluestone circles were finished a remarkable change of plan took place. Those stones already in position were dismantled and placed with those still awaiting erection, and the double ring of stone-holes was filled in. In view of the prodigious effort implicit in this grand design, some major ideological upset must have intervened. The dating of these events provides a possible clue. The pottery associated with the bluestone phase is Beaker. The relevant radiocarbon dates are *c.* 1620 bc from an uncompleted stone-hole in the double circle, *c.* 1728 bc for an antler pick from the bottom of the Avenue ditch, and *c.* 1720 bc for the raising of one of the great trilithons of the new plan, Phase III. Now these dates are statistically indistinguishable, and they coincide remarkably with the date of *c.* 1700 bc suggested for the emergence of cinerary urns and food vessels, the decline of Beakers and major social and political upheaval throughout these islands. New leaders emerged, and what more natural act could there be for a new régime than to demolish the great unfinished project of the old order, and institute an even more ambitious design?

Stonehenge III was an undertaking on an almost unbelievable scale, even for a society as well-organized as we know existed in Wessex. More than eighty great sarsen blocks, weighing up to fifty tons each, were dragged in from the Marlborough Downs near Avebury, twenty-five miles away. This in itself was a prodigious feat, for unless the holy men of Wessex knew of some power that has long since been lost to science, the whole operation would have to rely on human muscles, perhaps aided by draught oxen. To shift one fifty ton stone along the twenty-five mile route on a sled over rollers would require back-breaking effort from at least a thousand people, including those pulling, moving rollers, cutting new rollers, steering, greasing ropes, preparing food, and so on. Using oxen a smaller labour force would be required, but the feasibility of giant ox teams has been doubted, and this is a possibility only experiment could test. But using only human muscle power, it would take seven weeks just to drag one stone to the site, so clearly this was an undertaking that would have to be spread over years. (Figure 7.15.)

The sarsens, roughly shaped before their journey began, were carefully dressed on-site, and this operation alone would have kept 50 masons busy working a 10 hour, 7 day week, for 2 years and 9 months. This does not include the time taken to form the mortice and tenon joints which seated lintels on uprights, nor the tongue and groove joints which held the lintels of the sarson circle together, nor any polishing. A single tenon would have occupied two masons for a month. In practice the joints could probably not be formed until the uprights had been raised and given a year or so to settle.

Having prepared the great stones they were erected in a massive lintelled circle, nearly 5 metres high and 30 metres across, surrounding an inner horseshoe of even more enormous trilithons, the tallest soaring to 7.3 metres. These are the great stones which dominate the site today, and for most people *are* Stonehenge. Raising these thirty and forty ton blocks in their ramped holes was no doubt achieved by pulling from one side and levering from the other. The lintels could have been raised by using a timber crib progressively raised in easy stages, the lintel being jacked up at each new level in the staging.

The next step, when the great sarsens were in position, was to dress more than twenty of the discarded bluestones and erect them in an oval setting inside the sarsen horseshoe. This feature included at least two small-scale copies of the trilithons, but its precise form is unknown because of further modifications—how long after is uncertain. These involved the digging of the Y and Z holes, two rings dug outside the sarsen circle to take the remaining sixty bluestones (*c.* 1240 bc). But the plan was changed even as the last of these holes was being excavated, and events were overtaken by the developments of Phase IIIc. The oval bluestone setting was dismantled, the uprights,, their tenons battered and obliterated, were set up in the present bluestone horseshoe in the centre, while the lintel stones, and the sixty undressed bluestones intended for the Y and Z holes, were set up in their present position as a circle between the sarsen circle and horseshoe. The altar stone was set up as a tall pillar in front of the central sarsen trilithon. One of the last chapters in the long history of Stonehenge was the carving of representations of bronze implements on the sarsen uprights. Flanged axes of Arreton type can easily be recognized, and indicate a date towards the close of the Bedd Branwen period, around 1500 BC. More famous are the carvings supposed to represent square-shouldered Mycenaean daggers, which would belong to roughly the same period. Until the last few years it was widely held that the architecture of sarsen Stonehenge, unique north of the Alps, showed strong Mycenaean influence. In particular the form of the trilithons, and their mortice and tenon jointing, was matched in gate structures of Mycenae itself, so that the presence of Mycenaean dagger carvings on the stones seemed to clinch the argument. The Stonehenge

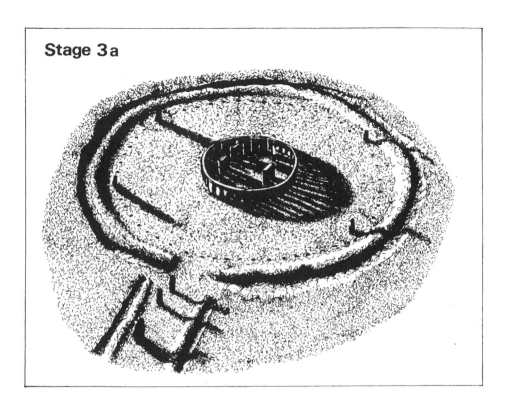

Stage 3a

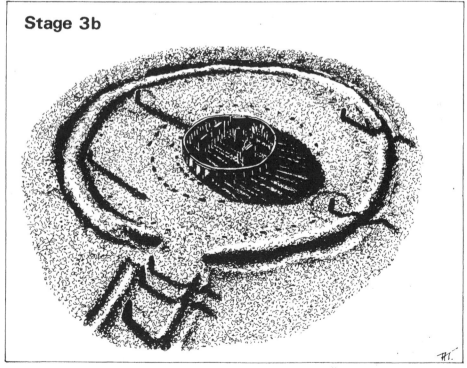

Stage 3b

Figure 7.15 Stonehenge: reconstructions of phases 3a and 3b

evidence in fact formed a major prop in the argument that linked 'Early Bronze Age' Wessex and the Mediterranean world. However in recent years the re-dating of the European early 'Bronze Age' has severed these Mediterranean links. Stonehenge is now seen to be much too early to have been influenced by Mycenaean architecture, so that the 'Mycenaean dagger' theory is no longer popular. However, another, clearer, Mycenaean dagger is carved on a stone from the Badbury barrow, Dorset, and an actual Mycenaean dagger comes from Pelynt, Cornwall, so the original identification is still the most likely one.

The scientific implications of Stonehenge fall under two headings, astro-archaeology and engineering. Its implications in socio-political terms have already been touched on, and no one can doubt the power and sophistication of a society that could expend over 30,000,000 man hours on erecting the sarsen monument alone. There can be little doubt, too, about the engineering skills of these people. The precise methods used for the various operations may be uncertain, but that is hardly the point. Here was a society that could carry out a major engineering project that would be daunting even today.

Not even scientists can agree about the astronomical and mathematical significance of Stonehenge. A mere fraction of the claims that have been made in these areas would comfortably fill this book, so clearly only some of the main points can be touched on. Speculation about the possible astronomical func-tions of Stonehenge go back at least to the remarkable eighteenth century antiquary William Stukeley, but serious debate was only sparked off with the publications of Thom and Hawkins in the 1960s.

Firstly, astronomical significance has been seen in the siting of Stonehenge. The monument lies at a singularly interesting latitude, where the directions of the midsummer rising solstitial sun and the midsummer rising full moon at its extreme southerly standstill position are at right angles. These orientations are incorporated in the rectangle provided by the Four Stations, a rectangle which was therefore accurate enough also to be of use in setting out the site. Only a few miles north or south and these alignments would be skewed. This position, too, gave the optimum horizon all around for viewing celestial events. It seems likely that observations on the spot were made for years, perhaps over a century, before the henge was built, for the bristling array of stakes in the Phase I entrance would have blocked access, and they are best seen in terms of earlier activity. They can be sorted out into a slightly fan-shaped arrangement of eleven now incomplete rows, six deep from front to back. Viewed from what later was to be the centre of Stonehenge, they would orientate on the extremes of the midwinter risings of the full moon, from maximum to coincidence with midsummer sunrise nine years later. This would fix the timing of midwinter nocturnal ceremonies and midsummer daylight celebrations, and eventually everything was placed on a more formal footing with the building of the henge.

Most astronomical claims made for Stonehenge relate to its use as a solar and lunar observatory. For distant sightings the position was carefully chosen with the all-round horizon in mind. It has long been known that the different heights of certain stones, such as the Heel Stone and Station Stone 91, are not arbitrary, for viewed from the centre the tops of these stones coincide with the distant horizon. This in itself suggests observations and alignments. Markers outside the henge would have been required for certain celestial events, and it is therefore interesting to note that the three large post-holes recently discovered in the Stonehenge car-park would have given alignments on midsummer sunset and midwinter moonset. Even without exterior markers, the various isolated stones placed within the henge bank are so situated as to give orientations of all the major events of the sun and moon viewed from the centre and from the Stations. In some cases features have been located on the distant horizon which could have provided foresights for some of these orientations. The alignment on midsummer sunrise may be the most obvious and best known astronomical property of Stonehenge, but it was by no means the only one.

The most sophisticated claim for Stonehenge was that the Aubrey Holes were designed as an eclipse predictor, but the premises on which this suggestion was based subsequently foundered both on astronomical and archaeological grounds. Nevertheless we can be sure that we are only just beginning to grasp the implications, not only of this remarkable site, but of all its remarkable contemporaries. The profound interest of many ancient societies in the heavens is well-known, and some of the postulated astronomical functions of Stonehenge are no more exceptional than the engineering skills implicit in its construction.

The chronology of Stonehenge is very much that of henges as a whole. The bulk of pottery finds from sites all over the country are Grooved ware and Beaker, suggesting that they flourished in the Meldon Bridge and Mount Pleasant periods. Radiocarbon dates are very much in agreement with this evidence. Beginnings at the opening of our period are suggested by dates of *c.* 2790, 2530 and 2470 bc for the Class I site of Llandegai A in north Wales, *c.* 2490 bc for the Class I site at Arminghall, Norfolk, *c.* 2416 bc for the complex segmented ditch site at Barford, Warwickshire, and *c.* 2356 and 2238 bc for the Class I Stenness in the Orkneys. Next comes the date of *c.* 2180 bc for Stonehenge I. That Class I, multiple-ditched and segmented sites were developed before Class II is confirmed by the pottery finds, for Beaker sherds are absent from primary contexts at most Class I sites, but plentiful in Class II sites. At Mount Pleasant there is direct site evidence that Class I and Class II sites were built at about the same time, for the great enclosure here (*c.* 2108–2006 bc), producing only Grooved ware in primary context, enclosed a ditch-encircled post structure of Woodhenge type (*c.* 2038–1961 bc) which also yielded Grooved ware. The other great enclosures of Wessex, Durrington

Walls, Avebury and Marden, were built at about the same time as the Mount Pleasant main enclosure, and also have strong Grooved ware associations.

All these large enclosures have provided proof of activity continuing down to the Bedd Branwen period, but this consists mainly of patches of occupation debris and hearths, especially in the partly silted ditches. At Mount Pleasant these run down to *c.* 1324 bc, and at Durrington Walls to *c.* 1610 bc, but whatever they represent need not have been connected with the original function of these sites. The latest major development at Mount Pleasant was not matched at the other three enclosures: at about the same time that bluestone Stonehenge was scrapped in favour of the sarsen plan, the great timber structure at Mount Pleasant was replaced by a setting of sarsens (*c.* 1680 bc), and a massive palisade was constructed around the hill-top (*c.* 1695, 1687 bc).

Unfortunately there are few radiocarbon dates for the smaller Class II sites, but many have produced Beaker material including Llandegai B, Maiden's Grave in Yorkshire, Cairnpapple, Ballymeanoch in Argyll and Fargo Plantation. An external pit at Llandegai B gave a date of *c.* 1790 bc. Some of these finds suggest activity continuing well down into the Overton period, for the Beakers are sometimes late examples, as at Llandegai B, while that at Fargo Plantation was found in the same grave as a food vessel. Stonehenge tells much the same story, with the unfinished Phase II around the transition from the Mount Pleasant to the Overton period, and Phase IIIA firmly in the Overton period. But with these smaller sites as with the larger enclosures the overriding impression is that by the Overton period the nature of the activity was changing, becoming more overtly sepulchral in character. Small hengiform sites continued to be built into the Bedd Branwen period, but these appear to have been designed purely as burial sites.

Throughout Britain and Ireland there are major concentrations of 'public' monuments in which henges and cursūs figure prominently. Stonehenge, Dorchester-on-Thames, Llandegai, Maxey in Northamptonshire, and Rudston and Thornborough in Yorkshire are but a few of the best-known examples. Cursus monuments consist of parallel lengths of bank and external ditch, usually 40–80 metres between ditches, extending for anything up to several miles across country. They frequently run in astonishingly straight lines, although at intervals they may change course slightly, and their hair-pin ends have often been squared off with remarkable accuracy. Overall they exhibit a very high standard of field surveying.

Cursūs were frequently aligned on pre-existing long barrows and mortuary enclosures, either cutting through them, as happens in the case of the Dorchester cursus, or incorporating them in the cursus line, as at the Dorset cursus. They also provide convenient terminals, the Dorset, North Stoke and Stonehenge cursūs being among those which end at long barrows. Where a relationship can be demonstrated, the cursus is always later than the long barrow. Some cursūs pass by or incorporate round barrows in much the same way, as at Aston-on-Trent, Derbyshire, or have round barrows at their ends, as at Scorton in north Yorkshire, but these relationships cannot be worked out as easily. The chronology of cursus monuments seems very much the same as that of henges: they were an innovation of the Meldon Bridge period and the earliest examples may have been built as the long barrow tradition was coming to an end. Among the earlier cursūs may be that at Maxey, which was earlier than circles of pits producing Fourth Millennium pottery of Mildenhall style; also the Dorchester-on-Thames example, which produced Ebbsfleet ware of about the same date in its upper ditch fill. On the other hand the Stonehenge cursus is likely to be contemporary with the bluestone phase at Stonehenge, while one of the Rudston cursūs produced Beaker sherds from a primary ditch context.

The construction of cursūs as of henges, probably lasted to the end of the Mount Pleasant period, but not long thereafter. Their use is very much a mystery, but in view of their scale and their close relationship to henges, it seems logical to suppose that they shared some of the latter's communal functions. Suggestions have ranged from processional ways to racetracks, and a combination of functions may well have been involved. They, too, may have had astronomical functions. The Dorset Cursus, in fact two joined end to end to make the longest cursus of all, may incorporate alignments that would be useful for tracking the lunar orbit, predicting lunar eclipses, and establishing the winter solstice. However, knowledge of these interesting sites and their purpose is even more rudimentary than our knowledge of henges.

Stone circles, settings and rows

Hundreds of stone circles and settings exist throughout Britain and Ireland, mainly on the stony areas of the west and north, with notable concentrations in eastern Scotland, Cumbria, the Peak District, Dartmoor, northern Ireland and south-west Ireland. They occur in all shapes and sizes, from great rings of massive stones weighing up to fifty tons and four hundred metres in diameter, as at Avebury, to small settings a few yards across, consisting of stones only a foot or two high. This suggests considerable variation in the purpose of the monuments. (Figure 7.16.)

Many henges incorporate stone circles, so the two must overlap in function and chronology. Both originated in the Meldon Bridge period, flourished in the Mount Pleasant period, but then declined. Unfortunately few stone circles have been extensively and scientifically excavated, and, like so many henges, they tend to produce few datable finds in primary contexts. The evidence for early beginnings rests largely on the apparent contemporaneity of the passage grave and surrounding stone circle at Newgrange, and the C14 dates of c. 2238 bc and c. 2356 bc for the Stones of Stenness. There was a dramatic upsurge in stone circle construction in the Mount Pleasant period to judge from their

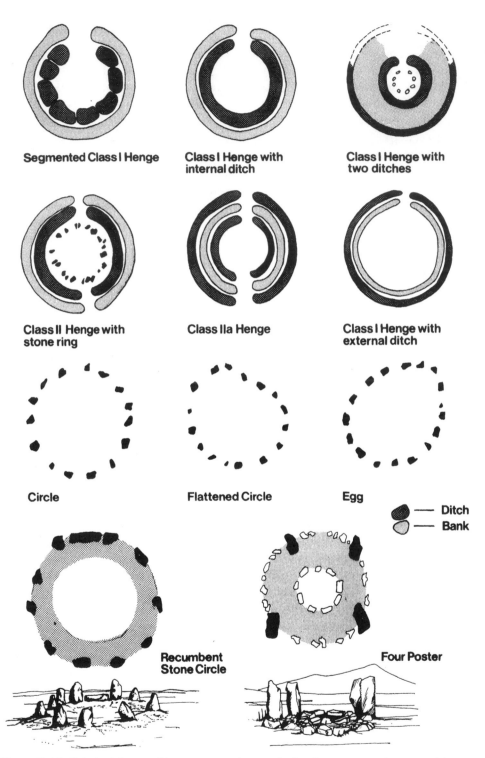

Segmented Class I Henge

Class I Henge with internal ditch

Class I Henge with two ditches

Class II Henge with stone ring

Class IIa Henge

Class I Henge with external ditch

Circle

Flattened Circle

Egg

— Ditch
— Bank

Recumbent Stone Circle

Four Poster

Figure 7.16 Principal forms of henges, stone rings and related monuments (not to scale)

association with Class II henges, and the Stonehenge evidence shows they were still being built at the turn of the Mount Pleasant period. Thereafter the focus switches to ring cairns and related monuments, and the survival of the tradition into the Bedd Branwen period rests on the date of *c.* 1200 bc for a small oval setting of stones at Scone, Perthshire.

In classifying stone circles an immediate distinction can be drawn between those associated with an embanked ring of some kind, and 'free-standing' circles. Henge circles are an obvious example of the first variety, but must be distinguished from embanked stone circles, which are more closely connected with ring cairns, in that their stones are set usually at the inner edge of a ring bank. Often they have an entrance marked by portal stones. In contrast the recumbent stone circles of eastern Scotland usually surround a ring cairn.

That many stone circles are in fact far from circular has always been apparent, but until recently this was put down to the deficient planning of their builders. Only since the 1960s, with the remarkable surveys of Thom, has it become clear that the seemingly haphazard shapes of stone circles were in fact carefully contrived. Not surprisingly the majority are indeed roughly circular, the circle being a very simple shape to set out with the aid of a rope attached to a central peg. Well-known circular sites include the Merry Maidens in Cornwall, Stanton Drew in Somerset and the Rollright Stones in Oxfordshire. Thom has distinguished four other principal shapes, flattened circles (e.g. Long Meg and Her Daughters and Castlerigg in Cumbria; Twelve Apostles, Dumfries), ellipses (e.g. Cultoon, Islay; Druid's Circle, Penmaemawr, Caernarvonshire), eggs (e.g. Arbor Low, Derbyshire; Cairnpapple), and complex circles (notably Avebury) in descending order of frequency. To these can be added rectangular settings, in particular 'four-posters'.

The recumbent stone circles and four-posters so common in eastern Scotland form, together with the Clava passage graves and Clava cairns, a complex spiritual and ceremonial fabric that has much in common with the mix of stone circles and ring cairns in the Pennines and Wales. Recumbent stone circles consist of a ring of standing stones, graded in height, the two tallest, often in the south-west quadrant, flanking a large recumbent block. Frequently the stones are set round the outer edge of a ring cairn, with an open space at the centre. Burials are not always present, and are nowhere sufficiently numerous or elaborate to suggest they were more than a part of the ritual for which these sites were intended. Some examples have a central cremation pit, but others, such as that at Loanhead of Daviot, Aberdeen (not to be confused with the famous cremation cemetery), have produced a black, charcoal-rich burnt layer with patches of bone, a pattern familiar in other categories of east Scottish ring monuments. As in the Welsh ring cairns, pits and deposits have frequently been recorded round the inner edge of the ring cairn. Unfortunately the pottery is usually undistinguished 'flat-rim ware' but Beaker sherds, including

AOC fragments, have come from Old Keig and Loanhead of Daviot, suggesting their origins go back at least to the Mount Pleasant period.

The small rectangular settings of standing stones known as four-posters occur mainly in eastern Scotland, but scattered examples spread southwards into England. These monuments are sometimes set on the edge of a small ring cairn, as at the Three Kings in Northumberland, or set into an existing cairn, as at Lundin Farm, Perth, where the original mound covered an AOC Beaker. At most sites the form of the cairn and its relationship to the stones is uncertain. Recorded burials are cremations, with Collared Urns at Lundin Farm and Carse Farm in Perth, and a Cordoned Urn at Glenballoch, Perth. Four-posters seem to be more explicitly burial sites than were the stone circles, and the associated pottery links some at least with the Bedd Branwen period.

One four-poster is known from south-west Ireland, where there is also a local group of recumbent stone circles to pose questions about relationships with eastern Scotland. The Irish sites lack the inner ring cairn of the Scottish sites and may have a central stone. Sporadic cremations are recorded, often token deposits, suggesting that the Irish recumbent stone circles, like those in Scotland, were not primarily sepulchral. The Irish finds, too, are usually unhelpful 'flat-rim ware' sherds.

Stone circles: metrology, geometry and astronomy

It is central to Thom's thesis that the builders of stone circles employed a standard unit of measurement, the so-called megalithic yard of 2.72 feet, and that they had a considerable knowledge of field geometry which they used in setting out the different shapes. That stone circles occur in a regularly recurring range of different shapes there is no doubt, but it is the means used to arrive at these shapes which have generated such fierce controversy in recent years. Firstly, the validity of the megalithic yard itself has been challenged, and the suggestion made that it represents no more than the length of an average pace. There is slight regional variation in the theoretical units of measurement used in stone circles, which argues strongly that an average pace was indeed a basis for measurement. Given the territorial social and political situation existing in the country, the idea of a national megalithic yard in Thom's sense, with a central headquarters supplying standard measuring rods, is inherently unlikely. But there is no reason why a standard unit should not have existed in each region, based on a local average pace, and standardized in local measuring rods. Megalithic builders were clearly capable of field engineering of a high standard, so the likelihood that they were versed in basic numeracy and used standard units and measuring rods might be considered likely, even inevitable. Just such a measuring rod, of hazel, was found in a Middle Bronze Age grave at Borum Eshøj in Denmark. This measured 0.79 of a metre in length, less than the 0.829 of a metre of the megalithic yard, but well within the limits of variation in the human pace.

Undoubtedly stone circle measurements frequently do fall in multiples of Thom's megalithic yard, for example sites as far apart as Newgrange, the Ring of Brodgar in the Orkneys and the inner circles of Avebury, all measure 125 megalithic yards in diameter. The megalithic yard seems to be valid for sites scattered in areas as far apart as Dartmoor, Argyll and Caithness, but equally there are regions where rather different standards seem to apply. In eastern Scotland different groups of monuments seem to be based on slightly different standards, 0.820 of a metre for the recumbent stone circles, 0.838 of a metre for the Clava passage graves, and 0.826 of a metre for the ring cairns.

So, while it seems entirely plausible that megalithic builders had their own local units and measuring rods based on their version of the average pace, the idea that they were sufficiently versed in geometry to perform some of the intricate mensuration suggested by Thom is an entirely different matter. They certainly could cope with some of the required manoeuvres, for example the precisely squared off ends of some cursūs show they knew how to lay out right angles. But if they were capable of doing much more than this, and setting out straight lines and circles, then a greater match between circle plans and theoretical shapes might be expected than actually exists. Use of the simple steps above, coupled with empirical knowledge, might be sufficient to produce at least some of the shapes involved, but practical experiment is needed to explore the various possibilities.

Apart possibly from the four-posters and some ring cairns stone circles do not seem to have been primarily concerned with burial. We have seen how sites as far apart as Welsh ring cairns and east Scottish recumbent stone circles produce scattered cremations, but never more than seem an adjunct to the principal function of the sites concerned. More formal burials are found, for example the inhumations with Beakers at the foot of some of the Avebury stones, the food vessel-accompanied inhumations in cists at the Machrie stone circle on Arran, and the cremations in enlarged food vessels in the Druid's Circle, Penmaemawr. It is important to stress in the last two cases at least that these burials need not relate to the building and main use of these sites. Indeed there is good reason to think that the food vessel and urn burials from many stone circles were late insertions, and represent a change in the use of stone circles. If not sepulchral monuments, what were the aims of stone circle builders? Thom's work has been directed towards demonstrating their role as celestial observatories, principally of the sun and moon, but also of lesser astronomical events such as the rising and setting of planets and bright stars. An interest in celestial matters is common to all peasant societies, if only for agricultural purposes, but the farmers of our period could have observed all they needed to in the heavens without going to the lengths of setting up stone circles. If celestial observation is involved then it is likely to have been for magico-religious rather than practical reasons. Indeed, given the structured society of the day, and the often staggering requirement in human labour involved in erecting stone circles, they look increasingly like devices used by leaders of society, both secular and spiritual, to keep their subjects busy and keep them submissive. All dynasties need their great monuments, and this is perhaps how the stone circles should be viewed.

Celestial observation could well have been part of the mystique of this process. An ability to predict events in the sky would give prestige to the holy men, especially the more unusual events such as eclipses. The use of the Stonehenge Aubrey Holes as an eclipse predictor has not been confirmed, but this is the sort of activity we should perhaps consider when examining stone circles. Undoubtedly sighting on significant celestial events can be found at many stone circles, but this is not the same as saying that such alignments were deliberately conceived, and that the stones were used in this way. This is also true of standing stones, to which we will turn below.

Stone avenues and rows

Stone 'avenues', twin lines of stones, lead away from stone circles in many parts of the country. They may extend from one site to another, for example the West Kennet Avenue from Avebury to the Sanctuary on Overton Hill, or they may terminate in higher terminal stones, as at Callanish on Lewis. Many are too ruinous for useful comment, as at Stanton Drew. Stone avenues are perhaps counterparts of earthen avenues, like those which lead from Stonehenge and Arbor Low; and of timber avenues which are coming to light in increasing numbers, some leading up to long barrows, as at Kemp Howe in Yorkshire, others up to round barrows, as at Poole, Dorset. Timber avenues and rows also occur in the great enclosures. At Durrington Walls a timber avenue approached a large circular timber structure, and there were rows of timber uprights. The remarkable out-turned timber avenue entrances at Meldon Bridge and Forteviot must also be relevant.

It may be that these avenues took over some of the functions of the cursūs. Stone avenues are frequently not connected to a circle, as in the case of such Welsh examples as Cerrig Duon in Breconshire. This leads on to the related phenomenon of stone rows, which are common in many upland areas, especially in south-west England. Here they occur as single, double and treble lines, frequently terminating in taller pillars and often leading from, or incorporating in their line, cairns and cists. They may wander across the moors for anything up to two miles, in which case they must have served very different purposes from the 'lines' of three stones so familiar in western Scotland and northern Ireland. While an astronomical function for the latter seems possible, the straggly rows of the south-west have no obvious celestial significance.

If there is any one site which epitomizes the remarkable stone monuments of Britain and Ireland it is the astonishing complex at Beaghmore in Co. Tyrone, where stone circles, cairns, rows and avenues have been revealed over an area of *c.* 150 metres by up to 60 metres by peeling back the peat. Even then the rows run on under the bog, so that the full extent of this ritual agglomeration is unknown. Who can doubt that complexes like Beaghmore, or Stanton Drew, or Callanish were major territorial centres for ritual and ceremony, a necessary part of the fabric of a highly organized and structured society where such monuments may have been a vital part of the means of power. Their precise function may always prove elusive, but at least some of their implications should be quite obvious.

Standing stones

Standing stones, monoliths or the 'menhirs' of the early antiquaries, are amongst the most widespread of our antiquities, but have been raised in practically every period for all manner of reasons. Some were erected for the most mundane purposes, as cow scratching posts, for example, while others have marked boundaries between estates, parishes and even countries, such as the Stob Stones in the Cheviots, which were set up in the early Medieval period to mark the border between England and Scotland. Thus it is dangerous to dogmatize about individual monuments, even though many are genuinely prehistoric. Excavation is one answer, but is by no means guaranteed to provide a solution. A rule of thumb guide is to regard the larger examples, say over 2 metres high, as less likely to be recent agricultural devices and boundary markers than the smaller ones, but this in no way indicates how many of the latter were raised in our period. Juxtaposition to a genuine prehistoric monument, such as a cairn or stone circle, may be an indication, but not an infallible one.

The largest, tallest monolith in these islands is that in Rudston churchyard on the Yorkshire Wolds, standing about 8 metres high and weighing 26 tons, a gritstone block which must have been hauled from Cayton Bay about 10 miles away. For this reason, because of its size, and because it stands as the focus of a remarkable convergence of cursus monuments, it can be confidently assigned to the earlier part of our period. Towering spire though it seems, it is a pygmy compared with the vast menhirs of Brittany. The tallest still standing there, at Kerloas, soars to nearly 11.7 metres, but the prostrate Grand Menhir Brisé, never raised, is 20.6 metres long and weighed nearly 350 tons.

That a great many of the standing stones of Britain and Ireland were raised in our period is clear from their often intimate connection with cairns and stone circles. The most explicit relationship is where a standing stone was incorporated in a burial mound, as at Bedd Branwen, a more certain association than examples raised on top of cairns, such as that on the mound at Llanfachreth, Merioneth. Upright stones were frequently used as grave markers, for example under the barrow at Rhoscrowther, in Pembrokeshire. Many isolated standing stones had burials of various kinds at their foot including a cremation at Drumnahare, Co. Down, a cremation in a Bipartite Urn at

Glynllifon, Caernarvonshire, and an inhumation in a cist at the foot of the Carn Tulach stone, Perth. There were also cists at the base of the Punchestown and Longstone Rath stones in Co. Kildare. The latter, 6.4 metres high, stands within a typical Irish 'henge', and its cist contained multiple cremations accompanied by a stone bracer. In some cases a monolith was left standing on the edge of a burial mound, as at Ystrad Hynod, Montgomeryshire. Other explicit dating evidence is provided by cup and ring markings, as on a stone at Nether Largie, Argyll. Less precision is afforded by simple cup marks such as occur on a stone at Swinburn Castle, Northumberland, 3.7 metres high.

Standing stones frequently lie at the centre of, adjacent to, or are outliers of, stone circles. Such famous circles as the Stripple Stones and Boscawen-Un in Cornwall have central uprights, as do several of the Irish recumbent stone circles. Famous circles with adjacent monoliths include Long Meg and her Daughters in Cumbria, where a slender pillar is decorated both with cup and ring marks and a spiral in passage grave style. More distant outliers are also common, like the 5.6 metres high Watch Stone near the Stones of Stenness, and these may have formed markers for celestial observations from the circle. Some outliers are visible from circles, others are not, for example at the Merry Maidens, Cornwall, the Goon Rith stone only 2.7 metres high can be seen from the circle, but the bigger Pipers, 4.6 and 4 metres high, cannot. There are also famous standing stones, in ones, twos and threes, which it is claimed provided alignments on celestial events. One of the most famous, at Ballachroy on the Kintyre coast, consists of three slender pillars in a line, theoretically providing alignments on the west end of Cara Island to give an orientation on midwinter sunset at about 1800 BC. Another possibility is the orientation of the central stone to Corra Beinn on the island of Jura, 30 kilometres away across the water, which would provide an alignment on midsummer sunset at about 1800 BC. On the island of Islay, the tall monolith at Ballinaby, a thin, elegant slab 5.4 metres high, can be aligned on prominent crags and has been claimed as a lunar observatory. Thom has described many such sites in Scotland, but in at least some cases the configuration of the surrounding landscape makes it difficult to support his claims. One has the feeling that in these western coastal districts it would be almost impossible to erect an upright which could not be aligned on some distant horizon notch or celestial event.

The function of some groups of stones is less obvious, such as the trio of great monoliths known as the Devil's Arrows near Boroughbridge in Yorkshire. Pairs of stones are also common, from Yarrows in Caithness to Orwell in Kinross, where both stones had cremations at their feet, and Bryngwyn on Anglesey. It has been claimed that in Wales pairs of standing stones up to *c*. 8 metres apart form a specific type of field monument. One such pair, at Rhos-y-clegyrn, Pembrokeshire, was the scene of one of the few area excavations around standing stones. Here the stones were at the centre of a ritual complex which yielded cremated bones and food vessel sherds, a complex of pits, some of which may have held further uprights, and stone rings. There were also traces of an underlying settlement of sub-rectangular huts.

Cup and ring marks

Amongst the most impressive field monuments of north Britain are rock outcrops, often of enormous size, decorated with cup and ring markings pecked and pounded into the rock and rubbed smooth (Plate III). The range of motifs used in this type of rock art is very limited; essentially concentric circles, often with a gap or tail, the simple cup-mark, and a combination of ring or rings surround a central cup. Numerous designs appear less frequently including spirals, concentric arches and a fan of short lines projecting from a circle, but the essence of cup and ring art is its simplicity. This is in marked contrast to the passage grave art of Ireland, with its great range of motifs, which is based as much on the spiral as cup and ring art is on the concentric circle. The impact of cup and ring carvings is achieved by the way in which the limited motifs are used in a bewildering number of combinations, and splashed across great rock surfaces. Thus tails and channels link one design to the next, great panels of cups may be set within a deep rectangular frame, and rings may be set in multiples on waving stalks like bunches of flowers.

The cup and ring outcrops cannot of course be dated in themselves, except where burial mounds were raised over them, as at Fowberry Moor in Northumberland. Fortunately smaller slabs decorated in this manner were frequently incorporated as capstones or sidestones in cists containing Beakers and food vessels, so it is known that cup and ring carvings were being executed by the Overton period. The problem is to know how much earlier their origins can be placed and what the relationship is between the cup and ring slabs in the graves and the great outcrops.

In examining many cup and ring marked outcrops one is struck by the frequency with which designs at the edges are incomplete, as if bits have been struck or levered off. On turning to the cist examples we find that here too individual motifs are often incomplete, and have the appearance of having been prized off larger rocks. This suggests that the cist slabs were broken off the great decorated outcrops, but it does not tell us whether they were removed and used in the cists because of their spiritual significance, or simply because the outcrops were convenient sources of stone for building tombs. Since so little care was taken in breaking off the small lumps and slabs there is much in favour of the latter.

This admits the possibility that the cup-and-ring decorated natural rock surfaces had been a feature of the landscape for some time before the Overton period. Simple cup markings undoubtedly have a very long ancestry, stretching back long before our period. For example, a cup-marked slab was found in the mortuary structure underneath the long barrow at Dalladies, Kincardine.

Cup markings occur sporadically throughout the Fourth Millennium. Ring marks are less common in this period, but in the Meldon Bridge period some of the elements of cup and ring art are found in passage grave contexts in Ireland, especially carved on some of the stones at Newgrange. It is possible that the concept of decorating stones was carried across the Irish Sea in a simplified form as part of the intensive traffic connecting Ireland and Britain at this time. Cup and ring rocks in north-west England and western Scotland show a much greater use of passage grave motifs than those in eastern areas, particularly the spiral, wheel, and depressed geometric designs. Notable examples include the slab with triangles used as a cist cover for a burial with a late Beaker at Carnwath, Lanarkshire; and the slab with wheel designs from Aspatria in Cumberland. The mixture of cup and rings and spiral on Long Meg has already been mentioned. Cup and ring markings are found quite regularly on the stones of stone circles, even more so cup marks, which are abundant on the Clava tombs and their surrounding stone rings, and on the recumbent stone circles, four posters and other ring monuments of eastern Scotland. A special relationship is indicated here, and this is bound up with the whole question of the meaning of cup and ring art.

Outside Britain and Ireland stones decorated in superficially similar styles to our cup and ring rocks are found sporadically from Scandinavia to central Europe, but it is Iberia which has produced some of the most remarkable parallels, notably Galicia. Here there are rock surfaces covered with rings, tails and cups in a manner very similar to that found in classic British cup and ring areas such as western Scotland and Northumberland. It is hard to deny some connection between the two areas, but difficult to find a convincing context for such contacts. The answer could lie in the stream of traffic up and down the Atlantic sea routes in the Third Millennium, reflected, for example, in passage grave architecture and the possible Atlantic contribution to the Irish Beaker tradition. But unless the Irish manifestations of cup and ring designs are seen as a common source, it is difficult to explain why north Britain, and not Ireland, shows the closer similarities to the Galician rocks.

The meaning of cup and ring art is a mystery. Some spiritual significance is assumed, but all manner of suggestions of a more practical nature have been put forward, from rock maps to the identification of metal sources, on no great evidence. The use of cup and ring marks on stone circles and ring monuments suggests that, like passage grave art, they were part of the total religious fabric of the Third Millennium. The fact that broken-off bits were being incorporated in graves as structural elements in the Overton period *could* mean no more than an attempt to transfer the magic significance of the parent rock to the tomb. But equally it could constitute just one more example of changing spiritual attitudes in the Second Millennium.

Engineering and manpower

The manpower requirements of many of the monuments of our period were quite modest, and well within the capabilities of a single family. But the greatest engineering feats would have consumed millions of man-hours, and an effort spread over years, even with a labour force of hundreds.

The basic tools available to the prehistoric navvy were antler picks, wooden shovels, such as those which left marks in the fields at Gwithian, ox scapulae shovels and scrapers, wood and antler wedges, stone axes and axe-hammers and baskets for carrying spoil. Later on bronze axes may have been used as mattocks. Experiment has shown that workers using such tools could probably shift 5 hundredweight of spoil per man hour, working in a team on chalk, or put in another way, 5 cubic feet of chalk per man hour. Thus a small bowl barrow 40 feet in diameter heaped up from a ditch 6 feet wide and 4 feet deep, would require approximately 700 man hours of work, so that a family group with 10 able-bodied workers could build such a barrow in a week of 10-hour days. On the other hand one of the large bell barrows of Wessex, such as may have housed a local dignitary and his family, would require cooperative labour. One with a mound 140 feet in diameter, piled up from a ditch 10 feet wide and 5 feet deep, would entail 4,650 man hours, or about 50 workers putting in 10-hour days for 10 days. In practice these figures would be amplified by finishing processes, and would grow with organization problems as the size of the job increased. For burial mounds had a tiny labour requirement compared with some of the major monuments.

Even some of the smaller chambered tombs of the Meldon Bridge and Mount Pleasant periods could have been built in under 10,000 man hours. But then there is a big leap to 20–25,000 man hours required for just a small, one hectare, hill-fort with timber-revetted ramparts at the end of our period, such as Rams Hill. Such figures were modest compared with the hundreds of thousands of man hours required for the great Wessex enclosures, and the millions involved in the construction of the great cursus monuments, Silbury Hill and the sarsen phase at Stonehenge. Obviously these major undertakings would have required labour forces of hundreds working for years: even a project of just 1 million man hours would keep 200 men busy for 18 months.

The use of stone circles and other ring monuments, stone avenues and rows and monoliths, can be traced down to *c.* 1250 bc, but their decline probably set in much earlier, during the Overton period. Their use seems to have changed in character as cremation ousted inhumation. But the whole fabric of prestigious burial as represented by Collared Urns and other specialized cinerary vessels, rich grave groups and fancy burial monuments was itself at an end by *c.* 1250 bc. It is tempting to see social upheaval in its passing, and to link this in its turn with the final abandonment of megalithic sites. For the muscles which sweated and strained over fifty ton blocks of stone belonged to those masses who came to the fore after *c.* 1250 bc. Those who caused the great stone monuments to be built, and thereafter made use of them, were those buried in the fancy burial sites with fancy burial pottery, and it was these elements which vanished now from the archaeological record. In the decline of megaliths we may be seeing a reaction against a tradition which depended on the labour of the majority for the satisfaction of a minority. One other possibility is that megalithic sites became increasingly difficult to use in the face of a deteriorating climate. The major concentrations of stone rings and linear monuments are in upland areas which would be amongst the first to feel the effects of a changing climate. So many of these sites are today on moorland or buried in peat which has formed since the Second Millennium. Waterlogging would have become increasingly troublesome, and if they were centres of celestial observation then this facility, too, would have been affected. The careful observations postulated at so many megalithic sites would be feasible only in a climate warmer and drier than today, requiring prolonged cloudless periods, and still, dry and clear atmospheric conditions for good visibility. Such a climate is known to have prevailed in the earlier part of our period, but had deteriorated by its end. What is not clear at present is how soon the effects of this deterioration were felt. In areas rich in megalithic remains such as Dartmoor and Bodmin Moor, waterlogging was clearly being experienced, and peat developing, at settlements such as Stannon Down and Holne Moor by *c.* 1000 bc, but whether this began early enough to have influenced the abandonment of the stone monuments, the evidence cannot yet tell us.

Water cults, pomp and display

The Knighton Heath period saw the aftermath of long-lived religious traditions which had focussed on great circular and linear monuments. What replaced them is not clear, but water-orientated cults are one possibility.

Springs, lakes and other watery places were an important element in the religion of the Celts of later prehistory. This is vouched for both by classical writers such as Posidonius and by the votive offerings which were regularly deposited in sacred pools and springs, for example at the source of the Seine at Saint-Germain, and in Lake Neuchatel in Switzerland.

There is good evidence that a similar interest in water developed among the societies of Britain and Ireland as the megalithic tradition declined. The first hints come from the siting of ring monuments in Wales and other upland areas, around springs and rising streams. But much more dramatic evidence comes from the increasing quantities of the very finest bronze-work which are found in rivers and other watery places from the beginning of the Knighton Heath period. The Bann, Shannon, Trent, and especially the Thames, have been particularly prolific in finds. The fact that so much of this material is weaponry, and that the domestic equipment of everyday life is poorly represented, argues against accidental loss. It is a question not only of the finest weapons being discovered in wet places, but also the proportion of total finds which have come from rivers, bogs and the like. Thus about 70–80 per cent of all the dirks and rapiers of Britain and Ireland have been recovered from water.

This trend became even more pronounced in later periods, when there are also whole classes of weapons which are impractical for combat and seem to have been made purely for display, parades and casting into water. Such are the outlandish barbed spearheads of the Ewart Park phase, practically all of which have come from wet sites, and for which no satisfactory utilitarian function has ever been suggested. At the end of our period, in the Penard period, the sheet metal shields may be viewed in the same way. These would have been fine on parade and in the posturings before combat, but were too flimsy to withstand serious attack. Practically all of them have come from bogs and rivers, and some, in addition, bear holes and cuts suggesting they were ritually 'killed' before deposition.

With the increased precipitation and waterlogging after 1500 BC a development of water cults makes good sense. One other element which may have been combined with the deposition of votive offerings is the casting of bodies, or bits of bodies, into the water. With the metalwork dredged up from rivers and bogs there are often human bones, including skulls. Of course associations in watery contexts are practically impossible to prove, but some finds are particularly suggestive. One such came to light on the banks of the Trent at Clifton, where an extensive area of piles produced both skulls and a fine series of spearheads, rapiers and other weapons, dating to the Penard period.

The classical writers, Celtic tradition and archaeological finds all have much to say about the heroic side of Celtic society, and make clear the importance of martial pomp and display in the Celtic ethos. Battles were preceded by much feasting and carousing, the fighting by noisy parades and posturings, and by individual combat between champions. Warfare in the Second Millennium must have had something of this flavour. Many weapons are much too ornate or impractical to have been used in actual fighting. For example, remarkably long and slender triple-arris (Group III) rapiers such as that from Lissane, Co. Derry, may have been the greatest achievement of the Second Millennium armourer, but would quickly have snapped if put to the test. Similarly many basal-looped spearheads would have flashed splendidly on parade, but when it came to battle would have been exchanged for something more practical. Some were much too large, such as one from Croydon, Surrey, 90 centimetres long, while others were too ornate and valuable to be risked. These might be handed on from father to son through generations, such as the examples with decorative gold bands round their sockets from Harrogate in Yorkshire and Pyot-dykes, Angus. These may have been made as early as the Penard period, but were finally deposited in the ground in hoards of the Ewart Park phase.

Sensible warriors would also exchange their sheet metal shields for more practical leather shields when the parading gave way to actual fighting. But this martial ostentation was not limited either to metal weapons or to the end of our period. Many of the impressive stone battle-axes wielded by warriors in the Mount Pleasant and Overton periods were also only for show, too ornate to risk in battle, or with shaft holes too small to admit handles of utilitarian thickness.

After all the preliminaries, when it came to actual fighting there was nothing half-hearted about these prehistoric warriors, and no doubt about the efficacy of their weapons. The point is made by grisly finds of the slain, represented, for example, by the skeleton found at Queensford Mill, Dorchester, Oxfordshire, its pelvis pierced by a basal-looped spearhead (Plate XVIII). For all the advances made in the age of Stonehenge, strife and uncertainty were ever present, never more so than in the time of troubles with which this account must end.

Epilogue

If there is anything calculated to make prehistorians irate it is the linking of Stonehenge with Druids in the popular imagination. It is a sobering thought that the Druids known to the Romans were as far removed in time from the building and use of Stonehenge as they are from us in the 1980s AD. As Atkinson has remarked in his authoritative work on Stonehenge, if the Druids had still venerated the site two thousand years ago then it would probably have been destroyed by the Romans, for Druidism was one of the few religions which they felt was dangerous enough to suppress with the utmost violence.

So if Caesar's Druids had no known interest in Stonehenge still less reason is there for the 'druidic' cavortings which have gone on there in modern times. It is legitimate to ask, with ideas of continuity in prehistory so much to the fore, how different were the sages who masterminded the construction of Stonehenge and Avebury – Callanish and Beaghmore – from those who twenty centuries later screamed defiance across the Menai Straits at the assembled cohorts of Suetonius Paulinus. Caesar stressed the importance of oral tradition to the Druids, how all they knew was passed on from generation to generation. Given the much greater degree of continuity which we now envisage in later prehistory, how far back could Druidic tradition reach? It is suspected from modern ethnographic studies that oral learning can preserve a record of an event or the mood of an era for centuries, perhaps millennia. It has been claimed that epic Irish literature provides a window on the 'Iron Age'. But if the only major differences between the 'Bronze' and 'Iron' Ages were technological, can we glean at least something of the flavour of our period from the Irish traditions? The evidence for a major immigration of iron-using Celts into these islands towards the middle of the First Millennium has largely evaporated, and more and more the transition from bronze to iron-using societies appears an insular affair, with the emphasis on continuity. On this basis, if the Irish tales illuminate the later First Millennium, do they not also throw light on the early First Millennium, or even the Second? The picture of the Celtic world to be gleaned from Irish tradition is one of lands rent by tribal rivalries, of fiercely maintained ancestral territories, a world of rigidly stratified societies, guided by sages, ruled by great warrior chiefs forever in combat with rivals, performing prodigious feats of arms, against a background of drinking, feasting, women and song. This is a picture which comes over as much in the earlier as in the later part of the First Millennium, for already by the ninth to eighth centuries there was the weaponry, the buckets, cauldrons and flesh-hooks, the horns and horse-gear, the hill-forts, the chiefs and all the evidence for strict territorial division. Can this picture be pushed back still further, to breathe life into what we know of the Second Millennium? Until recently there would have been no question about the essential continuity of bronze-using societies from the Second into the First Millennium. In that case if one had accepted the relevance of Irish traditions for early First Millennium societies then plausibly they would have had some relevance for the Second Millennium too. It would then have been possible to argue that Caesar's Druids were linked, by oral tradition at least, with the seers who watched the great sarsens rise at Stonehenge.

What now weighs against these romantic possibilities are the upheavals of the Penard period. It is an interesting commentary on prehistoric studies that what has hitherto seemed a period of insular continuity now emerges as the most important time of change in later prehistory. It shows that secure dating, of sites and artefacts, is still vital to a fuller understanding of the past.

While the extent of the social, economic and spiritual disruptions of the Penard period has yet to be established, it must be stressed that one important tradition had already petered out. The megalithic tradition, which had Stonehenge as its most monumental achievement, had disappeared two or three hundred years before. If it was already a folk memory by the Penard period, it seems most unlikely that anything more than folk tales could have been handed down to the historic Druids. Clearly the spiritual interests of post-Penard Britain and Ireland were very different from those manifested in the great stone monuments, and the wealth of barrows and cairns which still litter our countryside. One has a strong impression that society in the Age of Stonehenge was very different from society in the Age of Hillforts, certainly more so in southern Britain than in north Britain, although the differences have yet to be quantified.

How different will our concepts of Third and Second Millennium society be in five years time, in ten years, in a century from now?

That they lived in an organized condition of society may be considered as quite certain and, as a necessity of such a state, they must have been under the government of a head, most probably the chief of a sept or clan. They had unquestionably long passed beyond the stage when the family is the only community, and they were ruled by an order and constraint embracing wider bounds than those comprised within the authority of relationship in its more limited sense. The magnitude of the burial-mounds would in itself imply this, as, from the amount of continued labour bestowed upon them, they could never have been erected except by a community which included several families. The very extensive and strongly constructed defensive arrangements . . . are strongly indicative of a combination which necessitates an union of very considerable bodies of men. . . . Within what may perhaps be designated as the larger federation, held together by a common origin and mutual interest, there were doubtless several smaller tribal divisions, ruled over by their respective chiefs, either independent, or more or less under the authority of the federal head. It may also be that there were still more minute sub-divisions, where the family government might prevail, and where the interest and property in the land would be parcelled out into tracts . . . not more extensive perhaps than the present parishes. To the heads of these smaller communities . . . the greater number of the barrows must probably be attributed, if the supposition is correct which regards them as the burial-places, not of the mass of the people, but of those who occupied a position of authority . . . it cannot be supposed for a moment that the whole population was buried in the sepulchral mounds. These mounds must be regarded as the places of sepulture of chiefs of tribes, clans, and families . . . and of those who were nearly connected with them, as wives, children and personal dependents.

These sentiments, echoing those which pervade these pages, were published a century ago by the great nineteenth century barrow digger and antiquary Canon Greenwell, in the introduction to his *British Barrows* (1877). In a sense they signal the failure of prehistorians, or perhaps the hopelessness of their task, in that with all the lavish expenditure of human and material resources, and despite being able to draw on a battery of scientific aids, their view of the prehistoric past in many essentials has changed little in a hundred years. Their failure in another sense has been even greater. The average schoolboy of 1980 has no greater appreciation of the prehistoric past than his counterpart of 1880. For too many education authorities history still begins at 1815, or perhaps 1603 in enlightened cases. Before this time the ordinary citizen can only hop from one fragmentary recollection to another, all of uncertain relationship, from Henry and his wives, via John and Magna Carta, William and Hastings and Alfred and his cakes, back to Caesar's expeditions and the standard bearer of the tenth Legion leaping boldly into the sea. How many people, even those supposedly educated, have any knowledge at all of what happened before 55 BC? A few might have a dim and distorted recollection of woad-painted savages gleaned from Caesar's commentaries, some might know from their television programmes that mighty monuments were raised and fabulous treasures lost, but not many will have the slightest idea of what happened in prehistory, or, indeed, that we had a prehistory. I have tried to show in these pages that a lot did happen, that the prehistorian can assemble some sort of picture of our early ancestors stretching back over thousands of years before Caesar came, wrote regrettably little down of what he saw, and failed dismally to conquer. Prehistory was a continuum with history, and cannot be separated from it in the story of these islands. If history has any value for the present and the future, then so does prehistory, and the problem is to demonstrate its relevance to all and not just to a few cognoscenti. This is a challenge which our schools and colleges are only now beginning to take up, and it is the key to the prehistorian's success or failure.

Abbreviations

AA Archaeologia Aeliana

AC Archaeologia Cambrensis

Annable and Simpson, *Devizes Collections* Annable, F. K. and Simpson, D. D. A., 1964. *Guide Catalogue of the Neolithic and Bronze Age Collections in Devizes Museum*. Devizes.

Ant Antiquity

Ant J Antiquaries Journal

Arch Archaeologia

Archaeol Atlantica Archaeologia Atlantica

Archaeol Austriaca Archaeologia Austriaca

Arch J Archaeological Journal

Atkinson et al, *Dorchester* R. J. C. Atkinson, C. M. Piggott and N. K. Sandars, 1951. *Excavations at Dorchester, Oxon*. Oxford

BAJ Berkshire Archaeological Journal

BAR British Archaeological Reports

Bateman, *Ten Years Diggings* Bateman, T., 1861. *Ten Years Diggings in Celtic and Saxon Grave Hills*

Bateman, *Vestiges* Bateman, T., 1848. *Vestiges of the Antiquities of Derbyshire*

BBCS Bulletin of the Board of Celtic Studies

Boon and Lewis, *Welsh Antiquity* Boon, G. C. and Lewis, J. M. (eds.), 1976. *Welsh Antiquity: Essays Mainly On Prehistoric Topics Presented to H. N. Savory Upon His Retirement As Keeper of Archaeology*. Cardiff

BRGK Bericht der Römisch-Germanischen Kommission

Briard, *Les Dépôts Bretons* Briard, J., 1965. *Les Dépôts Bretons et L'Age du Bronze Atlantique*. Rennes

Burl, *Stone Circles* Burl, A., 1976. *The Stone Circles of the British Isles*. London and New Haven.

CLAJ County Louth Archaeological Journal

Clarke, *Beakers* Clarke, D. L., 1970. *Beaker Pottery of Great Britain and Ireland*. Cambridge

Colchester Arch Gp Bull   Colchester Archaeological Group Bulletin

Coles and Simpson, *Ancient Europe*   Coles, J. M. and Simpson, D. D. A., 1968. *Studies in Ancient Europe.* Leicester

Coll Ayr Archaeol Natur Hist Soc   Collections of the Ayrshire Archaeological and Natural History Society

Cornish Archaeol   Cornish Archaeology

Curr Arch   Current Archaeology

CW   Transactions of the Cumberland and Westmorland Antiquarian and Archaeological Society

DAJ   Derbyshire Archaeological Journal

Davies, *Denbighshire*   Davies, E., 1929. *The Prehistoric and Roman Remains of Denbighshire.* Cardiff

Denbigh Hist Trans   Denbighshire Historical Transactions

DE Scot   Discovery and Excavation in Scotland

ERA   East Riding Archaeologist

Evans, *ABI*   Evans, J., 1881. *The Ancient Bronze Implements, Weapons, and Ornaments of Great Britain and Ireland.* London

GAJ   Glasgow Archaeological Journal

Gall. Préhist.   Gallia Préhistoire

Gerloff, *Daggers*   Gerloff, S., 1975. *The Early Bronze Age Daggers in Great Britain and a Reconsideration of the Wessex Culture = Prähistorische Bronzefunde* vol. 1/2. München

Glob, *Bog People*   Glob, P. V., 1971. *The Bog People.* London

Glob, *Mound People*   Glob, P. V., 1974. *The Mound People.* London

Greenwell, *British Barrows*   Greenwell, W., 1877. *British Barrows.* Oxford

Grimes, *Prehistory of Wales*   Grimes, W. F., 1951. *Prehistory of Wales.* Cardiff

Grimes, *Defence Sites*   Grimes, W. F., 1960. *Excavations on Defence Sites, 1939–45 I.* London

Harding, *Hillforts*   Harding, D. (ed.), 1976. *Hillforts: Later Prehistoric Earthworks in Britain and Ireland.* London

Henshall, *Chambered Tombs*   Henshall, A. S., 1963, 1972. *Chambered Tombs of Scotland.* Edinburgh, 2 vols

Herity, *Passage Graves*   Herity, M., 1974. *Irish Passage Graves.* Dublin

IARF   Irish Archaeological Research Forum

Inv Arch   Inventaria Archaeologica

JBAA   Journal of the British Archaeological Association

JCHAS   Journal of the Cork Historical and Archaeological Society

J Hist Astron   Journal for the History of Astronomy

JKAS   Journal of the Kildare Archaeological Society

JRSAI   Journal of the Royal Society of Antiquaries of Ireland

Jutland Archaeol Soc Publ   Jutland Archaeological Society Publications

L'Anthrop   L'Anthropologie

Lincs Hist Archaeol   Lincolnshire History and Archaeology

London Arch   London Archaeologist

LPA   British Museum, 1953, *Later Prehistoric Antiquities of the British Isles.* London

Lynch, *Anglesey*   Lynch, F., 1970. *Prehistoric Anglesey.* Llangefni

May, *Lincolnshire*   May, J., 1976. *Prehistoric Lincolnshire.* Lincoln

Moore and Rowlands, *Salisbury Metalwork*   Moore, C. N. and Rowlands, M., 1972. *Bronze Age Metalwork in Salisbury Museum.* Salisbury

Mortimer, *Forty Years Researches*   Mortimer, J. R., 1905. *Forty Years' Researches in British and Saxon Burial Mounds of East Yorkshire.* London

NAG NEWS   Northumberland Archaeological Group Newsletter

New Phytol   New Phytologist

Oakley et al, *Farnham District*   Oakley, K. P. (ed.), 1939. *A Survey of the Prehistory of the Farnham District.* Guildford

Oxon   Oxoniensia

Palaeo   Palaeohistoria

PBNHPS   Proceedings of the Belfast Natural History and Philosophical Society

PCAS   Proceedings of the Cambridge Antiquarian Society

PDAES   Proceedings of the Devon Archaeological Exploration Society

PDAS   Proceedings of the Devon Archaeological Society

PDNHAS   Proceedings of the Dorset Natural History and Archaeological Society

PHFC   Proceedings of the Hampshire Field Club

Piggott, *Ancient Europe*   Piggott, S., 1965. *Ancient Europe.* Edinburgh

Piggott, *Neolithic Cultures*   Piggott, S., 1954. *The Neolithic Cultures of the British Isles.* Cambridge

Pitt-Rivers, *Cranborne Chase*   Pitt-Rivers, A. *Excavations in Cranborne Chase* II (1887), IV (1898)

PPS   Proceedings of the Prehistoric Society

PPSEA   Proceedings of the Prehistoric Society of East Anglia

PRIA   Proceedings of the Royal Irish Academy

PSAL   Proceedings of the Society of Antiquaries of London

PSANHS   Proceedings of the Somerset Archaeological and Natural History Society

PSAS   Proceedings of the Society of Antiquaries of Scotland

PSIA   Proceedings of the Suffolk Institute of Archaeology

PUBSS   Proceedings of the University of Bristol Spelaeological Society

RCAHM   Royal Commission on Ancient and Historical Monuments

Records of Bucks   Records of Buckinghamshire

Renfrew, *British Prehistory*   Renfrew, C. (ed), (1974). *British Prehistory: A New Outline*. London

SAC   Sussex Archaeological Collections

SAF   Scottish Archaeological Forum

SANH   Somerset Archaeology and Natural History

Scarborough Distr Archaeol Soc Res Rep   Scarborough District Archaeological Society Research Report

Simpson, *Economy and Settlement*   Simpson, D. D. A. (ed), 1971. *Economy and Settlement in Neolithic and Early Bronze Age Britain and Europe*. Leicester

Slov Arch   Slovenska Archeologia

Soc Ant London Res Rep   Society of Antiquaries of London Research Report

Sussex Co Mag   Sussex County Magazine

TAASND Transactions of the Architectural and Archaeological Society of Durham and Northumberland

Tait, *Beakers*   Tait, J., 1965. *Beakers from Northumberland*. Newcastle upon Tyne

TBAS   Transactions of the Birmingham Archaeological Society

TCNS   Transactions of the Cardiff Naturalists Society

TDA   Transactions of the Devon Association

TDGNHAS   Transactions of the Dumfries and Galloway Natural History and Antiquarian Society

TGAS   Transactions of the Glasgow Archaeological Society

Thom, *Megalithic Sites*   Thom, A., 1967. *Megalithic Sites in Britain*. Oxford

TLCAS   Transactions of the Lancashire and Cheshire Antiquarian Society

TPPSNS   Transactions and Proceedings of the Perthshire Society of Natural Science

Trans Hunter Archaeol Soc   Transactions of the Hunter Archaeological Society

Trans London Middlesex Archaeol Soc   Transactions of the London and Middlesex Archaeological Society

Travaux Lab d'Anthrop Rennes   Travaux de Laboratoire d'Anthropologie Préhistorique − Faculté des Sciences de Rennes

T St Albans Archit Archaeol Soc   Transactions of the St. Albans Architectural and Archaeological Society

UJA   Ulster Journal of Archaeology

ULIAAR   University of London Institute of Archaeology Annual Report

VCH   Victoria County History
WAM   Wiltshire Archaeological Magazine
Worth, *Dartmoor*   Worth, R. H., 1953. *Dartmoor*. Newton Abbot
YAJ   Yorkshire Archaeological Journal

List of Principal Sites Mentioned

Aberdour Road, Dunfermline, Fife: *PSAS*, 104 (1971–2), 121–36.
Abingdon, Berkshire. Causewayed camp: *Ant J*, 36 (1956), 1–30.
Deverel-Rimbury site: Unpublished.
Acklam Wold 92, 204, Yorkshire: J. R. Mortimer, *Forty Years Researches*, 84–7.
Acton Park, Denbighshire: *AC*, 4, 6 (1875), 70–3.
Aglionby, Cumberland: *CW*, 2, 56 (1956), 12–17.
Aldbourne, Wiltshire: *PPS*, 4 (1938), 74, Figure 12.
Aldro 52, 54, 94, Yorkshire: J. R. Mortimer, *Forty Years Researches*, 61–6; 82.
Alfriston, Sussex: *PPS*, 41 (1975), 119–52.
Alton, Hampshire: *WAM*, 68B (1973), 120–2.
Amberley Mount, Sussex: *SAC*, 104 (1966), 6–25.
Amesbury G 71, Wiltshire: *PPS*, 33 (1967), 336–66.
Angle Ditch, Dorset: A. Pitt-Rivers, *Cranborne Chase: IV*
Annaghkeen, Co. Galway: *JRSAI*, 99 (1969), 71, Figure 4.
Annaghmare, Co. Armagh: *UJA*, 28 (1965), 3–46.
Anner Tol III, Netherlands: *Helinium*, 12 (1972), 225–41.
Antofts Windypit, Yorkshire: J. McDonnell (ed.), *A History of Helmsley, Rievaulx and District* (1963). York. 20–2, 355–65.
Arbor Low, Derbyshire: *DAJ*, 88 (1968), 100–3.
Arminghall, Norfolk: *PPS*, 2 (1936), 1–51.
Arreton Down, Isle of Wight. Hoard: *PPS*, 29 (1963), 284–91, 317–18. Round barrow: *PPS*, 26 (1960), 263–302.
Ashford, Kent: *ULIAAR*, 10 (1954), 39, 45, Figure 1.2.
Ashford Common, Middlesex: *Trans London and Middlesex Archaeol Soc*, 24 (1973), 111–34.
Ashgrove, Fife: *PSAS*, 97 (1963–4), 166–79.
Ash Tree Cave, Derbyshire: *DAJ*, 76 (1956), 57–64.
Aspatria, Cumberland: *SAF*, 4 (1972), 91–2, 101, Figure 7:34.
Aston-on-Trent, Derbyshire: *DAJ*, 88 (1968), 68–81.
Auchnacree, Angus: *Inv Arch*, 5 (1958), GB. 27.
Auchterhouse, Angus: Coles and Simpson, *Ancient Europe*, 180–1, 188, Figure 43.
Avebury, Wiltshire: I. Smith, *Windmill Hill and Avebury* (London, 1965.) A. Burl, *Prehistoric Avebury* (London, 1979.)
Aylesford, Kent: Gerloff, *Daggers*, 61, 68, Plate 44F.

Badbury, Dorset: *Ant J*, 19 (1939), 291–9.

Balbirnie, Fife: *Arch J*, 131 (1974), 1–32.

Ballachroy, Argyll: A. Thom, *Megalithic Sites in Britain* (Oxford, 1967), 151. A. Thom, *Megalithic Lunar Observatories* (Oxford, 1971), 36.

Ballaharra, Isle of Man: *BAR*, 54 (1978), 141–64.

Ballinaby, Islay: *J Hist Astron*, 5 (1974), 50–1.

Ballinderry Crannog 2, Co. Offaly: *PRIA*, 47 C (1942), 1–76.

Ballintubbrid, Co. Wexford: *JRSAI*, 105 (1975), 132–9, 145–6.

Ballyglass, Co. Mayo: *JRSAI*, 102 (1972), 49–57.

Ballymacdermot, Co. Armagh: *UJA*, 27 (1964), 3–22.

Ballymeanoch, Argyll: Atkinson et al, *Dorchester*, 85, 89–91, 99.

Ballynagilly, Co. Tyrone: *JRSAI*, 99 (1969), 165–8. *IARF*, 2 (1975), 1–6.

Ballyscullion, Co. Antrim: *Science*, 172 (1971), 560–2.

Ballyutoag, Co. Antrim: *PBNHPS*, 5 (1936–7), 43–9.

Ballyvalley, Co. Down: *PRIA*, 67 C (1968), 42, Figure 5.

Ballyvourney, Co. Cork: *JRSAI*, 84 (1954), 105–55.

Balmashanner, Angus: *PSAS*, 26 (1892), 174, 182–8.

Balneil, Wigtown: *PSAS*, 50 (1915–16), 302–5.

Barbrook II, Derbyshire: *DAJ*, 86 (1966), 115–17.

Barclodiad y Gawres, Anglesey: T. G. E. Powell and G. E. Daniel, *Barclodiad y Gawres* (Liverpool, 1956.)

Barford, Warwickshire: *TBAS*, 83 (1966–7), 1–64.

Barmston, Yorkshire: *ERA*, 1 (1968), 12–26.

Barnack, Northamptonshire: *Durobrivae*, 4 (1976), 14–17.

Barton, Hampshire: J. Abercromby, *Bronze Age Pottery*, II (1912), Figure 382.

Baunogenasraid, Co. Carlow: *PRIA*, 74 C (1974), 277–312.

Baux-Saint-Croix, Normandy, France: *BAR*, 31 ii (1976), Plate 52.

Beacharra, Argyll: *PPS*, 30 (1964), 134–58.

Beaghmore, Co. Tyrone: *UJA*, 3 ser. 32 (1969), 73–91.

Beaquoy, Orkney: *PSAS*, 106 (1974–5), 39–98.

Bedd Branwen, Anglesey: *AC*, 120 (1971), 11–83.

Beddgelert, Caernarvonshire: *RCAM Caernarvon*, II, *liv*, *Figure 13*.

Beedon, Berkshire: *ULIAAR*, 10 (1954), 39, 57, Figure 1.

Bee Low, Derbyshire: *Ant J*, 50 (1970), 186–215.

Behy-Glenulra, Co. Mayo: *BAR*, 48 (1978), 138–9.

Belderg Beg, Co. Mayo: *BAR*, 48 (1978), 140.

Belle Tout, Sussex: *PPS*, 36 (1970), 312–79.

Benie Hoose, Shetland: *PSAS*, 94 (1960–1), 28–45.

Berwick St. John, Wiltshire: *VCH Wiltshire* I (1957), no. 10. A. Pitt-Rivers, *Cranborne Chase*: II (1887), Plate 86.

Billingborough Fen, Lincolnshire: *Curr Arch*, 67 (1979), 246–8.

Bircham, Norfolk: R. R. Clarke, *East Anglia* (London, 1960), 75.

Birkrigg, Lancashire: *CW*, 2, 12 (1912) 262; Burl, *Stone Circles*, 63, 346.

Birchover, Derbyshire: Gerloff, *Daggers*, 168, Plate 54A.

Bishopsland, Co. Kildare: *PPS*, 30 (1964), 272–88, Figure 5.

Bishop's Waltham 'Great Barrow', Hampshire: *PPS*, 23 (1957), 137–66.

Blackheath Todmorden, Yorkshire: *TLCAS*, 71 (1961), 41, Figure II.

364 *The Age of Stonehenge*

Black Moss of Achnacree, Argyll: *BAR*, 33 (1976), 283–7.
Black Patch 3, Sussex: J. H. Pull, *Flint Miners of Blackpatch* (1932), 69–72.
Blackpatch, Sussex: *PPS*, 44 (1978), 455–6.
Blackwaterfoot, Arran: Coles and Simpson, *Ancient Europe*, 183, Figure 42.
Blanch, Yorkshire: J. R. Mortimer, *Forty Years Researches*, 322–32.
Bleasdale, Lancashire: *Ant J*, 18 (1938), 154–71.
Blissmoor, Devon: *PPS*, 20 (1954), 87–102.
Bodrifty, Cornwall: *Arch J*, 113 (1956), 1–32.
Bodwrdin, Anglesey: *PPS*, 29 (1963), 285, 291–2; 32 (1966), 349.
Boles Barrow, Wiltshire: R. J. C. Atkinson, *Stonehenge* (London, 1960), 110.
Bolton House, Northumberland: *AA*, 4, 47 (1969), 168–71.
Borum Eshøj, Denmark: P. V. Glob, *Mound People*, 31–49.
Boscawen-un, Cornwall: A. Burl, *Stone Circles*, 124–5.
Boscombe Down, Wiltshire: *PPS*, 8 (1942), 48–61.
Bos Swallet, Mendips: *PUBSS*, 10 (1964), 98–111.
Bow Hill, Sussex: M. Jesson and D. Hill (eds.), *The Iron Age and its Hill-forts* (Southampton, 1971), 56–7.
Bowsden, Northumberland: *AA*, 4, 47 (1969), 168–71.
Brackmont, Fife: *PSAS*, 76 (1941–2), 84–93. 83 (1948–9), 224–9. 99 (1966–7), 60–92.
Breach Farm, Glamorgan: *PPS*, 4 (1938), 107–201.
Breiddin, Montgomery: *AC*, 92 (1937), 186–228. Harding, *Hillforts*, 293–302.
Brenig, Denbighshire: *Denbigh Hist Trans*, 23 (1974), 1–56; 24 (1975), 1–25.
Bridged Pot, Somerset: *Ant J*, 8 (1928), 198.
Brigg, Lincolnshire: *Lincs Hist Archaeol*, 10 (1975), 5–13.
Brockagh, Co. Kildare: *JKAS*, 13 (1961–3), 458–62.
Bromfield, Shropshire: C. Thomas (ed.), *The Iron Age in the Irish Sea Province* (CBA, London, 1972), 32–3, 36.
Broome Heath, Norfolk: *PPS*, 38 (1972), 1–97.
Broomrigg C, Cumberland: *CW*, 2, 50 (1950), 30.
Brough-on-Humber, Yorkshire: Gerloff, *Daggers*, 74, Plate 46 C.
Bryn Celli Ddu, Anglesey: *Arch*, 80 (1930), 179–214. *AC*, 86 (1931), 216–50; 118 (1969), 17–48.
Bryn Crug, Caernarvonshire: REM Wheeler, *Prehistoric and Roman Wales* (Oxford, 1925), 146, Figure 48.
Brynford, Flintshire: W. F. Grimes, *Prehistory of Wales* (Cardiff, 1951), 86–7, 200.
Bryn yr Hen Bobl, Anglesey: *Arch*, 85 (1935), 253–92.
Buchau, Württemberg: M. Gimbutas, *Bronze Age Cultures in Central and Eastern Europe* (The Hague, 1965), 301–5.
Buckstone Road, Edinburgh: *PSAS*, 105 (1972–4), 281–4.
Bught Park, Inverness: *PSAS*, 88 (1954–6), 7–10, Plates II–III.
Burton Latimer, Nottinghamshire: Nottingham Univ. Mus.
Burythorpe, Yorkshire: Min. of Public Building and Works, *Archaeological Excavations* 1968 (1969), 14.
Bush Barrow, Wiltshire: Annable and Simpson, *Devizes Collections*, 45–6, 99, 168–78.

Butterwick, Yorkshire: Greenwell, *British Barrows*, 186–91, Figures 4, 37, 38, 104, 105.

Cae Mickney, Anglesey: Lynch, *Anglesey* 160–3.
Caherguillamore, Co. Limerick: in E. Rynne (ed.), *North Munster Studies* (Limerick, 1967), 20–42.
Cairnpapple, West Lothian: *PSAS*, 82 (1947–8), 68–123.
Čaka, Czechoslovakia: *Slov Arch*, 8 (1960), 59–124. *PPS*, 29 (1963), 217–19, Figures 2–5.
Calais Wold 24, 114, Yorkshire: J. R. Mortimer, *Forty Years Researches*, 156, 169.
Callanish, Lewis: G. and M. Ponting, *The Standing Stones of Callanish* (Callanish, 1977).
Callis ('Calais') Wold, Yorkshire: *Ant*, 50 (1976), 130–1. *BAR*, 33 (1976), 143–50.
Caltragh, Co. Galway: *JRSAI*, 91 (1961), 45–51.
Camerton, Somerset: *PPS*, 4 (1938), 76, Figure 14.
Camster, Caithness: Piggott, *Neolithic Cultures*, 234–41. Renfrew, *British Prehistory*, 141–2. *PPS*, 44 (1978), 459.
Carn Brea, Cornwall: *Cornish Archaeol*, 9 (1970), 53–62. 11 (1972), 5–8.
Carn Creis, Cornwall: *Arch J*, 101 (1946), 31, Figure 6.
Carn Tulach, Perth: *PSAS*, 44 (1909–10), 154–6.
Carnwath (Wester Yardhouses), Lanarkshire: *TDGAS*, 47 (1970), 137–80.
Carrowkeel, Co. Sligo: *PRIA*, 29 C (1911–12), 311–47.
Carrowmore, Co. Sligo: *JRSAI*, 100 (1970), 185–90.
Carse Farm, Perth: Burl, *Stone Circles*, 192, 362.
Cassington, Oxfordshire: *Ant J* 14 (1934), 268–76; *BAR*, 526 (1977), 98.
Castell Bryn Gwyn, Anglesey: *AC*, 111 (1962), 25–58.
Castlerigg, Cumberland: Burl, *Stone Circles*, 39, 56–61, 74–5, 342.
Castletown Roche, Co. Cork: *PRIA*, 67c (1968), 45 Figure 11.
Catfoss, Yorkshire: *ERA*, I (1968), 1–10.
Cerrig Duon, Breconshire: Burl, *Stone Circles*, 261–4, 369.
Chalton, Hampshire: *Ant J*, 50 (1970), 1–13.
Cham, South Germany: *Germania*, 29 (1951), 5.
Chapel Brampton, Northamptonshire: G. C. Boon and J. M. Lewis (eds.), *Welsh Antiquity* 89.
Charmy Down, Somerset: *Ant J*, 30 (1950), 34–46.
Chatton Sandyford, Northumberland: *AA*, 4, 46 (1968), 5–50.
Cheselbourne, Dorset: P. Fowler (ed.), *Recent Work in Rural Archaeology* (Bradford on Avon, 1975), 51–3.
Chippenham, Cambridgeshire: *Ant J*, 15 (1935), 61–3; 213. *PCAS*, 36 (1936), 134–55.
Cholwich Town, Devon: *PDAS*, 31 (1973), 1–21.
Church Dale Cave, Derbyshire: *PPS*, 19 (1953), 228–30.
Churchfield, Co. Mayo: *PPS*, 28 (1962), 160, 175–81, 186, Plate XXIV.
Church Hill, Findon, Sussex: *Sussex Co Mag*, 28 (1953), 15–21.
City Farm, Hanborough, Oxfordshire: *Oxon*, 29–30 (1964–5), 1–98.

Clacton, Essex: in G. Sieveking (ed.), *Prehistoric and Roman Studies* (1971), London. 93–124.
Clandon, Dorset: Gerloff, *Daggers*, 74, no. 127, Plate 46D.
Clava, Inverness: *PSAS*, 88 (1954–6), 173–207. Burl, *Stone Circles*, 161–7.
Clayton Hill, Sussex: *Arch*, 85 (1935), 248, Figures 2, 5.
Clifton, R. Trent, Nottingham: *Ant J*, 21 (1941), 133–43.
Clonbrin, Co. Longford: *PPS*, 28 (1962), 175–7, Plate XXIII.
Cock Hill, Sussex: *SAC*, 99 (1961), 78–101.
Cockleswood Cave, Somerset: *PSANHS*, 96 (1952), 193.
Codicote, Hertfordshire: *T St Albans Archit Archaeol Soc* (1961), 5–20.
Colleonard, Banff: *Inv Arch*, 5th set (1958), GB 29.
Colwinston, Glamorgan: *AC*, 5, 5 (1888), 83–93.
Coney Island, Lough Neagh: *UJA*, 28 (1965), 78–101.
Cookestown, Co. Tyrone: Coles and Simpson, *Ancient Europe*, 205–6, Figure 42:2.
Coolmore, Co. Kilkenny: *JRSAI*, 93 (1963), 122.
Copt Hill, Houghton-le-Spring, Co. Durham: *AA*, 3, 11 (1914), 123–30.
Corbury Hill, Lanarkshire: *RCAHM Lanark Inventory* (1978), 81, no. 187.
Corby's Crags, Northumberland: *AA*, 5, 4 (1976), 11–16.
Corlona, Co. Leitrim: *JRSAI*, 85 (1955), 77–83.
Corrower, Co. Mayo: *PRIA*, 61 C (1960), 79–93.
Corston, Somerset: *Ant J*, 21 (1941), 151.
Craig Law, Peebles: *RCAHM Peebles Inventory* (1967), 72, no. 157.
Craignish, Argyll: Coles and Simpson, *Ancient Europe*, 206–7, Figure 49:6.
Crawfurd, Lanark: *PSAS*, 17 (1882–3), 451.
Creag na Caillich, Killin, Perthshire: Coles and Simpson, *Ancient Europe*, 126–8.
Cressingham, Norfolk: *PPS*, 4 (1938), 92–3, Figure 22.
Crichel Down, Dorset: *Arch*, 90 (1944), 47–80.
Crickley Hill, Gloucestershire: *Ant*, 46 (1972), 49–52. 47 (1973), 56–9. in Harding, *Hillforts*, 161–75.
Crig-a-mennis, Cornwall: *PPS*, 26 (1960), 76–97.
Cromaghs, Co. Antrim: *PRIA*, 26 C (1906), 119–24.
Crosby Garrett, Westmorland: Greenwell, *British Barrows*, 389–91.
Croydon, Surrey: *PSAL*, 2, 18 (1901), 353.
Crug yr Avan, Glamorgan: *BBCS*, 20 (1962), 75–94.
Culbin Sands, Moray: *PSAS*, 102 (1969–70), 87–100.
Culduthel Mains, Inverness: National Mus. of Antiquities, Edinburgh.
Cullyhanna Lough, Co. Armagh: *UJA*, 21 (1954), 7–13.
Cultoon, Islay: Burl, *Stone Circles*, 46, 150, 359.
Culver Hole, Glamorganshire: *AC*, 107 (1958), 45, 49, Figure 4:8, 10.
Cuxwold, Suffolk: *Arch J*, 14 (1857), 92. Gerloff, *Daggers*, 180–1, 257, Plate 57N.

Dainton, Devon: R. J. Silvester, *Dainton Excavations, 1975: Interim Report*.
Dalkey Island, Co. Dublin: *PRIA*, 66 C (1968), 53–233.
Dalladies, Kincardine: *PSAS*, 104 (1971–2), 23–47.
Dalmore, Easter Ross: *PSAS*, 13 (1878–9), 252.

Danes Pad, Lancashire: *TLCAS*, 3 (1850), 60–1, 113.

Dean Moor, Devon: *TDA*, 89 (1957), 18–77.

Deverel, Dorset: W. A. Miles, *A description of the Deverel Barrow* (1826).

Devil's Arrows, Boroughbridge, Yorkshire: I. H. Longworth, *Yorkshire* (London, 1966), 33–4, 85, Figure 17.

Dinorben, Denbigh: W. Gardner and H. N. Savory, *Dinorben* (Cardiff, 1964). *Ant*, 45 (1971), 251–61. H. N. Savory, *Excavations at Dinorben 1965–9* (Cardiff, 1971).

Doll Tor, Derbyshire: Bateman, *Ten Years Diggings*, 84. *DAJ*, 13 (1939), 116.

Dorchester Henges, Cursus, Oxfordshire: Atkinson et al., *Dorchester.*

Dorset Cursus: *Arch J*, 130 (1973), 44–76.

Dover Harbour, Kent: *Archaeol Atlantica*, I (1975), 193–5.

Dowel Cave, Derbyshire: *DAJ*, 79 (1959), 97–107.

Downpatrick, Co. Down: *UJA*, 27 (1964), 31–58.

Dowth, Co. Meath: Herity, *Passage Graves*, 30–4.

Drimnagh, Co. Dublin: *JRSAI*, 69 (1939), 190–220.

Drombeg, Co. Cork: Circle *JCHAS*, 64 (1959), 1–27. Cooking place *JCHAS*, 65 (1960), 1–17.

Druid's Temple, Lancashire: Burl, *Stone Circles*, 5–6, 63, 346, Figure 9.

Drumnahare, Co. Down: *UJA*, 20 (1957), 37–42.

Duff House, Banff: *PSAS*, 17 (1882–3), 446; 97 (1963–4), 150, Plate VI.

Duggleby Howe, Yorkshire: Mortimer, *Forty Years Researches*, 23–42.

Dundrum, Co. Down: *UJA*, 15 (1952), 2–30. 22 (1959), 5–20.

Dunnottar, Kincardine: *PSAS*, 88 (1954–6), 1–6.

Dunragit, Wigtown: *PSAS*, 66 (1931–2), 19. Coles and Simpson, *Ancient Europe*, 185, 193, Figure 42:17.

Durrington Walls, Wiltshire: G. J. Wainwright and I. H. Longworth, *Durrington Walls . . . = Soc Ant London Res Rep*, 29 (1971).

Dyffryn Ardudwy, Merioneth: *Arch*, 104 (1973), 1–49.

Earls Barton, Northamptonshire: *Curr Arch*, 3 (1972), 238–40.

East Kennet, Wiltshire: Clarke, *Beakers*, 398, no. 948.

Easton Down, Wiltshire: *WAM*, 46 (1933), 218–24.

Eaton Heath, Norfolk: *Arch J.*, 130 (1973), 1–43.

Ebbesbourne Wake, Wiltshire: Moore and Rowlands, *Salisbury Metalwork*, 63–4, Plate XV.

Ebnal, Shropshire: F. Lynch and C. Burgess, *Prehistoric Man in Wales and the West* (Bath, 1972), 167–81.

Edmondsham, Dorset: *PPS*, 29 (1963), 395–425.

Edmondstown, Co. Dublin: *JRSAI*, 100 (1970), 116.

Eggardon, Dorset: Atkinson et al, *Dorchester*, 102.

Egtved, Denmark: Glob, *Mound People*, 51–64.

Elbolton Cave, Yorkshire: *YAJ*, 45 (1973), 41–54.

Eldon's Seat, Dorset: *PPS*, 34 (1968), 191–237.

Embo, Sutherland: *PSAS*, 96 (1962–3), 9–36.

Eriswell, Suffolk: Barrow: *PSIA*, 33 (1973), 1–18. Hoard: *Ant J*, 35 (1955), 218–19.

Eschenz, Switzerland: *Ant*, 49 (1975), 132–3.

Eynsham, Oxfordshire: *Oxon*, 3 (1938), 10, 18–19, 22, 28. *Inv Arch*, 3 (1956), GB.14. *BAR*, S 26 (1977), 98–9, Figure 4:5.

Fargo Plantation, Wiltshire: *WAM*, 48 (1938), 357.

Farleigh Wick, Wiltshire: *WAM*, 51 (1947), 447–52. 52 (1948), 270–1.

Farnham, Surrey: Oakley et al, *Farnham District*, 169–79.

Faversham, Kent: Gerloff, *Daggers*, 28, Plate 41F.

Fengate, Peterborough: *BAR*, 33 (1976), 29–49. F. Pryor, *Excavation at Fengate, Peterborough, England*: First Report (1974); Second Report (1978). Royal Ontario Museum, Toronto.

Ffridd Faldwyn, Montgomery: *AC*, 97 (1942), 1–57.

Ffynhonnau, Breconshire: *AC*, 107 (1958), 27–8, Figure 3.

Findon, Sussex: *Sussex Co Mag*, 28 (1953), 15–21.

Flamborough, Yorkshire: *YAJ*, 41 (1963), 191–202.

Ford, Northumberland: *AA*, 4, 12 (1935), 148–57.

Fordy, Cambridgeshire: *New Phytol.*, 39 (1940), 370–400.

Forteviot, Perth: *Ant*, 52 (1978), 47–50.

Fort Harrouard, Eure-et-Loir, France: *L'Anthrop*, 46 (1936), 257–301; 541–612. 47 (1937), 253–308. N. K. Sandars, *Bronze Age Cultures in France* (Cambridge, 1957), passim.

Fowberry Moor, Northumberland: S. Beckensall, *Prehistoric Carved Rocks of Northumberland* (Newcastle upon Tyne, 1974).

Fowey, River. Cornwall: *Ant J*, 49 (1969), 1–21.

Frampton G4, Dorset: *PDNHAS*, 80 (1958), 111–32.

Frankford (Birr), Co. Offaly: *CLAJ*, 16 (1966), 85–90.

Fritzdorf, Germany: *Germania*, 33 (1955), 319.

Frøjk, Denmark: *Palaeo*, 9 (1963), 73 and passim, Figure 16, Plate VIa.

Furzey, Hampshire: *Arch J*, 119 (1962), 30–1, Figure 12:6.

The Gairdie, Shetland: *PSAS*, 89 (1955–6), 369, no. 28, Figure 9.

Galbally, Co. Tyrone: Evans, *Ancient Bronze Implements*, 252–3, Figure 319.

Garlands, Cumberland: *CW*, 2, 56 (1956), 1–17.

Garrowby Wold C69, Yorkshire: Mortimer, *Forty Years Researches*, 138–40.

Garton Slack 75, 141, Yorkshire: Mortimer, *Forty Years Researches*, 222–4, Plates LXXVI, LXXVII; 259, Figures 723–5.

Gavel Moss, Renfrew: *Inv Arch*, 5 (1958), GB.28.

Gazely, Suffolk: *PSIA*, 33 (1973–4), 19–46.

Giants' Hills, Skendleby, Lincolnshire: *Arch* 85 (1936), 37–106.

Gilchorn, Angus: *PSAS*, 25 (1890–1), 447–63. Coles and Simpson, *Ancient Europe*, 178, 190, Figure 44.

Girvans, Ayrshire: *Coll Ayr Archaeol Natur Hist Soc*, 2, 7 (1961–6), 9–27.

Glarryford, Co. Antrim: *PRIA*, 76C (1976), 343–4, Figures 11c, 18:17.

Glenballoch, Perth: *PSAS*, 15 (1880–1), 89. Burl, *Stone Circles*, 67, 192, 194, 363.

Glenforsa, Isle of Mull: *PSAS*, 9 (1870–2), 537–8. Clarke, *Beakers*, 185–6, 232, 513, Figures 676–7.

Glenluce, Wigtown: *RCAHM Wigtown*, xliii. *PSAS*, 86 (1951–2), 43–69.

Glenwhappen Rig, Peebles: *RCAHM Peebles*, I, 76, no. 198.

Glynllifon, Caernarvonshire: *AC*, 87 (1932), 199–200.

Goatscrag, Northumberland: *AA* 4, 50 (1972), 15–69.

Goldberg, South Germany: *Ausgrabungen in Deutschland I* (1975) (Römisch-Germanisches Zentralmuseum, Mainz), 98–114.

Goodland, Co. Antrim: *JRSAI*, 99 (1969), 39–53. in G. Daniel and P. Kjaerum (eds.), *Megalithic Graves and Ritual,* = *Jutland Archaeol Soc Publ*, 11 (1973), 173–96.

Gop Cave, Flintshire: *Arch J*, 58 (1901), 322–41. *AC*, 90 (1935), 194–200. G. Daniel, *Prehistoric Chambered Tombs of England and Wales* (Cambridge, 1950), 46.

Gorsey Bigbury, Somerset: *PUBSS*, 14 (1976), 155–83.

Grassington, Yorkshire: *YAJ*, 33 (1937), 166–74. *BAR*, 48 (1978), 109–14, Figure 14.2.

Grandtully, Perth: *Ant*, 43 (1969), 216–17.

Grauballe, Denmark: P. V. Glob, *The Bog People* (London, 1971), 33–48.

Great Ayton, Yorkshire: *Scarborough Distr Archaeol Soc Res Rep*, 7 (1967).

Great Langdale, Westmorland: *PPS*, 15 (1949), 1–20.

Green Knowe, Peebles: *PSAS*, 94 (1960–1), 79–85. *DE Scot*, 1977. *PPS*, 44 (1978), 459–60.

Grey Croft, Seascale, Cumberland: *CW*, 2, 57 (1957), 1–8.

Grimes Graves, Norfolk: *PPS*, 39 (1973), 182–218. *BAR*, 33 (1976), 101–11.

Grimspound, Devon: R. H. Worth, *Dartmoor*, 142–4.

Grimthorpe, Yorkshire: *PPS*, 34 (1968), 148–90.

Gristhorpe, Yorkshire: W. C. Williamson, *The Bronze Age Tree Trunk Coffin Burial Found at Gristhorpe . . .*, 3rd ed. (Scarborough, 1872).

Gruting School, Shetland: *PSAS*, 89 (1955–6), 340–97.

Gwithian, Cornwall: C. Thomas, *Gwithian – Ten Years Work* (1958). *BAR*, 33 (1976), 51–79.

Haldon, Devon: *PDAES*, 2 (1936), 244–63; 3 (1937), 33–43.

Hambledon Hill, Dorset: *Curr Arch*, 48 (1975), 16–18. *PPS*, 43 (1977), 393–4; 45 (1979), 334.

Handley Down, Dorset: A. Pitt-Rivers, *Cranborne Chase IV*.

Handley Hill 24, Dorset: A. Pitt-Rivers, *Cranborne Chase IV*, 49.

Hanging Grimston 55, Yorkshire: Mortimer, *Forty Years Researches*, 100–2, Figures 240–7.

Hardelot, Pas-de-Calais, France: *Helinium*, 1 (1961), 229–32.

Harland Edge, Derbyshire: *DAJ*, 86 (1966), 31–53.

Harlyn Bay III, Cornwall: *Arch J*, 101 (1944), 31, Figure 6. Gerloff, *Daggers*, 108, Plate 50B.

Harristown, Co. Waterford: *JRSAI*, 71 (1941), 130–47.

Harrogate, Yorkshire: *PPS*, 30 (1964), 192, Plate XVIII.

Harrow Hill, Sussex: *SAC*, 78 (1937), 230–52.

Hatton Mill, Angus: *PSAS*, 102 (1969–70), 82–6.

Hedderwick, East Lothian: *PSAS*, 63 (1929), 29–98. *PSAS*, 80 (1945–6), 141–3.

High Knowes, Alnham, Northumberland: *AA*, 4, 44 (1966), 5–48.

Holne Moor, Devon: *Curr Arch*, 5 (1976), 250–2. 6 (1979), 234–7.

Horridge Common, Devon: *PPS*, 35 (1969), 220–8.

Horsbrugh Castle Farm, Peebles: *PSAS*, 105 (1972–4), 43–62.

Houndslow, Cheshire: W. Varley and J. W. Jackson, *Prehistoric Cheshire* (Chester, 1940), Figure 18.

Hove, Sussex: E. C. Curwen, *The Archaeology of Sussex* (London, 2 ed., 1954), 33, Plate 9. Gerloff, *Daggers*, 105, Plate 49C.

Hoveringham, Nottinghamshire: Nottingham University Museum.

Huggate Wold 216, 254, Yorkshire: Mortimer, *Forty Years Researches*, 309–10, 320–1.

Hunstanton, Norfolk: Unpublished: I. Kinnes, various lectures.

Hurlers, The, Cornwall: *PPS*, 4 (1938), 319. Burl, *Stone Circles*, 115–20, 341.

Hurst Fen, Mildenhall, Suffolk: *PPS*, 26 (1960), 202–45.

Hvorslev, Denmark: *Tools and Tillage*, I (1968), 56–8. J. G. D. Clark, *Prehistoric Europe: The Economic Basis* (Cambridge, 1952), 102–3, Figure 49.

Ilsmoor, Kr. Stade, Germany: Palaeo, 9 (1963), 50–63, Figure 10.

Inch Island, Co. Donegal: *Sibrium*, 6 (1961), 234, Figure 22.

Ingleby Greenhow, Yorkshire: *Ryedale Historian*, No. 5 (June, 1970), 12–25.

Irton Moor, Yorkshire: *YAJ*, 45 (1973), 55–95.

Island, Co. Cork: *JRSAI*, 88 (1958), 1–23.

Itford Hill, Sussex: Settlement: *PPS*, 23 (1957), 167–212. Barrow: *SAC*, 110 (1972), 70–117.

Ivinghoe Beacon, Buckinghamshire: *Records of Bucks*, 18 (1968), 187–260.

Jarlshof, Shetland: JRC Hamilton, *Excavations at Jarlshof, Shetland* (Edinburgh, 1956).

Jerpoint West, Co. Kilkenny: *PRIA*, 73 C (1973), 107–27.

Kaimes, Midlothian: *GAJ*, 1 (1969), 7–28.

Kate's Pad, Pilling, Lancashire: *Radiocarbon*, 2 (1960), 69–70.

Keenogue, Co. Meath: *PPS*, 3 (1937), Plate 27. *JRSAI*, 100 (1970), 127.

Kelleythorpe, Driffield, Yorkshire: Mortimer, *Forty Years Researches*, 271–5.

Kemp Howe, Yorkshire: Mortimer, *Forty Years Researches*, 336–8.

Kerguevarec, Brittany: *PPS*, 5 (1939), 193.

Kerlagat, Morbihan: *L'Anthrop*, 44 (1934), 504, Figure 19.

Kerloas, Brittany: P. R. Giot, *Menhirs et Dolmens* (Chateaulin, n.d.), 4, Plate.

Kestor, Devon: *PPS*, 20 (1955), 87–102.

Kilellan Farm, Islay, Argyll: *BAR*, 33 (1976), 181–207.

Kilhoyle, Co. Derry: *PBNHPS*, 2, I (1937–8), 34–48. *PPS*, 27 (1961), 199–229, 206, Figure 24.

Killaha East, Co. Kerry: *PRIA*, 67c (1968), 52–3, Figures 24–5.

Killeaba, Isle of Man: *BAR*, 54 (1978), I, 203, 205, 207–16.

Killeens, Co. Cork: *JRSAI*, 84 (1954), 105–55.

Killymaddy, Co. Antrim: *Sibrium*, 6 (1961), 232–3, 239–41, tav. 8–9, 16–17, 19–20.

Kilskeery, Co. Tyrone: *UJA*, 2 (1939), 65–71.

King's Barrow, Stowborough, Dorset: J. Hutchins, *History and Antiquities of the County of Dorset*, I (1774), 26–7, Figure. Gerloff, *Daggers*, 179, 258, Plate 57P.

Kinniel Mill, Stirling: *PSAS*, 100 (1967–8), 86–99.

Kirkburn, Lockerbie, Dumfriesshire: *PSAS*, 96 (1962–3), 107–35.

Kirkcaldy, Fife: *Inv Arch*, 5 (1958), GB. 32.

Kirkhaugh, Northumberland: *AA*, 4, 13 (1936), 207–17.

Knackyboy, Scillies: *Ant J*, 32 (1952), 21–34.

Knighton Heath, Dorset: *BAR*, 33 (1976), 291, 300.

Knipton, Leicestershire: *Inv Arch*, 4 (1957), GB 20.

Knockadoon, Lough Gur, Co. Limerick: *PRIA*, 56 C (1954), 297–459.

Knockast, Co. Westmeath: *PRIA*, 41 C (1934), 232–84.

Knockboy, Co. Antrim: *UJA*, 27 (1964), 62–6.

Knocknague, Co. Galway: *PRIA*, 67 C (1968), 53, Figure 26.

Knowth, Co. Meath: *BAR*, 33 (1976), 251–66. *PRIA*, 66 C (1968), 299–400. 74 C (1974), 11–112. *Ant*, 43 (1969), 8–14.

Labbamolaga, Co. Cork: *JCHAS*, 55 (1950), 15–20.

Lacra, Cumberland: *CW*, 2, 48 (1948), 1–22.

Lakenheath, Suffolk: *PCAS*, 42 (1949), 101. 53 (1960), 1–7.

Lambourn Seven Barrows, Berkshire: *BAJ*, 55 (1956), 15–31.

Lancaster Moor, Lancashire: *TLCAS*, 13 (1895), 132. *JBAA*, 21 (1865), 159–61; 28 (1872), 80–2.

Lannion, 'La Motta', Brittany: *Palaeo*, 16 (1974), 152–63.

Largs, Ayr: *Arch*, 62 (1910), 239–46.

Latch Farm, Hampshire: *PPS*, 4 (1938), 169–87.

Law Park, Fife: *PSAS*, 41 (1906–7), 410–14.

Legis Tor, Devon: *TDA*, 28 (1896), 174–99. Worth, *Dartmoor*, 113–14, 117, 121–32, 144–9, Figures 23, 25, 28–9, 38.

Lescongar, Finistère: *Gall Préhist*, 11 (1968), 247–59.

Lesser Garth Cave, Glamorgan: *TCNS*, 93 (1964–6), 18–39.

Liddle, Orkney: *PSAS*, 106 (1974–5), 39–98.

Liffs Low, Derbyshire: Bateman, *Vestiges*, 41. *DAJ*, 75 (1955), 99–101.

Lilliesleaf, Roxburgh: *TGAS*, 14 (1956), 31–4.

Linch Hill, Oxfordshire: Grimes, *Defence Sites*, 154–64.

Linkardstown, Co. Carlow: *JRSAI*, 74 (1944), 61–2.

Links of Noltland, Orkney: *Curr Arch*, 6 (1978), 44–6.

Lissane, Co. Derry: Evans, *ABI*, 252, Figure 318.

Llanarth, Cardiganshire: Grimes, *Prehistory of Wales*, 211, Figure 78.

Llanarthney, Carmarthenshire: Boon and Lewis, *Welsh Antiquity*, 86–7, Figure 1d.

Llanddyfnan, Anglesey: Lynch, *Anglesey*, 136–45, Figures 46–8.

Llandegai, Caernarvonshire: *Ant*, 42 (1968), 216–21. Boon and Lewis, *Welsh Antiquity*, 55–62.

Llandegla, Denbighshire: Grimes, *Prehistory of Wales*, 211, Figure 78.

Llanfachreth, Merioneth: *AC* 7, 6 (1926), 406–9.

Llangwm, Denbighshire: Davies, *Denbighshire*, 275–81.

Llyn Cerrig Bach, Anglesey: C. F. Fox, *A Find of the Early Iron Age from Llyn Cerrig Bach, Anglesey* (Cardiff, 1946). Lynch, *Anglesey*, 249–77, Figures 82–90.
Loanhead of Daviot, Aberdeen: *PSAS*, 70 (1935–6), 278–310.
Lockerbie, Dumfriesshire: *TDGNHAS*, 41 (1962–3), 116.
Long Bennington, Lincolnshire: May, *Lincolnshire*, 85–9, Figure 50.
Long Meg and her Daughters, Cumberland: Thom, *Megalithic Sites*, 151. Burl, *Stone Circles*, 64, 89–92, 343, Figures 8, 14, Plate 10.
Loose Howe, Yorkshire: *PPS*, 15 (1949), 87–106.
Lough Gur, Co. Limerick: *PRIA*, 54 C (1951), 37–74. 56 C (1954), 297–459.
Lundin Farm, Perth: *PSAS*, 98 (1964–6), 126–49.

Machrie, Arran: *BAR*, 48 (1978), 133–6. Burl, *Stone Circles*, 143–7.
Maes Howe, Orkney: Henshall, *Chambered Tombs: 2*.
Maiden Bower, Bedfordshire: *VCH Bedfordshire: I* (1904), 163–70. *PSAL*, 27 (1915), 143–61. *Arch J*, 88 (1931), 90–2. *BAR*, 29 (1976), 1–3, 9, 160–2.
Maiden Castle, Dorset: R. E. M. Wheeler, *Maiden Castle, Dorset* = Soc of Ant London Res Rep 12, 1943.
Maiden's Grave, Rudston, Yorkshire: *Ant*, 38 (1964), 217–19.
Mains of Culduthel, Inverness: National Museum of Antiquities, Edinburgh.
Mains of Daltulich, Nairn: *PSAS*, 104 (1971–2), 283–5.
Malassis, Cher, France: *Gall Préhist*, 13 (1969), 37–73.
Mam Tor, Derbyshire: *Curr Arch*, 3 (1971), 100–2. Harding, *Hillforts*, 147–52.
Manton, Wiltshire: Annable and Simpson, *Devizes Collections*, 47, 101, Figures 195–210.
Marden, Wiltshire: *Ant J*, 51 (1971), 177–239.
Martin Down, Hampshire: Pitt-Rivers, *Cranborne Chase IV*, 185–215.
Martinstown, Dorset: *PPS*, 16 (1950), 152–3.
Masterton, Fife: *PSAS*, 96 (1962–3), 145–54.
Maumbury Rings, Dorset: *Arch*, 105 (1976), 1–97.
Maxey, Northamptonshire: *Ant*, 41 (1967), 138. *Curr Arch*, 1 (1967), 2–4.
Mayburgh, Westmorland: *RCAHM Westmorland*.
Meldon Bridge, Peebles: *BAR*, 33 (1976), 151–79.
Mere G 6a, Wiltshire: Annable and Simpson, *Devizes Collections*, 40, 92, nos. 93–6.
Merry Maidens, Cornwall: Burl, *Stone Circles*, 42, 53, 120–6, 341, Figure 5, Plate 6.
Merthyr Mawr Warren, Glamorgan: *AC* 6, 19 (1919), 323–52. Grimes, *Prehistory of Wales*, passim. *TCNS*, 82 (1955), 39–42.
Mid Gleniron, Wigtown: *TDGNHAS*, 45 (1968), 73–9.
Migdale, Sutherland: *Inv Arch*, 5 (1958), GB. 26.
Mildenhall, Suffolk: *Ant J*, 16 (1936), 29–50.
Milfield, Northumberland: *BAR*, 33 (1976), 113–42.
Mill of Laithers, Aberdeen: *PPS*, 30 (1964), 428. *PSAS*, 101 (1968–9), 50–1, 102, Figure 39.
Mill of Marcus, Forfar: *PSAS*, 12 (1889–90), 470.
Millstreet, Co. Cork: *JRSAI*, 84 (1954), 143.
Milton Loch, Kirkcudbright: *Ant*, 48 (1974), 154–6.

Minnis Bay, Kent: *PPS*, 9 (1943), 28–47.
Misk Knowes, Ayrshire: *PSAS*, 40 (1905–6), 378–402.
Moelfre Uchaf, Denbigh: *AC*, 92 (1937), 335.
Moel y Gaer, Flintshire: Harding, *Hillforts*, 465–73. *PPS*, 41 (1975), 203–21.
Mold, Flintshire: *PPS*, 19 (1953), 161–79.
Monamore, Arran: *PSAS*, 97 (1963–4), 1–34.
Moneen, Co. Cork: *PRIA*, 54 C (1952), 121–59.
Monknewtown, Co. Meath: *PRIA*, 76 C (1976), 25–72.
Monkton, Pembrokeshire: *AC* 6, 8 (1908), 114–15.
Mont-Saint-Aignan, Normandy, France: G. Verron, *Musée des Antiquités de la Seine Maritimes*: *Antiquités Préhistoriques et Protohistoriques* (1971), 47, 49, Plate.
Moor Divock, Westmorland: *CW*, 8 (1886), 323–47.
Morges-les-Roseaux, Switzerland: Gerloff, *Daggers*, 184, 239, 265, Plate 59A.
Mosley Heights, Lancashire: *TLCAS*, 52 (1951), 204–8.
Mound of the Hostages, Tara, Co. Meath: *PPS*, 21 (1955), 163–73.
Mount Gabriel, Co. Cork: *JCHAS*, 77 (1972), 25–7. *Archaeol Austriaca*, 43 (1968), 92–114.
Mount Pleasant, Dorset: *Curr Arch*, 2 (1970), 320–4. *PPS*, 38 (1972), 389–407.
Mount Stewart, Co. Down: *PPS*, 3 (1937), 29–42.
Mount Vernon, Glasgow: *TDGNHAS*, 42 (1965), 41, Figures 7–8, nos. 56–61.
Muckhatch farm, Thorpe, Surrey: Pers. comm. B. Johnson.
Mucking, Essex: in R. Bruce-Mitford (ed.), *Recent Archaeological Excavations in Europe* (London, 1975), 133–87.
Mühltal, Germany: Piggott, *Ancient Europe*, 105, Figure 58.
Mullaghfarna, Co. Sligo: M. Herity, *Irish Passage Graves*, 157–8, Figure 109.
Mycenae, Shaft Graves Iota, Omicron: Piggott, *Ancient Europe*, 134. G. E. Mylonas, *Ancient Mycenae* (London, 1957), 151. G. E. Mylonas, *Mycenae and the Mycenaean Age* (London, 1966), 104. *PPS*, 38 (1972), 297.
Mynydd Carn Goch, Glamorgan: *AC*, 3, 2 (1856), 63–7; 14 (1868), 252–5.

Nant Ffrancon, Caernarvonshire: *Radiocarbon*, 15 (1973).
Ness of Gruting, Shetland: *PSAS*, 89 (1955–6), 340–97.
Nether Criggie, Kincardine: *PSAS*, 88 (1954–6), 1–14.
Nether Largie, Argyll: E. W. MacKie, *Scotland: An Archaeological Guide* (London, 1975), 150–3.
New Barn Down, Sussex: *SAC*, 75 (1934), 137–70.
Newborough Warren, Anglesey: Lynch, *Anglesey*, 80–2, 87–9, Figures 32–3.
Newgrange, Co. Meath: *Ant.*, 42 (1968), 40–2. 46 (1972), 226–7. G. Daniels and P. Kjaerum (eds.), *Megalithic Graves and Ritual = Jutland Archaeol Soc Publ*, 11 (1973), 137–46. *PRIA*, 74 C (1974), 313–83.
Nieuwe Dordrecht, Holland: Piggott, *Ancient Europe*, 95, 110, Plate IX.
Nine Ladies, Stanton Moor, Derbyshire: Bateman, *Vestiges*, 112. Burl, *Stone Circles*, 290–1, 344, Figure 48.
Nine Stones, Dorset: Burl, *Stone Circles*, 290, 299, 345, Figure 48.
Normangill, Lanarkshire: *PPS*, 35 (1969), 128.
North Carnaby Temple, Rudston, Yorkshire: *BAR*, 9 (1974), 37–63.

North Ferriby, Yorkshire: E. V. Wright, *The North Ferriby Boats: a Guide Book* (1976). Greenwich, Nat. Maritime Mus.
Northton, Harris: *BAR*, 33 (1976), 221–31.
Norton Fitzwarren, Somerset: *Curr Arch*, No. 28 (1971), 116–20.
Nutbane, Hampshire: *PPS*, 25 (1959), 15–51.

Oddendale, Westmorland: *JBAA*, 35 (1879), 369; Burl, *Stone Circles*, 62, 93, 348.
Offham Hill, Sussex: *PPS*, 43 (1977), 201–41.
Ogbourne Down, Wiltshire: *PPS*, 8 (1942), 48–61.
Ogof-yr-Esgyrn, Breconshire: *AC*, 117 (1968), 18–71.
Old England, Brentford, Middlesex: *Ant*, 3 (1929), 20–32.
Old Keig, Aberdeen: *PSAS*, 68 (1934), 372.
Ord, The, Sutherland: *PPS*, 39 (1973), 344–5, Figure 11.
Orsett, Essex: Hoard: Causewayed enclosures: *PPS*, 44 (1978), 219–308. *BAR*, 31 ii (1976), 234–5, Plate 23.
Orwell, Kinross: *PSAS*, 98 (1964–6), 140.
Ostenfeld, North Germany: *Palaeo*, 9 (1963), 73 and passim, Figure 16.

Painsthorpe Wold 4, 83, Yorkshire: Mortimer, *Forty Years Researches*, 113–17, 119.
Pangbourne, Berkshire: *PPSEA*, 6 (1929), 30–9.
Park Brow, Sussex: *Arch*, 76 (1927), 14–40.
Pelynt, Cornwall: *PPS*, 17 (1951), 95. 18 (1952), 237–8. *Cornish Archaeol*, 12 (1973), 19–23.
Penard, Glamorgan: *Arch*, 71 (1920–1), 138.
Penmaenmawr Circles, Caernarvonshire: *PPS*, 26 (1960), 303–39.
Penn Moor, Devon: *PDAS*, 31 (1973), 1–21.
Pentridge Hill, Dorset: Simpson, *Economy and Settlement*, 171–2, Figure 35 B.
Pewit Farm, Berkshire: *Trans Newbury District Field Club*, 8 (1938), 110.
Pilsgate, Lincolnshire: *PCAS*, 65 (1974), 1–12.
Pitnacree, Perthshire: *PPS*, 31 (1965), 34–57.
Plas Penrhyn, Anglesey: *AC*, 79 (1929), 229–36. Lynch, *Anglesey*, 163–5, Figure 57.
Playden, Sussex: *Ant. J.*, 15 (1935), 152–64. F. Pryor, *Excavations at Fengate: Second Report* (Toronto, 1978), 219–23.
Plumpton Plain A and B, Sussex: *PPS*, 1 (1935), 1–59.
Pokesdown, Hampshire: *Ant J*, 7 (1927), 465–84.
Pontavert, Aisne, France: *Gall Préhist*, 17 (1974), 439–41.
Poole, Dorset: *PPS*, 18 (1952), 148–59.
Ports Down, Hampshire: *PHFC*, 24 (1967), 20–41.
Portrieux, Brittany: Briard, *Les Dépôts Bretons*, Figure 38.
Portsdown Hill, Hampshire: *PHFC*, 24 (1967), 42–58.
Preshute, Wiltshire: *PPS*, 8 (1942), 48–61.
Priddy, Somerset: *PUBSS*, 11 (1966–7), 97–125.
Puddlehill, Bedfordshire: *BAR*, 29 (1976), 25–150.
Punchestown, Co. Kildare: Burl, *Stone Circles*, 234.

Punds Water, Shetland: Henshall, *Chambered Tombs I*, 138–47, 171–2, Figure 8, Plate 25A.
Pyotdykes, Angus: *PPS*, 30 (1964), 186–98.

Quanterness, Orkney: *Ant*, 50 (1976), 194–204.
Queensford Mill, Oxfordshire: *Bar*, 34 (1977), 37, Plate 1.
Quoyness, Orkney: *Ant*, 50 (1976), 194–204.

Raddick Hill, Devon: Worth, *Dartmoor*, 113–14. *AC*, 101 (1951), 167–8. *PPS*, 18 (1952), 63, 84.
Radley, Berkshire: *Inv Arch*, 1 (1955), GB.2.
Rainsborough, Northamptonshire: *PPS*, 33 (1967), 207–306.
Rams Hill, Berkshire: *BAR*, 19 (1975).
Rathgall, Co. Wicklow: *Ant*, 44 (1970), 51–4. 45 (1971), 296–8. 47 (1973), 293–5. Harding, *Hillforts . . .*, 339–57.
Reaverhill Farm, Barrasford, Northumberland: *AA*, 4, 43 (1965), 65–75.
Red Shore, Alton, Wiltshire: *WAM*, 68 B (1973), 120–2.
Reffley Wood, Norfolk: *LPA*, 40, 46, Figure 16.
Retz, Brittany: *Annales de Bretagne*, 72 (1965), 75–85.
Rhoscrowther, Pembrokeshire: *AC*, 7, 6 (1926), 1–32.
Rhos-y-Clegyrn, Pembrokeshire: *AC*, 123 (1974), 13–42.
Rhuddlan, Flintshire: *Curr Arch*, 3 (1972), 245–8.
Rider's Rings, Devon: Worth, *Dartmoor*, 115–16, 149, Figures 24, 40–1.
Rillaton, Cornwall: *Arch J*, 24 (1867), 189. Gerloff, *Daggers*, 107, 178–82, 190–3, Plate 50 A.
Rimbury, Dorset: *Ant J*, 13 (1933), 446–7; L. V. Grinsell, *Dorset Barrows* (Dorchester, 1959, 142).
Ring of Brodgar, Orkney: *J Hist Astron*, 4 (1973), 111–23. Burl, *Stone Circles*, 99–102, 362, Plate 3.
Ringwould, Kent: *Arch*, 45 (1877), 53–6. *Helinium*, 1 (1961), 101–3, Figure 1.
Rinyo, Orkney: *PSAS*, 73 (1938–9), 6–31; 81 (1947–8), 16–42.
Rippon Tor, Devon: *PPS*, 20 (1954), 87–102.
Robin Hood's Ball, Wiltshire: *WAM*, 59 (1959), 1–27.
Rockbarton, Co. Limerick: *PRIA*, 48 C (1942), 255–72.
Rockbourne Down, Hampshire: *PHFC*, 16 (1946), 156–62.
Roke Down, Dorset: Evans, *ABI*, 233–4, Figure 290.
Rollright Stones, Oxfordshire: Burl, *Stone Circles*, 292–7, 347, Figure 49, Plate 33.
Ronaldsway, Isle of Man: *PPS*, 13 (1947), 139–60. *BAR*, 54 (1978), 177–218.
Rook Reave, Devon: *PDAS*, 31 (1973), 9–10, Figure 4.
Rosinish, Benbecula: *BAR*, 33 (1976), 209–20.
Ross Links, Northumberland: *AA*, 4, 5 (1928), 13–25. Tait, *Beakers*, 14–15, 65, Figures 1–25.
Rothesay, Bute: *Ant*, 42 (1968), 296–7.
Rough Tor, Cornwall: *Cornish Archaeol*, 9 (1970), 18.
Roundway G8, Wiltshire: Annable and Simpson, *Devizes Collections*, 38, 88, nos. 59–63.

Rowbarrow Cavern, Somerset: *PUBSS*, 2 (1926), 190–209.
Rudston, Yorkshire: (pit sites) *BAR*, 9 (1974). *YAJ*, 47 (1975), 23–59.
Rudston (Cursus), Yorkshire: *PPS*, 32 (1966), 86–95.
Rudston LXII, LXIII, Yorkshire: Greenwell, *British Barrows*, 234–5; 245–51. *YAJ*, 42 (1969), 254–8; 44 (1972), 1–22.
Rülow, Mecklenburg, Germany: Palaeo, 9 (1963), 60–1, 73, Plate VIa.
Runnymede Bridge, Surrey: *London Arch*, 3 (1976), 10–17.
Rybury, Wiltshire: *Ant*, 4 (1930), 38–40. *WAM*, 59 (1964), 185; 60 (1965), 127.
Rylston, Yorkshire: Greenwell, *British Barrows*, 376. *PPS*, 16 (1950), 131.
Ryton-on-Dunsmore, Warwickshire: *Radiocarbon*, 10 (1968), 204; 13 (1971), 154.

Salcombe, Devon: *Youth Hostelling News*, No. 23 (1977), 1.
Sant-y-Nyll, Glamorgan: *TCNS*, 89 (1959–60), 9–25.
Scone, Perthshire: *TPPSNS*, 11 (1966), 7–23.
Scorton, Yorkshire: *NAG NEWS* 2 (1), (1978), 12. Excavated P. Topping, pers. comm. *YAJ*, 38 (1955), 434.
Scratchbury, Norton Bavant, Wiltshire: Moore and Rowlands, *Salisbury Metalwork*, 49–50, Plate IV:1.
Sculptor's Cave, Covesea, Moray: *PSAS*, 65 (1930–1), 177–216.
Sewell, Bedfordshire: Clarke, *Beakers (2)*, 574, Plate 3.
Shap Centre, Gunnerkeld, Westmorland: *CW*, 4 (1878–9), 537.
Shave Hill, Somerset: *SANH*, 117 (1973), 116–19.
Shearplace Hill, Dorset: *PPS*, 28 (1962), 289–328. 35 (1969), 345–51.
Sheep Down, Winterbourne Steepleton, Dorset: *Arch J* 108 (1952), 1–24.
Sheepland, Co. Down: *UJA*, 27 (1964), 31–58.
Shell Top Reave, Devon: *PDAS*, 31 (1973), 10, Figure 4.
Silbury Hill, Wiltshire: *Ant*, 41 (1967), 259–62. 44 (1970), 313–14.
Simons Ground, Dorset: *BAR*, 33 (1976), 291–3.
Six Wells 271, Glamorgan: *Ant J*, 21 (1941), 99–125.
Skara Brae, Orkney: V. G. Childe, *Skara Brae: A Pictish Village in Orkney* (London, 1931). D. V. Clarke, *The Neolithic Village at Skara Brae . . . 1972–73 excavations* (Edinburgh, 1976).
Skrydstrup, Denmark: H. C. Broholm and M. Hald, *Skrydstrupfundet* (Copenhagen, 1939). Glob, *Mound People*, 65–73.
Slieve Gullion, Co. Armagh: *UJA*, 26 (1963), 19–40. 35 (1972), 17–21.
Sluie, Moray: *Inv Arch*, 5 (1958), GB.30.
Snowshill, Gloucestershire: *Arch*, 52 (1890), 70–2.
Soldier's Hole, Cheddar, Somerset: *Ant J*, 8 (1928), 204.
Sonning, Berkshire: *BAJ*, 61 (1963–4), 4–19.
Sopron, Hungary: Piggott, *Ancient Europe*, 198–9, 213, Figure 111.
South Cadbury, Somerset: L. Alcock, *By South Cadbury is that Camelot* (London, 1973).
South Lodge, Dorset: A. Pitt-Rivers, *Cranborne Chase IV. Curr Arch*, 6 (1978), 54–6.

South Street, Wiltshire: *Ant*, 42 (1968), 138–42. Simpson, *Economy and Settlement*, 40–52, 162–3.

Sprouston, Roxburgh: *PSAS*, 83 (1948–9), 220–4.

Stainsby, Lincolnshire: May, *Lincolnshire*, 77–9, Figures 42–3.

Stancombe Downs, Berkshire: *Arch*, 75 (1924–5), 95.

Stanlake, Oxfordshire: *Arch*, 37 (1857), 368.

Standlow, Derbyshire: *PPS*, 42 (1976), 319–22.

Stannon Down, Cornwall: *Cornish Archaeol*, 9 (1970), 17–46.

Stanton Drew, Somerset: *PUBSS*, 11 (1965–6), 40–2. Burl, *Stone Circles*, 103–6, 347.

Stanton Harcourt, Oxfordshire: *Oxon*, 28 (1963), 1–52.

Stanton Moor, Derbyshire: *DAJ*, 4 (1930), 1–45; 10 (1936), 21–40; *Arch J*, 123 (1966), 13–16.

Stanydale, Shetland: *PSAS*, 89 (1955–6), 340–97.

Stathern, Lincolnshire: Nottingham University Museum.

Stenness, Stones of, Orkney: *PSAS*, 107 (1975–6), 1–60.

Steyning, Sussex: *PPS*, 24 (1958), 158–64.

Stob Stones, Roxburgh: *RCAHM Roxburgh II*, 460; I, Plate 3.

Stockbridge Down, Hampshire: *Ant J*, 20 (1940), 39–51.

Stonehenge, Wiltshire: R. J. C. Atkinson, *Stonehenge* (London, 1956, 1960, 1979). Burl, *Stone Circles*, 302–16, 348. *Nature*, 233 (1971), 3035. 243 (1973), 214–16. F. Hoyle, *On Stonehenge* (London, 1977).

Stoke Flat, Derbyshire: Bateman, *Vestiges*, 114.

Store Kongehøj, Denmark: Glob, *Mound People*, 84–5, 88–9.

Streatley, Bedfordshire: Simpson, *Economy and Settlement*, 123, Figure 20.

Stripple Stones, Cornwall: *Arch*, 61 (1908), 1–60. Burl, *Stone Circles*, 119–22, 341.

Stromness, Orkney: *PPS*, 16 (1950), 153.

Sturminster Marshall, Dorset: *Arch J*, 119 (1964), 34, 60, Figure 14.

Sumburgh, Shetland: *DE Scot* (1974), 87.

Sunbrick, Cumberland: *CW* 2, 27 (1927), 100.

Sun Hole, Cheddar, Somerset: *PUBSS*, 3 (1928), 84–97.

Sutton 268, Glamorgan: *Arch*, 89 (1943), 89–125.

Swarkeston, Derbyshire: *DAJ*, 80 (1960), 1–48.

Swinburn Castle, Northumberland: *History of Northumberland XV* (Newcastle upon Tyne, 1940), 40, 62, Figure 15.

Swine Sty, Derbyshire: *Trans Hunter Archaeol Soc*, 10 (1971), 5–13; 10 (1975), 204–11.

Talaton, Devon: *Arch J*, 24 (1867), 110.

Talbenny, Pembrokeshire: *Arch J*, 99 (1943), 1–32.

Tallington, Lincolnshire: *PPS*, 42 (1976), 215–39.

Tarrant Launceston 4, Dorset: *Arch*, 90 (1944), 74–5.

Taunton, Somerset: *Inv Arch*, GB 7th set (1959), GB 43.

Tentsmuir, Fife: *PSAS*, 99 (1966–7), 6–92.

Thickthorn, Dorset: *PPS*, 2 (1936), 77–96.

Thirlings, Northumberland: *BAR*, 33 (1976), 113–42.

Thornborough, Yorkshire: *YAJ*, 38 (1955), 425–45.
Thorne Moor, Yorkshire: *Nature*, 241 (1973), 405–6.
Thorny Down, Wiltshire: *PPS*, 7 (1941), 114–33.
Three Kings, Northumberland: *AA*, 4, 49 (1971), 37–51. 50 (1972). 1–14.
Throwley, Staffordshire: Bateman, *Ten Years Diggings*, 130.
Thwing, Yorkshire: *Ant*, 42 (1968), 130–1, Plate XX. *Curr Arch*, 67 (1979),
240–1.
Tickenham, Somerset: *SANH*, 117 (1973), 33–44.
Tollund, Denmark: P. V. Glob, *The Bog People* (London, 1971), 21–32.
Tonfannau, Merioneth: *AC*, 87 (1932), 395–7.
Tooth Cave, Gower, Glamorgan: *BBCS*, 23 (1967), 277–90.
Topped Mountain, Co. Fermanagh: *PRIA*, 20 (1896–8), 651–8.
Totley, Derbyshire: *Arch J*, 123 (1966), 1–26.
Totternhoe, Bedfordshire: *Ant J*, 20 (1940), 487–91.
Tourony, Côtes-du-Nord: Briard, *Les Dépôts Bretons*, 290–1, Figure 110.
Towthorpe 18, 21, Yorkshire: Mortimer, *Forty Years Researches*, 9–12.
Tréboul, Finistère: *Travaux Lab d'Anthrop Préhist Rennes*, 1956, 1958. Briard, *Les
Dépôts Bretons*, 79–108.
Treiorwerth, Anglesey: *AC*, 120 (1971), 11–83.
Trevisker, Cornwall: *PPS*, 38 (1972), 302–81.
Trindhøj, Denmark: Glob, *Mound People*, 25–9.
Twelve Apostles, Dumfries: *RCAHM Dumfries*, no. 284. Burl, *Stone Circles*,
102–3, 357.

Udal, North Uist: *Ant*, 51 (1977), 124–36.
Unival, North Uist: *PSAS*, 82 (1950), 1–49.
Upton Lovell, Wiltshire: Annable and Simpson, *Devizes Collections*, 48, 103, nos.
225–33.
Urbalreagh, Co. Antrim: *UJA*, 31 (1968), 25–32.
Urswick, Cumbria: *CW*, 2, 57 (1957), 9.

Vinces Farm 3, Ardleigh, Essex: *Colchester Arch Gp Bull*, 4 (1961), 33–53.
Voorhout, Netherlands: *BRGK*, 31 (1941), Taf. 26. *Palaeohistoria*, 9 (1963),
Figure 11.

Walker, Newcastle upon Tyne: *AA*, 4, 43 (1965), 77–86.
Walney Island, Furness: *CW*, 2, 50 (1950), 15; 55 (1955), 1.
Warren Farm, Milton Keynes, Buckinghamshire: *Arch J*, 131 (1974), 75–139.
Watern Oke, Devon: *PPS*, 18 (1952), 67–70.
Wasbister, Orkney: Coles and Simpson, *Ancient Europe*, 177, 191, Figure 44.
Watch Hill, Cornwall: *Cornish Archaeol*, 14 (1975), 5–81.
Waulud's Bank, Bedfordshire: *Curr Arch*, 30 (1972), 173–6.
Wayland's Smithy, Berkshire: *Ant*, 39 (1965), 126–33.
Weird Law, Peebles: *PSAS*, 99 (1966–7), 93–103.
West Furze, Yorkshire: *Arch*, 61 (1911), 593–607.
West Kennet, Wiltshire: S. Piggott, *The West Kennet Long Barrow* (London,
1962).

West Overton G6b, Wiltshire: *PPS*, 32 (1966), 122–55.
Whiteleaf, Buckinghamshire: *PPS*, 20 (1954), 212–30.
White Meldon, Peeblesshire: *RCAHM Peeblesshire I*, nos. 192, 193. *PPS*, 39 (1973), 338, 340, Figure 5.
Whitesheet Hill, Wiltshire: *WAM*, 54 (1952), 404–10.
Whitestanes Moor, Dumfriesshire: *TDGNHAS*, 42 (1965), 51–60.
Willerby Wold CCXXXV, Yorkshire: *Arch*, 52 (1890), 2–4. *PPS*, 4 (1938), 283–5, Figure 12.
Willings Walls, Devon: *PDAS*, 31 (1973), 1–5, Figure 2.
Willington, Derbyshire: *Ant*, 46 (1972), 314–16.
Wilsford G8, Wiltshire: Annable and Simpson, *Devizes Collections*, 46, 100, nos. 179–92.
Wilsford Shaft, Wiltshire: *Ant*, 37 (1963), 116–20. 40 (1966), 227–8.
Wimborne St. Giles G9, Dorset: Annable and Simpson, *Devizes Collections*, 39, 90, nos. 77–85.
Windmill Hill, Wiltshire: I. F. Smith, *Windmill Hill and Avebury* (Oxford, 1965).
Winnall, Hampshire: *PHFC*, 26 (1969), 5–18.
Winterborne Came 18b, Dorset: C. Warne, *Celtic Tumuli of Dorset* (1866), no. 12. L. V. Grinsell, *Dorset Barrows* (Dorchester, 1959), 148.
Winterborne St. Martin, 5c, 34b, Dorset: *Arch*, 30 (1844), 331–2, Plate XVII.
Winterbourne Abbas, Dorset: *RCHM Dorset II* (1970), 461–3. Simpson, *Economy and Settlement*, 171–2, Figure 35A.
Winterbourne Kingston, Dorset: *PDNHAS*, 94 (1973), 37–43.
Winterbourne Steepleton, Dorset: *Arch J*, 108 (1952), 1–24.
Winterbourne Stoke G28, Wiltshire: Annable and Simpson, *Devizes Collections*, 62, 117, nos. 485–6.
Winterslow, Wiltshire: *WAM*, 52 (1947), 126.
Wolstonbury, Sussex: *SAC*, 71 (1930), 237–45.
Woodend, Co. Tyrone: *UJA*, 3 (1940), 162.
Woodhead, Cumberland: *CW*, 2, 40 (1940), 162–6.
Woodhenge, Wiltshire: M. E. Cunnington, *Woodhenge* (Devizes, 1929).
Worgret, Dorset: *PDNHAS*, 87 (1966), 119–25.
Wykeham Forest, Yorkshire: *YAJ*, 45 (1973), 55–95.

Yarrows, Caithness: Henshall, *Chambered Tombs I*, 70–9, 88–94, 291–4, Figure 51.
Yes Tor Bottom, Devon: *TDA*, 30 (1898), 99–104. Worth, *Dartmoor*, 146–9, Figure 39.
Yoxie, Shetland: *PSAS*, 94 (1960–1), 28–45.
Ystrad Hynod, Montgomeryshire: *AC*, 122 (1973), 35–54.

Bibliography

Chapter I Before Stonehenge

APSIMON, A. M., 1969 The earlier Bronze Age in the north of Ireland, *UJA*, 32, 28–72.

ASHBEE, P., 1970 *The Earthen Long Barrow in Britain*. London.

BRIARD, J., 1965 *Les Dépôts Bretons et L'Age du Bronze Atlantique*. Rennes.

BURGESS, C. B., 1969 Chronology and Terminology in the British Bronze Age, *Ant J*, 49, 22–9.

BURGESS, C. B., 1970 The Bronze Age, *Curr Arch*, 2, 8, 208–15.

BURGESS, C. B., 1974 The Bronze Age, in C. Renfrew (ed.), *British Prehistory – A New Outline*. London, 165–232, 291–329.

BUTLER, J. J., 1963 *Bronze Age Connections Across the North Sea*, = *Palaeohistoria*, 9. Groningen.

CASE, H. J., 1961 Irish Neolithic Pottery: distribution and sequence, *PPS*, 27, 174–233.

CASE, H. J., 1969 Settlement patterns in the North Irish Neolithic, *UJA*, 32, 3–27.

CLARK, J. G. D., 1966. The invasion hypothesis in British archaeology, *Ant*, 40, 172–89.

CLARK, R. M., 1975. A calibration curve for radiocarbon dates, *Ant*, 49, 251–66.

EVANS, J. G., 1975 *The Environment of Early Man in the British Isles*. London.

EVANS, J. G., LIMBREY, S. and CLEERE, H. (eds.), 1975 *The Effect of Man on the Landscape: The Highland Zone*. London, CBA Res. Rep. 11.

FOX, C., 1959 *The Personality of Britain*. Cardiff, 4 ed.

GAUCHER, G., and MOHEN, J. P., 1974. *L'Age du Bronze dans le Nord de la France*. Amiens.

GIMBUTAS, M., 1965 *Bronze Age Cultures in Central and Eastern Europe*. The Hague.

GODWIN, H., 1975 *The History of the British Flora*. Cambridge, 2 ed.

GUILAINE, J. (ed.), 1976 *La Préhistoire Française II*. Paris.

HARBISON, P., 1973 The earlier Bronze Age in Ireland – late 3rd millennium to *c*. 1200 BC, *JRSAI*, 103, 93–152.

HAWKES, C. F. C., 1960 *A scheme for the British Bronze Age*, duplicated precis of an address to the CBA Bronze Age Conference, London, December, 1960.

HENSHALL, A. S., 1963, 1972 *Chambered Tombs of Scotland*. Edinburgh, 2 vols.

HERITY, M. and EOGAN, G., 1977 *Ireland in Prehistory*. London.

LAMB, H. H., 1967 Britain's changing climate, *Geogr J*, 133, 445–68.

LYNCH, F., 1970 *Prehistoric Anglesey*. Llangefni.

LYNCH, F. and BURGESS, C. (eds.), 1972 *Prehistoric Man in Wales and the West*. Bath.

MAY, J., 1976 *Prehistoric Lincolnshire*. Lincoln.

MOORE, C. N. and ROWLANDS, M., 1972 *Bronze Age Metalwork in Salisbury Museum*. Salisbury.

PIGGOTT, S., 1954 *The Neolithic Cultures of the British Isles*. Cambridge.

PIGGOTT, S., 1965 *Ancient Europe*. Edinburgh.

PIGGOTT, S., 1972 A note on climatic deterioration in the first millennium BC in Britain, *SAF*, 4, 109–13.

PIGGOTT, S., DANIEL, G. and McBURNEY, C. (eds.), 1974 *France before the Romans*. London.

POWELL, T. G. E. et al, 1969 *Megalithic Enquiries in the West of Britain*. Liverpool.

RENFREW, C., 1973 *Before Civilisation: The Radiocarbon Revolution and Prehistoric Europe*. London.

RENFREW, C. (ed.), 1974 *British Prehistory: A New Outline*. London.

WADDELL, J., 1974 On some aspects of the Late Neolithic and Early Bronze Age in Ireland, *IARF*, 1 (1), 32–8.

WADDELL, J., 1978 The Invasion hypothesis in Irish prehistory, *Ant*, 52, 121–8.

WATKINS, T. (ed.), 1975 *Radiocarbon: Calibration and Prehistory*. Edinburgh.

WHITTLE, A. W. R., 1977 *The Earlier Neolithic of Southern England and its Continental Background* = *BAR*, supp. ser. 35.

Chapter II The Prehistory of the Third Millennium: The Meldon Bridge and Mount Pleasant periods

BRITTON, D., 1963 Traditions of metal-working in the later Neolithic and Early Bronze Age of Britain: Part 1, *PPS*, 29, 258–325.

BURGESS, C. B., 1976 Meldon Bridge: a Neolithic defended promontory complex near Peebles, in Burgess and Miket (eds), *Settlement and Economy in the Third and Second Millennia BC* = *BAR*, 33, 151–79.

BURGESS, C. B., 1979 The background of early metalworking in Ireland and Britain, in M. Ryan (ed.), *The Origins of Metallurgy in Atlantic Europe* = *Proceedings of the Fifth Atlantic Colloquium, Dublin, 1978*.

BURGESS, C. B. and SHENNAN, S., 1976 The Beaker phenomenon: some suggestions, in C. B. Burgess and R. Miket (eds), *Settlement and Economy in the Third and Second Millennia BC* = *BAR*, 33, 309–31.

BURLEIGH, R., LONGWORTH, I. H., WAINWRIGHT, G. J., 1972 Relative and absolute dating of four late Neolithic enclosures: an exercise in the interpretation of radiocarbon determinations, *PPS*, 38, 389–407.

CASE, H. J., 1967 Were Beaker people the first metallurgists in Ireland? *Palaeohistoria*, 12, 141–77.

CLARKE, D. L., 1970 *Beaker Pottery of Great Britain and Ireland*. Cambridge, 2 vols.

COLES, J. M., 1968–9 Scottish Early Bronze Age metalwork, *PSAS*, 101, 1–110.
HARBISON, P., 1968 Catalogue of Irish Early Bronze Age associated finds containing copper or bronze, *PRIA*, 67 C, 35–91.
LANTING, J. N. and VAN DER WAALS, J. D., 1972 British Beakers as seen from the Continent, *Helinium*, 12, 20–46.
MANBY, T. G., 1974 *Grooved Ware Sites in the North of England* = *BAR*, 9.
MANBY, T. G., 1975 Neolithic occupation sites on the Yorkshire Wolds, *YAJ*, 47, 23–59.
MERCER, R. (ed.), 1977 *Beakers in Britain and Europe: Four Studies* = *BAR*, suppl. ser. 26.
PIGGOTT, S., 1962 *The West Kennet Long Barrow*. London.
PIGGOTT, S., 1963 Abercromby and after: the Beaker cultures of Britain re-examined, in Foster, I. and Alcock, L., *Culture and Environment*, 53–91. London.
RENFREW, C., 1976 Quanterness, radiocarbon and the Orkney cairns, *Ant*, 50, 194–204.
SMITH, I. F., 1965 *Windmill Hill and Avebury*. Oxford.

Chapter III The Prehistory of the Second Millennium: The Overton, Bedd Branwen and Knighton Heath periods

APSIMON, A. M. and GREENFIELD, E., 1972 The excavation of the Bronze Age and Iron Age settlements at Trevisker Round, St. Eval, Cornwall, *PPS*, 38, 302–81.
BARRETT, J., 1975 The later pottery: (2) Types, affinities, chronology and significance, in Bradley, R., Ellison, A., *Rams Hill* = *BAR*, 19, 101–18.
BARRETT, J., 1976 Deverel-Rimbury: problems of chronology and interpretation, in Burgess, C. B. and Miket, R. (eds), *Settlement and Economy in the Third and Second Millennia BC* = *BAR*, 33, 289–307.
BRADLEY, R. and ELLISON, A., 1975 *Rams Hill: A Bronze Age Defended Enclosure and its Landscape* = *BAR*, 19.
BUTLER, J. J., and SMITH, I. F., 1956 Razors, urns and the British Middle Bronze Age, *ULIAAR*, 12, 20–52.
BURGESS, C. B., 1968 *Bronze Age Metalwork in Northern England* c. 1000–700BC Newcastle upon Tyne.
BURGESS, C. B., 1968 The later Bronze Age in the British Isles and north-western France, *Arch J*, 125, 1–45.
BURGESS, C. B., 1968 Bronze Age dirks and rapiers as illustrated by examples from Durham and Northumberland, *TAASDN*, N.S. 1, 3–26.
BURGESS, C. B., 1976 The Gwithian mould and the forerunners of South Welsh axes, in Burgess, C. B. and Miket, R. (eds), *Settlement and Economy in the Third and Second Millennia BC* = *BAR*, 33, 69–75.
BURGESS, C. B. and COWEN, J. D., 1972 The Ebnal hoard and Early Bronze Age metal-working traditions, in Lynch, F., and Burgess, C. B. (eds), *Prehistoric Man in Wales and the West*. Bath.
CALKIN, J. B., 1962 The Bournemouth area in the Middle and Late Bronze Age, with the 'Deverel-Rimbury' problem reconsidered, *Arch J*, 119, 1–65.

COLES, J. M., 1963–4 Scottish Middle Bronze Age Metalwork, *PSAS*, 97, 82–156.

COLES, J. M. and TAYLOR, J., 1971 The Wessex Culture! a minimal view, *Ant*, 45, 6–14.

COWEN, J. D., 1951 The earliest bronze swords in Britain and their origins on the Continent of Europe, *PPS*, 17, 195–213.

EOGAN, G., 1964 The Later Bronze Age in Ireland in the light of recent research, *PPS*, 30, 268–351.

FLEMING, A., 1971 Territorial patterns in Bronze Age Wessex, *PPS*, 37 (1), 138–66.

FLEMING, A., 1973 Models for the development of the Wessex Culture, in Renfrew, C. (ed.), *The Explanation of Culture Change*, 571–85. London.

GERLOFF, S., 1975 *The Early Bronze Age Daggers in Great Britain and a Reconsideration of the Wessex Culture* = Prähistorische Bronzefunde VI/2. München.

LONGWORTH, I. H., 1961 Origins and development of the Collared Urn tradition in England and Wales, *PPS*, 27, 263–306.

MCKERRELL, H., 1972 On the origins of British faience beads and some aspects of the Wessex-Mycenae relationship, *PPS*, 38, 286–301.

PIGGOTT, S., 1938 The Early Bronze Age in Wessex, *PPS*, 4, 52–106.

RENFREW, C., 1968 Wessex without Mycenae, *Annual of the British School of Archaeology at Athens*, 63, 277–85.

ROWLANDS, M. J., 1976 *The Organisation of Middle Bronze Age Metalworking* = BAR, 31, 2 vols.

SAVORY, H. N., 1971 A Welsh Bronze Age hill-fort, *Ant*, 45, 251–61.

SAVORY, H. N., 1958 The Late Bronze Age in Wales, *AC*, 107, 3–63.

SIMPSON, D. D. A., 1968 Food Vessels: associations and chronology, in Coles, J. M. and Simpson, D. D. A., (eds), *Studies in Ancient Europe*, 197–211. Leicester.

SMITH, M. A., 1959 Some Somerset hoards and their place in the Bronze Age of southern Britain, *PPS*, 25, 144–87.

WADDELL, J., 1976 Cultural interaction in the insular Early Bronze Age: some ceramic evidence, in De Laet, S. J. (ed.), *Acculturation and Continuity in Atlantic Europe* (Papers presented at the IV Atlantic Colloquium, Ghent, 1975). 284–94. Brugge.

Chapter IV People, population and social organization

ATKINSON, R. J. C., 1968 Old mortality: some aspects of burial and population in Neolithic England, in Coles, J. M., and Simpson, D. D. A., *Studies in Ancient Europe*, 83–93. Leicester.

ATKINSON, R. J. C., 1972 Burial and population in the British Bronze Age, in Lynch, F. and Burgess, C. B. (eds), *Prehistoric Man in Wales and the West*, 107–16. Bath.

BROTHWELL, D. R., 1972 Palaeodemography and earlier British populations, *World Archaeol*, 4, 75–87.

BROTHWELL, D. R., and KRZANOWSKI, W., 1974 Evidence of biological differences between early British populations from Neolithic to medieval times, *J. Archaeol Sci*, 1, 249–60.

CIPOLLA, C. M., 1974 *The Economic History of World Population*. Harmondsworth.

GLOB, P. V., 1974 *The Mound People*. London.

GREEN, H. S., 1974 Early Bronze Age burial, territory and population in Milton Keynes, Buckinghamshire, and the Great Ouse valley, *Arch J*, 131, 75–139.

HAMILTON, J. R. C., 1968 Iron Age forts and epic literature, *Ant*, 42, 103–8.

HAWKES, C. F. C., 1972 Europe and England: fact and fog, *Helinium*, 12, 105–16.

POWELL, T. G. E., 1958 *The Celts*. London.

RENFREW, C., 1973 Monuments, mobilization and social organization in neolithic Wessex, in Renfrew, C. (ed.), *The Explanation of Culture Change: Models in Prehistory*. 539–57. London.

Chapter V   Settlement and agriculture

BOWEN, H. C., 1961 *Ancient Fields*. London.

BOWEN, H. C. and FOWLER, P. J. (eds), 1978 *Early Land Allotment in the British Isles = BAR*, 48. Oxford.

BRADLEY, R., 1978 *The Prehistoric Settlement of Britain*. London.

BURGESS, C. B. and MIKET, R. (eds), 1976 *Settlement and Economy in the Third and Second Millennia BC = BAR*, 33.

DENNELL, R. W., 1976 Prehistoric crop cultivation in southern England: a reconsideration, *Ant J*, 56, 11–23.

FEACHEM, R. W., 1973 Ancient agriculture in the highland of Britain, *PPS*, 39, 332–53.

FIELD, H. N., MATTHEWS, C. L. and SMITH, I. F., 1964. New Neolithic sites in Dorset and Bedfordshire, with a note on the distribution of Neolithic storage pits in Britain, *PPS*, 30, 352–81.

FLEMING, A., 1978 The prehistoric landscape of Dartmoor. Part I. South Dartmoor, *PPS*, 44, 97–124.

FOWLER, P. J. (ed.), 1975 *Recent Work in Rural Archaeology*. Bradford-on-Avon.

FOX, A., 1973 *South West England, 3500 BC–AD 600*. 2 ed. Newton Abbot.

HEDGES, J., 1974–5 Excavations of two Orcadian burnt mounds at Liddle and Beaquoy, *PSAS*, 106, 39–98.

HELBAEK, H., 1952 Early crops in southern England, *PPS*, 18, 194–233.

PRYOR, F., 1974, 1978 *Excavation at Fengate, Peterborough, England*: First Report and Second Report. Royal Ontario Museum Archaeological Monographs. Toronto.

RENFREW, J. M., 1973 *Palaeoethnobotany: The Prehistoric Food Plants of the Near East and Europe*. London.

REYNOLDS, P. J., 1976 *Farming in the Iron Age*. Cambridge.

SIMPSON, D. D. A., 1971 *Economy and Settlement in Neolithic and Early Bronze Age Britain and Europe*. Leicester.

TAYLOR, C., 1975 *Fields in the English Landscape*. London.

WHITTLE, A. W. R., 1978 Resources and population in the British Neolithic, *Ant*, 52, 34–42.

WIJNGAARDEN-BAKKER, L. H. Van, 1974 The animal remains from the Beaker settlement at Newgrange, Co. Meath: first report, *PRIA*, 74 C, 313–83.

Chapter VI Crafts, industry, and communications

CLARK, J. G. D., 1952 *Prehistoric Europe: the Economic Basis*. London.
COGHLAN, H. H. and RAFTERY, J., 1961 Irish prehistoric casting moulds, *Sibrium*, 6, 223–44.
COLES, J. M., 1978 Music of Bronze Age Europe, *Archaeology*, 31 (2), 12–21.
COLES, J. M., HEAL, S. V. E., and ORME, B. J., 1978 The use and character of wood in prehistoric Britain and Ireland, *PPS*, 44, 1–46.
COLES, J. M., et al, 1975 onwards *Somerset Levels Papers*, 1–.
HENSHALL, A. S., 1950 Textiles and weaving appliances in Prehistoric Britain, *PPS*, 16, 130–62.
HODGES, H. W. M., 1976 *Artifacts*, 2 ed. London.
JOHNSTONE, P., 1972 Bronze Age sea trial, *Ant*, 46, 269–74.
McGRAIL, S., 1978 *Logboats of England and Wales = BAR*, 51.
ROWLANDS, M. J., 1971 The archaeological interpretation of prehistoric metalworking, *World Archaeol*, 3, 210–24.
TYLECOTE, R. F., 1962 *Metallurgy in Archaeology*. London.
WRIGHT, E. V., 1976 *The North Ferriby Boats, Nat. Maritime Museum Monograph and Report*, 23. London.

Chapter VII Burial, ritual and ceremony

ANNABLE, F. K., and SIMPSON, D. D. A., 1964 *Guide Catalogue of the Neolithic and Bronze Age Collections in Devizes Museum*. Devizes.
ATKINSON, R. J. C., PIGGOTT, C. M., and SANDARS, N. K., 1951. *Excavations at Dorchester, Oxon*. Oxford.
ATKINSON, R. J. C., 1979 *Stonehenge*, 2 ed. Harmondsworth.
ASHBEE, P., 1960 *The Bronze Age Round Barrow in Britain*. London.
BAITY, E. C., 1973 Archaeoastronomy and ethnoastronomy so far, *Current Anthropology*, 14, 389–449.
BATEMAN, T., 1848 *Vestiges of the Antiquities of Derbyshire*.
BATEMAN, T., 1861 *Ten Years' Diggings in Celtic and Saxon Grave Hills*.
BURL, A., 1976 *The Stone Circles of the British Isles*. New Haven and London.
BURL, A., 1969 Henges: internal features and regional groups, *Arch J*, 126, 1–28.
BURL, A., 1976 Intimations of numeracy in the Neolithic and Bronze Age societies of the British Isles, *Arch J*, 133, 9–32.
BURL, A. and FREEMAN, P. R., 1977 Local units of measurement in prehistoric Britain, *Ant*, 51, 152–4.
COLES, J. M., 1973 *Archaeology by Experiment*. London.
GREENWELL, W., 1877 *British Barrows*. Oxford.
GRINSELL, L. V., 1953 *The Ancient Burial Mounds of England*, 2 ed.
HADINGHAM, E., 1975 *Circles And Standing Stones*. London.
HODSON, F. R. (ed.), 1974 *The Place of Astronomy in the Ancient World*. London.
HOYLE, F., 1977 *On Stonehenge*. London.

LYNCH, F., 1972 Ring-cairns and related monuments in Wales, *SAF*, 4, 61–80.

LYNCH, F., 1974, 1975 Brenig Valley excavations, 1973, 1974, *Denbigh Hist Trans*, 23, 1–56; 24, 1–25.

MACKIE, E. W., 1977 *Science and Society in Prehistoric Britain.* London.

MORRIS, R. W. B., and BAILEY, D. C., 1977 *The Prehistoric Rock Art of Argyll.* Poole.

MORTIMER, J. R., 1905 *Forty Years' Researches in British and Saxon Burial Mounds of East Yorkshire.* London.

NEWHAM, C. A., 1972 *The Astronomical Significance of Stonehenge.* Leeds.

PETERSEN, F., 1972 Traditions of multiple burial in later Neolithic and Early Bronze Age England, *Arch J*, 129, 22–55.

RITCHIE, J. N. G., and MACLAREN, A., 1972 Ring-cairns and related monuments in Scotland, *SAF*, 4, 1–17.

SIMPSON, D. D. A., and THAWLEY, J. E., 1972 Single-grave art in Britain, *SAF*, 4, 81–104.

THOM, A., 1967 *Megalithic Sites in Britain.* Oxford.

THOM, A., 1971 *Megalithic Lunar Observatories.* Oxford.

THOM, A., 1974 Stonehenge, *J Hist Astron*, 5, 71–90.

WADDELL, J., 1970 Irish Bronze Age cists: a survey, *JRSAI*, 100, 91–139.

WAINWRIGHT, G. J., 1969 Review of henge monuments in the light of recent research, *PPS*, 35, 112–33.

WAINWRIGHT, G. J., and LONGWORTH, I. H., 1971 *Durrington Walls.* Society of Antiquaries, London.

Sources acknowledged in the captions and not otherwise included in the Bibliography

ANATI, E., 1965 *Camonica Valley*. London.

APSIMON, A. M., 1958 Food Vessels, *ULIAAR*, 1, 24–36.

AVERY, M., and CLOSE-BROOKS, J., 1969 Shearplace Hill, Sydling St. Nicholas, Dorset, House A: a suggested re-interpretation, *PPS*, 35, 345–51.

BARING-GOULD, S., 1902 (ed.) Eighth Report of the Dartmoor Exploration Committee, *TDA*, 34, 160–5.

BU'LOCK, J. D., 1961 The Bronze Age in the North West, *TLCAS*, 71, 1–42.

BURSTOW, G. P., and HOLLEYMAN, G. A., 1957 Late Bronze Age Settlement on Itford Hill, Sussex, *PPS*, 23, 167–212.

CAULFIELD, S., 1978 Neolithic fields: the Irish evidence, in H. C. Bowen and P. J. Fowler (eds), *Early Land Allotment = BAR*, 48, 137–43.

CHENEY, H. J., 1935 An Aeneolithic occupation site at Playden, near Rye, *Ant J*, 15, 152–64.

CHRISTIE, P. M., 1960 Crig-a-Mennis: a Bronze Age barrow at Liskey, Perranzabuloe, Cornwall, *PPS*, 26, 76–97.

CHRISTIE, P. M., 1967 A barrow-cemetery of the Second Millennium BC in Wiltshire, England, *PPS*, 33, 336–66.

CLARK, J. G. D., and PIGGOTT, S., 1970 *Prehistoric Societies* 2 ed. Harmondsworth.

CLARK, J. G. D., 1963 Neolithic bows from Somerset, England, and the prehistory of archery in north-western Europe, *PPS*, 29, 50–98.

COWIE, T. G., 1978 *Bronze Age Food Vessel Urns = BAR*, 55.

CUNLIFFE, B., 1974 *Iron Age Communities in Britain*. London.

CURWEN, E. C., 1934 A Late Bronze Age farm and a Neolithic pit-dwelling on New Barn Down, Clapham, near Worthing, *SAC*, 75, 137–70.

DAVIES, E., 1949 *Prehistoric and Roman Remains of Flintshire*. Cardiff.

ERITH, F. H., and LONGWORTH, I. H., 1960 A Bronze Age urnfield on Vinces Farm, Ardleigh, Essex, *PPS*, 26, 178–92.

FLEMING, A., COLLIS, J., and JONES, R. L., 1973 A late prehistoric reave system near Cholwich Town, Dartmoor, *PDAS*, 31, 1–21.

FOX, A., 1954 Celtic fields and farms on Dartmoor, in the light of recent excavations at Kestor, *PPS*, 20, 87–102.

FOX, A., 1957 The prehistoric monuments of Dartmoor, *Arch J*, 114, 152–9.

FOX, A., and BRITTON, D., 1969 A Continental palstave from the ancient field system on Horridge Common, Dartmoor, England, *PPS*, 35, 220–8.

GAUCHER, G., and ROBERT, Y., 1967 Les dépôts de bronze de Cannes-Écluse, *Gallia Préhist*, 10, 169–223.

GILKS, J. A., 1973 The Neolithic and Early Bronze Age pottery from Elbolton Cave, Wharfedale, *YAJ*, 45, 41–54.

GRIMES, W. F., 1938 A barrow on Breach Farm, Llanbleddian, Glamorgan, *PPS*, 4, 107–21.

HAMLIN, A., and CASE, H., 1963 Excavation of ring-ditches and other sites at Stanton Harcourt. Notes on the finds and on ring-ditches in the Oxford region, *Oxon*, 28, 1–52.

HAWKES, J., 1941 Excavation of a megalithic tomb at Harristown, Co. Waterford, *JRSAI*, 71, 130–47.

HENSHALL, A., and McINNES, I., 1967–8 A Beaker grave at Springwood, Kelso, Roxburghshire, *PSAS*, 100, 79–85.

HOLLEYMAN, G. A., and CURWEN, E. C., 1935 Late Bronze Age lynchet settlements on Plumpton Plain, Sussex, *PPS*, 1, 16–38.

HUXTABLE, J., HEDGES, J. W., RENFREW, A. C., and AITKEN, M. J., 1976 Dating a settlement pattern by thermoluminescence: the burnt mounds of Orkney, *Archaeometry*, 18, 5–17.

JOBEY, G., 1968 Notes on some food vessels from north Northumberland, *TAASDN*, NS 1, 103–5.

KAVANAGH, R. M., 1973 The Encrusted Urn in Ireland, *PRIA*, 73 C, 507–617.

LANGMAID, N., 1971 Norton Fitzwarren, *Curr Arch*, 3, no. 28, 116–20.

LONGWORTH, I. H., 1969 Five sherds from Ford, Northumberland, and their relative date, *YAJ*, 42, 258–61.

LYNCH, F., 1969 The Megalithic tombs of north Wales, in Powell, T. G. E., et al, 1969. *Megalithic Enquiries in the West of Britain*. Liverpool. 107–48.

MACHIN, M. L., 1971 Further excavations of the enclosure at Swine Sty, Big Moor, Baslow, Derbyshire, *Trans Hunter Archaeol Soc*, 10 (1), 5–13.

MACHIN, M. L., 1975 Further excavations of the enclosure at Swine Sty, Big Moor, Baslow, *Trans Hunter Archaeol Soc*, 10, 204–11.

MANBY, T., 1957 Food Vessels of the Peak District, *DAJ*, 57, 1–29.

MARSDEN, B. M., 1970 The excavation of the Bee Low round cairn, Youlgreave, Derbyshire, *Ant J*, 50, 186–215.

McINNES, I. J., 1968 The excavation of a Bronze Age cemetery at Catfoss, east Yorkshire, *ERA*, I, 1–10.

McINNES, I., 1971 Settlements in later Neolithic Britain, in D. D. A. Simpson (ed.), *Economy and Settlement in Neolithic and Early Bronze Age Britain and Europe*. Leicester. 113–20.

MEGAW, B. R. S., and HARDY, E. M., 1938 British decorated axes and their diffusion during the earlier part of the Bronze Age, *PPS*, 4, 272–307.

MEGAW, J. V. S., 1976 Gwithian, Cornwall: some notes on the evidence for Neolithic and Bronze Age settlement, in C. Burgess and R. Miket (eds.), *Settlement and Economy in the Third and Second Millennia BC = BAR*, 33, 51–79.

MERCER, R. J., 1970 The excavation of a Bronze Age hut-circle settlement, Stannon Down, St. Breward, Cornwall, 1968, *Cornish Archaeol*, 9, 17–46.

MORRISON, A., 1968 Cinerary urns and pygmy vessels in south-west Scotland, *TDGNHAS*, 45, 80–140.

MORRISON, A., 1971 Cist burials and food vessels: some recent discoveries and rediscoveries in western Scotland, *GAJ*, 2, 8–26.

O'KELLY, M. J., 1954 Excavations and experiments in ancient Irish cooking places, *JRSAI*, 84, 105–55.

PATAY, P., 1968 Urnenfelderzeitliche Bronzeschilde im Karpatenbecken, *Germania*, 46, 241–8.

PHILLIPS, C. W., 1941 Some recent finds from the Trent near Nottingham, *Ant J*, 21, 133–43.

PIGGOTT, C. M., 1938 A Middle Bronze Age barrow and Deverel-Rimbury urnfield, at Latch Farm, Christchurch, Hampshire, *PPS*, 4, 169–87.

PIGGOTT, C. M., 1942 Five late Bronze Age enclosures in north Wiltshire, *PPS*, 8, 48–61.

PIGGOTT, S., 1953 Church Dale Cave, Derbyshire, *PPS*, 19, 228–30.

POWELL, T. G. E., 1953 The gold ornament from Mold, Flintshire, north Wales, *PPS*, 19, 161–79.

PROUDFOOT, E. V. W., 1963 Report on the excavation of a bell barrow in the parish of Edmondsham, Dorset, England, *PPS*, 29, 395–425.

PRYOR, F., 1976 Fen-edge land management in the Bronze Age: an interim report on excavations at Fengate, Peterborough, 1971–75, in C. B. Burgess and R. Miket (eds), *Settlement and Economy in the Third and Second Millennia BC* = *BAR*, 33, 29–49.

RAFTERY, B., 1974 A prehistoric burial mound at Baunogenasraid, Co. Carlow, *PRIA*, 74 c, 277–312.

RAFTERY, J., 1960 A Bronze Age tumulus at Corrower, Co Mayo, *PRIA*, 61 c, 79–83.

RAHTZ, P. A., and APSIMON, A. M., 1962 Excavations at Shearplace Hill, Sydling St. Nicholas, Dorset, England, *PPS*, 28, 289–328.

RILEY, D. N., 1957 Neolithic and Bronze Age pottery from Risby Warren and other occupation sites in north Lincolnshire, *PPS*, 23, 40–56.

ST. JOSEPH, J. K., 1978 Air reconnaissance: recent results, 44, *Ant*, 52, 47–50.

SAVORY, H. N., 1957 A corpus of Welsh Bronze Age pottery II. Food Vessels and Enlarged Food Vessels, *BBCS*, 18, 196–233.

SCHAUER, P., 1971 *Die Schwerter in Süddeutschland, Österreich und der Schweiz: I* =PBF, IV/2. München.

SCOTT, W. L., 1950–1 Eilean an Tighe . . ., *PSAS*, 85, 1–37.

SIMPSON, D. D. A., 1965 Food vessels in south-west Scotland, *TDGNHAS*, 3, 42, 25–50.

SMITH, I. F., and SIMPSON, D. D. A., 1966. Excavation of a round barrow on Overton Hill, north Wiltshire, England, *PPS*, 32, 122–55.

STEVENSON, R. B. K., 1956–7 A bone ring from a Beaker burial at Mainsriddle, Kirkcudbrightshire, *PSAS*, 90, 229–31.

STONE, J. F. S., 1936 An enclosure on Boscombe Down East, *WAM*, 47, 466–89.

SWEETMAN, P. D., 1976 An earthen enclosure at Monknewtown, Slane, Co. Meath, *PRIA*, 76 c, 25–72.

SWITSUR, R., 1974 The prehistoric longbow from Denny, Scotland, *Ant*, 48, 56–8.

TAIT, J., 1965 *Beakers from Northumberland.* Newcastle upon Tyne.

WAINWRIGHT, G. J., 1972 The excavation of a Neolithic settlement on Broome Heath, Ditchingham, Norfolk, England, *PPS*, 38, 1–97.

WORTH, R. H., 1935 Dartmoor Exploration Committee, Twelfth Report, *TDA*, 67, 115–30.

WORTH, R. H., 1953 *Dartmoor.* Newton Abbot.

Radiocarbon Date List

Abbots Way Track,	GaK-1940	2090 bc ± 90	Blackpatch,			
Westhay Level	Q-926	2068 bc ± 80	Sussex	BM-290	3140 bc ± 130	
	Q-908	2014 bc ± 60	Brenig 42,			
	Lu-298	1990 bc ± 65	Denbighshire	HAR-713	1660 bc ± 70	
	BM-386	1984 bc ± 111	Brenig 44,	HAR-501	1680 bc ± 100	
Achnacree,			Denbighshire	HAR-500	1540 bc ± 70	
Black Moss	SRR-219	1359 bc ± 50		HAR-502	1520 bc ± 70	
Amesbury G. 71	NPL-77	2010 bc ± 110		HAR-505	1520 bc ± 80	
	NPL-75	1640 bc ± 90		HAR-504	1340 bc ± 80	
Amesbury 39	HAR-1237	1670 bc ± 90		HAR-503	1280 bc ± 70	
Annaghmare,			Brenig 45,	HAR-712	1670 bc ± 60	
Co. Armagh	UB-241	2445 bc ± 55	Denbighshire	HAR-657	1620 bc ± 100	
Anner Tol III,			Brenig 51,			
Netherlands	GrN-6753	1450 bc ± 45	Denbighshire	HAR-801	1560 bc ± 70	
Arminghall,			Brigg,	Q-1199	680 bc ± 100	
Norfolk	BM-129	2490 bc ± 150	Lincolnshire	Q-1200	593 bc ± 100	
Ballaharra,	BM-769	2283 bc ± 59	Broome Heath,			
Isle of Man	BM-768	2275 bc ± 67	Norfolk	BM-755	2217 bc ± 78	
Ballymacdermot,	UB-207	1710 bc ± 60	Chalton,			
Co. Armagh	UB-705	1565 bc ± 85	Hampshire	BM-583	1243 bc ± 69	
Ballynagilly,	UB-555	2100 bc ± 50	Church Hill,			
Co. Tyrone	UB-558	2060 bc ± 80	Findon, Hampshire	BM-181	3390 bc ± 150	
	UB-556	1910 bc ± 50	Cissbury, Sussex	BM-185	2780 bc ± 150	
	UB-557	1830 bc ± 70		BM-183	2770 bc ± 150	
Ballyscullion,				BM-184	2700 bc ± 150	
Co. Antrim	UB-111	2250 bc ± 85	Coney Island,			
Ballyutoag,			Lough Neagh	UB-43	1400 bc ± 80	
Co. Antrim	D-48	2170 bc ± 300	Creag Na Caillich,	UB-371	2510 bc ± 90	
Barbrook II,			Perthshire	UB-372	2250 bc ± 90	
Derbyshire	BM-179	1500 bc ± 150	Crig-a-Mennis,			
Barford,			Cornwall	NPL-193	1565 bc ± 90	
Warwickshire	Birm-7	2416 bc ± 64	Dinorben,	V-123	945 bc ± 95	
Barmston,	BM-122	1010 bc ± 150	Denbighshire	V-122	895 bc ± 95	
Yorkshire	BM-123	940 bc ± 150	Downpatrick,	UB-472	1845 bc ± 75	
Bedd Branwen,	BM-456	1403 bc ± 60	Co. Down	UB-471	1625 bc ± 70	
Anglesey	BM-455	1307 bc ± 80		UB-474	1375 bc ± 75	
	BM-453	1274 bc ± 81		UB-473	1315 bc ± 80	
Behy-Glenulra,			Drombeg,	D-64	430 ad ± 120	
Co. Mayo	SI-1464	2510 bc ± 115	Co. Cork	D-63	560 ad ± 120	

Durrington Walls,	BM-400	2050 bc ± 90
Wiltshire	BM-399	2015 bc ± 90
	BM-398	1977 bc ± 90
	BM-285	1610 bc ± 120
Earls Barton,	BM-681	1264 bc ± 64
Northamptonshire	BM-680	1219 bc ± 51
Easton Down,		
Wiltshire	BM-190	2530 bc ± 150
Edmondsham,		
Dorset	BM-708	1119 bc ± 45
Embo, Sutherland	BM-442	1920 bc ± 100
Fengate,	HAR-397	2030 bc ± 100
Cambridgeshire	HAR-774	2030 bc ± 100
	HAR-399	2020 bc ± 70
	HAR-401	2010 bc ± 90
	HAR-404	1930 bc ± 80
	HAR-780	1900 bc ± 120
	HAR-409	1860 bc ± 150
	HAR-778	1830 bc ± 90
	HAR-400	1460 bc ± 120
	HAR-784	1040 bc ± 70
	HAR-783	1040 bc ± 80
	HAR-781	990 bc ± 90
	HAR-782	980 bc ± 80
	HAR-785	940 bc ± 60
Grandtully,		
Perthshire	GaK-603	1270 bc ± 100
Great Langdale,		
Westmorland	BM-281	2730 bc ± 135
Green Knowe,	1200–1000 bc pers. comm.	
Peebles	G. Jobey	
Grimes Graves,		
Norfolk	BM-97	2340 bc ± 150
	BM-87	2320 bc ± 150
	BM-377	2300 bc ± 130
	BM-944	2203 bc ± 64
	BM-943	2154 bc ± 55
	BM-775	1865 bc ± 60
	BM-778	1831 bc ± 67
	BM-777	1814 bc ± 60
	BM-1037	1053 bc ± 49
	BM-1035	1044 bc ± 40
	BM-1036	1005 bc ± 39
	BM-1038	986 bc ± 43
Gwithian,		
Cornwall	NPL-21	1120 bc ± 103
Hove, Sussex	BM-682	1239 bc ± 46
Hunstanton,		
Norfolk	BM-704	1736 bc ± 63
Island, Co. Cork	D-49	1160 bc ± 140
Itford Hill, Sussex	GrN-6167	1000 bc ± 35
Kaimes,		
Midlothian	GaK-1970	1191 bc ± 90
Killeaba,	BM-839	2431 bc ± 58
Isle of Man	BM-840	2350 bc ± 52
Killeens, Co. Cork	C-877	1556 bc ± 230
	C-878	1763 bc ± 270
Knowth,	UB-337	2795 bc ± 165
Co. Meath	BM-1078	2449 bc ± 67
	BM-785	2208 bc ± 126
Llandegai,	NPL-220	2790 bc ± 150
Caernarvonshire	NPL-224	2530 bc ± 145
	NPL-221	2470 bc ± 140
	NPL-222	1790 bc ± 145
Liddle, Orkney	SRR-701	876 bc ± 75
Maes Howe,	SRR-505	2185 bc ± 65
Orkney	Q-1482	2020 bc ± 70
Mam Tor,	Birm-202	1180 bc ± 132
Derbyshire	Birm-192	1130 bc ± 115
Marden, Wiltshire	BM-557	1988 bc ± 48
Meldon Bridge,	SRR-644	2736 bc ± 90
Peebles	SRR-643	2726 bc ± 180
	SRR-646	2336 bc ± 50
	HAR-796	2330 bc ± 80
	SRR-647	2290 bc ± 85
	HAR-797	2150 bc ± 130
	SRR-645	2132 bc ± 80
	GU-1059	2020 bc ± 85
	GU-1051	1200 bc ± 55
	GU-1050	1170 bc ± 50
Milton Loch,	K-1394	400 bc ± 100
Kircudbrightshire	K-2027	490 bc ± 100
Moel y Gaer,		
Flintshire	SRR-498	1015 bc ± 35
Monamore, Arran	Q-676	2240 bc ± 110
Monknewtown,		
Co. Meath	UB-728	1860 bc ± 45
Mound of the	D-43	2310 bc ± 160
Hostages,	D-42	2130 bc ± 160
Co. Meath	D-44	1930 bc ± 150
Mount Gabriel,		
Co. Cork	VRI-66	1500 bc ± 120
Mount Pleasant,	BM-792	2108 bc ± 71
Dorset	BM-793	2098 bc ± 54
	BM-667	2038 bc ± 84
	BM-794	2006 bc ± 45
	BM-663	1961 bc ± 89
	BM-646	1778 bc ± 59
	BM-665	1695 bc ± 43
	BM-662	1687 bc ± 63
Nant Ffrancon,		
Caernarvonshire	Q-907	2306 bc ± 50

Ness of Gruting,			Skendleby,	BM-191	2460 bc ± 150	
Shetland	BM-441	1564 bc ± 120	Lincolnshire	BM-192	2370 bc ± 150	
Newgrange,	UB-361	2585 bc ± 105	Slieve Gullion,			
Co. Meath	GrN-5462	2550 bc ± 45	Co. Armagh	UB-180	2005 bc ± 75	
	GrN-5463	2465 bc ± 40	South Cadbury,	I-5973	985 bc ± 90	
North Ferriby,	Q-837 ⎱	1443 bc ± 210	Somerset	I-5971	925 bc ± 90	
Yorkshire		1556 bc ± 110	South Street,			
	Q-1197	1430 bc ± 100	Wiltshire	BM-356	2810 bc ± 130	
	Q-1217	1362 bc ± 100	Star Carr,	Q-14	7607 bc ± 210	
Pitnacree,			Yorkshire	C-353	7583 bc ± 350	
Perthshire	GaK-601	2860 bc ± 90	Stenness, Orkney	SRR-350	2356 bc ± 65	
Playden, Sussex	BM-450	1740 bc ± 115		SRR-351	2238 bc ± 70	
Quanterness,	Q-1294	2640 bc ± 75	Stonehenge,	I-2328	2180 bc ± 105	
Orkney	Q-1363	2590 bc ± 110	Wiltshire	C-602	1848 bc ± 275	
	SRR-754	2410 bc ± 50		BM-1164	1728 bc ± 68	
	Pta-1626	2350 bc ± 60		BM-46	1720 bc ± 150	
	Q-1479	2220 bc ± 75		I-2384	1620 bc ± 110	
	Pta-1606	2180 bc ± 60		I-2445	1240 bc ± 105	
	Q-1451	2160 bc ± 100	Thorne Moor,			
	Q-1480	1955 bc ± 70	Yorkshire	Birm-336	1140 bc ± 90	
	SRR-755	1920 bc ± 55	Tinney's Tracks,	HAR-681	1090 bc ± 70	
Quoyness, Orkney	SRR-753	2315 bc ± 50	Somerset	HAR-684	1070 bc ± 70	
	SRR-752	2240 bc ± 50	Warren Farm,			
Rothesay, Bute	GaK-1714	2120 bc ± 100	Buckinghamshire	I-7148	1500 bc ± 90	
	Q-1223	2390 bc ± 65	Watch Hill,	HAR-654	1520 bc ± 70	
Rousay, Orkney	Q-1224	2350 bc ± 60	Cornwall	HAR-655	1470 bc ± 80	
	Q-1222	2060 bc ± 60	Weird Law,			
	Q-1221	2355 bc ± 60	Peebles	NPL-57	1490 bc ± 90	
	Q-1227	2055 bc ± 60	Westhay Track,			
Scone, Perthshire	GaK-787	1200 bc ± 150	Somerset	Q-308	850 bc ± 110	
Shearplace Hill,			Whitestanes			
Dorset	NPL-19	1180 bc ± 180	Moor, Dumfries	GaK-461	1360 bc ± 90	
Silbury Hill,	SI-910A	2725 bc ± 110	Wilsford,			
Wiltshire	SI-910C	2620 bc ± 120	Wiltshire	NPL-74	1380 bc ± 90	
	SI-910D	2580 bc ± 110	Woodhenge,	BM-677	1867 bc ± 74	
	SI-910CH	2515 bc ± 130	Wiltshire	BM-678	1805 bc ± 54	
	SI-910B	2365 bc ± 110	Worgret, Dorset	NPL-199	1740 bc ± 90	
	I-4136	2145 bc ± 95				

Index

    goldwork 110–11, 114–15
    halberds 111
    metalwork 106
    Mycenaean connections 108, 109

ornaments 104, 106, 108, 109, 111
pottery 100, 103, 104
radiocarbon dates 106, 108
territories 168–9
Woodworking 32, 267–9